PHILOSOPHICAL ANALYSIS
IN THE TWENTIETH CENTURY

PHILOSOPHICAL ANALYSIS

in the

TWENTIETH

CENTURY

VOLUME I

THE DAWN OF ANALYSIS

Scott Soames

PRINCETON UNIVERSITY PRESS

PRINCETON AND OXFORD

Copyright © 2003 by Princeton University Press

Published by
Princeton University Press,
41 William Street,
Princeton, New Jersey 08540

In the United Kingdom:
Princeton University Press,
3 Market Place,
Woodstock, Oxfordshire OX20 1SY

Second printing, and first paperback printing, 2005
Paperback ISBN 0-691-12244-X

The Library of Congress has cataloged the cloth edition of this book as follows

Soames, Scott.
Philosophical analysis in the twentieth century/Scott Soames.
p. cm.
Includes bibliographical references and index.
Contents: v. 1. The dawn of analysis.
ISBN: 0-691-11573-7 (v. 1: alk. paper)
1. Analysis (Philosophy). 2. Methodology—History—20th century.
3. Philosophy—History—20th century. I. Title.
B808.5 .S63 2003   2002042724
146'.4—dc21

British Library Cataloging-in-Publication Data is available

This book has been composed in Galliard

Printed on acid-free paper. ∞

pup.princeton.edu

Printed in the United States of America

7   9   10   8   6

ISBN-13: 978-0-691-12244-1 (pbk.)

THIS VOLUME IS DEDICATED
TO MY SON
GREG

CONTENTS

ACKNOWLEDGMENTS

THE TWO VOLUMES of this history grew out of two lecture courses given at Princeton University, the one that led to the first volume for a period of many years, the one that spawned the second in 1998, 2000, and 2002. The idea for the volumes was originally suggested to me by my one-time student, now friend and professional colleague, Jonathan Vogel, on a walk across the Brooklyn Bridge one hot summer evening sometime in the mid-nineties. The genesis of the volumes in the courses is reflected both in the topics taken up, and in the level at which they are discussed. Although the origin of the work has resulted in omissions of some philosophically important technical material—e.g., from Frege, Tarski, Carnap, and Kripke (which I hope to cover in later work)—it has also made for a more widely accessible finished product. All the material in these volumes has been presented to upper-division undergraduates and beginning graduate students—a fact which, I would like to think, has led to an emphasis on large, comprehensible themes with a minimum of inessential detail.

I am grateful to four people for reading and commenting on the manuscript for volume 1—my Princeton colleague, Mark Greenberg, my longtime friend and philosophical confidant, Ali Kazmi, a reader for the Princeton University Press, John Hawthorne, and my student, Jeff Speaks. All four read the manuscript carefully and provided me with detailed and helpful criticisms. In addition to discussing important philosophical issues with me, Jeff played a large role in helping to produce the manuscript, and in making significant stylistic suggestions, such as the outline at the beginning of each chapter. I would also like to thank my editor at the Press, Ian Malcolm, for his stewardship of the volumes. Finally, I can't thank Martha Dencker enough for her unselfish and untiring support throughout the time it took me to write the two volumes, and for the happiness that she has brought into my life.

INTRODUCTION TO THE TWO VOLUMES

THIS WORK presents an introductory overview of the analytic tradition in philosophy covering roughly the period between 1900 and 1975. With a few notable exceptions, the leading work in this tradition was done by philosophers in Great Britain and the United States; even that which wasn't written in English was, for the most part, quickly translated, and had its greatest impact in the world of English-speaking philosophers. Fortunately, the philosophy done in this period is still close enough to speak to us in terms we can understand without a great deal of interpretation. However, it has begun to recede far enough into the past to become history. Looking back, we are now in a position to separate success from failure, to discern substantial insights, and to identify what turned out to be confusions or dead ends. The aim of this work is to do just that. This will involve not only explaining what the most important analytic philosophers of the period thought, and why they thought it, but also arguing with them, evaluating what they achieved, and indicating how they fell short. If the history of philosophy is to help us extend the hard-won gains of our predecessors, we must be as prepared to profit from their mistakes as to learn from their achievements.

To my mind the two most important achievements that have emerged from the analytic tradition in this period are (i) the recognition that philosophical speculation must be grounded in pre-philosophical thought, and (ii) the success achieved in understanding, and separating one from another, the fundamental methodological notions of logical consequence, logical truth, necessary truth, and apriori truth. Regarding the former, one of the recurring themes in the best analytic work during the period has been the realization that no matter how attractive a philosophical theory might be in the abstract, it can never be more securely supported than the great mass of ordinary, pre-philosophical convictions arising from common sense, science, and other areas of inquiry about which the theory has consequences. All philosophical theories are, to some extent, tested and constrained by such convictions, and no viable theory can overturn them wholesale. Analytic philosophers are, of course, not the only philosophers to have recognized this; nor, as we shall see, have they always been able to resist the seductions of unrestrained, and sometimes highly counterintuitive, theorizing. Still, the tradition has had a way of correcting such excesses, and returning to firmer foundations. Regarding (ii), no philosophical advance of the twentieth century is more significant, more far-reaching, and destined to be more long-lasting than the success achieved in distinguishing logical consequence, logical truth, necessary truth, and apriori truth from one another, and in understanding the special character of each. The struggle that led to this success was long and arduous, with many missteps along the way. But the end result has transformed the philosophical landscape in ways that have become apparent only now, when we look back at our great twentieth-century predecessors from a position that they helped us to achieve.

It is a measure of the importance of these achievements that they have reverberated across all areas of philosophy in the analytic tradition. Accompanying them have been significant advances in more specialized areas of philosophy as well—most notably in the philosophy of logic, the philosophy of language, the philosophy of mind, the philosophy of science, and epistemology. Indeed, the very organization of the subject into separate and specialized areas such as these is, in part, a product of the analytic tradition. With this organization has come increasing interaction between philosophers with specialized interests and theorists in related fields. This interaction has, in turn, fed a number of important intellectual developments. One of the most striking of these involves the growth and development of symbolic logic into a largely autonomous discipline with important philosophical applications, and significant interest to philosophy. A second involves the emergence of modern linguistics and the scientific study of the natural languages, to which developments in the philosophy of language and logic have made, and continue to make, significant contributions.

Despite the engagement of analytic philosophers with important scientific and mathematical developments in the twentieth-century, the analytic tradition in philosophy has often been misunderstood by those outside the field, especially by traditional humanists and literary intellectuals. One persistent misconception has been to think of analytic philosophy as a highly cohesive school or approach to philosophy, with a set of tightly knit doctrines that define it. As the reader of these volumes will see, at various times in its history, analytic philosophy has contained within it systems and movements that did purport to have more or less the final truth about philosophy in general, philosophical methodology, or the nature of analysis; or about some large area within the subject. However, none of these systems or movements formed the basis of any lasting consensus. Invariably, the harshest and most effective opponents of any analytic philosopher have always been other analytic philosophers. In some cases, the harshest criticism has been self-criticism. One movement—logical positivism—is widely regarded to have been refuted by its own proponents. As chronicled in volume 1, the logical positivists articulated their basic conception, formulated it in terms that were clear and precise enough to allow it to be tested, and then found counter-arguments that in the end undermined it. Events like these, which constitute real progress, are unfortunately far too rare in the history of philosophy. For that reason, the rise and fall of logical positivism is viewed by many philosophers today as a proud chapter in the analytic tradition.

If analytic philosophy is not a unified set of doctrines adhered to by the broad range of philosophers, what is it? The short answer is that it is a certain historical tradition in which the early work of G. E. Moore, Bertrand Russell, and Ludwig Wittgenstein set the agenda for later philosophers, whose work formed the starting point for the philosophers who followed them.[1] The work done today in analytic philosophy grows out of the work done yesterday, which in turn can often be traced back to its roots in the analytic philosophers of the early part of the twentieth-century. Analytic philosophy is a trail of influence.

Although there are no fixed doctrines throughout the history of analytic philosophy, there are certain underlying themes or tendencies that characterize it. The most important of these involve the way philosophy is done. The first is an implicit commitment—albeit faltering and imperfect—to the ideals of clarity, rigor, and argumentation. This commitment is well illustrated by the very first paragraph of G. E. Moore's enormously influential book, *Principia Ethica*, written at the dawn of the analytic movement in philosophy.

> It appears to me that in Ethics, as in all other philosophical studies, the difficulties and disagreements, of which its history is full, are mainly due to a very simple cause: namely to the attempt to answer questions, without first discovering precisely *what* question it is which you desire to answer. I do not know how far this source of error would be done away, if philosophers would *try* to discover what question they were asking, before they set about to answer it; for the work of analysis and distinction is often very difficult: we

---

[1] Although the work of the German mathematician and philosopher, Gottlob Frege, could well be added to this list, his concerns were, on the whole, more specialized and technical than the others, and for many years this limited his influence.

may often fail to make the necessary discovery, even though we make a definite attempt to do so. But I am inclined to think that in many cases a resolute attempt would be sufficient to ensure success; so that, if only this attempt were made, many of the most glaring difficulties and disagreements in philosophy would disappear. At all events, philosophers seem, in general, not to make the attempt, and, whether in consequence of this omission or not, they are constantly endeavoring to prove that 'Yes' or 'No' will answer questions, to which *neither* answer is correct, owing to the fact that what they have before their minds is not one question, but several, to some of which the true answer is 'No', to others 'Yes'.[2]

This paean to clarity expresses a central ideal to which philosophers in the analytic tradition continue to aspire today, every bit as much as they did nearly a century ago, in 1903, when it was written.

However, clarity is not the whole story. Equally important is the analytic philosopher's commitment to argument. Philosophy done in the analytic tradition attempts to establish its conclusions by the strongest rational means possible. Whether the philosopher offers a general view of the world, or only attempts to resolve some conceptual confusion, he or she is expected to do so by formulating clear principles and offering rigorous arguments for the point of view being advanced. It is not enough to lay out speculative possibilities about what the world might be like, without offering cogent reasons for believing that looking at the world in this way is rationally superior to looking at it in other ways. Even if in the end there turns out to be no one way of viewing things that commands everyone's assent, the goal is to push rational means of investigation as far as possible.

This is connected with a second underlying theme running through analytic philosophy throughout the period. In general, philosophy done in the analytic tradition aims at truth and knowledge, as opposed to moral or spiritual improvement. There is very little in the way of practical or inspirational guides in the art of living to be found, and very much in the way of philosophical theories that purport to reveal the truth about a given domain of inquiry. In general, the goal in analytic philosophy is to discover what is true, not to provide a useful recipe for living one's life.

---

[2] Preface to *Principia Ethica*, (Cambridge: Cambridge University Press), originally published in 1903.

The third general tendency in analytic philosophy has to do with the scope of fruitful philosophical inquiry. Throughout its history, analytic philosophy has been criticized by outsiders for being overly concerned with technical questions and matters of detail, while neglecting the perennial big questions of philosophy and giving up on the ideal of developing comprehensive philosophical systems. As the reader will see, this criticism is largely inaccurate; analytic philosophy is no stranger to grand, encompassing systems, or to grandiose philosophical ambitions. However, it is true that philosophy in the analytic tradition also welcomes and accommodates a more piecemeal approach. There is, I think, a widespread presumption within the tradition that it is often possible to make philosophical progress by intensively investigating a small, circumscribed range of philosophical issues while holding broader, systematic questions in abeyance. What distinguishes twentieth-century analytical philosophy from at least some philosophy in other traditions, or at other times, is not a categorical rejection of philosophical systems, but rather the acceptance of a wealth of smaller, more thorough and more rigorous, investigations that need not be tied to any overarching philosophical view.

This last tendency in analytic philosophy—the acceptance of small-scale philosophical investigations—grew more pronounced in the second half of the century than it was in the first. To a certain somewhat more limited extent, a similar trend can be observed in twentieth-century western philosophy in general—no matter what the approach. Much of this has to do with the institutionalization of the profession, the enormous growth in the number of people employed teaching and writing philosophy, the expansion of the audience for philosophy, and the explosion in outlets for publication. All of this has led to a degree of specialization very much like that found in other contemporary disciplines. The result, and not just in analytic philosophy, is that the field has gotten too big, too specialized, and too diverse to be encompassed by a single mind. We have gotten used to thinking of other disciplines in this way. As unsettling as it might at first seem, we will have to get used to thinking of philosophy in this way too. The careful, specialized investigations that have come in recent years to characterize much of analytical philosophy are here to stay.

Of course, this isn't the whole story. At the beginning of the twenty-first century, we can, in my opinion, no longer expect the development of the kind of grand, deductive philosophical systems that in the past attempted to provide simple, yet comprehensive, views of the world and our place in it. However, we can, and should, continue to try to develop broad, informative pictures of substantial parts of the philosophical landscape. The way to do this, I believe, is **not** to forswear the disciplined, meticulous approach to circumscribed philosophical problems that has, over time, proved so enlightening. Instead, this approach must be supplemented with attempts to synthesize and abstract general themes and lessons from the wealth of existing analytic detail. We need to become better at creating illuminating overviews of large areas of philosophical investigation by working from the ground up—moving from the trees to the forest, rather than the other way around. These volumes are dedicated to the idea that one of the areas of philosophical investigation that needs to be illuminated in this way is the history of analytic philosophy itself.

The books—which grew out of two of my regular lecture courses at Princeton—are aimed at two main audiences. The first consists of upper-level undergraduates and beginning graduate students in philosophy, who, with some effort, should be capable of working through the material presented here, even if they have had little or no previous acquaintance with the philosophers discussed. The second consists of advanced graduate students and professors, who, while being familiar with much of the material covered, may appreciate the opportunity to fill in gaps in their knowledge, while profiting from the larger evaluative and interpretive stance taken towards different philosophers, and the tradition as a whole. For both groups, the overarching goal is to help forge a common understanding of the recent philosophical past that illuminates where we now stand, as well as where we may be heading in philosophy.

I would be pleased if, in addition, these volumes succeed in making analytic philosophy more understandable to interested non-philosophers. In philosophy, as in any other discipline, it is not necessary for non-specialists to be concerned with the most advanced and abstruse matters of concern to experts. However, in the case of philosophy it is especially important that its leading ideas be made at least somewhat comprehensible to non-specialists. Contemporary philosophy touches on intellectual endeavors of all kinds. If, in the long run, it is to be of continuing value, it must both inform and be informed by those endeavors. In order for this to happen, there must be a healthy dialog between philosophers and non-philosophers of many different sorts. I would like to think that these volumes may make a contribution to that dialog.

Of course, my project is not without its limitations. It certainly is not intended to be an exhaustive study of analytic philosophy in the first 75 years of the twentieth-century. The field is far too large for that—encompassing more published work in philosophy than was done in all the previous centuries combined. Of necessity, many significant analytic philosophers have been left out, and some important works of the philosophers discussed have had to be slighted, or even go unmentioned. This is inevitable in any introductory overview of the period. By way of compensation, I have tried to provide clear, focused, and intense critical examinations of some of the most important and representative works of each major philosopher discussed. In all, I have tried to provide enough detail to allow one to understand and properly evaluate the main philosophical developments of the period. However, on no issue and no philosopher is the discussion intended to be exhaustive.

One particular omission deserves special notice. An important tradition of work in logic, the foundations of logic, and the application of logical techniques to the study of language has had to be treated rather sparingly. The tradition may be viewed as starting with Gottlob Frege, continuing through Bertrand Russell, the early Ludwig Wittgenstein, the logical positivists, Kurt Gödel, Alonzo Church, Alfred Tarski, Rudolf Carnap, C. I. Lewis, Ruth Barcan Marcus, the early Saul Kripke, Richard Montague, David Kaplan, Robert Stalnaker, David Lewis, Donald Davidson, and the Kripke of *Naming and Necessity*. Although much of this work is discussed in the two volumes, the more highly technical parts of the tradition—which deserve a separate volume of their own—have had to be left out. This includes a highly productive, historically integrated line of research starting with Frege's formalization of the modern conception of logic in the late nineteenth century and Tarski's work on truth and logical consequence in formalized languages in the early 1930s. This line of research continued with Carnap's extension and reinterpretation of Tarskian techniques in the development of modal logic, and with the contributions of C. I. Lewis, Ruth Marcus, Saul Kripke and others, resulting in the development of a well-understood, systematic model theory for modal logics. On the philosophical side, this formal work prompted battles pitting skeptics against proponents of the notions of necessity and possibility and their deployment in philosophy. In the end the proponents prevailed, and sophisticated applications of these notions were made by Montague, Kaplan, Lewis, Stalnaker, and others to semantic theories of natural languages, enriched logical languages, and pragmatic theories of language use. This tradition of formal work took up a number of problems and themes found in Russell, the early Wittgenstein, and the logical positivists, discussed in volume 1, and produced results that made their way back into the less formal mainstream of analytic philosophy in ways discussed both at the end of volume 1 (in connection with Quine's attack on the analytic/synthetic distinction) and in volume 2 (where the works of Davidson, and Kripke's *Naming and Necessity* are treated at length). Apart from these points of contact, however, the fascinating history of this formal interlude and its broader significance for mainstream analytic philosophy could not be included here. That is a story that I hope to tell at another time.

Finally, a word about how to use these volumes. My aim in writing them was to build up a broad, synthetic overview from a connected series of deep, critical investigations of the central philosophical developments of the period. For this reason, the volumes are best used in conjunction with the primary sources they discuss. For those new to the subject, my recommendation when encountering a new philosopher, or a new philosophical problem, is first to read my discussion for perspective, next to read the primary sources examined in that discussion, and finally to reread my discussion in order to reach one's final assessment of the material. Such a method is ideal for courses in which these volumes are used as texts. However, it may also be used by diligent students working on their own. Those who wish to go further are encouraged to delve into the Suggested Further Reading listed at the end of each major part of the text.

A Word about Notation

In what follows I will use either single quotation or italics when I want to refer to particular words, expressions, or sentences—e.g., 'good' or *good*. Sometimes both will be used in a single example—e.g., *'Knowledge is good' is a true sentence of English iff knowledge is good.* This italicized sentence refers to itself, a sentence the first constituent of which is the quote name of the English sentence that consists of the word 'knowledge' followed by the word 'is' followed by the word 'good'. In addition to using italics for quotation, sometimes I will use them for emphasis, though normally I will use boldface for that purpose. I trust that in each case it will be clear from the context how these special notations are being used.

In addition when formulating generalizations about words, expressions, or sentences, I will often use the notation of boldface italics, which is to be understood as equivalent to the technical device known as "corner quotes." For example, when explaining how simple sentences of a language L are combined to form larger sentences, I may use an example like (1a), which has the meaning given in (1b).

1a. For any sentences A and B of the language L, *A & B* is a sentence of L.

  b. For any sentences A and B of the language L, the expression which consists of A followed by '&' followed by B is a sentence of L.

Given (1), we know that if 'knowledge is good' and 'ignorance is bad' are sentences of L, then 'knowledge is good & ignorance is bad' and 'ignorance is bad & knowledge is good' are also sentences of L.

Roughly speaking, a generalization of the sort illustrated by (2a) has the meaning given by (2b).

2a. For any (some) expression E, . . . *E* . . . is so and so.

  b. For any (some) expression E, the expression consisting of '. . .', followed by E, followed by '. . .', is so and so.

One slightly tricky example of this is given in (3).

3a. For any name n in L, *'n' refers to n* expresses a truth.

  b. For any name n in L, the expression consisting of the left-hand quote mark, followed by n, followed by the right-hand quote mark, followed by 'refers to,' followed by n, expresses a truth.

Particular instances of (3a) are given in (4).

4a. *'Brian Soames' refers to Brian Soames* expresses a truth.

  b. *'Greg Soames' refers to Greg Soames* expresses a truth.

Finally, I frequently employ the expression *iff* as short for *if and only if.* Thus, (5a) is short for (5b).

5a. For all x, x is an action an agent ought to perform iff x is an action that produces a greater balance of good over bad consequences than any alternative action open to the agent.

5b. For all x, x is an action an agent ought to perform if and only if x is an action that produces a greater balance of good over bad consequences than any alternative action open to the agent.

PART ONE

G. E. MOORE ON ETHICS, EPISTEMOLOGY, AND PHILOSOPHICAL ANALYSIS

CHAPTER 1

COMMON SENSE
AND PHILOSOPHICAL ANALYSIS

George Edward Moore was born the son of a doctor, in 1873, in a
suburb of London. He studied classics—Greek and Latin—in school,
and entered Cambridge University in 1892 as a classical scholar. At the
end of his first year he met Bertrand Russell, two years his senior, who
encouraged him to study philosophy, which he did with great success.
He was especially drawn to ethics and epistemology, which remained
his primary philosophical interests for most of his career. After his
graduation in 1896, he held a series of fellowships at Trinity College
for eight years, by the end of which he was recognized as a rising star
in the philosophical world. Along with Bertrand Russell and Ludwig
Wittgenstein, he would remain one of the three most important and
influential philosophers in Great Britain until his retirement from
Cambridge in 1939.

Although highly regarded for his many contributions to philosophy, G. E. Moore was probably best known as the leading philosophical champion of common sense. His commonsense view, expressed in
a number of his works, is most explicitly spelled out in his famous paper, "A Defense of Common Sense," published in 1925.[1] There, he
identifies the propositions of "common sense" to be among those that
all of us not only believe, but also feel certain that we know to be true.

---

[1] G. E. Moore, "A Defense of Common Sense," in J. H. Muirhead, ed., *Contemporary
British Philosophy* (2nd Series), 1925, reprinted in G. E. Moore, *Philosophical Papers* (London:
Collier Books, 1962), 32–59. (All references will be to the Collier edition.)

Examples of commonsense propositions that Moore claimed to know with certainty are given in (1):

1a. that he [Moore] had a human body which was born at a certain time in the past, which had existed continuously, at or near the surface of the earth, ever since birth, which had undergone changes, having started out small and grown larger over time, and which had coexisted with many other things having shape and size in three dimensions which it had been either in contact with, or located at various distances from, at different times;

1b. that among those things his body had coexisted with were other living human bodies which themselves had been born in the past, had existed at or near the surface of the earth, had grown over time, and had been in contact with or located at various distances from other things, just as in (1a); and, in addition, some of these bodies had already died and ceased to exist;

1c. that the earth had existed for many years before his [Moore's] body was born; and for many of those years large numbers of human bodies had been alive on it, and many of them had died and ceased to exist before he [Moore] was born;

1d. that he [Moore] was a human being who had had many experiences of different types—e.g., (i) he had perceived his own body and other things in his environment, including other human bodies; (ii) he had observed facts about the things he was perceiving such as the fact that one thing was nearer to his body at a certain time than another thing was; (iii) he had often been aware of other facts which he was not at the time observing, including facts about his past; (iv) he had had expectations about his future; (v) he had had many beliefs, some true and some false; (vi) he had imagined many things that he didn't believe, and he had had dreams and feelings of various kinds;

1e. that just as his [Moore's] body had been the body of a person [namely, Moore himself] who had had the types of experiences in (1d), so many human bodies other than his had been the bodies of other persons who had had experiences of the same sort.

Finally, in addition to the truisms in (1) that Moore claimed to know about himself and his body, he claimed to know with certainty the following proposition about other human beings:

2. that very many human beings have known propositions about themselves and their bodies corresponding to the propositions indicated in (1) that he [Moore] claimed to know about himself and his body.

The propositions indicated by (1) and (2) constitute the core of what Moore called the "Common Sense view of the world."[2] His position regarding the propositions of common sense is that they constitute the starting point for philosophy, and, as such, are not the sorts of claims that can be overturned by philosophical argument. Part of his reason for specifying these propositions in such a careful, painstaking way, was to make clear that he was **not** including among them every proposition that has commonly been believed at one or another time in history. For example, propositions about God, the origin of the universe, the shape of the earth, the limits of human knowledge, the difference between the sexes, and the inherent goodness or badness of human beings are **not** included in what Moore means by the truisms of Common Sense—no matter how many people may believe them.

Although he did not attempt any precise characterization of what makes certain propositions truisms of Common Sense, while excluding from this class other commonly believed propositions, the position he defended was designed and circumscribed so as to make the denial of his Common Sense truisms seem absurd, or even paradoxical. Of course, he fully recognized that none of the propositions in (1) are such that their denials are contradictory; none are necessary truths— i.e., propositions that would have been true no matter which possible state the world had been in. Nevertheless the propositions in (1) about Moore would have been very hard for **him** to deny, just as the corresponding propositions about other human beings, mentioned in (2), would be hard for **them** to deny. This is not to say that no philosophers have ever denied such propositions. Some have. However, Moore maintains that if any philosopher ever goes so far as to deny that there are any true propositions at all of the sort indicated in (1), and mentioned in (2), then the mere fact that the philosopher has de-

---

[2] Moore, "A Defense of Common Sense," see especially pp. 32–45.

nied this provides a convincing refutation of his own view. Assuming, as Moore does, that any philosopher is a human being who has lived on the earth, had experiences, and formed beliefs, we can be sure that if any philosopher has doubted anything, then some human being has doubted something, and so has existed, in which case many claims about that philosopher corresponding to the claims Moore makes about himself surely must be true. Moore expresses this point (in what I take to be a slightly exaggerated form): "the proposition that some propositions belonging to each of these classes are true is a proposition which has the peculiarity, that, if any philosopher has ever denied it, it follows from the fact that he as denied it, that he must have been wrong in denying it."[3]

But what about Moore's claim that he **knows** the propositions in (1) to be true, and his further, more general, claim (2)—that many other human beings **know** similar propositions about themselves to be true—can these claims be denied? Certainly, the things claimed to be known aren't necessary truths, and their denials are not contradictory. Some philosophers have denied that anyone truly knows any of these things, and this position is not obviously inconsistent or self-undermining. Such a philosopher might consistently conclude that though no one knows the things wrongly said in (2) to be known, these things may nevertheless turn out to be true after all. Though scarcely credible, this position is at least coherent. However, such a philosopher must be careful. For if he goes on to confidently assert, as some have been wont to do, that claims such as the proposition that human beings live on the Earth, which has existed for many years, are commonly believed, and constitute the core of the commonsense conception of the world, then he is flirting with contradiction. For one who confidently asserts this may be taken to be implicitly claiming to know that which he asserts—namely that certain things are commonly believed by human beings generally. But that means he is claiming to **know** that there are human beings who have had certain beliefs and experiences; and it is hard to see how he could do this without taking himself to **know** many of the same sorts of things that Moore was claiming to know in putting forward the propositions in (1). Finally, unless the philosopher thinks he is unique, he will be hard pressed to deny that others are in a position to know such things as well, in which case he will be well on his way to accepting (2).

[3] Ibid., p. 40.

Considerations like these were offered by Moore in an attempt to persuade his audience that the commonsense view of the world, as he understood it, should be regarded as so obviously correct as to be uncontentious. In this, it must be said, he was very persuasive. It is very hard to imagine anyone sincerely and consistently denying the central contentions of Moore's commonsense point of view. Moore himself was convinced that no one ever had. For example he says:

> I am one of those philosophers who have held that the 'Common Sense view of the world' is, in certain fundamental features, *wholly* true. But it must be remembered that, according to me, *all* philosophers, without exception, have agreed with me in holding this [*i.e., they have all believed it to be true*]: and that the real difference, which is commonly expressed in this way, is only a difference between those philosophers, who have *also* held views inconsistent with these features in 'the Common Sense view of the world,' and those who have not.[4]

After all, Moore would point out, philosophers live lives that are much like those of other men—lives in which they take for granted all the commonsense truths that he does. Moreover, this is evidenced as much in their profession of skepticism as in anything else. In propounding their skeptical doctrines, they address their lectures to other men, publish books they know will be purchased and read, and criticize the writings of others. Moore's point is that in doing all this they presuppose that which their skeptical doctrines deny. If he is right about this, then his criticism of their inconsistency is quite a devastating indictment. Reading or listening to Moore, many found it hard not to agree that he was right.

Despite its obviousness, Moore's view was, in its own way, extraordinarily ambitious, and even revolutionary. He claimed to know a great many things that other philosophers had found problematic or doubtful. What is more, he claimed to know these things without philosophical argument, and without directly answering the different skeptical objections that had been raised against such knowledge. How he was able to do this is something we will examine carefully in the next chapter.

For now, I wish to emphasize how Moore's stance is to be contrasted with a different, more skeptical, position that philosophers have sometimes adopted toward the claims of common sense. The skeptic's

---

[4] Ibid., p. 44.

position is that of being the ultimate arbiter or judge of those claims. The philosopher who takes this stance prides himself on **not** taking pre-philosophical knowledge claims at face value. Given some pre-theoretically obvious claims of common sense—e.g., that material objects are capable of existing unperceived, that there are other minds, and that perception is a source of knowledge about the world—the skeptical philosopher typically asks how we could possibly know that these claims are true. He regards this question as a challenge to **justify** our claims; if we in the end can't give **proofs** that satisfy his demands, he is ready to conclude that we don't know these things, after all.

Worse yet, some philosophers have claimed to be able to show that our most deeply held commonsense convictions are false. When Moore was a student at Cambridge just before the turn of the century, this radically dismissive attitude toward common sense was held by several leading philosophers who were his professors and mentors. Among the views advocated by these philosophers were:

the doctrine that time is unreal (and so our ordinary belief that some things happen before other things is false),

the doctrine that in reality only one thing exists, the absolute (and so our ordinary conception of the world as containing a variety of different independent objects is false), and

the doctrine that the essence of all existence is spiritual (and so our view that there are material objects with no capacity for perceptual or other mental activity is false).

As a student, Moore was perplexed by these and related doctrines.[5] He was particularly puzzled about how the philosophers who advocated them could think themselves capable of so completely overturning our ordinary, pre-philosophical way of thinking about things. From what source did these speculative philosophers derive their alleged knowledge? How could they, by mere reflection, arrive at doctrines the certainty of which was so secure, that they could be used to refute our most fundamental pre-philosophical convictions?

As Moore saw it, conflicts between speculative philosophical principles and the most basic convictions of common sense confront one

---

[5] See Moore's "An Autobiography," in *The Philosophy of G. E. Moore*, vol. 1, edited by P. A. Schilpp (La Salle, IL: Library of the Living Philosophers, 1968).

with a choice. In any such case, one must give up either one's common-sense convictions, or the speculative philosophical principle. Of course, one ought to give up whichever one has the least confidence in. But how, Moore wondered, could anyone have more confidence in the truth of a general philosophical principle than one has in the truth of one's most fundamental commonsense convictions—convictions such as one's belief that there are many different objects, and many different people, that exist independently of oneself? In the end, Moore came to think that one's confidence in a general principle of philosophy never could outweigh one's confidence in convictions such as these. In other words, Moore came to think that philosophers have no special knowledge that is prior to, and more secure than, the strongest examples of what we all pre-theoretically take to be instances of ordinary knowledge. As a result philosophers have nothing that could be used to undermine the most central and fundamental parts of what we take ourselves to know.

The effect of Moore's position was to turn the kind of philosophy done by some of his teachers on its head. According to him, the job of philosophy is not to prove or refute the most basic propositions that we all commonly take ourselves to know. We have no choice but to accept that we know these propositions. However, it is a central task of philosophy to **explain** how we do know them. And the key to doing this, Moore thought, was to analyze precisely **what it is that we know** when we know these propositions to be true.

Moore turned his method of analysis on two major subjects—our knowledge of the external world, and ethics. Regarding the former, the basic problem, as Moore saw it, may be expressed as follows: (i) knowledge of the external world is based on our senses; but (ii) the basic data provided by our senses are sense experiences, which are merely private events in the consciousness of the perceiver; while (iii) our knowledge of the external world is knowledge of objects that are not private to us, but rather are publicly available to all; thus (iv) there is a gap between the privacy and observer-dependence of our evidence, on the one hand, and the publicity and observer-independence of the things we come to know about on the basis of this evidence, on the other. Moore struggled for most of his professional life trying to explain how this gap could be filled.

The second area in which he employed his method of analysis was ethics. He thought that the central task of ethics was to answer two fundamental questions: *What kinds of things are good (bad) in them-*

selves? and *What actions ought (ought not) we to perform?* Answers to the first question were to be provided by theories of the form:

> For all x, x is good (bad) in itself iff x is so and so.

Answers to the second question were regarded as parasitic on answers to the first. According to Moore, the rightness or wrongness of an action is determined solely by the goodness or badness of its consequences. Thus, on his view, if we could determine precisely what is good and what is bad, we could, in principle, decide which acts are right and which are wrong—or rather, we could decide this, if we also had full knowledge of the total consequences of different actions. Of course, we don't, and never will, have such knowledge. Still, if Moore is right about the connection between the moral character of an action and the goodness or badness of its consequences, then we might be in an enviable position. If, in such a position, we could settle questions about what is good and bad (in itself), then our moral uncertainties about which acts to perform would be reduced to ordinary empirical ignorance about what their consequences are. Although we might not know what was morally required of us in a particular case, we would know precisely what factual considerations would settle the matter; and in cases of particular importance we might set out to gather the evidence needed to make our moral obligation clear.

In the end, however, Moore could not fully endorse this picture. Rather, he believed, there was an intractable problem preventing one from proving, or providing compelling arguments for, any philosophical theory of the form *For all x, x is good in itself (bad in itself) iff x is so and so.* For reasons we will explore, he thought that one could give arguments for such a theory only if one could analyze goodness (and badness) into simpler, component parts. However, he also thought he had found a way of demonstrating that this is impossible, because goodness is a simple property that cannot be further broken down into any conceptually more basic constituents. Although goodness may be directly apprehended, it cannot be defined, or analyzed. Because of this, Moore thought, we can no more prove that one thing is good, whereas another is not, by philosophical argument, than we can prove that one thing is yellow, and another is not, by philosophical argument. In the case of the color, we must simply look; in the case of goodness we can only consult our moral intuition. We cannot **prove** any philosophical theory of the good. The most we can do is to clear away conceptual confusions, and thereby allow our moral intuition to work properly. This devastating and perplexing conclusion occupied a central position in ethical theory in the analytic tradition for the next fifty years.

Our task in the next three chapters will be to carefully examine and evaluate the central tenets of Moore's position regarding knowledge of the external world, the analysis of moral notions, and the role of reason and argument in ethics.

CHAPTER 2

MOORE ON SKEPTICISM, PERCEPTION, AND KNOWLEDGE

Moore's Proof of an External World

We begin with what may be G. E. Moore's best-known article, his famous "Proof of an External World."[1] The article appeared in 1939, the same year that Moore retired from Cambridge University at the age of 65. The paper, though late in his career, was not his final piece of work. He continued to lecture at various universities and to publish off and on for nearly two decades until his death in 1958. Although "Proof of an External World" was one of his later works, its main ideas

---

[1] Moore, "Proof of an External World," *Proceedings of the British Academy*, vol. 25, 1939; reprinted in his *Philosophical Papers*. All page references will be to this work.

had been familiar fixtures of his philosophical outlook for at least thirty years prior to its publication. For example, these ideas were touched on in his paper, "Hume's Philosophy,"[2] published in 1909, and elaborated in considerable detail in chapters 1, 5, and 6 of his book *Some Main Problems of Philosophy*,[3] which reproduces in published form lectures he gave in London in 1910–11. Thus, by the time "Proof of an External World" appeared in print, the central views presented so clearly and forcefully there had been in circulation among leading analytic philosophers for decades, and had already had a lasting impact.

What Is to Be Proved and Why

Moore begins the article with a quote from the preface to the second edition of Immanuel Kant's *Critique of Pure Reason*.

> "It still remains a scandal to philosophy . . . that the existence of things outside of us . . . must be accepted merely on faith, and that, if anyone thinks good to doubt their existence, we are unable to counter his doubts by any satisfactory proof."

Moore points out that if this is a scandal to philosophy, then Kant evidently must have thought that it is the job of philosophy to give a satisfactory proof of the existence of things outside of us, and that such a proof really can be given. Kant was not alone in this view; it is a position that has been taken by a number of philosophers, especially since the great seventeenth-century philosopher, René Descartes. The task Moore sets for himself is (i) to find out exactly what it is that these philosophers have thought should be proved, and (ii) to determine what sort of proof, if any, could be given for the desired conclusion.

We may begin, by way of background, by recalling the legacy of Descartes, who begins his *Meditations* by introducing a method of radical doubt. He proposes to doubt, or at least suspend judgment upon, everything he can imagine the slightest reason for doubting. He ends up doubting the existence of tables, chairs, other people, his own body— indeed everything except himself and, as he puts it, his thoughts. Now it might initially seem at best artificial, and at worst pathological, to

---

[2] Moore, "Hume's Philosophy," *New Quarterly*, November 1909; reprinted in Moore, Philosophical Studies (Totowa, NJ: Littlefield, Adams & Co.), 1968.

[3] Moore, *Some Main Problems of Philosophy* (New York: Macmillan, 1953; reprinted by Collier in 1962). All page references will be to the Collier edition.

doubt all that Descartes suspends judgment on. Nevertheless, his method played an important preparatory role in furthering his goal of grounding all our knowledge on a foundation of utter certainty. In addition, Descartes finds theoretical reasons for his doubts. He says that he might be dreaming—he might always be in one long dream so that when he thinks he is seeing, hearing, touching, tasting, or smelling something, he is really experiencing nothing more than very vivid dreams. He even considers the possibility that an evil demon might be causing him to have these dreams, thereby deceiving him. This is rather like thinking that you may be in a deep coma all of your life, during which time a brilliant scientist has electrodes attached to your brain that cause you to have just the sensations you would have if you were leading a normal life.

By considering scenarios like these, Descartes reaches a point at which the only things he can be completely certain of are that he thinks, that he exists, and that he has certain ideas, thoughts, sensations, and experiences. The task he sets for himself is to show how, starting from this meager foundation, one can reconstruct, and justify, all, or nearly all, of what we ordinarily take ourselves to know. His goal was to show how the structure of our ordinary knowledge could be firmly grounded on an absolutely certain foundation. Not surprisingly, there were serious problems in the reasoning by which Descartes attempted to reach this goal. It is, I think, fair to say that in the end, he didn't succeed in getting much beyond his severely restricted starting point. As a result, one of his most important legacies was a method of doubt that, hypothetically at least, could lead one to a highly skeptical position—a position from which Descartes himself had no convincing means of escape.

From this an epistemological program was born—namely, escaping from something like the skeptical position of Descartes's First Meditation. As a first approximation, then, what Kant seems to be saying in the passage quoted by Moore is that it is a scandal to philosophy that no one has succeeded in refuting the Cartesian skeptic. Not that there really are any living, breathing skeptics to refute; it is hard to imagine anyone sincerely and consistently accepting the skeptic's incredible conclusion. Rather, Kant seems to be saying that it is a scandal that no one has refuted the hypothetical skeptical position outlined by Descartes and other philosophers.

Moore's "Proof of An External World" should be seen as a comment on this epistemological program. Note, I have **not** said that Moore's proof is something that **succeeds** in refuting the Cartesian skeptic in terms that even the skeptic would have to recognize. I have not even said that it is an **attempt** to do so. As I see it, Moore's "proof" is an attack on the presuppositions of such attempts. His goal is first, to understand what the skeptic is asking for and why he is asking for it, and second, to undermine the skeptic's position by questioning the implicit assumptions that lead him to question our knowledge of the external world in the first place, and to demand the sort of proof that never could be given. His aim is not so much to answer the skeptic as to change philosophers' perspective on the skeptic's problem.

Moore begins by asking what it is exactly that philosophers have been trying to prove. In the passage quoted from Kant the question at issue is the existence of *things outside of us*. However, Moore notes that for Kant the phrase *things outside of us* is ambiguous. According to Kant, one of its meanings is *thing-in-itself, distinct from us*, which presumably involves independence from us. The second meaning that Kant attaches to the phrase can be expressed in a variety of ways: *things belonging to external appearance, empirically external objects, things to be met with in space*, and *things presented in space*.

The contrast between these two meanings may seem strange. We normally take many things that are met with in space to be things that exist in their own right, distinct from and independent of us. However, on Moore's interpretation, this was not the way that Kant thought of them. There is a natural way of reading Kant according to which he does not regard the objects met with, or presented, in space to be wholly distinct from us. On this reading, they are seen as mind-dependent entities the organization and constitution of which are due in part to our cognitive categories of perception and understanding. Since space, for Kant, is one of these categories, it is natural for him to use the phrases *things to be met with in space* and *things presented in space* to indicate a class of mind-dependent entities that he calls *external appearances*.

Although Moore doesn't dwell on this, he may well think that Kant could be criticized for trading on the ambiguity in his use of the term *things outside us*. On the interpretation in which things outside us are **not** dependent for their existence on our minds, one can understand why a philosopher might claim that it is a scandal that no one has been able to prove their existence. Ordinarily we think of material objects like the earth, rocks, and trees as things which, if they exist, exist independently of us. With this in mind, one naturally interprets Kant's remark about the alleged scandal to philosophy as the claim that it is a scandal to philosophy that, prior to Kant, no one was able to prove to the Cartesian skeptic that things independent of our minds, like the earth, really exist. Similarly, one naturally takes Kant's claim to have provided a rigorous proof of the existence of things outside of us as a proof of the existence of mind-independent objects, like the earth, that would satisfy even the Cartesian skeptic. However, it is not obvious that Kant really tried to prove this. Instead, on one natural interpretation, he sets out to demonstrate a variety of things about the existence and constitution of a world of mind-dependent appearances. The problem, of course, is that the existence of such appearances is **not** what philosophers since Descartes have tried to prove.

Although this is not the place to go into it, there is another, more charitable, interpretation of Kant in which what he tried to prove was neither about cognitively inaccessible things-in-themselves nor about mind-dependent appearances, but rather about tables and chairs in the sense that we ordinarily think about them. On this interpretation, Kant didn't so much attempt to prove that these ordinary objects exist; rather he attempted to prove that the very ability to formulate and take seriously the skeptical question presupposes that one already is implicitly committed to the existence of such objects—i.e., objects that are external to, and independent of, oneself. Such a position is quite interesting. Unfortunately, however, Kant himself did not carefully distinguish it from other, more problematic, interpretations, with the result that his distinction between things-in-themselves, on the one hand, and external appearances, on the other, has been subject to serious confusion.

This confusion illustrates why it is important to be clear about what one is asking when one asks for a proof of the existence of *things outside us*, or *things external to our minds*, or *things to be met with in space*. Thus, a necessary preliminary for Moore's proof is the clarification of what **he** means by these phrases.

External Objects vs. Objects Internal to, or Dependent on, Our Minds

Moore approaches this task by distinguishing two classes of things: *things to be met with in space* vs. *things presented in space*. Examples of *things to be met with in space* are tables, chairs, bubbles, rocks, trees, and the earth. Examples of *things presented in space* are pains (such as the throbbing I sometimes feel just behind my eyes when I have a headache), afterimages (such as the bright gold circle that gradually changes to blue in the middle of my visual field that I seem to see when I close my eyes after staring at a bright light against a dark background), and double images (such as the images I see when I hold a pencil close to my face and press my finger against one of my eyes until I see double). Moore notes two general differences between these classes of things.

First, he notes that afterimages, double images, and pains are logically (conceptually) private. This may be defined as follows:

> x is logically (conceptually) private to y iff it is conceptually possible for y to perceive or experience x, but conceptually impossible for someone other than y to perceive or experience x.

Consider pains, for example. Moore would say that although the pain you feel may be very similar to the pain I feel, it cannot be the very same pain. It is a consequence of this view that if you have a pain in your leg and I have one in mine, then two pains exist, not one that is simultaneously in both of our legs. I don't feel the pain in your leg and you don't feel the pain in mine; we each feel our own pains, no matter how similar they may be. According to Moore, and to many other philosophers, this is no accident of nature. Rather, it is part of what we mean by *pain* that it is conceptually impossible for two people to experience the same one. Moore holds that the same is true of afterimages and double images. They are all logically (conceptually) private.

This is not true of things met with in space—like tables, chairs, and bubbles. Some bubble may in fact be perceived by only one person y. But no bubble is such that it is conceptually absurd or impossible for it to be perceived by someone other than y. Thus bubbles, along with other things to be met with in space, are **not** logically (conceptually) private.

The second difference between *things to be met with in space* and *things presented in space*, as Moore uses these terms, is that for things presented in space, but not things to be met with in space, **to exist is to be perceived**. That is, afterimages, double images, and pains can only exist when they are perceived or experienced. After my foot stops hurting, we normally don't suppose that the pain still exists without my feeling it (though the cause of the pain might). Similarly, when my afterimage goes away we don't suppose that it still exists somewhere unperceived. Again, this is no accident of nature. According to Moore, these are kinds of things about which it is inconceivable that they could exist unperceived or unexperienced. As before, this is not true of tables, chairs, and soap bubbles. Bubbles, Moore says, are notorious for often existing only as long as they are perceived. But no soap bubble is such that it is inconceivable that it might exist unperceived. Indeed, we commonly suppose that a great many things of this type do in fact exist without anyone perceiving them.

Thus, Moore is going to try to prove that there are things to be met with in space, where it is understood that if x is to be met with in space, then x is the sort of thing which could exist unperceived, and which could be perceived by more than one person (assuming it could be perceived at all). Now surely, if tables, chairs, rocks, trees, hands, or shadows exist, then they are the sorts of things that are capable of existing unperceived; and they are also capable of being perceived by more than one person. Consequently, if there are tables, chairs, hands, or shadows, then there are things to be met with in space (in Moore's sense).

Next, consider the phrase *things external to our minds*. According to Moore, philosophers have used this expression in accordance with the following definitions:

> x is **in my mind** iff it is conceptually impossible for x to exist at a time when I am having no experiences—in particular, at a time in which I am not experiencing x.

> For x to be **external**, not only to my mind, but to all human minds, is for it to be conceptually possible for x to exist without anyone perceiving or experiencing x.

Notice, however, that this last was also a criterion for something to be met with in space. Thus, Moore uses the phrases *thing to be met with in space* and *thing external to our minds* in such a way that it follows that anything to be met with in space **is** external to our minds.

The Proof

We have already seen that if there are tables, chairs, hands, or shadows, then there are things to be met with in space. We now see that if there are tables, chairs, hands, or shadows, then it follows that there are things external to our minds. What then is Moore's proof that there are things external to our minds? It is very simple.

Premise 1.   Here (holding up one hand) is one hand.

Premise 2.   Here (holding up his other hand) is another hand.

Conclusion 1. Therefore, there are at least two hands.

Conclusion 2. Since there are two hands, there are at least two things to be met with in space.

Conclusion 3. Therefore, there are at least two things external to our minds.

This argument is so simple that one might wonder whether it really is a proof.[4] Moore insists that it is. He cites three requirements that an argument must satisfy if it is to count as a proof.

The first requirement is that the premises in the argument must be different from the conclusion. This criterion is satisfied by the proof Moore gives. His premises are: (i) that this (holding up one hand) is one hand, and (ii) that this (holding up the other) is another hand. His conclusion is that at least two things external to the mind exist. This conclusion could be true even if the premises were not. For example, it would be true if Moore's feet existed, even though his hands didn't. Since the conclusion could be true in a situation in which the premises were false, the conclusion differs from the premises, and Moore's first requirement is satisfied.

The second requirement an argument must satisfy in order to be a proof is that the conclusion must follow from the premises. That is to say, it must be **impossible** for the premises to be true while the conclusion is false. Moore's argument also satisfies this condition. He has explained that he is using the expressions *hand, thing to be met with in space*, and *thing external to our minds* in such a way that it follows that **if** there are hands, then there are things to be met with in space, and hence there are things external to our minds. Consequently, Moore's conclusion **does** follow from his premises.

Moore's final requirement that an argument must satisfy in order to qualify as a proof is that the premises must be known to be true. Thus, the question arises, "Does Moore really know when he holds up his hands that they are hands?" Moore recognizes this to be the crucial consideration. Surely any skeptic who thought that we couldn't know of the existence of the external world would deny that Moore knew that he had hands. Thus, we must pay close attention to Moore's claim that his proof satisfies this requirement.

---

[4] Moore could, of course, have skipped the intermediate step, and moved directly from Conclusion 1 to Conclusion 3. Conclusion 2 is included here only to preserve that pattern of his discussion.

In defending this claim, Moore starts out in a way that might initially seem simplistic and unsophisticated. He says that, of course, he knows that he has hands. It would be as absurd to suggest that he didn't as it would be to claim that you don't know that you are reading these words. Moore thinks that nothing could be more obvious than that we know such things. If he is right, then his argument satisfies all three of his requirements for being a proof, and he has reason to conclude that he has indeed proven the existence of the external world.[5] But is he right?

Moore insists that he is, in part by pointing out the ordinary nature of the proof he has given. He does this by offering a comparison. He asks us to imagine someone claiming that there are three misprints on a certain page, and someone else disputing this. The first person then **proves** that there are three misprints on the page by reading through the page and pointing them out. "Here is a misprint, there is another misprint, and there is a third, therefore there are at least three misprints on the page." Moore points out that it would be absurd to suppose that no such proof could ever be legitimate. Any of us would be perfectly happy to accept such a proof in real life. But if one can prove in this way that there are three misprints on a page, then one can **know** the premises of the proof to be true. That is, one can know that such and such is a misprint. But surely, if one can know this, then one can know that certain things are hands.

What should we make of this defense on Moore's part? On the one hand, what he says seems compelling. No one in daily life would seriously deny that we can know that something is a misprint. So, surely the same should hold true for hands. Why, one might ask, should proofs in philosophy be held to some different, and absurdly high, standard that proofs in other areas of life are not held to? The skeptic in philosophy asks for a proof of the external world. Very well,

---

[5] Some philosophers have contended that there is a fourth requirement for being a proof that Moore's argument does not satisfy—roughly, that the premises must be knowable prior to, or independently of, knowing the conclusion to be true. The contention is that though Moore's premises—that he has hands—are indeed knowable, knowing them to be true depends on already knowing the conclusion to be true. For a development of this idea, see Martin Davies, "Externalism and Armchair Knowledge," in Paul Boghossian and Christopher Peacocke, eds., *New Essays on the Apriori* (Oxford: Clarendon Press, 2000). For further discussion, plus a defense of the claim that Moore's argument (or at least one very much like his) does, in fact, satisfy this fourth requirement, see James Pryor, "Is Moore's Argument an Example of Transmission-Failure?" (forthcoming).

Moore implicitly replies, let us first figure out what counts as a proof. How do we do this? One thing we do is look around at what everyone routinely regards as a proof. The example about misprints is such a case. But then, since such proofs are genuine, Moore's so-called proof of the external world should also count as genuine. Of course, the skeptic might reply that that isn't what he means by a proof—what he means is something much stricter and more rigorous. But what point is there in that? Wouldn't taking such an exalted attitude toward philosophy be a sure way to rob it of significance and seriousness? One might argue that it would not, if philosophers had some special source of insight that allowed them to live up to such exalted standards. But they don't. Hence, there seems to be something right about Moore's defense.

On the other hand, what Moore says might also seem ineffective, and even paradoxical. Surely, Moore recognizes that any philosopher who was initially skeptical about whether we could know that external objects exist would be skeptical of Moore's claim that he knows his premises to be true. Any philosopher who thought that a proof of the external world was needed in the first place would reject Moore's attempted proof on the grounds that his premises required proof. Moore has no sympathy with this reply. According to him, his premises don't need proof, and in any case no proof of them can be given that would satisfy the hypothetical skeptic. Thus, Moore rejects the view that if you can't prove you have hands in a way that would satisfy the skeptic, then you don't know that you have hands.

Defense of Moore's Proof against Skeptical Attack

At this point it might seem as if we had reached an impasse. The skeptic claims that Moore's so-called proof is no proof, and is worthless unless Moore can justify his claim to know that he has hands by proving that he does. Moore rejects the skeptic's demand and claims that he can know that he has hands without proof. What are we to think? Is Moore really responding to the skeptic, or simply dismissing him?

I believe that Moore does have a real response, but it is not one that he explicitly gives in his "Proof of an External World." The response is briefly touched upon in his earlier article "Hume's Philosophy" (1909), and it is developed at greater length in lectures he gave the following year, and published much later as chapters 5 and 6 of *Some Main Problems of Philosophy*. In effect, Moore's response is to ask the skeptic to justify **his claim** that we can't know that there are hands.

As Moore saw it, philosophical skeptics have typically based their skepticism about such knowledge on restrictive philosophical theories regarding what counts as knowledge. He cites David Hume as an example, and he spends considerable time explicating what he takes Hume's theory to be. For our purposes the details of this particular theory are less important than the way theories of this general sort are used in skeptical arguments. Such arguments may be reconstructed as having the following form:

1. All knowledge is thus and so. (For example, to know p, one's evidence must logically or conceptually entail p—and so completely rule out the possibility that p is not true. Moreover, nothing counts as evidence unless one couldn't possibly be mistaken about it under any conceivable circumstances—even if one turned out to be a brain in a vat, or to be dreaming, or to be deceived by an evil demon. On this picture, one's evidence ends up being restricted to certain basic statements about oneself, one's thoughts, and one's private sense experience—statements such as the statement that one exists, that one seems to be seeing something red, and so on.)

2. Alleged knowledge of hands, etc., is not thus and so.

3. Thus, no one ever knows that there are hands, etc.

Moore's reply to all such arguments is "How do **you** know that the premises of **your** argument are true?"

It should not be thought that restrictive principles like Hume's, which have more or less the force of (1), are themselves entirely without intuitive support. If one builds the case in the right way, one can give a skeptical argument that has some appeal to what we would ordinarily take to be commonsense views about knowledge—after all, we would normally be quite uncomfortable with the claim *I know that S, but it is possible, given my evidence, that not S*. Nevertheless, Moore thinks that no argument of the above sort could ever establish its conclusion. Since the conclusion does indeed follow from the premises, what the argument shows is that one cannot simultaneously accept statements (1), (2), and (4):

4. I know that this is a hand.

At least one of these statements must be given up. **However, nothing in the argument dictates which one should be rejected**. What one must do is decide which statement one has the least confidence in, or the least reason to accept, and reject it, while retaining those statements one has the most confidence in, or the most reason to accept. Moore's point seems to be that if one honestly asks oneself which of these statements one has the most confidence in, or most reason to accept, one will find that it is (4). Thus, one must reject either (1) or (2).

According to Moore, the problem with the skeptic is that he has adopted a philosophical theory about what knowledge consists in that is far too restrictive. **The skeptic assumes that we can be certain about what knowledge is before we decide whether what we all ordinarily take to be paradigmatic cases of knowledge really are genuine.** But this is backwards. Moore would say that one fundamental way to test any theory about what knowledge consists in is to determine whether it is consistent with what we all recognize to be the most basic and paradigmatic examples of knowledge. If the theory is not consistent with these examples, then Moore would insist that this result constitutes strong evidence against it. Once we see that the skeptic's assumptions about knowledge are themselves typically unsupported, and far less plausible than the commonsense convictions they conflict with, we will have no choice but to reject the way in which the skeptic poses the problem of the external world in the first place. The real philosophical problem, according to Moore, is not to prove that we know that there are hands, or to deny this, but to construct a theory of knowledge that is consistent with obvious instances of knowledge such as this, and that explains how such knowledge arises.

What then is Moore's ultimate diagnosis of the skeptical problem? On his view, both the skeptic and the philosopher who tries to provide the proof demanded by the skeptic accept an unjustified theory of what knowledge consists in. This diagnosis brings out the ironic nature of Moore's presentation. Would anyone who believed that a proof of the external world was needed by satisfied by Moore's proof? No. Anyone who demanded such a proof would already have accepted the skeptic's restrictive conception of what knowledge is, and so would deny that Moore knew that he was holding up his hand. What then was Moore's purpose in presenting his proof? It was to show that there is no need for such a proof in the first place. What he wants us to see is that if there is scandal to philosophy in all of this, it is not the inability of philosophers to satisfy the demands of the skeptic; rather it is their uncritical acceptance of the legitimacy and presuppositions of those demands.

Perception, Sense Data, and Analysis

Sense Data

In giving his proof of an external world, Moore claims to know the truth of his premises simply by perception, without further proof. Although this seems plausible, it raises important questions. What exactly is perception and how does it give us knowledge? Moore was acutely concerned with this question throughout much of his philosophical career. Most of his discussion of it focused on visual perception. We will follow him in this.

We will begin by taking up Moore's views regarding sense data, as presented in chapter 2 of *Some Main Problems of Philosophy*, dating from 1910. The doctrine Moore presents there is one that he calls *the accepted view*, on the grounds that it was widely accepted by the philosophers of his time, and earlier. Moore himself was inclined to think that this view was plausible, though he never felt entirely certain of it, and he changed his mind about aspects of it at various times. Nevertheless, the view he outlines was something like the default view of perception held by many analytic philosophers throughout much of the first 50 years of the century.

It is helpful when first considering this theory to begin with certain kinds of unusual, nonstandard visual experiences such as hallucinating a dagger. Imagine yourself standing before a blank wall and hallucinating that there is a dagger before you. In describing such a case there is a temptation to say that although you are not seeing a real dagger, and although no material object is looking to you like a dagger, nevertheless you are seeing something that has the visual characteristics of a dagger. Such an object—the thing that looks like a dagger but is not any material object—if in fact there is one, is what Moore and many other philosophers would call *a visual sense datum*.

Two other cases mentioned earlier provide examples in which it is tempting to say that what one sees is not a material object, but a sense datum. One of these cases involves afterimages; the other seeing double. For example, if I close my eyes after staring directly at a bright light against a dark background, I have an experience that is naturally described as one of seeing a bright gold circle that gradually changes to blue in the middle of my visual field. Or, if I press my finger against the side of my eye so that I see double while looking at a pencil, it is natural to say that what I see are two images of the pencil. Since there is only one pencil before me, it seems that at least one of the images is not the pencil, or any other material object looking like a pencil. In the case of the afterimage it seems even more evident. If I saw a circle at all, then surely that circle wasn't a material object.

In each of these cases Moore would say that I saw a sense datum—in one case an hallucinatory dagger, in another an afterimage, and in the third a double image. Moore draws attention to four general characteristics that these sense data have often been assumed to have.[6]

1. For each, to be is to be perceived.

For example, when my afterimage fades away, we don't think that the circle I saw continues to exist somewhere unperceived. The same is true of the hallucinatory dagger and the double image.

2. Each is logically (conceptually) private.

It is impossible for these sense data to be seen by more than one person. For example, suppose two people both hallucinate rats running across the floor. Suppose further that one says that the rats he sees are pink, while the other says that the rats he sees are white. In such a case we wouldn't say that one of the two must be misperceiving the hallucinatory rats that both are seeing. Rather we would say that their hallucinations were different. But if differing perceptual reports always lead to the conclusion that different hallucinatory objects are involved, then it seems reasonable to suppose that two people can't ever see the same hallucinatory objects. In other words, these objects are logically (conceptually) private. The same reasoning applies to afterimages and double images.

3. When it comes to sense data there is no distinction between appearance and reality.

For them to seem to be so and so is for them to be so and so; they are what they seem. Many philosophers have supposed that sense data such as hallucinatory objects, afterimages, and double images have all and only the observational properties they appear to have. If one person's hallucinatory rats seem pink, then they are pink. If another's seem white, then they are

---

[6] In the text Moore gives prominence only to (1), (2) and (4). However, he appears also to be implicitly accepting (3).

white.It should be clear what is going on. Talk of hallucinations, afterimages, and the like, is talk about how things appear to one. If, in these cases, one insists that one is always seeing **something**, then it is natural to suppose that what one is seeing is **an appearance**. But then, the description of the appearance will match the description of how things appear. If, after looking at a bright light and turning toward a blank wall, it appears to you that you are seeing a bright gold circle, then Moore will say, you are seeing an appearance that is bright, gold, and circular. Similarly for hallucinations and double images.

4.　Sense data do not exist in any public space.

Your visual sense data are in your private visual space and mine are in mine. Thus, your sense data can never be in the same place as mine.

So far we have considered only unusual cases of visual perception. In these cases Moore and other philosophers hold that what we see are not material objects, but rather are sense data. Moreover, as is indicated by the four general characteristics just listed, sense data are **mind-dependent** entities. They are private to each observer, they exist only as long as they are perceived, and they have precisely the properties they appear to the observer to have.

But now, supposing that we see such sense data in unusual cases of perception, we must ask whether there is any reason to believe that we also see them in normal cases. Moore thinks that there is. To illustrate this he holds up an envelope in front of his class. He insists, quite rightly, that each student sees the same envelope. He also maintains that the envelope looks different to each student depending upon where he is sitting. To someone in the back of the room it looks quite small, whereas to someone in the front it looks larger. To someone off to one side it looks as if it has one shape, whereas to someone directly in front of it, it looks to have another. Even the colors seen by different students vary slightly, depending on the lighting, the strength of their eyes, and other factors. Moore expresses this by saying that a student in the front of the room sees a white patch, rectangular in shape that occupies a large part of his visual field. Someone in the back and to the side sees a smaller, slightly darker patch. But now, since the patch seen by someone in the front has different properties from the patch seen by someone in the back, the person in the front and the person in the back must see two different patches.

Moore then argues as follows:

P1. Each student sees a different patch.

P2. Each student sees the same envelope.

  C. Therefore, at most one student sees a patch that is identical with the envelope seen by all the students.

Note, this argument has the same form as the following argument:

  (i) Each student has a different faculty advisor.

 (ii) Each student has the same analytic philosophy teacher.

(iii) Therefore, at most one student has a faculty advisor who is identical with his or her analytic philosophy teacher.

These arguments are logically valid; so if their premises are true, their conclusions must be true. Since Moore argues for the truth of the premises of the first argument, he is committed to its conclusion.

In fact, he is prepared to go further. He points out that it would be implausible to suppose that only one of the students sees a patch that is identical with the envelope, while all the other students see something else. Surely, it would be arbitrary to say that just one student does this, since we have no criterion for saying of which student this is true. Thus, Moore concludes, it is most plausible to suppose that each student sees a patch that is distinct from the envelope they all see. These patches are, of course, sense data. They are things that exist only when perceived, are private to different observers, have all and only the observable properties they appear to have, and exist in spaces private to different observers. Thus, Moore concludes that what we have before our minds in both normal and abnormal perceptual experiences are mind-dependent entities.

But this raises a problem. If what we have before our minds both in cases of hallucination and in cases of normal perception are sense data, then what is the difference between the two? What is the difference between hallucinating a dagger and really seeing one? We want to say that in the case of hallucination we only think that there is a real dagger in front of us, while in the case of seeing a dagger there really is a dagger present. But if the sense data in the two cases are indistinguishable, what does this difference amount to, and how do we ever know that we are not just hallucinating?

The Analysis of Perceptual Statements

We can now see the tension in Moore's epistemology. On the one hand, he insists that he knows that there are material objects and that this knowledge rests on perception. On the other hand, his analysis of perception may make it seem difficult for him to explain how this knowledge is possible. How can this tension be resolved? Moore admits that he was never able to resolve it in a fully satisfactory way. However, he did have certain suggestions about the direction in which any satisfactory solution must lie. He discusses these suggestions in section 4 of "A Defense of Common Sense."

His first and most basic suggestion is that in order to understand how perception can give us knowledge that there are material objects, we must **analyze** exactly what we mean by such elementary claims as:

A. I see this and this is a table.

According to Moore, it is not the job of philosophy to try to decide whether or not such propositions are true. Of course, many are true. Rather, philosophers must accept that they are true, and provide an analysis of these propositions that explains how we are able to come to know that they are true. How, then, are we to analyze propositions like A? Moore suggests three alternatives among which he cannot make up his mind.[7]

The first alternative is Direct Realism, which involves scrapping sense data for cases of normal perception. On this alternative, what I perceive are not sense data at all, in the sense in which afterimages are. Rather, what I see is the table and nothing more. In addition, there is no more basic proposition that gives the content of A. Although Moore grants that this view might possibly be correct, he cites two objections to it that make him doubtful. First, it requires giving up the analysis of normal perception as involving sense data, which he did not want to do. One reason he was reluctant to do this was that he was inclined to accept principle B.

---

[7] I will omit here the distinction between talking about a table and talking about the surface of the table. Although Moore spends quite a bit of time on this, the distinction does not affect the central philosophical questions at stake.

B. Whenever something looks white, rectangular, small, etc., to you, you are seeing something that is white, rectangular, small, etc.

This was the principle that led him to conclude from the fact that the envelope looked different to different students that they must have been seeing different patches—i.e., sense data. Since Direct Realism denies this, and since Moore was inclined to accept B, he took this to be an objection to Direct Realism—though not necessarily a fatal one, since he admitted that he was not completely sure of B. Of course, if one doesn't think that B is plausible in the first place, as many now do not, then one won't see this as a real problem. However, Moore also had another objection to Direct Realism. He thought that it was plain that in cases involving hallucination, after-images, and double images, we really do see sense data. Furthermore, he thought that what we see in these cases is very like what we see in normal perception—so much like it that the most plausible explanation for the similarity is that we always see sense data. If that is so, then Direct Realism is out.

The second alternative is that in normal, veridical cases (in which, unlike cases of hallucination, things really are the way they seem to be), what we see are, in reality, mind-dependent sense data that are related to material objects in a certain way. On this alternative, statement A is analyzed as meaning the same as some version of A*.

A*. There is exactly one thing of which it is true both that it is a table and that it bears R to this sense datum that I am now seeing.

We get different versions of this alternative for different choices of R. On one familiar version, R is the causal relation. On this version, to see a table is to see a sense datum caused by a table. Moore himself did not accept this version, but rather preferred a version according to which R is an unanalyzable relation that holds between x and y iff y is an appearance of x.

But no matter how we characterize R, on this alternative one's justification for believing that one sees a table is based on one's perceptual knowledge of sense data. One must be able to justifiably infer from the fact that one is perceiving sense datum that there is something that bears R to the sense datum one is perceiving. Although Moore thinks that this analysis might be correct, he notes that the basis for the inference is problematic. If all that we ever directly perceive are sense data, how do we know that anything bears R to them, or, if some things do, how do we know what those things are like? Having posited intermediaries between us and material objects, this alternative has no obvious explanation of how we get beyond the intermediaries.

Moore takes this to be a powerful objection. However, he doesn't regard it as absolutely conclusive. For example, he notes at the end of chapter 2 of *Some Main Problems of Philosophy* that there are cases in which it is clear that we know, on the basis of mental images that are presently before our minds, of the existence of other things that are not immediately present to your minds. His example is memory. He says that he can remember today that he saw something red yesterday, even though the red sense datum the existence of which he remembers is not identical with any memory image that he now has. Moore takes this to show that sometimes our direct awareness of certain images or sense data makes it possible for us to know of the existence of other things to which those images or sense data are related. According to the second alternative view of perception, our knowledge of the existence of material objects on the basis of our perception of sense data is analogous to this. Moore acknowledges that this might be the correct account, but he admits that he is not certain that it is.

So far we have considered two alternatives. The first alternative scraps sense data for normal perception and claims that a statement like A doesn't have any more fundamental analysis. The second alternative posits sense data as objects perceived in all cases of perceptual experience, and takes the meaning of A to be given by A*. As we have seen, Moore thinks that there are substantial, but not absolutely conclusive, objections to each. At this point it is worth bringing out an additional consideration that may have made both alternatives seem unattractive to him, though he doesn't mention it himself. This consideration is based on the reason that he is looking for what he calls an analysis of statements like A in the first place.

The main reason why Moore wants an analysis of these propositions is to help explain how we can come to know that they are true. In my view, the key problem in providing such an explanation will arise no matter whether one takes sense data to be the objects of perception or not. Either way, one must admit that people sometimes have hallucinatory experiences that seem to them to be qualitatively indistinguishable from cases of normal perception. People sometimes are fooled by hallucinations. But if they are sometimes fooled, how can we be sure that we are not always fooled?

To make the problem vivid, we may ask how any person can know that he is not now just a brain in a bottle, a brain whose sensory pathways are being electronically stimulated by a computer in just the ways they would be if the person were living a normal life. It doesn't seem to matter very much whether we describe the brain as seeing sense data to which no material objects correspond, or as not really seeing anything (including sense data), but only seeming to see things. The point is that it is possible for me to have experiences indistinguishable from those I am now having without there being any table, computer, or wall in front of me. But if that is so, how does my actual experience ensure that I know that these things are really there? This question is crucial, and difficult to answer, whether or not the objects of perception are sense data.

If, according to Direct Realism, statements like A do not have any more fundamental analysis, then analyzing **what we know** when we know A to be true doesn't help us answer this question about **how we know**. The same is true of the second alternative. If A is analyzed as A*, then the job of explaining how we can know it to be true doesn't seem to get any easier. Since Moore hoped, rightly or wrongly, that the analysis of statements like A would help with such an explanation, he had reason to be dissatisfied with both of these alternatives.

This brings us to the final, very radical alternative, that Moore thought might provide a correct analysis. On this alternative, material objects are **not** fundamentally different from sense data, but rather are what John Stuart Mill called *permanent possibilities of sensation*. On this view, the meaning of a statement like A is given by a long list of categorical and hypothetical statements about sense data. Roughly speaking, A means something like the following:

> A** I am seeing a certain table-like visual sense datum; and if I were to walk a little to the side, then I would have certain other slightly different table-like visual sense data; and if I were to put my hand down, then I would have certain tactile sense data of hardness and smoothness; and so on, and so on, and so on.

Moore doesn't say what the virtues of this analysis are supposed to be. However, it is pretty clear what he has in mind. According to the analysis, to say that I am seeing a table is just to say something about my own sense data—the ones I am having now, and the ones I would have if certain conditions were fulfilled. I know what sense data I am having now because I perceive them, and because they are the kinds of things I can't be mistaken about. Do I know what sense data I would perceive if certain conditions were fulfilled? Well, if in a particular case of "seeing a table" I gather enough visual and tactile sense data, then because I have experienced such combinations of sense data in the past, and seen what other sense data follow from them, it is plausible to suppose that I am justified in believing that all the conditions for "seeing a table" are fulfilled. If they are fulfilled, then it is natural to suppose that I know this. Thus, if *I am seeing a table* is really a statement about my own sense data, then it is understandable how I can come to know that such a statement is true.

Is this, then, the correct analysis? Moore is dubious. For one thing, he notes that it seems doubtful that the conditions specified in the analysis of material object statements like A can be spelled out without again referring to material objects. Note, in providing A** as the analysis of A, I said such things as *If I were to walk a little to the side . . .* , and *If I were to put my hand down. . . .* But walking is something that implies that I have a body, and putting my hand down implies that I have a hand. If all material objects are supposed to be permanent possibilities of sensation, then these references to hands, bodies, and the rest would themselves have to be spelled out completely in terms of sense data. Moore doubts that this could be done. Second, Moore seems to think that statements about one's own sense data—no matter how complex—can never be fully equivalent to statements about material objects. He seems to think (for good reason) that there is an irreducible residue in our talk about material objects that cannot be captured by talk about sense data.

Thus, he was unsatisfied with all the analyses of statements like A that he could think of. As a result he was left without an answer to his central problem: *Granted that we do know about material objects, how is this knowledge to be explained?* However, the fact that he left this question unanswered was a stimulus to other philosophers. Three aspects of his position that were particularly influential were:

a. his conviction that we do know that there are material objects and other people,

b. his insistence that the job of philosophy is not to dispute this but to explain how such knowledge is possible, and

c. his belief that any satisfactory explanation must rest on a philosophical analysis of the meanings of statements about material
objects, other people, and so on.

This was an important legacy. But as important as it was, it may not
have been his most influential contribution. His views on ethics had a
profound effect, not only on his contemporaries, but on generations of
philosophers to come. It is no exaggeration to say that the moral philosophy of G. E. Moore defined the basic framework for much of the
discussion of ethics in analytic philosophy for more than half a century.

CHAPTER 3

MOORE ON GOODNESS AND THE FOUNDATIONS OF ETHICS

Overview: Moore's Main Theses about Goodness and Rightness

In this chapter we turn to Moore's ground-breaking views on ethics, presented in his classic work Principia Ethica, published in 1903.[1] In the preface to that work, Moore distinguishes two kinds of ethical questions.

A. What kinds of things **ought to exist for their own sakes?**
are good in themselves?
have intrinsic value?

B. What kinds of actions **ought we to perform?**
are right?
are duties?

He takes the different versions of A to be equivalent. The same is true of the B questions, with the exception of a slight difference between what he means by calling an action our duty, or one that we ought to perform, on the one hand, and what he means by calling it right. For Moore, acts that are duties and acts we ought to perform are one and the same. Every such act is right. However, in some cases it is possible for our duty to be to perform either one or the other of two different acts. In such cases both acts are right, though neither is, by itself, a duty or one we ought to perform. But for this small exception, Moore regards the different versions of B to be equivalent.

Corresponding to these two kinds of questions are two classes of ethical statements—those that purport to give answers to A-questions and those that purport to give answers to B-questions. Purported partial answers to questions of type A are:[2]

The apprehension of beauty is (intrinsically) good.

Knowledge is (intrinsically) good.

Friendship is (intrinsically) good.

Purported partial answers to questions of type B are:

Keeping one's promises is right.

[1] G. E. Moore, Principia Ethica (Cambridge: Cambridge University Press, 1903; revised edition, 1993).
[2] Here and in the discussion of Moore that follows, I will always use *good* to mean *good in itself*, or *good as an end*, rather than as *good as a means to some end*.

Telling the truth is right.

Helping others is right.

In the preface, Moore announces two theses about the class of A-statements and the class of B-statements.[3]

> T1. If the conclusion of an argument is an A-statement, but none of the premises are, then the premises do not entail the conclusion and, moreover, their truth does not provide any evidence for the conclusion, or any compelling reason to think it is true.

> T2. If the conclusion of an argument is a B-statement, then the premises entail the conclusion only if they include both an A-statement and a "causal statement" (or another B-statement).

Thesis 2 expresses Moore's commitment to **consequentialism**—the view that the rightness of an action is wholly dependent on the goodness or badness of its consequences. On this view, our ethical evaluation of the rightness of an action is conceptually dependent on our evaluation of the goodness of the states of affairs that the action brings about.

The classical **utilitarianism** of Bentham and Mill is a theory of this kind.

> 1a. An act is right iff it produces more good consequences than any alternative act open to the agent.

> b. Happiness and happiness alone is good.

> c. Therefore, an act is right iff it produces more happiness than any alternative act open to the agent.

The first premise here is common to all consequentialist theories, and expresses an idea much in keeping with Moore's T2. The second premise, about happiness, is a moral statement of type A. Different versions of consequentialism result from selecting different A-statements to play the role of the second premise. On Moore's view, principles of type A form the foundation of all ethical judgments. Since

---

[3] In articulating these theses, Moore is, of course, painting with a broad brush, and putting aside technical niceties. For example, some statement containing a predicate distinct from, but defined in terms of, *good* might entail an A-statement without itself being an A-statement. Moore should be regarded as implicitly excluding such cases.

they are the most fundamental principles, they are the ones with which he is most concerned.

They are also the subject of his central thesis, T1, which, from the moment it was enunciated, was quite naturally viewed as a bold and startling claim. Ordinarily, one would suppose that the claim that something is good can, at least sometimes, be supported by evidence and argument. In such cases, one is inclined to think, one may truly say that x is good because x is so and so—where the claim that x is so and so is not itself an explicitly evaluative claim, requiring still further defense and justification. However, if T1 is correct, this natural idea is mistaken.

What, then, is Moore's reason for holding T1? The main premise supporting this thesis is Moore's T3.

T3. *Good* is indefinable.

Moore has an argument that he thinks demonstrates the truth of T3. In addition, he thinks that once T3 is established, we will see that T1 must also be true. Still, the connection between T1 and T3 is less than transparent. One way of making the connection explicit is by adding a further thesis that Moore suggests at the end of section 5 in chapter 1.[4]

T4. It is impossible to know what constitutes evidence for the proposition that something is good unless one knows the definition of *good*.

It might well seem that if both T3 and T4 were true, then T1 would also have to be true. For suppose that *good* is indefinable. Then, since there is no definition of *good*, no one can know the definition of *good*. If, in addition, T4 is true, then no one can know what constitutes evidence that anything is good. This in turn at least suggests that there can be no evidence for the proposition that a particular thing is good, or any compelling reason to think it is true. If that is so, then claim T1 is true.

This, I think, was Moore's view. In saying this, I should add four clarifications. First, Moore devotes several pages of chapter 1 to a discussion of what he means by *definition*. These pages are rather confusing and also, I think, somewhat confused.[5] Instead of going through them in detail, I will offer a reconstruction of what he is after. Although

---

[4] See also section 86, pp. 142–43 (pp. 192–93 of the revised edition).
[5] Part of the difficulty here is Moore's tendency to give credence to a certain tradition that distinguished between "real" definitions of a property and "nominal" definitions of a word

he does not put it this way himself, as I see it, he is looking for a
definition of the word 'good' that gives an analysis of the property
(concept) that we use the word to express. In general, Moore assumes
that when P is any predicate, a definition of P is a definition (or analysis) of the property we use P to express—a definition expressed by a
true sentence *The property of being (a) P is the property of being (a)
D,* where D is some word or phrase. For example, a definition, in this
sense, of the word 'square' tells us that the property of being a square
is the property of being a rectangle with four equal sides. On this view,
the word 'square' is standardly used to express a complex property the
constituents of which include the property of being a rectangle and the
property of having four equal sides. Since this property is also expressed
by the phrase 'rectangle with four equal sides', the word 'square' means
the same as this phrase, and one can be substituted for the other in any
sentence without changing its meaning, or the proposition it expresses.
In saying that *good* is indefinable, Moore is saying that the word 'good'
cannot be given a definition in this sense; the property we use it
to express is a simple, unanalyzable property that has no constituent
properties whatsoever.

The second clarification needed to understand Moore involves distinguishing between knowing the meaning of the word 'good', on the
one hand, and knowing its definition, on the other. If Moore is right
that the property of being good is a simple, indefinable one, then the
word 'good' has no definition in Moore's sense, but it still has a meaning. Indeed its meaning simply is the indefinable property it expresses.
Thus even if no one can know the definition of 'good', one can know
what 'good' means.

The third needed point of clarification involves the relationship
between knowing that something is good and having evidence that it is
good. For Moore, the statement that one can't know what is evidence
for the claim that x is good does not entail that one cannot know that x
is good. Moore thinks that there are some things we know without evidence—that is, without inferring their truth, or even their probable
truth, from other more basic claims. For example, Moore thinks that we
can know that something is yellow, not by inferring this proposition
from more basic claims that count as evidence for it, but simply by looking at the thing under proper conditions. Similarly, he thinks that it is

---

expressing the property. Fortunately, I think Moore's main points can be explicated without
getting into this complication.

possible, at least in some cases, to know that something is good, simply by considering the question of its goodness and properly distinguishing that question from other questions with which it might be confused.

Even with these necessary clarifications, Moore moves very quickly from T3 to T1, without spending much time considering the connection between the two. This is something we will examine closely when we critically evaluate his view. First, however, we need to understand Moore's claim that good is indefinable, and the argument for it.

The Argument That Good Is Indefinable

Definability and the Distinction between the Analytic and the Synthetic

We begin by determining what kinds of statements Moore takes to be definitions. Here it is helpful to focus on four different categories of statements, generated by two rough and ready distinctions. One distinction is between **analytic** and **synthetic** statements, the other is between **equivalences** and **generalities**. Accordingly, the four categories of statements are analytic equivalences, analytic generalities, synthetic equivalences, and synthetic generalities. A substantial portion of the first chapter of *Principia Ethica* is devoted to making these distinctions.

Moore begins his discussion of the subject matter of ethics by indicating that when we say things like *Jerry is a good man*, or *I ought to keep my promise to Jones*, we are making ethical statements. However, these statements are particular. We may become interested in ethics because we are interested in making particular evaluations like these; but we don't expect a moral philosopher to be concerned with each particular judgment one might make. Rather, Moore says, the moral philosopher is concerned with general ethical principles that cover a broad range of cases. For example, he thinks, the moral philosopher is concerned with generalizations such as (2a) and (2b).

2a. Pleasure is good.

  b. Pleasure and only pleasure is good.

The first of these statements is an example of a **generality**. It says that all pleasure is good, while leaving open whether or not other things are good. The second statement is an example of an **equivalence**.

It says that pleasure is good, and furthermore, nothing other than pleasure is good.

Next we need to understand how Moore distinguishes between analytic and synthetic statements. With this in mind, consider the following examples:

3a. For all x, if x is a U.S. senator, then x is a member of the U.S. Senate.

   b. For all x, if x is a U.S. senator representing New Jersey, then x is male.

Both of these statements are (now) true. However, (3a) is a necessary truth that is knowable apriori, whereas (3b) is a contingent truth that is knowable only on the basis of empirical evidence and investigation. Moore would say that it is part of our concept of being a U.S. senator that anyone to which it applies is a member of the U.S. Senate. Hence, he would hold that we can know, without following the election returns, that it is impossible for x to be a U.S. senator without being a member of the U.S. Senate. He would, therefore, classify (3a) as analytic. In the case of (3b), it is no part of our concept of being a U.S. senator representing New Jersey that x be male. Since it is possible to be a female senator, (3b) is a statement which, though true, could have been false. It is also a statement the truth of which cannot be known by reasoning and reflection alone, but rather requires empirical investigation. Therefore, Moore would classify it as synthetic.

Can we find examples of analytic and synthetic equivalences? Consider the following pair.

4a. For all x, x is a human iff x is a featherless biped.

   b. For all x, x is a human iff x is a rational animal.

Although (4a) is (let us assume) true, it is contingent, and knowable only on the basis of empirical evidence. Clearly it is possible for something to be a featherless biped without being a human. Thus, (4a) would be classified by Moore as synthetic, and the concepts, being a human and being a featherless biped, would not be regarded as necessarily equivalent. In the case of (4b), some philosophers are reputed to have held that it provides the definition of being a human. They have held that it is impossible to be a human without being a rational animal, and vice versa; in addition, they have maintained that we somehow know this apriori just by understanding the terms and reflecting on them. Although it seems highly doubtful that they are right about this, we at least have some idea of what they are claiming—namely, that (4b) is analytic. Other, more obvious, examples of analytic equivalences are (5a) and (5b).

5a. For all x, x is a square iff x is a rectangle with four equal sides.

   b. For all x, x is a brother of y iff x is a sibling of y and x is male.

In each case, the claims are both necessary and knowable apriori.

In claiming that *good* is indefinable, Moore takes himself to be saying something from which it follows that there is no analytic statement of the form (6), where the dots are filled in by a word or phrase expressing either a complex property (not itself involving goodness as a constituent) or a natural property like pleasure, which some philosophers have wanted to identify with goodness.

6. For all x, x is good iff x is . . . .

This does not mean that Moore thought that no statements of the form (6) are true. In fact he thought that something like (7) is true.

7. For all x, x is good iff x is the contemplation of a beautiful object, or x is the enjoyment of human companionship.

What he insists is that even though some such statements are true, none is analytic, where by analytic, he seems to mean, roughly, a statement that is necessarily true, knowable apriori, and true in virtue of an analysis of the concepts involved in the statement. (More on this later.)

A similar point holds for generalities involving goodness. According to Moore, no generality of the form

8. For all x, if x is . . . , then x is good.

is analytic, when the dots are filled in by a word or phrase standing for either a complex property (not itself containing goodness as a constituent) or a simple natural property. Moore expresses his view that statements about what is good are never analytic at the end of section 6 of chapter 1 of *Principia Ethica*.

If I am asked, 'What is good?' my answer is that good is good, and that is the end of the matter. Or if I am asked 'How is good to be defined?' my answer is that it cannot be defined, and that is all I have to say about it. But disappointing as these answers may appear, they are of the very last importance. To readers who are familiar with philosophic terminology, I can express their importance by saying that they amount to this: That propositions about the good are all of them synthetic and never analytic; and that is plainly no trivial matter. And the same thing may be expressed more popularly, by saying that, if I am right, then nobody can foist upon us such an axiom as that 'Pleasure is the only good' or that 'The good is the desired' on the pretence that this is 'the very meaning of the word.'[6]

It is this denial of the existence of analytic statements involving 'good' that leads Moore to think that no conclusion that something is good can ever be derived from premises not mentioning goodness. He does, however, think that some **synthetic** generalities involving goodness are true—e.g. he takes it to be true that the enjoyment of human companionship is good.

Simple, Indefinable Properties: The Analogy between Being Good and Being Yellow

As we have seen, Moore goes so far as to hold that premises that do not mention goodness can never provide **evidence** that something is good. This point about evidence can be made clearer by considering an example he discusses. According to Moore, the property of being good is analogous in certain respects to the property of being yellow. Consider the statement:

9a. Lemons are yellow.

One might say this without saying that to be a lemon is the same thing as to be yellow. One might even hold that it is not a necessary feature of lemons that they are yellow, since there seems to be nothing conceptually incoherent or impossible about a world in which lemons are orange. Thus, Moore would say that the statement that lemons are yellow is **synthetic**. This is analogous to Moore's claim that the statement (2a) is synthetic.

---

[6] Section 6, pp. 6–7 (pp. 58–59 of the revised edition). See also Section 86, p. 143 (p. 193, revised edition), where Moore characterizes all claims expressed by sentences of the form 'that is good' and 'that is bad' as synthetic.

A similar point can be made regarding equivalences. Consider the statement (9b).

9b. x is yellow iff x reflects light waves of frequency n.

Although this equivalence is, in fact, far too simplistic to be strictly true, let us ignore technicalities and imagine for the sake of argument that investigations into the physics of light established the truth of an equivalence of roughly this kind, for some specific n. Even then, Moore would not regard (9b) as analytic, or as a definition. He would maintain that the clause on the right does not give the meaning of the clause on the left. In support of this he would point out that the ordinary person might know that something is yellow without having the slightest idea about light waves, frequency, and the like. Thus, Moore would say, it is not part of our concept of being yellow that anything that is yellow must reflect light waves of a certain frequency. Rather, we use one set of criteria to determine whether something is yellow—namely just looking at it—and another set of criteria to determine the frequency of the light waves it reflects. It is a matter of empirical discovery, not conceptual or philosophical reflection, that the two sets of criteria end up being satisfied by the same objects. Thus, (9b), like (9a), is synthetic rather than analytic. Moore says that something analogous is true of equivalences involving 'good'. Although there are true statements of the form *x is good iff x is so and so,* none is a definition, and none is analytic.

According to Moore, the reason that the words 'good' and 'yellow' are alike in this way is that both the property of being good and the property of being yellow are simple, unanalyzable properties. They differ in that while we can tell that something is yellow by sense perception, the only way to determine that something is good is by intellectual intuition. Moore expresses this by saying that the property of being yellow is a **natural** property, whereas the property of being good is a **non-natural** property.

Given this view about the similarity of the words 'good' and 'yellow', we can better understand the nature of Moore's claim that conclusions to the effect that something is good are not entailed, nor in any way supported, by premises that do not mention goodness. This claim is analogous to one that could be made about being yellow.

T1y. If the conclusion of an argument is a statement that something is yellow, but none of its premises are, then the prem-

ises do not entail the conclusion and, moreover, they do not provide any evidence for the conclusion, or any compelling reason to think it is true.

This claim has some plausibility. How, after all, does one typically establish that something is yellow? Not by argument, but by looking. There are, of course, imaginable cases in which an argument might be given. Presumably, however, Moore would maintain that none of these falsifies T1y. For example, consider the following dialog. Q: *What's in the box? Is it something yellow?* A: *It's a lemon.* C: *Then it is probably something yellow.* Here it might seem that the premise *It's a lemon* provides evidence for the conclusion *It's yellow*, and hence a reason for thinking that it is true.

I doubt that Moore would regard this as a genuine counterexample to claim T1y. Rather, he would most likely reply, the argument relies on a suppressed premise, *All (most) lemons are yellow*, which itself depends ultimately on observation rather than demonstrative argument. Once this premise is added to the little argument in the dialog, the argument's premises will contain a statement about what things are yellow, and it will cease to be a counterexample to T1y. Although it is debatable whether this is the right way to think about such alleged counterexamples, I suspect that Moore would say the same thing about the following case.

What color is that object at the blast site?

It reflects light waves of frequency n.

Then, it must be yellow.

Supposing this argument is sound, Moore would probably say that is so only because it relies on a suppressed premise that has already been established—*Anything that reflects light waves of frequency n is yellow*. In fact, examples like this may have made it seem to him all the more plausible that conclusions about what is yellow must ultimately rest on simple observations, rather than on demonstrative arguments the premises of which don't mention being yellow.

On Moore's view, something similar is true of conclusions about what is good. The main difference is that we don't observe whether or not something is good in the same way we observe whether or not something is yellow. We observe that something is yellow with our eyes. We come to see that something is good with our intellect—simply by getting clear about what we are thinking about and coming to understand that it must be good.

Moore's Open Question Argument

So far we have elucidated the content of Moore's conclusions T1 and T3. However, we have not yet discussed precisely how he reaches these conclusions, nor have we criticized them. It is time to do this. We begin with the conclusion, T3, that 'good' is indefinable. Moore gives his famous "open question" argument for this conclusion in section 13 of *Principia Ethica*. He says that we can see that 'good' is indefinable, since no matter what definition is offered it is always meaningful to ask of whatever satisfies the defining complex whether it is good. He illustrates this point by considering a sample definition.

G. For all x, x is good iff x is what we desire to desire.

Moore reasons that if G were a genuine definition, then not only would it be true, it would also give us the meaning of 'good'—in which case 'good' and the phrase 'what we desire to desire' would express the same property, and so mean the same thing. But Moore thinks that we can easily show that 'good' does not mean this by considering Q1.

Q1. Granted that x is what we desire to desire, is x good?

No matter what you might think the answer to this question is, Moore says, it is clear that the question is just as intelligible, and makes just as much sense, as Q2.

Q2. Is x good?

But if 'good' and 'what we desire to desire' expressed the very same property, and so meant the very same thing, then we could always replace one of these expressions by the other in any sentence without changing the proposition, or question, it expresses. Thus if G were a genuine definition, the sentences Q1 and Q3 would mean the same thing, and express the same question.

Q3. Granted that x is what we desire to desire, is x what we desire to desire?

But this is absurd. The sentences Q1 and Q3 do not mean the same thing, and the questions they express are different. Hence G does not give us the meaning of 'good'.

With this in mind, we may reconstruct Moore's argument that 'good' is indefinable as follows:

P1. If (i) *for all x, x is good iff x is* D is a definition of 'good', then 'good' expresses the same property as D, and the two expressions mean the same thing.

P2. If 'good' expresses the same property as D, and the two expressions mean the same thing, then the sentences (ii) *Granted that x is D, is x good?* and (iii) *Granted that x is D, is x D?* express the same trivial, self-answering question (i.e. (ii) is on a par with (iv) *Granted that x is a male sibling of y, is x a brother of y?* in that properly understanding these sentences should be sufficient to know that the answer to the questions they express is 'yes').

P3. There is no complex property (not itself containing goodness as a constituent), or simple natural property P and expression D, such that D expresses P, and (ii) in P2 expresses the same trivial, self-answering question as (iii); nor could we introduce such an expression D.

C1. Therefore, there is no definition of 'good', *for all x, x is good iff x is D*, in which D expresses either a complex property, or a simple natural property.

C2. Thus 'good' is indefinable, and hence must express a simple non-natural property.[7]

The premises of this argument are intuitively rather plausible. P2 embodies the natural assumption that the meaning of a sentence (in these and other relevant cases) is a function of the meanings of its parts, while P1 is a reasonable statement of what we want from at least one significant kind of definition. Although not beyond question, these assumptions are attractive, and, for our purposes, may be accepted. Given this, our assessment of the argument depends on our assessment of P3. Here it is helpful to articulate a principle that Moore may well have been relying on, even though he never made it explicit.

THE TRANSPARENCY OF MEANING

If two expressions α and β mean the same thing (e.g., if two predicates express the same property), and if, in addition, an individual x (fully) understands both α and β then (i) x will know that α and β mean the same thing, and (ii), x will know that any two sentences (of the sort Moore is considering)

---

[7] This last clause assumes both (i) that if 'good' is meaningful, then it expresses a property, and (ii) that if the property expressed by 'good' were complex, or if it were a simple natural property, we could find, or introduce, some word or phrase D expressing that property such that *for all x, x is good iff x is D* would be a definition of 'good'. Although we will later call (i) into question, for now we will provisionally accept both (i) and (ii).

that differ only in the substitution of one of these expressions for the other mean the same thing, and thereby express the same proposition (in the case of declarative sentences) or question (in the case of interrogatives).

Moore seems, tacitly, to be relying on this, or some similar, principle when he takes it for granted that if D gave the meaning of *good*, then anyone who (fully) understood both could simply see by introspection that the interrogative sentences (ii) and (iii) of P2 meant the same thing, and so expressed the same question.[8] Since it is quite plausible both that we do (fully) understand *good* and related expressions, and that we wouldn't judge the questions to be related in this way, he takes P3 to be correct.

As well he should, given that he accepts the transparency principle. As for the principle itself, the situation is more complicated. On the one hand, the principle has intuitive appeal, and was accepted, either explicitly or implicitly, not only by Moore, but also by the great majority of analytic philosophers in the early to mid-twentieth century who dealt with substantial questions about meaning. On the other hand, in the last two decades important counterexamples to the principle have been brought forward—many involving proper names and natural kind predicates, understood in accordance with an approach to semantics known as *direct reference theory*.[9] In my opinion, these counterexamples, though genuine and quite important in other contexts, have a limited relevance to Moore's implicit reliance on the principle.[10] Thus, although the transparency principle is in my opinion ultimately incorrect, and therefore provides no basis for P3, the latter still remains plausible, and need not be challenged here. This puts us in a position to accept, at least provisionally, Moore's conclusion that *good* is indefinable.

[8] He speaks of our being able to find out things like this "by inspection," p. 16 (p. 67 in the revised edition).

[9] See chapters 3 and 10 of my *Beyond Rigidity* (New York: Oxford University Press, 2002) for discussion of such counterexamples.

[10] On my view, the only counterexamples to the principle involving natural kind predicates are those in which both α and β are simple natural kind terms (typically single words), like *groundhog* and *woodchuck*; when one of the terms is simple (e.g., *water*) and the other is compound (e.g., H_2O, or *substance molecules of which have two hydrogen atoms and one oxygen atom*), the two expressions α and β never mean the same thing. (See chapter 10 of *Beyond Rigidity*.) Thus, even if *good* turned out to behave like a natural kind predicate, the corresponding result would ensure that it was indefinable by any compound expression D that expressed a complex property. This is not the end of the matter—there are further cases that could be considered in evaluating this principle. However, since there are other, more pressing problems with Moore's overall argument, we need not enter into such complications here.

The appeal of Moore's result may be enhanced by citing the existence of meaningful and widespread controversy about goodness among philosophers and others. The very fact that philosophers argue so persistently about questions like Q1 indicates that they can hardly be trivial in the way in which the question (iv) of P2 is. In the particular case of Q1, we can see how such controversy might arise by asking who the *we* is that is supposed to be doing the desiring. Does it include people like Hitler, Stalin, Mao, or Pol Pot? If so, then it is certainly not clear that what they desire to desire is good. If not, on what basis is it decided whom to include and whom to exclude? Difficulties like these suggest that Q1 is not trivial, but has real force. Thus, Moore concludes that 'good' does not mean the very same thing as 'what we desire to desire.' It is plausible to suppose that a similar defect could be found in all proposed philosophical definitions of 'good,' and hence that 'good' really is indefinable, in Moore's strict sense of definition.

The Role of the Indefinability Thesis in Moore's Argument for T1

The indefinability thesis, T3, is the first step in Moore's (implicit) argument for T1. That argument may be reconstructed as follows, where in giving the argument, we take a relevant D to be any word or phrase that stands for either a complex property or a simple natural property. (S4 restates and elaborates T1 in accordance with Moore's views.)

The Argument

S1. There is no relevant D such that *for all x, x is good iff x is D* is a definition of 'good'.

S2. There are no analytic equivalences, *for all x, x is good iff x is D*, and no analytic generalities, *if x is D, then x is good*, for any relevant D.[11]

S3. There is no entailment of the statement (expressed by) *α is good* by the corresponding statement (expressed by) *α is D*, for any relevant D.

---

[11] We exclude from consideration terms that are themselves defined in terms of 'good'.

S4. No statement (expressed by) *α is D*, for any relevant D, provides any evidence for the conclusion (expressed by) *α is
good*, or any compelling reason to think it is true. The claim
that a particular thing is good can sometimes be derived from
a general principle which states that all members of a certain
class are good. But the fundamental principles of ethics—
which state that all, or all and only, members of a certain class
are good, and which provide the basis for justifying all other
ethical claims—are self-evident propositions for which no justification is either needed or possible; such propositions must
simply be seen to be true.[12]

Interpretation 1:
Restricted Conceptions
of Analyticity and Entailment

Given Moore's very strict sense of what counts as a definition, his
argument that 'good' is indefinable is quite plausible. I therefore propose we accept S1. However, there are serious questions about his
move from S1 to S2–S4. We begin with the transition from S1 to S2.
Moore treats his argument that there is no definition of 'good' as if it
were sufficient to establish that there are no analytic equivalences or
generalities connecting goodness with the properties expressed by any
relevant D. In order to assess this move, we need to further clarify
what he means by an **analytic** truth. It is striking that he devotes so
little attention to this and other closely related notions that are so
important to his overall argument. On the few occasions in *Principia
Ethica* in which he talks about analyticity, he seems to indicate that he
takes analytic truths to be necessary truths the falsity of which is
"inconceivable" to us, and the negations of which are "contradictory."[13]
What he means by these terms is never spelled out in detail; but they
may plausibly be read as indicating a rather narrow conception of ana-

[12] See chapter 5, section 86, pp. 143–44 (pp. 193–194, revised edition).
[13] A similar, slightly longer discussion of the notion of an analytic truth can be found in
Moore's paper, "The Refutation of Idealism," published in the same year as *Principia
Ethica*, but reprinted in Moore, *Philosophical Studies* (Totowa, NJ: Littlefield, Adams & Co.,
1968). (See pp. 12 and 13 in that volume, where Moore discusses analytic truths
as necessary truths the falsity of which are inconceivable, and the negations of which are
self-contradictory.)

lyticity. He may well have assumed that analytic truths are those that can be turned into formal logical truths by replacing synonyms with synonyms. On this view, *if John is a brother of Mary, then John is a male sibling of Mary* is an analytic truth, since by substituting a synonym for *is a brother of* one can generate the logical truth *if John is a male sibling of Mary, then John is a male sibling of Mary*, which is of the form *if p then p*. Since the negation of this, or any other, logical truth is logically equivalent to a simple contradiction p & $\sim p$, the sense in which the negations of analytic truths are contradictory, is, on this interpretation, straightforward. If one did hold this view of analyticity, then given Moore's very restrictive conception of what counts as a definition, and hence what counts as synonymy, one would end up characterizing the set of analytic truths as a highly restricted subset of the set of necessary truths that express propositions that are knowable apriori (assuming, as Moore did, that logical truths are necessary and apriori). On this interpretation, the gap between S1 and S2 in Moore's argument is small, and the move from the first to the second is plausible and understandable.

However, there is reason to be suspicious of this interpretation. Its chief problem is that the narrow conception of analyticity used to validate the move from S1 to S2 makes problems for the move from S2 to S3 and S4. To get to S3 one needs to say something about the notion of entailment. Moore tended to speak of this relation as being that of *logical implication*—a proposition p entails a proposition q iff p logically implies q—i.e., iff q is a logical consequence of p. However, by *logical implication* and *logical consequence*, he did not mean what is now meant by these notions in formal symbolic logic. For one thing, logical implication and logical consequence were, for Moore, relations between propositions or sets of propositions; whereas in formal logic they are relations between sentences or sets of sentences. Propositions, for Moore, are pieces of information that sentences encode and claims that assertive utterances of sentences are used to make—where it is understood that different but synonymous sentences express (encode) the same proposition, and that different propositions may be expressed (encoded) by different uses of the same sentence, if the sentence contains an indexical expression like 'I' or 'now'.[14]

---

[14] In explicating Moore's ethical theses I will avoid sentences containing indexicals, and (unless otherwise indicated) I will set aside complications that can arise from different utterances of the same sentence expressing different propositions.

Another point showing the difference between what Moore meant by *logical implication* and *logical consequence* and what these terms now mean in modern symbolic logic is that whereas Moore regarded S3 as a momentous philosophical thesis, its counterpart S3$_1$, involving the modern notion of logical implication, is nothing more than a triviality.

S3$_1$. For any relevant D, and name n, the sentence *n is D* does not logically imply *n is good.*

S3$_1$ is a triviality, since the mere fact that the word *good* does not appear in D is enough to ensure that *n is D* does not logically imply *n is good* in the sense of modern logic. This point may be illustrated with the help of a simple example. In modern logic, the sentence *the <u>object</u> is neither <u>round</u> nor <u>square</u>* logically implies the sentence *the <u>object</u> isn't <u>round</u>* because **any** interpretation assigned to the underlined, non-logical words in these two sentences that made the first sentence true would make the second sentence true as well. This is reflected by the fact that the result of uniformly replacing the underlined non-logical vocabulary with other non-logical words, while leaving the remaining logical vocabulary intact, would never yield a pair of sentences in which the first was true and the second untrue. By this criterion the sentence *a <u>square</u> is <u>inside</u> the <u>circle</u>* **does not** logically imply *a <u>rectangle</u> is <u>inside</u> the <u>circle</u>*, since the modern definition of logical implication doesn't constrain the words replacing *square* and *rectangle* to be related. Since Moore would insist that the proposition that a square is inside the circle **does** entail the proposition that a rectangle is inside the circle, the entailment relation in Moore's S3 cannot be logical implication in the modern sense.

At this point in the interpretation of Moore, one is pulled in two directions—one aimed at validating the move from S2 to S3, and one aimed at validating the move from S3 to S4. First the former. Recall our provisional interpretation of Moorean analyticity—a sentence is analytic iff it can be turned into a formal logical truth by putting synonyms for synonyms. (S is a formal logical truth iff S comes out true no matter how its non-logical vocabulary is interpreted, and no matter which of its non-logical vocabulary is uniformly replaced with other non-logical vocabulary.)[15] This definition of analyticity can be

---

[15] For more on the modern notions of logical truth and logical consequence, see chapter 3 and pp. 101–2 of my *Understanding Truth* (New York: Oxford University Press, 1999).

extended to propositions by defining a proposition to be analytic iff it is expressed by some analytic sentence. Entailment might then be defined in terms of analytic implication.

ANALYTIC IMPLICATION: SENTENCES

A sentence, or set of sentences, S analytically implies a sentence R iff there is a sentence, or set of sentences, S' and a sentence R' that arise from S and R by replacing synonyms with synonyms, and S' logically implies R' (in the sense of modern symbolic logic).

ENTAILMENT: PROPOSITIONS

A proposition (or set of propositions) p entails a proposition q iff there is a sentence (or set of sentences) S that expresses p (or if p and S are sets, the sentences in S express the propositions in p) and there is a sentence R, such that R expresses q, and S analytically implies R.

On this interpretation of what entailment and analyticity amount to, S3 follows unproblematically from S2.

However, these notions of entailment and analyticity are very restrictive. For example, the set of analytic propositions is nothing more than the set of propositions expressed by purely formal logical truths, and the entailment relation holds only between those propositions p and q that are expressed by sentences s_p and s_q, one of which logically implies the other (in the modern formal sense). Moreover, the move from S3 to S4 now becomes hopeless. In order to reach that desired conclusion, Moore must, at the very minimum, rule out the possibility that for some relevant D,

10. If α is D, then α is good.

expresses something that is necessary, knowable apriori, and validated by the kind of reasoning available in philosophy. For if there is such a D, then the claim expressed by *α is good* will be an apriori, necessary, and philosophically validated consequence of the claim expressed by *α is D*, in which case the claim expressed by *α is D* might well constitute a proof of the claim expressed by *α is good*, or at least a compelling reason for drawing that conclusion. Such a result would falsify Moore's most important meta-ethical view about goodness; namely that there can be no proofs of, or compelling arguments for, claims about goodness.

Moore's vulnerability on this point can be illustrated by considering the following example.

11.   For all x, if x is chartreuse, then x is colored.

(11) is necessary, it expresses something knowable apriori, and it is self-evidently obvious. Someone like Moore, who believed in the transparency of meaning, might even maintain that a competent speaker who knew the meanings of both *chartreuse* and *colored* would thereby realize that (11) expresses a truth, and that anyone who entertained the proposition it expresses would be in a position to judge it to be true. (11) might be claimed to have these properties despite the fact *chartreuse* isn't **defined** in terms of *colored*, and *colored* isn't **defined** in terms of *chartreuse*. One can know what it is for something to be colored without knowing all the colors, or even knowing that all the colors can be gotten from certain primary colors. In light of this, it is plausible to suppose that we could establish that the predicate *colored* cannot be defined, in Moore's strict sense of definition, using any relevant word or phrase D mentioning individual colors.

Combining this result with the provisional definitions of analyticity and entailment mentioned above, we could get all the way to $S3_C$.

S3$_C$.   For any relevant D, and name n, the statement expressed by **n is D** does not entail the statement expressed by **n is colored.**

But from this, nothing interesting follows. The claim that something is chartreuse provides both evidence for, and compelling reason to believe, the claim that it is colored. In fact, one could **prove** or **establish** that a thing is colored by showing that it is chartreuse. Thus, the version of S4 involving the predicate *colored* is false, even though $S3_C$ is true. Since the move from the one to the other in this case is completely parallel to the original move from S3 to S4, in the case of *good*, S4 does not follow from S3. Thus, on this interpretation, Moore fails to establish his most important methodological conclusion.

Interpretation 2:
Expanded Conceptions
of Analyticity and Entailment

It is natural to think that the problem with the above interpretation lies in its unduly narrow conceptions of analyticity and entailment. Examples like (11) illustrate that two expressions can be conceptually connected even though neither is defined in terms of the other. Similarly, two sentences can be such that the proposition expressed by one is a necessary and apriori consequence of the proposition expressed by the other even though neither sentence is transformable into the other by putting synonyms for synonyms, and no chain of definitions relates the two. One natural response to these observations might be to maintain that we need more expansive notions of analyticity and entailment—notions that recognize conceptual connections, even when they are not grounded in definitions. Perhaps, using such notions, we could validate the move from S3 to S4 in Moore's argument.

With this in mind, let us examine the following more expansive notions.

ANALYTIC OBVIOUSNESS:
SENTENCES AND PROPOSITIONS

Let S be any sentence that is necessary, that expresses something knowable apriori, and that is so obvious that anyone who understands it is disposed to accept it, and anyone who entertains the proposition it expresses is inclined to judge it to be true. Call any such sentence, as well as the proposition it expresses, *analytically obvious.*

ANALYTICALLY OBVIOUS CONSEQUENCE:
SENTENCES AND PROPOSITIONS

We will say that a sentence R is an *analytically obvious consequence* of a (finite) set S of sentences iff the conditional sentence the consequent of which is R and the antecedent of which is the conjunction of the sentences in S is analytically obvious. A proposition q is an analytically obvious consequence of a (finite) set p of propositions iff there is some sentence S_Q that expresses q and some set S_P of sentences that express the propositions in p, and S_Q is an analytically obvious consequence of S_P.

I suspect that Moore would have been willing to characterize (11) as analytically obvious, and (12b) as an analytically obvious consequence of (12a).

12a. n is chartreuse.

12b. n is colored.

Next we define some more expansive notions. First we need the notion of a sentence or proposition that can be derived from other sentences or propositions by a series of analytically obvious steps.

EXTENDED ANALYTIC CONSEQUENCE:
SENTENCES AND PROPOSITIONS

A sentence R is an *extended analytic consequence* of a set S of sentences iff it is possible to construct a proof of R each line of which is either a member of S or an analytically obvious consequence of earlier lines in the proof. A proposition q is an extended analytic consequence of a set p of propositions iff some sentence S_Q expresses q, and the members of some set S_P of sentences express the propositions in p, and S_Q is an extended analytic consequence of S_P.

Next we introduce the notion of a sentence or proposition that is either analytically obvious, or can be derived from other analytically obvious sentences or propositions by a series of analytically obvious steps.

EXTENDED ANALYTICITY:
SENTENCES AND PROPOSITIONS

A sentence is *extendedly analytic* iff either it is analytically obvious, or it is an extended analytic consequence of some set of analytically obvious sentences. Extendedly analytic propositions are those expressed by extendedly analytic sentences.

Finally, we define extended entailment among propositions as the converse of extended analytic consequence. (p extendedly entails q just in case q is an analytic consequence of p.)

The difference between analytic obviousness and extended analyticity is illustrated by (13).

13. For all x, $x = 2^{11}$ iff $x = 2048$.

Notice that 2^{11} is not a **synonym** for *2048*. One can understand what both of these expressions mean without knowing that 2^{11} is 2048. Thus, the question

14a. Granted that n = 2048, does n = 2^{11}?

is a genuine, non-trivial question, and is certainly not the question (14b):

14b. Granted that n = 2048, does n = 2048?

This shows that (13) is not a definition in Moore's strict sense. Nevertheless it is true. Moreover, its truth is neither an empirical nor a contingent matter. Rather, (13) expresses a necessary truth that is knowable apriori. But it is not analytically obvious, since it is not the case that anyone who understands what the sentence means realizes that it is true, and it is not the case that anyone who entertains the proposition it expresses is thereby in a position to judge it to be true.

Nevertheless, (13) is, arguably, extendedly analytic, since it can be proved from obvious, self-evident premises by obvious, self-evident steps—where it is arguable that each step in the proof is either analytically obvious, or an analytically obvious consequence of previous steps. The idea, of course, is that exponentiation can be reduced to repeated multiplication, which can be reduced to repeated addition, which can in turn be reduced to repeated application of the function that takes a natural number to its successor—all in such a way as to make each step in the proof of (13) either itself analytically obvious, or an analytically obvious consequence of earlier lines in the proof. This idea is supported by the fact that principles like those in (15), which might be appealed to in such a proof, seem to be beyond rational dispute, in the sense that anyone who understands them can be expected to recognize their truth, if he pays careful attention and is not distracted.

15. 2^{11} = (2)(2)(2)(2)(2) (2)(2)(2)(2)(2)(2)

(2)(2)(2)(2)(2)(2)(2)(2)(2)(2)(2) = [(2)(2)(2)(2)(2)(2)(2)(2)(2)(2)
   + (2)(2)(2)(2)(2)(2)(2)(2)(2)(2)]

(2)(2)(2)(2)(2)(2)(2)(2)(2)(2) = [(2)(2)(2)(2)(2)(2)(2)(2)(2)
   +(2)(2)(2)(2)(2)(2)(2)(2)(2)]

etc.

2 + 2 = the successor of 2 + 1

2 + 1 = the successor of 2 + 0

$2 + 0 = 2$

the successor of $2 = 3$

the successor of $3 = 4$

etc.

If this is right, then (13) may well be extendedly analytic, in which case the proposition expressed by (16a) will extendedly entail the proposition expressed by (16b).

16a. There are 2048 so and so's.

  b. There are 2^{11} so and so's.

Similar points hold for other mathematical statements. For example, the same argument could be given to support the claims that (17) is extendedly analytic and that the proposition expressed by (18a) extendedly entails the proposition expressed by (18b).

17. For all x, x is an equilateral triangle iff x is an equiangular triangle.

18a. That is an equilateral triangle.

  b. That is an equiangular triangle.

The extended entailment relation used in making these claims is interesting for two reasons. First, if p extendedly entails q, then it is in principle possible to prove, establish, or come to know q by deriving it from p, provided one can prove, establish, or come to know p without first establishing q. Second, p can bear this relation to q, even though the connection between the two propositions is not initially evident, but may require considerable reasoning and analysis to discover. Thus, in a particular case it may be an important philosophical or mathematical discovery to learn that p does, or does not, extendedly entail q.

With this in mind, suppose that analyticity in S2 and entailment in S3 of Moore's overall argument were defined as extended analyticity and extended entailment. Then, S3 would both follow from S2, and provide a potentially reasonable basis for something approaching S4. In particular, if S2, and hence S3, could be established, it would follow that there could be no **proof** of the claim expressed by *α is good* from the premise expressed by *α is D*, for any relevant D, each step of which was either itself analytically obvious, and hence so obvious as to be essentially undeniable, or an analytically obvious consequence of earlier steps, and hence so obvious as to be undeniable given an acceptance of those earlier steps. Moreover, one can see how a philosopher might take this result to show that no **proof** of any claim to the effect that something is good is possible from premises not mentioning goodness. This, of course, is not quite Moore's S4, which talks about the inability of the claim expressed by α *is D* to provide any **evidence** for the conclusion expressed by α *is good*, or any **compelling reason** to a think that it is true. But at least a very significant step would have been taken toward that overall conclusion.[16]

Although this may at first appear rather promising for Moore, it presupposes that S2 can be validly inferred from S1, when analyticity is given the expansive interpretation as extended analyticity. However, it cannot. Moore's open question argument establishes at most that *good* is indefinable in Moore's very strict sense of definition. As we have already seen, a similar argument could be given that *colored* is indefinable in this sense, despite the fact that generalities like (11) may very well be extendedly analytic (if any sentences are). Thus, on this interpretation, Moore's overall argument fails to get beyond S1.

Can Moore's Argument Be Repaired?

The lesson to be learned is that one must stop trying to derive strong conclusions about what may, or may not, entail, or provide evidence for, interesting claims about goodness from theses about the lack of strict Moorean synonyms for the word 'good'. The lack of such strict synonyms is **not** the crucial point. Much more significant is the question of whether the claim expressed by α *is good* can be derived from the corresponding claim expressed by α *is D* by a series of individual steps each one of which is obvious in the way in which the statements in (15), appealed in the proof of (13), are obvious. The fact that interesting, non-obvious mathematical truths like (13) and (17) can be derived by a series of such utterly obvious steps is what makes it possible for many mathematical truths to be not only interesting, and even

[16] See section 86, pp. 143–44 (pp. 193–94, revised edition) of *Principia Ethica* for a discussion of what Moore means by *reason* and *evidence*.

surprising, but also rationally certain. If one could show that interesting claims about goodness can **never** be derived in this way from premises not mentioning goodness, then one would have taken a significant step toward the kind of strong meta-ethical conclusion that Moore was looking for.

The best hope I can see for doing this involves expanding and strengthening the original open question argument along the following lines.

EXPANDED OPEN QUESTION ARGUMENT

P1. If *for all x, if x is D, then x is good* is analytically obvious, then the question

   (i) *Granted that α is D, is α good?*
   is a trivial self-answering question on a par with (ii), (iii), and (iv).

   (ii) *Granted that α is a male sibling of β, is α a sibling of β?*

   (iii) *Granted that α is chartreuse, is α colored?*

   (iv) *Granted that the successor of n = the successor of m, is it the case that n = m?*

In each of these cases ((ii–iv)), the proposition corresponding to the question is an obvious necessary and apriori truth; moreover, anyone who truly understands the interrogative sentence, and thereby entertains the question it expresses, must realize that the answer to it is *yes*—failure to know this would be evidence that one doesn't fully understand the sentence, or grasp the question.

P2. There is no complex, or simple natural, property P and expression D, such that D expresses P, and the interrogative sentence (i) in P1 expresses a trivial, self-answering question on a par with (ii), (iii), or (iv).

C1. Therefore, there is no analytically obvious generality, *for all x, if x is D then x is good*, in which D expresses either a complex property, or a simple natural property.

C2. Thus, there is no extendedly analytic sentence, *for all x, if x is D then x is good*, in which D expresses either a complex property, or a simple natural property.

In this argument C1 follows from P1 and P2, and C2 follows from C1. In addition, S2 and S3 follow from C2 (when analyticity and entailment are taken to be extended analyticity and extended entailment, and the transparency of meaning is taken for granted), and a weakened version of S4 that limits itself to the claim that theses about goodness cannot be **proven** from claims not mentioning goodness might plausibly be taken to be established on the basis of S3. Thus, the weight of Moore's overall argument now rests on P1 and P2.

Where does Moore stand regarding these premises? In order to answer this question we must go back to his statement of the original "open question" argument. The conclusion there was that the property of being good is not any complex property, or any simple natural property. Moore argues for this by pointing out that the question expressed by *Granted that α is D, is α good?* is not the same question as that expressed by *Granted that α is D, is α D?* or the question *Granted that α is good, is α good?* for any D that expresses either a complex, or simple natural, property. So far so good. But does Moore think that *Granted that α is D, is α good?* and *Granted that α is good, is α D?* always express "open questions" (or that at least one of them does)?

That depends on what it means for a question to be "open." In the last sentence of section 13.1 of *Principia Ethica*, where he states the open question argument, Moore says that the mere fact that "we understand very well what is meant by doubting" whether everything we desire to desire is good "shows that we have two different notions before our minds." The suggestion here is that whereas it is **unimaginable** that anyone could doubt whether everything that is good is good, or whether everything that we desire to desire is something we desire to desire, it is quite definitely **imaginable** that someone could doubt whether everything we desire to desire is good. More generally, Moore seems to suggest that for any relevant D, it will always be imaginable that someone could doubt the proposition expressed by *Everything that is D is good*.

Were *good* truly definable, in the way that *brother* is definable as *male sibling* or *square* is definable as *rectangle with equal sides*, Moore would take this not to be so. No one, Moore seems to think, could

GOODNESS AND THE FOUNDATION OF ETHICS 61

doubt that which is expressed by *Everything that is a square is a rectangle with equal sides* because that is just the proposition that everything that is a square is a square. Someone might, of course, be unsure whether the **sentence** *Everything that is a square is a rectangle with equal sides* was true; presumably, however, Moore would maintain that this might happen only if the person was not a fully competent speaker of English, and failed to truly understand the sentence.

If this is right, then Moore may well have thought that for any relevant D, ***Granted that α is D, is α good?*** always expresses an open question, in the sense that it is possible to understand the sentence, and entertain the question it expresses, without realizing that the answer to it is 'yes' (if indeed that is the answer). If Moore was right about this, then it is enough to establish P2, and, indirectly, C1 and C2. The only remaining issue is whether Moore would have accepted the (implicit) characterization of the interrogative sentences (ii), (iii), and (iv) of P1 as **not** expressing "open questions" in the sense in which (i) supposedly does. In my opinion, the textual evidence in *Principia Ethica* does not unequivocally settle this matter. However, there is some reason to think that Moore would have been willing to accept these characterizations. He often speaks as if questions about goodness are substantial and open-ended in ways that trivial questions like those expressed by (ii), (iii), and (iv) are not. If there were no genuine contrast here, then his supposedly far-reaching conclusions S3 and S4 would either vanish or be drained of significance. Since he views them as of the highest importance, I am inclined to think that he would accept P1 and P2.

We have now arrived at the strongest reasonable reconstruction of Moore's argument for his main meta-ethical conclusion about goodness. This argument is a combination of the expanded version of the open question argument, the weakened version of S4 that limits itself to ruling out **proofs** of claims about goodness, plus the interpretation of steps S2 and S3 as involving extended analyticity and extended entailment (plus the transparency of meaning principle). We have seen that there is some reason to believe that Moore himself would have been willing to accept this reconstruction. In addition, it is clear that many philosophers who were influenced by him accepted something very much like it. However, as plausible as this position may have seemed to some, Moore did not really **establish** its correctness. In order to have done so, he would have had to show that there is a clear and definite contrast between questions like those expressed by (ii), (iii), and (iv) of P1, on the one hand, and questions about goodness expressed by (i) for all relevant D, on the other. This is something he neither did, nor seriously attempted. Moreover, the claim that there is such a contrast for all relevant D is simply not obvious. Thus, Moore's startling, and enormously influential, conclusion that one cannot establish by argument that something is good was itself insufficiently supported by argument. At best, we may regard it as an interesting, not altogether implausible, historically very influential conjecture.

Self-evidence

According to the Moorean conjecture (i), for any relevant D, it is always possible to understand the sentence **Things that are D are good**, without being inclined to accept it, and to entertain the proposition it expresses without being inclined to judge it to be true, and (ii) it is never possible to prove the claim expressed by **α is good** from a premise **α is D** by a series of steps that are so obvious that they cannot rationally be denied by anyone who carefully attends to those steps, understands the sentences that formulate them, and apprehends the propositions those sentences express. We may express this informally by saying that according to the Moorean conjecture, statements about goodness are never *analytically obvious,* nor are they *analytically provable* from statements not mentioning goodness. If one supposes that Moore really did accept this conjecture, one may be surprised to learn that he nevertheless believed that some very important propositions about goodness—including the most fundamental propositions of ethics—are self-evident.

Moore makes this clear in chapter 5 of *Principia Ethica*, when in the course of summing up his earlier investigation of what *good* means he says the following:

> We cannot tell what is possible, by way of proof, in favor of one judgment that 'This or that is good,' or against another judgement 'That this or that is bad,' until we have recognized what the nature of such propositions must always be. In fact, it follows from the meaning of good and bad, that such propositions are all of them, in Kant's phrase, 'synthetic': they all must rest in the end upon some proposition which must be simply accepted or rejected, which cannot be logically deduced from any other proposition. This result, which follows from our first investigation, may be

otherwise expressed by saying that the fundamental principles of Ethics must be self-evident.[17]

Among the fundamental ethical propositions that Moore takes to be self-evident are those in (19) and (20).

19. Pleasure is not the only (intrinsic) good.

20a. The appreciation of beautiful objects is (intrinsically) good.

  b. The pleasures of human companionship and interaction are (intrinsically) good.

  c. The appreciation of beautiful objects and the pleasures of human companionship and interaction are the only things that are (intrinsically) good.

(19) is declared by Moore to be self-evident in chapter 5, section 87. The examples in (20) are discussed in chapter 6, the main aim of which Moore describes as follows:

> Its main object is to arrive at some positive answer to the fundamental question of Ethics—the question: 'What things are goods or ends in themselves?' To this question we have hitherto obtained only a negative answer: the answer that pleasure is certainly not the *sole* good.[18]

Moore gives his positive answer in section 113.[19]

> Indeed, once the meaning of the question is clearly understood, the answer to it, in its main outlines, appears to be so obvious, that it runs the risk of seeming to be a platitude. By far the most valuable things, which we know or can imagine, are certain states of consciousness, which may be roughly described as the pleasures of human intercourse and the enjoyment of beautiful objects. No one, probably, who has asked himself the question, has ever doubted that personal affection and the appreciation of what is beautiful in Art or Nature, are good in themselves; nor, if we consider strictly what things are worth having *purely for their own sakes*, does it appear probable that any one will think that anything else has *nearly* so great a value as the things that are included

---

[17] P. 143 (p. 193, revised edition).
[18] Section 110, p. 184 (p. 233, revised edition).
[19] Pp. 188–89 (pp. 237–38, revised edition).

under these two heads. . . . What has *not* been recognized is that it is the ultimate and fundamental truth of Moral Philosophy. That it is only for the sake of these things—in order that as much of them as possible may at some time exist—that any one can be justified in performing any public or private duty; that they are the *raison d'être* of virtue; that it is they—these complex wholes *themselves*, and not any constituent or characteristic of them—that form the rational ultimate end of human action and the sole criterion of social progress: these appear to be truths which have been generally overlooked.

My concern here is not with the truth or falsity of (19) and (20), but with the claim that they are self-evident. In characterizing them in this way, Moore is claiming (i) that they can be known to be true, (ii) that our belief in them is justified even though they cannot be deduced (logically or analytically) from other more basic known or justified propositions, (iii) that their justification does not rest in any way on propositions other than themselves, and (iv) that their truth is potentially obvious to us once we attend to them and carefully distinguish them from other propositions with which they might be confused. One might, of course, doubt whether the particular propositions Moore selects—those in (19) and (20)—really are self-evident in this sense. We will return to that in a moment. However, before we do, we need to address a question about the relationship between self-evident propositions, on the one hand, and those that are analytically obvious, on the other. How, if at all, do these two differ?

For Moore, whether or not x has the non-natural property of being good (in itself) is necessarily dependent on x's natural properties; it is impossible for two things x and y with exactly the same natural properties to be such that x is good (in itself) and y is not. Thus, Moore is committed to the view that a self-evident truth like (20b) is necessary, as well as being both potentially obvious and knowable apriori. How then does (20b) differ from analytically obvious truths like (21a) and (21b), which are themselves necessary, knowable apriori, and potentially obvious?

21a. Red things are colored (i.e., for all x, if x is red, then x is colored).

  b. If a book has exactly 201 pages, then the number of pages in the book is the successor of 200.

Is there some way in which these non-ethical truths are obvious that self-evident truths of ethics are not?

One passage from *Principia Ethica* that touches on this point occurs in section 87.[20] There Moore reviews his earlier attempt to persuade the reader of the untruth of the proposition that pleasure is the only good by showing that it contradicts other propositions which appear equally true. He emphasizes (i) that he has offered no proof of his claim that pleasure is not the only good, since that claim is self-evident and therefore unprovable; he further emphasizes (ii) that while we are justified in holding that pleasure is not the only good, it is conceivable that we are wrong; and he says (iii) that though others have disagreed with him about the relationship between pleasure and goodness, this has typically been because they have not understood what question was really at issue. Points (i) and (ii) lend some weight to the idea that, for Moore, questions about goodness are always substantial, open-ended, and not open to proof in the way that mathematical questions are. However, in elaborating (iii) he says something that emphasizes the similarity between ethical and mathematical questions. He is anxious to show that the causes of disagreement about what is good in itself standardly involve the failure to make necessary distinctions and to clearly understand the question at issue; he further speculates that once the needed clarifications are made, **everyone** may agree about what is good. This leads him to compare ethics with mathematics. He says,

> Though, therefore, we cannot prove that we are right [about (19)], yet we have reason to believe that everybody, unless he is mistaken as to what he thinks, will think the same as we. It is as with a sum in mathematics. If we find a gross and palpable error in the calculations, we are not surprised or troubled that the person who made this mistake has reached a different result from ours. We think he will admit that his result is wrong, if his mistake is pointed out to him. For instance if a man has to add up $5 + 7 + 9$, we should not wonder that he made the result to be 34, if he started by making $5 + 7 = 25$. And so in Ethics, if we find, as we did, that 'desirable' is confused with 'desired', or that 'end' is confused with 'means', we need not be disconcerted that those who have committed these mistakes do not agree with us. The only

---

[20] Pp. 144–45 (pp. 194–95, revised edition).

difference is that in Ethics, owing to the intricacy of its subject-matter, it is far more difficult to persuade anyone either that he has made a mistake or that that mistake affects his result.[21]

Here Moore seems to be suggesting that the most basic principles of ethics are, when genuinely understood, as obvious and self-evident as those of mathematics. However, if that is so, how can these ethical principles **fail** to be analytically obvious in the sense of the Moorean conjecture, if the most basic mathematical axioms are?

Whereas later philosophers would answer this question by backing away from Moorean self-evidence, and emphasizing what they took to be the essentially motivating character of ethical principles, Moore neither took this position nor provided any clear answer to this question. It is possible that, if pressed, he would **not** have been willing to characterize the most basic axioms of mathematics (apart from trivial and explicit definitions) as analytically obvious in the sense defined here. In that case, however, the basic truths of ethics and mathematics would seem to be placed on a par, in which case it would be hard to accept his cautionary warnings about our inability to prove claims about goodness, or to attach much philosophical significance to his conclusion that goodness is unanalyzable. Similar deflationary judgments would hold if Moore were to maintain that the most basic truths of both disciplines were analytically obvious.

On the other hand, it is also possible that Moore thought that although the potential obviousness of self-evident ethical truths approaches that of fundamental mathematical axioms, the obviousness of the latter is tied to meaning and understanding in a way that the obviousness of the former is not. Perhaps, unlike mathematical axioms, sentences expressing self-evident ethical truths can be fully understood, and the propositions they express can be apprehended, without one's being inclined to judge that they are true, even though thinking more about these propositions and distinguishing them from other, related propositions, can bring one to appreciate how obvious they really are. If so, then the potential for agreement in ethics may approach that of mathematics, even if the epistemological sources of agreement in the two domains are different. Such a position is not inconsistent, and it is, I think, one way of interpreting Moore. However, if he did believe something like this, he certainly didn't establish it, or even do

[21] P. 145 (p. 195, revised edition).

much to make it clear. If this was his view, one would like to have been told more about what meaning and understanding amount to in a way that illuminates the alleged difference between mathematical axioms and self-evident ethical truths, and one would like to have it explained why, if both are self-evident in their own ways, it makes a significant difference to philosophy that one bears a connection to meaning and understanding that the other does not.

A General Lesson

As I see it, there is no resolution of these issues in Moore himself. We simply have a tension in his philosophy. On the one hand, he is sensitive to the fact that *good* is difficult if not impossible to define, and to the fact that interesting claims about goodness seem, for some reason, to be resistant to proof. On the other hand, he tries to do justice to the further fact that we standardly take claims about goodness to be the sorts of things that may not only be true or false, but may also, in some cases, be known to be so—a fact that is hard to explain unless some of these claims are self-evident. In my opinion, it was a strength of his philosophy that he was sensitive to these two sets of hard-to-reconcile facts, even though he failed to adequately explain them, or to show how to plausibly and coherently bring them together. As we will see, later philosophers who were strongly influenced by his views on ethics were themselves sensitive to this tension, and many responded by reaffirming Moore's indefinability and unprovability theses, while rejecting his view that fundamental ethical statements are self-evident, knowable, or even capable of being true or false. Thus, whether rightly or wrongly, it was his indefinability and unprovability theses that were historically most influential.

There is, however, a final point that should be made before leaving this topic. In my opinion, Moore's thesis that some ethical claims are self-evident is stronger, and more plausible, than it is often taken to be. One reason for this is that the particular examples he chose to illustrate his thesis are not the best candidates for the job. Claims like those in (20) are too broad, far-reaching, and contentious to have this status. Unfortunately, it is no accident that Moore chose examples like the ones he did; his choices were driven by an implicit conception of justification in ethics that led him to look in the wrong place.

In thinking about ethical justification, Moore was, I believe, guided by three overriding ideas. First, some ethical claims are both true and capable of being known to be true; hence they must either be self-evident or be capable of being justified. Second, the process of ethical justification always comes to an end with an appeal to certain ethical judgments which cannot themselves be justified, but rather must be accepted as self-evident. Third, ethical justification flows from the general to the particular. Ethical judgments about particular cases are justified by subsuming them under general moral principles. General principles are justified by appeal to still more general principles. For Moore, the process of justification stops when one arrives at absolutely general, self-evident moral principles—at equivalences, like (20c), which are equivalent to claims of the form *for all x, x is good iff x is D.* When Moore talks about there being no reason or evidence for any ethical claims, he is, I believe, thinking, in the first instance, that there is no reason or evidence supporting these fundamental principles upon which the justification of all other ethical judgments is based.

In my view, there is both something right about this, and something wrong. What is right is that all ethical justification rests, in the end, on self-evident ethical principles that cannot themselves be justified by appealing to anything more basic. What strikes me as wrong, or over-simplified, is Moore's implicit conception of ethical justification as always involving the subsumption of specific ethical principles and judgments under more general ones. By contrast, I would claim that the genuinely self-evident ethical judgments we are able to make are restricted generalities like those in (22).[22]

22a. Any man who habitually tortures children to death solely for the pleasure of watching them suffer and die is a bad man.

b. Any action that leads to widespread, avoidable suffering and the extinction of all life is wrong.

c. Any state of affairs in which every sentient being suffers alone in intense and continual pain with no relief of any kind, followed by death, is bad.

[22] In formulating these claims, I put aside Moore's thesis of the primacy of goodness, according to which other ethical notions are defined in terms of goodness, and other ethical claims all rest, at least in part, on claims about goodness.

d. Harming others is *prima facie* wrong—i.e., any such act is wrong unless it possesses some other right-making feature that outweighs its *prima facie* wrongness.

e. Keeping one's promises is *prima facie* right.

f. A good man is concerned with the rights and the welfare of others.

g. If one promises y that one will do x, then one has an obligation to do x, unless y releases one from the obligation.

As I see it, restricted generalizations like these are the platitudes that constitute our starting points in ethics. The central difficulty in ethics is that these restricted, self-evident generalities do not cover nearly all the cases for which evaluations need to be made. Thus our problem is to systematize and extend these judgments by forming more encompassing generalizations. These more encompassing generalizations are justified by appeal to a variety of factors—including making the right characterizations of what we antecedently take to be the self-evident cases, having significant independent plausibility themselves, and fitting in well with our already accepted principles. If this is right, then the most systematic and abstract generalizations in this area will not themselves be self-evident, but rather will be justified by how well they fit in with, and systematize, a whole array of more limited self-evident claims.

Had Moore adopted this picture, his conception of proper philosophical methodology in ethics would have been more in harmony with his views in other areas of philosophy than in fact it ended up being. Think of Moore's attitude toward philosophical theories of knowledge. Many philosophers of the past thought that we could start by establishing some general epistemological theory about what counts as knowledge, and then judge claims that one knows that one has hands, that one has a body, that there are other bodies, and so on, by whether they accord with the previously postulated general epistemological principle. Against this, Moore insisted that our pre-philosophical certainties about individual instances of knowledge provide the basis we must use in evaluating any such general principle. No idea is more associated with G. E. Moore than the idea of starting with pre-philosophical certainties about particular cases, and using them to confirm or disconfirm general philosophical principles, rather than going the other way around. None of his contributions to philosophy match this one for its lasting importance. How ironic, and what a pity, that he didn't follow this method in ethics. Had he done so, the crippling philosophical tension in his ethical views might have been, to some significant degree, alleviated.

CHAPTER 4

THE LEGACIES AND LOST OPPORTUNITIES
OF MOORE'S ETHICS

Sources of Tension in Moore's Moral Philosophy

At the end of the last chapter, we noted an important tension in
Moore's ethical views. On the one hand, he held that no ethical statements about what is or isn't good are analytic; in particular, no equivalences of the sort commonly put forward by philosophers are either
provable or analytic. On the other hand, he thought that some of these
statements are both true and capable of being known to be true; for
example, he thought that the equivalence *the appreciation of beautiful
objects and the pleasures of human companionship are (intrinsically)
good, and only those things are (intrinsically) good* is true and is capable
of being known to be so. Since, in his view, this was the most fundamental ethical principle, other ethical claims could be justified by appealing to it, but it could not be justified by appeal to anything. Thus,

he was driven to the view that this most general and fundamental ethical claim was self-evident. As a result, his final position should be understood as maintaining that there is a philosophically significant choice of D such that the equivalence *things that are D are good, and only those things are good* is self-evidently obvious, even though it is neither provable nor analytic, and even though, for any relevant D, the question expressed by *Granted that α is D, is α good?* is a genuinely open question in the sense that knowing the answer to it is not guaranteed by understanding the interrogative sentence and grasping the question it expresses. In short, these equivalences are self-evidently obvious, even though the question of whether they are true is genuinely open. How could that be?

Moore got himself into this predicament by holding fast to three general ideas:

(i) The most general ethical claims, *things that are D (and only those things) are good*, are neither analytic nor susceptible to philosophical proof, for any relevant D, and for any such D the question *Granted that α is D , is α good?* is genuinely open.

(ii) Some ethical claims are both true and capable of being known to be true; hence either they are self-evident, or they can be justified.

(iii) Justification of ethical claims flows from the general to the specific. Particular claims about this or that being good are justified by appeal to generalities under which they fall. Low-level generalities are justified by higher-level generalities and equivalences, until we reach a fundamental claim *things that are D (and only those things) are good*.

(ii) and (iii) together tell us that some high-level fundamental claims must be self-evident, since they serve as the justification for lower-level claims which, being knowable, must be capable of justification. Since there is nothing more fundamental on which to base the most fundamental claims—*Things that are D (and only those things) are good*—we have no choice but to regard them as self-evident. But it is hard to square this with (i). It is not easy to see how such claims could be self-evident without being either provable or analytically obvious. Unfortunately, Moore did next to nothing to explain how this tension could be resolved.

Historically, the most important group of moral philosophers to be influenced by Moore were the emotivists, whom we will discuss later in this volume. For now, I will simply note that they resolved the tension in Moore's view by giving up (ii). For them, no sentence *Things that are D are good* is analytic, because ethical sentences are not used to describe things, or to predicate properties of objects at all. Rather, ethical sentences are rhetorical devices for the expression of one's feelings and emotions, and nothing more. Since these sentences make no claim about the world, it makes no more sense to apply the categories of truth and falsehood to them, or to claim to know them to be true, than it makes sense to apply the categories of truth and falsity to the command *Close the door!* or to claim to know it to be true. Roughly speaking, on this view, the question *Granted α is D, is α good?* is always open because no matter what property you take an object to have, it is always open to you to respond to it either negatively, or with no emotion at all.

In this way, Moore's open question argument, and the conclusions he drew from it, fed forms of skepticism and non-cognitivism in ethics that he never endorsed or approved of. This is a pity, since there was an alternative available that both would have been more appealing to him and could have gone some way toward resolving the tension in his moral philosophy. As I pointed out at the end of chapter 3, he could have given up (iii). Instead of thinking that particular, or highly restricted, claims about goodness, badness, rightness, and wrongness have to be justified by appealing to self-evident equivalences, or highly abstract generalities, involving one or more of these notions, he could have held that the starting point for moral philosophy consisted in our pre-theoretic moral certainties about particular cases, and severely restricted generalities. These are self-evident moral claims, if any are.

From this point of view, the central difficulty in ethics is that these restricted, self-evident generalities do not cover nearly all the cases for which evaluations need to be made. Hence, our problem is to systematize and extend these judgments by forming more encompassing generalizations which may be justified by appeal to a variety of factors—including making the right characterizations of what we antecedently take to be the self-evident cases, having significant independent plausibility themselves, and fitting in well with our already accepted principles. On this conception—which we will examine when we discuss the moral philosophy of the great (Moorean influenced) cognitivist opponent of the emotivists in the 1930s, Sir David Ross—the most systematic and abstract generalizations in ethics are not themselves self-evident; rather, they are justified by how well they fit in with, and systematize, a whole array of more limited self-evident claims.

Although such an approach is promising, and although it does vindicate Moore's insight that the most important and far-reaching ethical claims of interest to the philosopher are highly resistant to straightforward proof, it must be admitted that the approach doesn't entirely resolve the tension in his moral philosophy. Certainly, Moorean appeals to self-evidence are far more plausible when they are directed at highly restricted claims involving fundamental moral notions, than when they are directed at far-reaching equivalences stating necessary and sufficient conditions for the application of those notions. But even plausible appeals to seemingly obvious and restricted moral claims raise troubling questions about Moore's meta-ethical theses about the unprovability and non-analytic status of all moral statements. If some moral truths are not only necessary and knowable apriori, but also self-evident, what does it mean to say that they are not analytic, and why does it matter whether or not they are? If one can, in principle, establish significant moral claims by appealing to self-evident moral truths, what is the significance of maintaining that these claims are not provable?

The fact that Moore had no answers to these questions was, in my opinion, connected to a fundamental defect in his thinking that he shared with virtually all analytic philosophers of his time. He did not understand the fundamental methodological notions—*analysis, definability, logical implication, entailment, logical consequence, logical consistency, logical truth, analyticity, necessity, possibility, meaning,* and *proof*—that played central roles in his arguments. At first glance, his use of these notions to discuss the central issues in ethics appears to be a model of clarity and precision, and there is no doubt that he strove mightily to live up to these ideals. However, the appearance of clarity and precision is misleading. As we saw in chapter 3, his theses and arguments—though laced with precise, technical-sounding terms—were anything but clear, precise, or well-understood. In the end, unclarity about these fundamental methodological notions eviscerated his most important meta-ethical conclusions. Because his confusion and unclarity was so widely shared, this was not appreciated for decades.

Lest this judgment seem harsh, one must remember that at the turn of the century, when Moore was writing *Principia Ethica*, the analytic approach to philosophy was not in the mature, self-conscious state it is in today. Then, it was struggling to be born, and unclarities about the central modalities of analysis were to be expected. Indeed, it will be one of the themes of these volumes that much of the progress achieved in analytic philosophy in the years since *Principia Ethica* is the story of the long and difficult struggle to understand these crucially important modalities.

We now turn, in the rest of this chapter, to a collection of important and historically significant, but somewhat independent, issues concerning Moore's ethics.

Did Moore Misunderstand *Good*?

The methodological issues we have been discussing have concerned how claims formulated using the word *good* are established. Our reason for focusing on *good* is that Moore takes it to be the most fundamental term in ethics—one that can be used to define other ethical terms, such as *duty, obligation,* and *morally right action.* So far, we haven't addressed this claim of the primacy of goodness among the moral notions. We will do so shortly. Before we do, however, two points are worth noting. First, in my opinion, our discussion of how ethical claims are established would **not** have been fundamentally changed if we had focused on claims formulated using other moral terms. The conclusions we have reached about goodness carry over naturally to other moral notions. Second, a certain aspect of Moore's treatment of *good* has been subjected to a historically important criticism of which students of the subject should be aware. This criticism, which was made by Peter Geach more than fifty years after the publication of *Principia Ethica,* had an important effect not only on the prevailing view of Moore's ethical theory, but also on a number of more contemporary ethical theories that had been influenced by Moore.[1]

Geach's criticism focuses on Moore's comparison of the word *good* to the word *yellow.* As we have seen, Moore commits himself to the view that both pick out properties, and thus to the view that a certain parallel holds. In the case of *yellow,* the sentence *That is a yellow N* is equivalent to the conjunction *That is yellow and that is an N*; thus, in the case of 'good', the sentence *That is a good N* should be equivalent

---

[1] Peter Geach, "Good and Evil," *Analysis* 17 (1956); reprinted in *Theories of Ethics,* edited by Philippa Foot (Oxford: Oxford University Press, 1967).

to the conjunction *That is good and that is an N*. In many cases, however, it is not, as is shown by the following example:

P1. α is a good driver.

C1. Therefore α is good and α is a driver.

C2. Therefore α is good.

P2. α is a man.

C3. Therefore α is good and α is a man.

C4. Therefore α is a good man.

If *α is a good N* were always equivalent to *α is good and α is an N*, then this would be a valid argument, and we could derive the conclusion that x is a good man from the premises that x is a good driver and x is a man. Since, in fact, this conclusion does not follow from the premises, *α is a good N* is not always equivalent to *α is good and α is an N*. This in turn means that *good*, as is used in the phrase *a good N*, does not stand for a property that is common to all and only good things. There is no significant property common to all good men, good carpenters, good burglars, good cooks, good houses, good cheese, and so on.

When *good* is used in these constructions it has an entirely different function from picking out a property. It is, in the words of Geach, an *attributive* predicate modifier rather than predicative adjective, or separate predicate itself. When one says *α is a good N*, one is saying, roughly, *α is an N that satisfies certain contextually relevant interests taken in N's, to a higher degree than most N's*.[2] Since it is often a straightforward matter to determine what the relevant interests are, one can often provide true, informative, and relatively uncontroversial statements of the conditions that are necessary and sufficient for the predicate *is a good N* to apply to something. For example, typically, someone is a good sprinter if and only if that person runs faster than most sprinters, something is a good watch if and only if it keeps the correct time, is durable, comfortable to wear, and so on. Similar results are forthcoming whenever N is a noun (or noun phrase) that stands for things with a highly specific function, or for things for which it is otherwise obvious what the interests taken in them are.

---

[2] What these interests are, and who takes these interests in N's, are often left implicit; they vary from one context of utterance to the next.

But when N is a noun standing for things with which no specific function is associated, it is often difficult, if not impossible, to specify what it is for the predicate *is a good N* to apply. For example, when N stands for a class of things that no one has any interest in—particles of dust, for example—the claim expressed by α *is a good N* (the claim that something is a good particle of dust) will seem strange and hard to make sense of (except, perhaps, in specialized or artificial contexts). Another class of problematic cases are those in which N stands for a class of things that people do have interests in, but interests of many different and varied kinds. A case in point is the predicate, *person*. One reason why it sometimes may be hard to get a handle on what it is to be a good person is that it may sometimes be hard to pin down precisely what the relevant interests taken in people are.[3] A similar point holds when N is a highly general or abstract predicate like *event*, or *state of affairs*. Since it is unclear and indefinite what, if any, the relevant interests taken in arbitrary events, or states of affairs, might be, it is understandably unclear and indefinite what sorts of events count as good events, and what sorts of states of affairs count as good states of affairs. One may even be tempted to think that there is nothing definite in these cases to get clear about.

The predicate *is a good state of affairs* was particularly significant for Moore, who regarded it as expressing the fundamental moral concept in terms of which the moral notions of duty, obligation, and morally right action could be defined. One problem with relying so heavily on this abstract predicate is that it is so difficult to figure out what counts as a good state of affairs. Of course, Moore had his own explanation of why it is so hard to establish claims about which states of affairs are good. On his view, since *good* stands for a simple, unanalyzable property common to all and only good states of affairs, claims about what is good cannot be established by abstract reasoning, or philosophical analysis. Since the property is non-natural, such claims cannot be settled by empirical observation either. For Moore, this left only intellectual intuition—something we scarcely understand. Later, the emotivists had their own explanation of why it is so hard to establish claims about which states of affairs are good. Such claims cannot be established because they are not really descriptive claims at all. For the emotivists,

---

[3] However, it does seem clear that some interests standardly taken in people—e.g., beauty, athletic ability, even intelligence—are virtually never the relevant dimensions for judging someone to be a good person.

good doesn't stand for any property; it is simply a rhetorical device used to express the feelings and evaluative attitudes of the speaker.

We now see, however, that there is another possible explanation of why the claim that x is a good state of affairs is so resistant to proof. If, as Geach maintains, *good* always functions as an attributive predicate modifier, rather than as a predicate or predicative adjective, then it may be perfectly descriptive without standing for any property at all. If, in addition, *a good N* means something like *an N that satisfies the contextually relevant interests taken in N's to a higher degree than most N's*, then the claim expressed by *α is a good N* will be unclear, open-ended, and hard to establish whenever it is unclear and indefinite what, if any, the relevant interests taken in things denoted by N are supposed to be. This is precisely what we find when we let N be the abstract predicate *state of affairs*. Since states of affairs have no function, and since there is no specific interest that we standardly take in arbitrary states of affairs, the claim that something is a good state of affairs is apt to seem vague and indefinite. No wonder one has a hard time seeing how to prove such claims.

As I see it, this is the most important criticism of Moore's discussion of goodness that can be extracted from Geach's analysis of *good* as an attributive predicate modifier. It is useful, in assessing its import, to separate uncontroversial matters of more or less established fact from issues that remain contentious, or unresolved. First, it is obvious that many, perhaps most, ordinary uses of the word *good* are uses in which it functions as an attributive predicate modifier in Geach's sense. Second, it seems clear that when *good* is used attributively it has an analysis of roughly the sort indicated above—one in which *good N* applies to things that satisfy certain interests taken in things denoted by N. However, the precise details of this analysis are debatable, and remain open to fine-tuning. Which interests in things denoted by N are the ones relevant to determining the denotation of *good N*, and whose interests are they? Are they the interests of everyone, the interests of those who may be choosing among things denoted by N, the interests of the speaker, the interests of an ideally situated observer who shares the speaker's values and knows all the relevant facts, or are they the interests of some group that the speaker has in mind and implicitly refers to? These (and other) options remain open.

Another matter that has not been conclusively resolved is whether *good* is always used attributively. Certainly it is sometimes used on its own, without an accompanying noun or noun phrase. In many of these cases it is clear from the context of utterance that some implicit N is intended. Geach maintains that this is always so.

> Even when *good* or *bad* stands by itself as a predicate, and is thus grammatically predicative, some substantive has to be understood; there is no such thing as being just good or bad, there is only being a good or bad so-and-so. (If I say that something is a good or bad *thing*, either 'thing' is a mere proxy for a more descriptive noun to be supplied from the context; or else I am trying to use 'good' or 'bad' predicatively, and its being grammatically attributive is a mere disguise. The latter attempt is, on my thesis, illegitimate.)[4]

Although Geach's claim is a bold one, it is not obvious that it is correct. If you say *Dick just got out of the hospital*, and I say *That's good*, my remark seems perfectly intelligible, even though it is not obvious what, if any, background noun or noun phrase *good* is modifying (short of the highly abstract and uninformative *event* or *state of affairs*). Could this be a genuinely predicative use of *good*? If so, is it the sort of use that Moore might appeal to in elucidating his notion of a good or desirable state of affairs? These questions are controversial, and remain unresolved. As valuable as Geach's contribution is to our understanding of the word *good*, it would, I think, be going too far to claim that he has established that there is no central notion in ethics akin to that of a good, or desirable, state of affairs, in roughly the sense understood by Moore.

Definability, Consequentialism, and the Primacy of Goodness

In chapter 3, we examined at length Moore's stringent conception of definition, and his argument that *good* is indefinable. According to Moore, no expression D counts as definitionally equivalent to *good* unless (i) it expresses the very same property as *good*, (ii) a competent speaker who understands both D and *good* would recognize that they mean the same thing, and (iii) substitution of one for the other in an ordinary declarative or interrogative sentence S preserves the propos-

---

[4] "Good and Evil," p. 65 in the Foote volume.

ition, or question, that S expresses. Philosophers who did not recognize that *good* is indefinable in this sense—those who maintained *good* could be defined, or that the property goodness could be analyzed—were regarded by Moore as guilty of having committed what he called *the naturalistic fallacy*, which he described as follows:

> It may be true that all things which are good are *also* something else, just as it is true that all things which are yellow produce a certain kind of vibration of light. And it is a fact that Ethics aims at discovering what are those other properties belonging to all things which are good. But far too many philosophers have thought that when they named these other properties they were actually defining good; that these other properties, in fact, were simply not 'other', but absolutely and entirely the same with goodness. This view I propose to call the 'naturalistic fallacy' and of it I shall endeavor to dispose.'[5]

By contrast, Moore claims that the notions of an act being right, being our duty, and being one that we ought to perform **are definable**—in terms of goodness. Not only does he think that all and only right actions share the property of causing consequences the goodness of which is not exceeded by those that would be caused by any alternative action open to the agent, he also believes that rightness is entirely the same as this property. Two places where he expresses this belief are sections 88 and 89 of *Principia Ethica*.

> To ask what kind of actions we ought to perform, or what kind of conduct is right, is to ask what kind of effects such action and conduct will produce. Not a single question in practical Ethics can be answered except by a causal generalization. All such questions do, indeed, also involve an ethical judgement proper—the judgement that certain effects are better, in themselves, than others. But they do assert that these better things are effects—are causally connected with the actions in question. Every judgement in practical Ethics may be reduced to the form: This is a cause of that good thing.[6]

> What I wish first to point out is that *right* does and can mean nothing but *cause of a good result*, and is thus identical with *useful*;

[5] *Principia Ethica*, section 10, p. 10 (p. 62 of the revised edition).
[6] Ibid., section 88, p. 146 (p. 196 of the revised edition).

whence it follows that the end always will justify the means, and that no action which is not justified by its results can be right.[7]

However, at this point a natural question arises. Can it really be that the two expressions *α is a right action* and *α is the cause of a good result*[8] satisfy Moore's stringent criteria for meaning the same thing? To suppose that they do is to suppose that any (fully) competent speaker of English who understands both will recognize (i) that they mean the same thing, and (ii) that Q1 expresses the same trivial, self-answering question as Q2.

Q1. Granted that $α$ causes a good result, is $α$ right?

Q2. Granted that $α$ causes a good result, does $α$ cause a good result?

But this simply does not seem to be so. Someone might feel unsure whether, in a particular case, lying or breaking a promise to produce a certain good result is right. Such a person might have no doubt that a good result would be achieved, while wondering whether the wrong-making features of the act itself, or its relation to past events, outweigh the goodness of the state of affairs that the action would cause to exist. Whatever the correct answer may be in a case like this, a person confronted with this dilemma may naturally use Q1 to express a genuine question that cannot be identified with the triviality expressed by Q2. Thus, it would seem that, by Moore's own standards, *a right act* is **not** definable as *a cause of a good result*.

In 1930, in his classic work *The Right and the Good*, Sir David Ross made precisely this argument. He accused Moore of being guilty of a fallacy with regard to *right* of the same type as the (supposed) naturalistic fallacy with regard to *good*. Here is an illustrative passage.

> The most deliberate claim that *right* is definable as *productive of so and so* is made by Prof. G. E. Moore, who claims in *Principia Ethica* that *right* means *productive of the greatest possible good*. Now it has often been pointed out against hedonism, and by no one more clearly than Prof. Moore, that the claim that *good* just means *pleasant* cannot seriously be maintained; that while it may or may not be true that the only things that are good are pleasant, the statement that the good is just the pleasant is a synthetic, not

---

[7] Ibid., section 89, p. 147 (pp. 196–97 of the revised edition).

[8] I.e., a result the goodness of which is not exceeded by the goodness of the result caused by any alternative action open to the agent.

an analytic proposition; that the words *good* and *pleasant* stand for distinct qualities, even if the things that possess the one are precisely the things that possess the other. If this were not so, it would not be intelligible that the proposition *the good is just the pleasant* should have been maintained on the one hand, and denied on the other, with so much fervor; for we do not fight for or against analytic propositions; we take them for granted. Must not the same claim be made about the statement *being right means being an act productive of the greatest good producible in the circumstances?* Is it not plain on reflection that this is not what we mean by *right*, even if it be a true statement about what is right? It seems clear for instance that when an ordinary man says it is right to fulfil promises he is not in the least thinking of the total consequences of such an act, about which he knows and cares little or nothing. 'Ideal utilitarianism' [i.e., consequentialism] is, it would appear, plausible only when it is understood not as an analysis or definition of the notion of *right* but as a statement that all acts that are right, and only these, possess the further characteristic of being productive of the best possible consequences, and are right because they possess this other characteristic.[9]

Given Moore's own standards of definition, one is hard pressed not to agree with Ross that the proposed definition of rightness of an action in terms of goodness of its consequences fails to satisfy them.

How could Moore have thought otherwise? He tells us most clearly in section 89 of *Principia Ethica*, where he says the following:

That the assertion *I am morally bound to perform this action* is identical with the assertion *This action will produce the greatest possible amount of good in the Universe* has already been briefly shown in Chap. 1 (section 17); but it is important to insist that this fundamental point is demonstrably certain. This may, perhaps, be best made evident in the following way. **It is plain that when we assert that a certain action is our absolute duty, we are asserting that the performance of that action at that time is unique in respect to value.** But no dutiful action can possibly have unique value in the sense that it is the sole thing of value in the world; since, in that case, *every* such action would be the *sole* good thing, which is a

---

[9] W. D. Ross, *The Right and the Good* (Oxford: The Clarendon Press, 1930), pp. 8–9.

manifest contradiction. And for the same reason its value cannot be unique in the sense that it has more intrinsic value than anything else in the world; since *every* act of duty would then be the *best* thing in the world, which is also a contradiction. **It can, therefore, be unique only in the sense that the whole world will be better, if it be performed, than if any possible alternative were taken. And the question whether this is so cannot possibly depend solely on the question of its own intrinsic value. For any action will also have effects different from those of any other action; and if any of these have intrinsic value, their value is exactly as relevant to the total goodness of the Universe as that of their cause.** It is, in fact, evident that, however valuable an action may be in itself, yet, owing to its existence, the sum of good in the Universe may conceivably be made less than if some other action, less valuable in itself, had been performed. But to say that this is the case is to say that it would have been better that the action should not have been done; and this again is obviously equivalent to the statement that it ought not to have been done—that it is not what duty required. . . .

Our 'duty,' therefore, can only be defined as that action, which will cause more good to exist in the universe than any possible alternative. And what is 'right' or 'morally permissible' only differs from this, as what will *not* cause *less* good than any possible alternative.[10]

In this passage, we see a remarkable transformation. Consequentialism is standardly understood as the doctrine that the rightness of an act depends **not at all** on the intrinsic character of the act itself, the agent's motivation in performing it, or the relation between the act and past actions or states of affairs, but **only** on the value of the consequences that come after, and are caused by the act. Moore's own language throughout *Principia Ethica* suggests this—for example, his repeated insistence that rightness is a matter of the goodness of that which an action **causes** (which must therefore come after the action). Certainly this is how Ross understood Moore's claim that *being right* simply means *being the cause of a good result*. Although this **is** the natural way to understand Moore's language throughout the work, it is clear that, at

[10] *Principia Ethica*, section 89, pp. 147–48 (pp. 197–98, revised edition), my boldface emphasis.

least in the passage, it is not what he really meant. There, in the process of defending the claim that consequentialism is true by definition, Moore transforms it from a highly interesting, but debatable, ethical thesis into something that approaches an uninformative triviality.

The gist of his argument in the passage is as follows: To say that an action is our duty is to say that it is the action that it would be best for us to perform, which is to say that it would be better, all things considered, for us to perform it than for us not to do so. Moreover, for it to be better, all things considered, for us to perform the action, rather than not, is for all the positive, morally relevant factors bearing on the action to outweigh the negative morally relevant factors associated with its performance. Here, by a *morally relevant factor* we mean anything that bears on the potential rightness or wrongness of the act—the value of the effects it causes, the intrinsic character of the act itself (e.g., whether or not it is a lie), the relation of the act to past actions and events (e.g., whether it involves doing what one has previously promised to do), the motivation it grows out of (e.g., gratitude for past service), or any number of other things. When, taking all these things into consideration, we judge it to be better to perform the act than not, we are saying that the universe would be better if the act were performed than if it weren't. Thus, when we say that an act is our duty we are saying that it maximizes value in the universe as a whole. In short, consequentialism is true by definition.

Like many sophistical arguments, this one confronts us with a choice. If one takes consequentialism to be the interesting, but debatable, thesis that the rightness of an action is determined solely by the goodness of the events or states of affairs that follow, and are causally produced by, it—and not at all by the intrinsic nature of the act itself, or its relations to past events—then the argument does **not** establish that consequentialism is true by definition; in fact it tacitly presupposes that consequentialism may well be false. By contrast, if one includes every state of affairs involving the action as among its consequences, while including every morally relevant feature of the action in the value of these "consequences," then one can understand how the conclusion that consequentialism is true by definition might seem tempting. However, the cost of adopting this strategy is to drain the doctrine of most of its philosophical significance. But whatever the merits of the strategy, the one thing that one must **not** do is combine the two options—treating consequentialism as a highly informative, and substantial, ethical doctrine, while regarding it as true by definition, in

Moore's sense. It is a defect of *Principia Ethica* that the overall impression given by the work is of just such a combination—which is precisely how Ross interpreted the work.

In fairness, it should be pointed out that, in time, Moore himself seemed to recognize the validity of this criticism. In his little book, *Ethics*, originally published in 1912, nine years after *Principia Ethica*, he vigorously defends consequentialism in its interesting, and debatable, form. As for the question of whether consequentialism about rightness or duty is true by definition, he says the following:

> [E]ven if we admit that to call an action expedient is the same thing as to say that it produces the best possible consequences, our principle still does not compel us to hold that to call an action expedient is *the same thing* as to call it a duty. All that it does compel us to hold is that whatever is expedient is always *also* a duty, and that whatever is a duty is always *also* expedient. That is to say, it *does* maintain that duty and expediency *coincide*; but it does *not* maintain that the meaning of the two words is the same. It is, indeed, quite plain, I think, that the meaning of the two words is *not* the same; for, if it were, then it would be a mere tautology to say that it is always our duty to do what will have the best possible consequences. Our theory does not, therefore, do away with the distinction between the *meaning* of the words 'duty' and 'expediency'; it only maintains that both will always apply to the same actions.[11]

The import of this change for Moore's overall position is that now he has the task of defending his fundamental consequentialist claims about rightness and duty in the same way—either by appeal to self-evident moral facts revealed by moral intuition, or in some other way— that he defends his fundamental claims about goodness.[12]

Moore's Argument against Subjectivism

In addition to containing this significant change in view, Moore's second book in moral philosophy, *Ethics*, contains an important chapter

---

[11] G. E. Moore, *Ethics* (London, Oxford, New York: Oxford University Press, 1912; reprinted 1965).

[12] Being the careful commentator that he was, Ross noted this change in Moore's position between *Principia Ethica* and *Ethics*, and even called attention to the passage from *Ethics* cited above.

devoted to the question of the objectivity of moral judgments. According to Moore, it is the essence of objectivity that if one person says of a given act *it is wrong* and another says of the same act *it is right* (or *not wrong*), then they cannot both be correct. Even if both are equally sincere and conscientious, x cannot be both wrong and right, and so, Moore thinks, one of them must be in error.

Recognizing that there are those who would dispute this, he points out that many who would do so believe that to assert of an act that it is right, or wrong, is to assert something about someone's feelings toward the act. A familiar version of this subjectivist view holds that

> whenever any man asserts an action to be right or wrong, what he is asserting is merely that he *himself* has some particular feeling towards the action in question. Each of us, according to this view, is merely making an assertion about *his own* feelings: when *I* assert that an action is right, the *whole* of what I mean is merely that *I* have some particular feeling towards the action; and when *you* make the same assertion, the *whole* of what you mean is merely that *you* have the feeling in question towards the action.[13]

Moore points out the following consequence of this view:

> If, whenever I judge an action to be right, I am merely judging that I myself have a particular feeling towards it, then it plainly follows that, provided I really have the feeling in question, my judgement is true, and therefore the action in question really is right. And what is true of me, in this respect, will also be true of any other man. . . . It strictly follows, therefore, from this theory that whenever *any man whatever* really has a particular feeling towards an action, the action really is right; and whenever *any man whatever* really has another particular feeling towards an action, the action really is wrong. . . . And now . . . it seems plainly to follow that, if this be so, one and the same action must quite often be both right and wrong.[14]

Although there is a slight mistake in this passage, it is correctable. The subjectivist described by Moore is committed to the view that two different men, one who says of a certain act x *it is right* and the other who says of x *it is wrong*, may both be correctly describing their

[13] *Ethics*, p. 37.
[14] Ibid., pp. 38–39.

feelings, and hence be speaking truly. But the subjectivist **is not** thereby committed to saying of x, *it is both right and wrong*. A Moorean subjectivist who said this would be saying of x that he, the subjectivist, had both the requisite right-making feeling about x and the requisite wrong-making feeling about x—feelings that he may well not have had. Depending on what the requisite feelings are, the subjectivist might even tell us that it is impossible for anyone to simultaneously have both toward the same act. Such a subjectivist would vigorously dissent from the sentence *one and the same action can be both right and wrong*.

Nevertheless, the subjectivist described by Moore does remain committed to the view that when one person says of x, *it is right*, and the other says, *it is wrong*, or even *it is not right*, the two speakers **do not** contradict each other, and both may be speaking truly. Moore, quite rightly, thinks that this alone is a fatal objection to the subjectivist view. He asks:

> Can it possibly be the case, then, that, when we judge an action to be right or wrong, each of us is only asserting that *he himself* has some particular feeling towards it?[15]

He answers:

> It seems to me that there is an absolutely fatal objection to the view that this is the case. It must be remembered that the question is merely a question of fact; a question as to the actual analysis of our moral judgements—as to what it is that actually happens, when we *think* an action to be right or wrong. And if we remember that it is thus merely a question as to what we *actually* think, when we think an action to be right or wrong—neither more nor less than this—it can, I think, be clearly seen that the view we are considering is inconsistent with plain facts. This is so because it involves a curious consequence, which those who hold it do not always seem to realize that it involves; and this consequence is, I think, plainly not in accordance with the facts. The consequence is this. If, when one man says, 'This action is right', and another answers, 'No, it is not right', each of them is always merely making an assertion about *his own* feelings, it plainly follows that there is never really any difference of opinion between them: the one of them is never really contradicting what the other is asserting. They

[15] Ibid., pp. 41–42.

are no more contradicting one another than if, when one had said, 'I like sugar', the other had answered, 'I don't like sugar'. In such a case, there is, of course, no conflict of opinion, no contradiction of one by the other: for it may perfectly well be the case that what each asserts is equally true; it may quite well be the case that the one man really does like sugar, and the other really does *not* like it. The one, therefore, is *never* denying what the other is asserting. And what the view we are considering involves is that when one man holds an action to be right, and another holds it to be wrong or not right, here also the one is *never* denying what the other is asserting. It involves, therefore, the very curious consequence that no two men can ever differ in opinion as to whether an action is right or wrong. And surely the fact that it involves this consequence is sufficient to condemn it. It is surely a plain matter of fact that when I assert an action to be wrong, and another man asserts it to be right, there sometimes is a real difference of opinion between us: he sometimes is denying the very thing which I am asserting. But, if this is so, then it cannot possibly be the case that each of us is merely making a judgement about his own feelings; since two such judgements never can contradict one another.[16]

What this argument shows is that a certain form of subjectivism cannot account for the reality of ethical disagreement, and therefore must be rejected. What the argument does **not** show is that **no** form of subjectivism can accommodate this reality, and hence that ethical judgments are "objective" in some robust sense. For example, a form of subjectivism which maintained that to say that an act is right is to say that everyone, or everyone who satisfies a certain condition, who considers the act will have a certain attitude toward it might well accommodate the fact that a person who says of x, *it is not right*, does indeed contradict a person who says of x, *it is right*. There may, of course, be other objections to such a subjectivist view, but at least it is compatible with Moore's argument. Later, when we discuss emotivism, we will see how Moore's argument against subjectivism played a historically important role in leading prominent emotivists like C. L. Stevenson to shape their emotivist brand of subjectivism in ways that allowed them to accommodate ethical disagreement.[17]

[16] Ibid., p. 42.
[17] C. L. Stevenson, "The Emotive Meaning of Ethical Terms," *Mind* 46 (1937); reprinted in *Logical Positivism*, edited by A. J. Ayer (New York and London: Free Press, 1959).

SUGGESTED FURTHER READING
FOR PART ONE

Main Primary Sources Discussed

Moore, G. E. "A Defense of Common Sense." In *Contemporary British Philosophy* (2nd Series), edited by J. H. Muirhead, 1925; reprinted in G. E. Moore, *Philosophical Papers* (London: Collier Books, 1962), 32–59. See especially sections 1 and 4.

———. *Ethics.* London, Oxford, New York: Oxford University Press, originally published in 1912; reprinted in 1965.

———. *Principia Ethica.* Cambridge: Cambridge University Press, 1903; revised edition, 1993. See especially the preface, chapter 1, chapter 5, and chapter 6.

———. "Proof of an External World." *Proceedings of the British Academy* 25 (1939); reprinted in his *Philosophical Papers*.

———. *Some Main Problems of Philosophy.* New York: Macmillan, 1953. See especially chapters 1, 2, 5, and 6.

Additional Primary Sources

Moore, G. E. "An Autobiography." In *The Philosophy of G. E. Moore*, volume 1, edited by P. A. Schilpp (La Salle, IL: Open Court, and London: Cambridge University Press, third edition, 1968), pp. 3–39.

———. "Hume's Philosophy," *The New Quarterly*, November 1909; reprinted in Moore, *Philosophical Studies*, (Totowa, NJ: Littlefield, Adams & Co., 1968).

Additional Recommended Reading

Davies, Martin. "Externalism and Armchair Knowledge." In Paul Beghossian and Christopher Peacocke, eds., *New Essays on the Apriori*, (Oxford: Clarendon Press, 2000).

Geach, Peter. "Good and Evil," *Analysis*, Vol. 17, 1956; reprinted in Philippa Foot, ed., *Theories of Ethics* (Oxford: Oxford University Press), 1967.

Pryor, James. "Is Moore's Argument an Example of Transmission-Failure?" Forthcoming.

———. "The Skeptic and the Dogmatist." *Noûs* 34 (2000).

Ross, W. D. *The Right and the Good.* Oxford: Clarendon Press, 1930.

PART TWO

BERTRAND RUSSELL

ON LOGICAL

AND LINGUISTIC ANALYSIS

CHAPTER 5

LOGICAL FORM, GRAMMATICAL FORM, AND THE THEORY OF DESCRIPTIONS

Bertrand Russell and G. E. Moore were contemporaries who influenced one another very significantly, particularly in the early stages of their careers. They met as students at Cambridge at the end of the nineteenth-century, where both began their studies in fields other than philosophy. Whereas Moore started his student days with a strong interest in classics, and was later won over to philosophy by Russell, Russell himself began as an undergraduate in mathematics, and was initially drawn to philosophy by an interest in the philosophical foundations of mathematics, to which he devoted the early part of his career. Among his most lasting contributions was his pioneering work in symbolic logic. However, he didn't confine himself to technical issues. Rather, his goal was to bring the rigor and scientific spirit found in mathematics to the philosophy of mathematics, and all of philosophy. Central to this goal was his use of certain results and techniques of logic to attack traditional philosophical problems.

Background of the Theory of Descriptions

One of the most important of those techniques is the use of his theory of descriptions. In order to understand what led Russell to this theory, one first must understand a little of the philosophical scene in which he developed the theory. At the time Russell and Moore first became interested in philosophy, the dominant school of thought at Cambridge was Absolute Idealism, a leading proponent of which was one of their teachers at Cambridge, J.M.E. McTaggart. Philosophers of this school typically held that all of reality is spiritual—that is what made them *idealists*. They also held that the whole of reality is a single unified object, either a divine mind or (depending on the idealist) an integrated system of interdependent minds—that is what made them *absolute* idealists. One idea that contributed to this overall picture was something called *the doctrine of the reality of internal relations*. In its most extreme form, the doctrine held that the nature and existence of each object is so dependent upon that of every other object, that had any entity lacked even a single property that it actually possesses, neither the universe itself, nor any part of it, would have existed. Although this view is startling, and certainly contradicts our ordinary ways of thinking, the argument for it given by the idealists had a degree of plausibility, and (and as we will see later) is not entirely without interest.

For a time while they were students, Moore and Russell were influenced by the idealist views of their teachers. However, they soon rebelled, with Moore leading the way. Some of his most interesting articles—for example, "The Refutation of Idealism" and "External and Internal Relations"—offered clear and powerful critiques of central

idealist doctrines.[1] Very early on, Moore's opposition to absolute idealism led him to an extreme version of a view known as *philosophical
realism*, but which might better be called *philosophical pluralism*. He
was followed in his adherence to this view by Russell.

The early realism of Moore and Russell consisted of three basic
ontological commitments. The first was a belief in the existence of
everyday objects—persons, bodies, material objects, and so on. Initially,
neither Moore nor Russell had any tendency to say that in reality there
are no such things as we commonly suppose, but only various constel-
lations of other, more basic elements. Their second realist commitment
was a belief in the existence of mathematical and logical entities such as
numbers, sets, relations, and properties—roughly what philosophers
have called *abstract objects*. The third commitment of their early realism
was the belief that, as they put it, *every object of thought* must possess
some kind of being (since otherwise we couldn't think about it). According to this belief, the fact that one can think of Pegasus, Santa Claus,
and the present king of France indicates that they must have some
kind of being, and hence that they are genuine constituents of reality.

These three ontological commitments are positions which Moore
and Russell initially held, but which they later modified or abandoned,
this time with Russell leading the way. In the end, he went much further in criticizing them than Moore ever did, eventually rejecting most
of what they expressed. This move away from philosophical pluralism
paved the way for new and more radical interpretations of the view
that philosophy is analysis, laying the foundations for the later schools
of logical atomism and logical positivism. We will trace Russell's progress down this path, beginning with the first step he took in this
direction: the development of his theory of descriptions.

This theory was central to his rejection of the view that every object
of thought must have being, and hence that there must be such things
as Pegasus, Santa Claus, and the present king of France. The key argument in favor of that doctrine was based on statements called *negative
existentials*. The argument is given in Russell's early book *The
Principles of Mathematics*, which was written in 1900 and published in
1903.[2]

[1] The former was originally published in *Mind* 12 (1903); the latter was originally published
in *Proceedings of the Aristotelian Society*, 1919–20; both are reprinted in G. E. Moore,
Philosophical Studies (Totowa, NJ: Littlefield and Adams, 1968).
[2] Bertrand Russell, *The Principles of Mathematics* (New York: Norton and Co.).

Early in the book, Russell explains some key terminology and antici-
pates the argument based on negative existentials to be given later.

> Whatever may be an object of thought, or may occur in any true
> or false proposition, or can be counted as *one*, I call a *term*. . . . A
> man, a moment, a number, a class, a relation, a chimera, or any-
> thing else that can be mentioned, is sure to be a term; and to deny
> that such and such a thing is a term must always be false.[3]

The argument for this conclusion is stated by Russell later in the book
as follows:

> *Being* is that which belongs to every conceivable term, to every
> possible object of thought—in short to everything that can possi-
> bly occur in any proposition, true or false, and to all such propo-
> sitions themselves. Being belongs to whatever can be counted. If
> A be any term that can be counted as one, it is plain that A is
> something, and therefore that A is. "A is not" must always be either
> false or meaningless. For if A were nothing, it could not be said
> not to be; "A is not" implies that there is a term A whose being is
> denied, and hence that A is. Thus unless "A is not" be an empty
> sound, it must be false—whatever A may be it certainly is. Numbers,
> the Homeric gods, relations, chimeras and four-dimensional spaces
> all have being, for if they were not entities of a kind, we could make
> no propositions about them. Thus being is a general attribute of
> everything, and to mention anything is to show that it is.[4]

In examining Russell's position, we will first reconstruct the argument
for his paradoxical conclusion, and then show how he later used his
theory of descriptions to block the problematic conclusion. The argument is based on *negative existentials*, which, for present purposes, we
may take to include any sentence of the form (a) or (b).

a. x doesn't exist.

b. x's don't exist.

Examples of negative existentials are (1–3).

1. Carnivorous cows don't exist.

---

[3] Ibid., p. 43.
[4] Ibid., p. 449.

2. The creature from the black lagoon doesn't exist.

3. Santa Claus doesn't exist.

With these examples in mind, Russell's 1903 argument may be reconstructed as follows:

P1. Meaningful negative existentials, such as (1–3), are subject-predicate sentences. For example, the subject of (1) is *carnivorous cows* and the predicate is *don't exist*.

P2. A meaningful subject-predicate sentence is true if and only if there is an object (or there are objects) to which the subject expression refers, and this object (or these objects) has (have) the property expressed by the predicate.

C1. Sentence (1) can be true only if there are objects—carnivorous cows—to which its subject expression, *carnivorous cows*, refers, and these objects have the property of not existing. Ditto for (2), (3), and all other meaningful negative existentials.

P3. No objects have the property of not existing. If there are objects to which the subjects of meaningful negative existentials refer, then they exist.

C2. Meaningful negative existentials cannot be true.

C3. So, there are no true, meaningful, negative existentials.

C4. In other words, true, meaningful, negative existentials don't exist.

C4 is itself both a meaningful negative existential and a consequence of P1–P3. Since these premises entail a general claim which is a counterexample to itself, at least one of them must be false. The question is which. Russell's original, 1903 "realist" (or "pluralist") solution located the difficulty in P3. According to the view he held then, being comes in degrees, including a category of nonexistent things that have being to a lower degree than do the things that exist. On this view there really are such things as carnivorous cows, the largest prime number, the 'f' in the word *philosophy*, the present king of France, the golden mountain, and even the existent golden mountain. There are such things; they have being, even though they don't exist. These are to be contrasted with things that really do exist, such as the queen of

England, the only even prime number, and Mount Vesuvius. As Russell put it then, *"being is a general attribute of everything, and to mention something is to show that it is. Existence, on the contrary, is the prerogative of some only amongst beings."*[5]

Although Russell was initially attracted to this view, he soon came to regard it as incredible. By 1905, he was already attributing it to another philosopher, Meinong, and criticizing it in the following way:

> This theory regards any grammatically correct denoting phrase as standing for an *object.* Thus 'the present King of France', 'the round square', etc. are supposed to be genuine objects. It is admitted that such objects do not *subsist,* but nevertheless they are supposed to be objects. This is in itself a difficult view; but the chief objection is that such objects, admittedly, are apt to infringe the law of contradiction. It is contended, for example, that the existent present King of France exists, and also does not exist; that the round square is round, and also not round, etc. But this is intolerable; and if any theory can be found to avoid this result, it is surely to be preferred.[6]

Years later, in the chapter entitled "Descriptions" of his book *Introduction to Mathematical Philosophy* (written while he was in prison protesting the first world war, and originally published in 1919), Russell expressed his objection to his early, 1903 view, as follows:

> For want of the apparatus of propositional functions [a central feature of Russell's 1905 theory of descriptions] many logicians have been driven to the conclusion that there are unreal objects. It is argued, e.g., by Meinong, that we can speak about "the golden mountain," "the round square," and so on; we can make true propositions of which these are the subjects; hence they must have some kind of logical being, since otherwise the propositions in which they occur would be meaningless. In such theories, it seems to me, there is a failure of that feeling for reality which ought to be preserved even in the most abstract studies. Logic, I should maintain, must no more admit a unicorn than zoology can; for logic is concerned with the real world just as truly as zoology,

[5] Ibid., p. 449.
[6] Russell, "On Denoting," *Mind* 14 (1905); reprinted in *Logic and Knowledge*, R. C. Marsh, ed. (New York: Capricorn Books, 1956), p. 45. All citations will be to the Marsh volume.

though with its more abstract and general features. To say that unicorns have an existence in heraldry, or in literature, or in imagination, is a most pitiful and paltry evasion. What exists in heraldry is not an animal, made of flesh and blood, moving and breathing of its own initiative. What exists is a picture, or a description in words. Similarly, to maintain that Hamlet, for example, exists in his own world, namely, in the world of Shakespeare's imagination, just as truly as (say) Napoleon existed in the ordinary world, is to say something deliberately confusing, or else confused to a degree which is scarcely credible. There is only one world, the "real" world: Shakespeare's imagination is part of it, and the thoughts that he had in writing Hamlet are real. So are the thoughts that we have in reading the play. But it is of the very essence of fiction that only the thoughts, feelings, etc., in Shakespeare and his readers are real, and that there is not, in addition to them, an objective Hamlet. When you have taken account of all the feelings roused by Napoleon in writers and readers of history, you have not touched the actual man; but in the case of Hamlet, you have come to the end of him. If no one thought about Hamlet, there would be nothing left of him; if no one had thought about Napoleon, he would have soon seen to it that some one did.[7]

It is evident, then, that Russell came to thoroughly reject the extreme "realist" view originally supported by his 1903 argument involving negative existentials. It was his theory of descriptions, first presented in "On Denoting" in 1905, that allowed him to do this. Central to that theory, and to his rejection of his earlier argument, was his famous distinction between *logical form* and *grammatical form*. According to Russell, sentences express thoughts, or propositions. Just as a sentence has a *grammatical form*, so the proposition (thought) expressed by the sentence has a *logical form*. Sometimes the logical form of the proposition expressed by S matches the grammatical form of S, and sometimes it doesn't. When S is grammatically of subject-predicate form and the logical form of the proposition it expresses **matches** the grammatical form of S, S is said to be *logically* of subject-predicate form. This is the case when the proposition P expressed by S can be exhaustively

[7] Bertrand Russell, *Introduction to Mathematical Philosophy* (New York: Dover, 1993), pp. 169–70. (First published by Allen and Unwin, London, and Macmillan, New York, 1919.)

divided into two parts: (i) the property expressed by the predicate, (ii) a constituent corresponding to the grammatical subject of S. For now we leave it open whether this constituent is the referent of the subject expression or a concept that determines the referent of the subject. (In the end Russell would insist that it must be the referent, but we need not insist on this now. In either case it is understood that the property expressed by the predicate is to be predicated of the referent of the subject expression.) The logical form of S (i.e., of the proposition expressed by S) plays an important role in determining the conditions under which S is true.

With this in mind, the paradox involving negative existentials can be restated as follows:

P1a.   Meaningful negative existentials, like (1–3), are logically of subject-predicate form.

P2a.   A sentence that is logically of subject-predicate form is true if and only if there is an object (or there are objects) to which the subject expression refers, and this object (or these objects) has (have) the property expressed by the predicate.

C1.   Sentence (1) can be true only if there are objects—carnivorous cows— to which its subject expression, *carnivorous cows*, refers, and these objects have the property of not existing. Ditto for (2), (3), and all other meaningful negative existentials.

P3.   No objects have the property of not existing. If there are objects to which the subjects of meaningful negative existentials refer, then they exist.

C2.   Meaningful negative existentials cannot be true.

C3.   So, there are no true, meaningful, negative existentials.

C4.   In other words, true, meaningful, negative existentials don't exist.

Russell's 1905 solution to this version of the paradox is to deny P1a. Although negative existentials such as (1–3) are grammatically of subject-predicate form, he claims that the propositions (thoughts) they express are not. His strategy is to produce, for each problematic negative existential sentence S, a logically equivalent sentence S_1 that is not of subject-predicate form—where the grammatical structure of

S_1 mirrors the logical structure of the proposition that both S and S_1 express. In the case of the negative existential C4, the relevant paraphrase might be C3 or C2. In the case of the negative existential (1) it might be something along the lines of (4).

4. Everything is such that either it isn't a cow or it isn't carnivorous.

When we look at (4), we see that no part of the sentence has the job of referring to something which is then said not to exist. Thus, there is nothing paradoxical about declaring it to be true. Finally, if sentence (1) expresses the same proposition as (4), then its truth is not paradoxical either.

Two things are needed in order to extend this approach to negative existentials generally, as well as to other philosophically problematic sentences. First, we need some conception of the logical form of propositions (thoughts) expressed by sentences, and some clear and unambiguous way of representing that form. Second, we need some precise and systematic way of deriving the logical form of a sentence of ordinary English from its evident grammatical form. Both are provided by Russell's theory of descriptions, which we will present in three stages. First, we will define a simple formal language for representing logical form, and provide a Russellian interpretation of that language in which the grammatical forms of its sentences mirror the logical structures of the propositions (thoughts) they express. Next, we will examine how Russell uses his formal language to provide analyses of problematic negative existentials. Finally, we will present Russellian rules for translating ordinary sentences of English containing names and descriptions of various sorts into sentences of the formal language that (purportedly) express the same propositions (thoughts) as the original English sentences do.

Russell's Formal Language and Its Interpretation

In specifying the formal language we first present its basic vocabulary, and then show how sentences are constructed from that vocabulary. Along the way we introduce the notion of a formula as a grammatical category mediating between vocabulary on the one hand, and sentences on the other. It is only sentences that (on their own) express complete thoughts, or propositions.

THE FORMAL LANGUAGE

I. Vocabulary

 1. Predicates
 = , *A, B, C,* . . . (The predicates are sorted into 1-place, 2-place, . . . n-place predicates. 1-place predicates, like *is red,* express properties of individuals; 2-place predicates, like *is heavier than,* express relations holding between pairs of individuals; and so on. An n-place predicate grammatically combines with n terms to form a formula.)

 2. Terms (These expressions designate or refer to single individuals.)

 a. Variables
 x, y, z, x′, y′, z′ . . .

 b. Names
 x, y, z, x′, y′, z′, . . . (Informally, underlining a variable will involve treating it as a name.)

II. Formulas
 1. Atomic Formulas
 An n-place predicate followed by n terms is a formula (in the case of '=' we let the terms flank, rather than follow, the predicate).

 2. Others
 If **Φ** and **Ψ** are formulas, so are *~Φ, (Φ ν Ψ), (Φ & Ψ), (Φ → Ψ),* and *(Φ ↔ Ψ).* If v is a variable and **Φ**(v) is a formula containing an occurrence of v, *∀ν Φ(ν)* and *∃ν Φ(ν)* are also formulas. (Sometimes parentheses will be dropped from formulas when no ambiguity results.)

 ~Φ, which is read or pronounced *not Φ,* is the negation of **Φ**; *(Φ ν Ψ),* which is read or pronounced *either Φ or Ψ,* is the disjunction of **Φ** and **Ψ**; *(Φ & Ψ),* which is read or pronounced *Φ and Ψ,* is the conjunction of **Φ** and **Ψ**; *(Φ → Ψ),* which is read or pronounced *if Φ, then Ψ,* is a conditional the antecedent of which is **Φ** and the consequent of which is **Ψ**; *(Φ ↔ Ψ),* which is read or pronounced **Φ** *if and only if Ψ,* is a biconditional connecting **Φ** and **Ψ**; *∀ν Φ(ν)* which is read or pronounced *for all ν Φ(ν),* is a universal generalization of **Φ**(v); and *∃ν Φ*(v), which is read or pronounced *there is at least one ν such that Φ(ν),* is an existential generalization of **Φ**(v). *∀ν* and *∃ν* are called quantifiers.

III. Sentences

1. A sentence is a formula that contains no free occurrences of variables.

2. Free occurrences of a variable
   An occurrence of a variable is free iff it is not bound.

3. Binding occurrences of variables
   An occurrence of a variable in a formula is bound iff it is within the scope of a quantifier using that variable.

4. The scope of an occurrence of a quantifier $\forall v$ or $\exists v$
   The scope of an occurrence of a quantifier in a formula is the quantifier together with the (smallest complete) formula immediately following it.

IV. Examples

$\forall x \ (Fx \rightarrow Gx)$ and $\exists x \ (Fx \ \& \ Hx)$ are each sentences, since both occurrences of 'x' in the formula attached to the quantifier are within the scope of the quantifier. Note, in these sentences (i) *Fx* does not **immediately** follow the quantifiers because '(' intervenes, and (ii) *(Fx* is not a **complete** formula because it contains '(' without an accompanying ')'. By contrast, *($\forall x \ Fx \rightarrow Gx$)* and *($\forall x \ (Fx \ \& \ Hx) \rightarrow Gx$)* are not sentences because the occurrence of 'x' following 'G' is free in each case.

A RUSSELLIAN INTERPRETATION OF THE LANGUAGE

I. Propositions and Propositional Functions

Sentences express propositions. Formulas that are not sentences ("open formulas") express propositional functions. A propositional function is a function that assigns propositions as values given objects as arguments. For example, if we use the predicate 'C' to mean 'is a cow', then the formula 'Cx' will express a function which, given any object o as argument, assigns as value the proposition that says of o that it is a cow. This proposition is true iff o is a cow, and is expressed by 'C$\underline{x}$' where '$\underline{x}$' names o.

II. Truth

1a. The proposition expressed by a sentence $\forall v \ \Phi(v)$ is true iff the propositional function expressed by $\Phi(v)$ is true for all values of v—i.e., iff that function assigns to each object o as argument a true proposition about o as value. This is the case iff for every object o, the result $\Phi(\underline{v})$ of taking all free occurrences of v to name o expresses a true proposition.

b. The proposition expressed by a sentence $\exists v\ \Phi(v)$ is true iff the propositional function expressed by $\Phi(v)$ is true for at least one value of v—i.e., iff there is at least one object o such that the function assigns a true proposition about o as value when applied to o as argument. This will be the case iff there is at least one object o such that the result $\Phi(\underline{v})$ of taking all free occurrences of v to name o expresses a true proposition.

2a. The proposition expressed by a sentence $\sim\!\Phi$ is true iff the proposition expressed by Φ is not true.

b. The proposition expressed by a sentence $(\Phi\ v\ \Psi)$ is true iff either the proposition expressed by Φ is true or the proposition expressed by Ψ is true.

c. The proposition expressed by a sentence $(\Phi\ \&\ \Psi)$ is true iff the proposition expressed by Φ is true and the proposition expressed by Ψ is true.

d. The proposition expressed by a sentence $(\Phi \rightarrow \Psi)$ is true iff it is not the case that (the proposition expressed by Φ is true and the proposition expressed by Ψ is false).

e. The proposition expressed by a sentence $(\Phi \leftrightarrow \Psi)$ is true iff the proposition expressed by Φ and the proposition expressed by Ψ are either both true or both false.

3. Predicates stand for properties (or relations). Names stand for objects. An atomic sentence consists of names plus a single predicate. The proposition expressed by such a sentence is true iff the object (or objects) named have the property (or bear the relation) indicated by the predicate. For example, if 'C' stands for the property of being a cow, the proposition expressed by the atomic sentence '$C\underline{x}$' is true iff the object named by '$\underline{x}$' is a cow. Every proposition that is not true is false.

The Structure of Propositions

Finally, we sketch Russell's theory of the structure of propositions. According to him, propositions constitute the information encoded by sentences. He thought of the information encoded by a sentence (in a logically perfect language) as a complex entity the structure of which mirrors the structure of the sentence. The propositions expressed by the sentences of his formal language are determined in the following way.

I.   The proposition expressed by an atomic sentence $P\ t_1 \ldots t_n$, consisting of a predicate followed by n names, is a complex $\langle P^*, O_1 \ldots O_n \rangle$ consisting of the property (or relation) expressed by the predicate, together with the referents of the names.

An atomic formula, $P\ t_1 \ldots t_n$, containing one or more free occurrence of a variable, does not, in and of itself, express a proposition. However, such a formula does express a proposition relative to an assignment of objects as (temporary) referents of its free variables. Thus, the proposition expressed by $P\ t_1 \ldots t_n$ relative to an assignment A of objects to its free variables is a complex, $\langle P^*, O_1 \ldots O_n \rangle$, consisting of the property (or relation) expressed by the predicate, together with the referents of the terms with respect to A (A being relevant only in the case of variables with free occurrences in the formula). The proposition is true iff the object (or objects) have the property (or stand in the relation) P^*.

II. The proposition expressed by the formula ~$\boldsymbol{\Phi}$ (relative to an assignment A) is the complex, $\langle$Neg, Prop $\boldsymbol{\Phi}\rangle$, where Prop $\boldsymbol{\Phi}$ is the proposition expressed by $\boldsymbol{\Phi}$ (relative to A) and Neg is the property of being a proposition that is not true. $\langle$Neg, Prop $\boldsymbol{\Phi}\rangle$ is true iff Prop $\boldsymbol{\Phi}$ is not true.

III. The proposition expressed by the formula $(\boldsymbol{\Phi}\ \&\ \boldsymbol{\Psi})$ (relative to an assignment A) is the complex $\langle$Conj, Prop $\boldsymbol{\Phi}$, Prop $\boldsymbol{\Psi}\rangle$, where Prop $\boldsymbol{\Phi}$ and Prop $\boldsymbol{\Psi}$ are the propositions expressed by $\boldsymbol{\Phi}$ and $\boldsymbol{\Psi}$, and Conj is a relation that holds between a pair of propositions iff both are true. Hence, $\langle$Conj, Prop $\boldsymbol{\Phi}$, Prop $\boldsymbol{\Psi}\rangle$ is true iff both Prop $\boldsymbol{\Phi}$ and Prop $\boldsymbol{\Psi}$ are true. Similar rules specify the propositions expressed by $(\boldsymbol{\Phi}\ v\ \boldsymbol{\Psi})$, $(\boldsymbol{\Phi} \rightarrow \boldsymbol{\Psi})$, and $(\boldsymbol{\Phi} \leftrightarrow \boldsymbol{\Psi})$.

IV. The proposition expressed by the formula $\exists v\ \boldsymbol{\Phi}(v)$ (relative to an assignment A) is the complex $\langle$SOME, g$\rangle$, where g is the propositional function that assigns to each object o the proposition expressed by $\boldsymbol{\Phi}(v)$ relative to an assignment A$'$ that assigns o as the referent of v (and is otherwise identical with A), and SOME is the property of being a propositional function that "is sometimes true", (i.e. that assigns a true proposition to at least one object). Hence, $\langle$SOME, g$\rangle$ is true iff at least one object "is Φ".

The proposition expressed by the formula $\forall \nu \; \Phi(\nu)$ (relative to an assignment A) is a complex $\langle$ALL, g$\rangle$, where g is the propositional function that assigns to each object o the proposition expressed by Φ(v) relative to an assignment A' that assigns o as the referent of v (and is otherwise identical with A), and ALL is the property of being a propositional function that "is always true", (i.e., that assigns a true proposition to every object). Hence, $\langle$ALL, g$\rangle$ is true iff all objects "are Φ".[8]

The Analysis of Negative Existentials

The Basic Idea

Having examined Russell's ideas about the structure of propositions, and his formal language for representing them, we are now in a position to understand how he applied those ideas to the paradox of negative existentials. In developing his theory of descriptions, he came to think that the paradox arises from uncritically taking **grammatical** form to be an accurate guide to **logical** form. A sentence *α doesn't exist* is grammatically of subject-predicate form. Often we assume that if a sentence is of subject-predicate form, then it will be true iff the subject expression refers to something that has the property expressed by the predicate. In the case of negative existentials this would mean that the statement is true iff α refers to an object that doesn't exist. But this seemed paradoxical, because it seemed that if there is something for α to refer to, then it must exist.

The way out of the paradox, Russell came to believe, is to recognize that the logical form of a sentence like

---

[8] The truth conditions given here (and in "A Russellian Interpretation of the Language") for propositions expressed by existential and universal generalizations, though Russellian in spirit, are more specific than any given by Russell himself. They employ ideas first explicitly developed by Alfred Tarski in the 1930s. A variant of the scheme given here takes SOME and ALL to be functions from propositional functions to truth values, and treats NEG, CONJ, etc. as functions from truth values to truth values. One advantage of this alternative is that it distinguishes the proposition expressed by $\exists x \; Fx$ from the proposition expressed by *The propositional function that assigns F-hood to objects is sometime true.*

1. Carnivorous cows don't exist.

is given by something like (a).

(a) $\forall x(\sim Cx \lor \sim Mx)$

Here, we let 'C' stand for the property of being a cow and 'M' stand for the property of being carnivorous. Then, the proposition expressed by (a) consists of the property ALL together with the propositional function g that assigns to each object o the proposition that says that either o isn't a cow or o isn't carnivorous. Thus, Russell regarded (a) as saying something that can roughly be paraphrased in English as (b) or as (4).

(b) The propositional function that assigns to each object the proposition that either it isn't a cow or it isn't carnivorous is always true.

4. Everything is such that either it isn't a cow or it isn't carnivorous.

This is what he thought is more misleadingly expressed by (1). He believed that once we saw this, we would no longer be tempted to think that (1) can be true only if there really are things—carnivorous cows—referred to by its grammatical subject that have the property of not existing.

Extending the Analysis to Cases Involving Singular Definite Descriptions

Our next step is to extend the analysis to other negative existentials, such as (2).

2. The creature from the black lagoon doesn't exist.

(2) differs from (1) in having a singular subject. In considering how Russell would treat this sentence, let us look at the corresponding positive existential.

5. The creature from the black lagoon exists.

For simplicity, we let 'C' stand for *is a creature*, and 'B' stand for *is from the black lagoon*. With this in mind, consider the logical formulation (6).

6. $\exists x(Cx \ \& \ Bx)$

According to Russell, (6) is true iff the propositional function expressed by *(Cx and Bx)* is true for at least one value of 'x'. In other words, (6) is true iff at least one object is a creature from the black lagoon. It should be noted, however, that this is not quite what (5) tells us. (6) leaves it open that there might be many creatures from the black lagoon. However, the use of the definite article *the* in (5) seems to indicate that there is supposed to be just one such creature.[9] We need to find a way of expressing this in Russell's formal language. As we will see, there are several different but logically equivalent ways of doing this.

First, consider the formula (7), in which '$\underline{x}$' is a name for me—Scott Soames.

7. $\forall y ((Cy \ \& \ By) \rightarrow y = \underline{x})$

This sentence says that every object is such that if it is a creature from the black lagoon, then it is me. This is compatible with two different possibilities: (i) No object is a creature from the black lagoon. (ii) Exactly one object is such a creature, namely me. The first of these possibilities is eliminated by (8a), which is equivalent to (8b).

8a. $\forall y((Cy \ \& \ By) \leftrightarrow y = \underline{x})$

b. $\forall y((Cy \ \& \ By) \rightarrow y = \underline{x}) \ \& \ \forall y \ (y = \underline{x} \rightarrow (Cy \ \& \ By))$

These sentences are true iff every object satisfies two conditions: (i) if it is a creature from the black lagoon then it is me, and (ii) if it is me, then it is a creature from the black lagoon. Since I am an object, and I am identical with myself, I satisfy the second condition only if I am a creature from the black lagoon. Thus (8a) and (8b) can be true only if I am such a creature. Now consider all other objects. No object other than me is identical with me. Hence these objects satisfy the first condition only if they are **not** creatures from the black lagoon. Therefore, (8a) and (8b) are true iff I—Scott Soames—am the one and only creature from the black lagoon.

Now consider (9).

---

[9] If I tell my class *the student who got an A on the homework assignment won't have to take the exam*, they will naturally assume that just one student got an A on the assignment (and that there will be one exam).

9. $\exists x \forall y ((Cy \& By) \leftrightarrow y = x)$
   There is an object x which is such that for any object y whatsoever, x is identical with y if and only if y is a creature from
   the black lagoon.

This sentence is true if and only if there is an object which is the one
and only creature from the black lagoon. The only difference between
(8a) and (9) is that (8a) tells you exactly which object satisfies the description—me. (9) tells you that there is one and only one such object,
but it doesn't identify it. Since the English sentence (5) says that there
is such an object without identifying it, Russell takes (9) to express
what (5) does.

Earlier I mentioned that there are several different, but **logically
equivalent**, ways of using our Russellian language to express what (5)
does. (9) is one of these ways. Two other ways are given by (10) and
(11).

10. $\exists x(Cx \& Bx) \& \forall y \forall z[((Cy \& By) \& (Cz \& Bz)) \rightarrow y = z]$
    There is at least one thing that is a creature from the black
    lagoon and for any pair of objects if both are creatures from
    the black lagoon, then the objects are one and the same—in
    other words, there is at least one creature from the black
    lagoon and at most one creature from the black lagoon.

11. $\exists x[(Cx \& Bx) \& \forall y((Cy \& By) \rightarrow y = x)]$
    There is at least one thing which both is a creature from and
    is identical with anything that is a creature from the black
    lagoon.

For Russell's purposes, any of the sentences (9), (10), or (11) will do
as a representation of the proposition expressed by (5). One question
that he never clearly addressed is whether (9), (10), and (11) all express the same proposition, or whether they express structurally different but logically equivalent propositions. Since, in general, Russell does
not identify logically equivalent propositions, it would be natural for
him to claim that (9), (10), and (11) express different, logically equivalent propositions. But then, one might ask, which of these propositions does (5) really express in English?

Russell never answers this question, and neither will we. However,
we may note two points: (i) For purposes of providing an analysis of
negative existentials, it doesn't matter which one we choose. Each allows

us to avoid the paradox posed by sentences like (2). (ii) Since (9) is the simplest sentence to work with, and since Russell often employs it, we will treat it as expressing the same proposition as (5).

Now that we have a Russellian analysis of (5), which is a positive existential, the analysis of the corresponding negative existential, (2), is automatic.

12. ~∃x ∀y ((Cy & By) ↔ y = x)

This says *It is not the case that there is exactly one object that is a creature from the black lagoon*, or, what comes to the same thing, *Every object is such that either it isn't a creature from the black lagoon or it is one of many such creatures.* According to Russell, this is what is expressed by (2).

The relation between the English sentence (2) and its Russellian logical form (12) is thought to be like the relation between the English sentence (1) about carnivorous cows and its logical form (4). Just as (1), on first glance, seems to make reference to several things and say of them that they don't exist, so (2), on first glance, seems to refer to a single thing and say of it that it doesn't exist. In both cases, Russell resolves the paradox by analyzing the logical form of the proposition expressed in such a way that no such reference, and no such predication of nonexistence, is involved.

Extending the Analysis to Sentences Involving Grammatically Proper Names

The next class of negative existentials to be considered are those like (3), the grammatical subjects of which are ordinary proper names.

3. Santa Claus doesn't exist.

Although this sentence is true, the same puzzle arises for it as arose over our earlier examples. Not surprisingly, Russell's solution to the puzzle regarding (3) parallels his solution to the earlier cases.

According to Russell, when we use a proper name like *Santa Claus* we always have some description in mind that we would be prepared to give, indicating how the name is being used. Precisely which description gives the content of the name may vary somewhat from speaker to speaker and time to time. However, whenever (3) is used there is always some description that may replace it. Thus, when we use (3), we always use it to mean something of the sort (3a).

3a. The old man who lives at the North Pole and . . . doesn't exist.

But since (3a) has the structure

3b. The so and so doesn't exist.

Russell can use his analysis of definite descriptions to give the logical form (3c) of the proposition expressed by (3).

3c. $\sim\exists x \,\forall y\,(y \text{ is so and so} \leftrightarrow y = x)$

As a result, on Russell's analysis the truth of (3) does not require any object to have the property of not existing, and the paradox dissolves.

Logically Proper Names

The key to this analysis of (3) is in the very first step—the claim that *Santa Claus* is simply short for a certain descriptive phrase, which in turn is analyzed by Russell in terms of quantifiers, logical symbols, and predicates. On this view, even ordinary proper names do not function logically as names. That is, their function is not simply to label, or directly refer to, anything. But if this is the case, one might wonder whether the notion of a name has any role at all to play in Russell's conception of logical form. We can put this another way. Are there any words in English the logical function of which is not to take the place of a description, but simply to label or refer to some object?

Russell thought that there was at least one such word—the word *this*. Consider the following example: I hold up my wallet and say *This is empty*. Here, the function of the word 'this' is simply to label or indicate what I am talking about. If my wallet weren't present, I wouldn't simply say *This is empty*, because my hearers wouldn't know what I was talking about. In that case, I would have to use a description like *the wallet I normally carry* to get them to understand my intention. In the present case, however, that isn't necessary, since they can all see what I am talking about. Here, the word 'this' is not functioning as a description, but rather as a bare label for what I am talking about.

One of the things that supports this view is the seeming absurdity of negative existentials involving 'this'.

13. This doesn't exist.

If I were to utter (13), directing my attention to something, or perhaps gesturing toward it, then it would be hard to make sense of my remark. My use of the demonstrative 'this', plus my gesture, would indicate that I took myself to be referring to something. But then I would be in the odd position of purporting to refer to something which I then went on to say didn't exist. Hence, (13) is a rare case of a negative existential that Russell really regarded as bizarre: to use it sincerely is to presume that it can't be true. Russell took this to indicate that the analysis of (13) is **not** like the analysis of our earlier examples. In the case of (13) its grammatical subject functions simply to name something, and not to describe it. He expresses this by saying that the word 'this' is a **logically proper name**.

I should add a complicating factor that I have not gone into up to now. It involves the question *What sorts of objects can be the referents of logically proper names?* Up to now, I have been talking as if material objects, like my wallet, can be the referents of logically proper names. In fact, Russell was dubious of this, and eventually denied it, holding instead that the only things one could name with a logically proper name were one's own sense impressions, thoughts, and other things that one is acquainted with in the most direct way (like abstract properties and relations). Thus, when *this* is used as a logically proper name, it always names one of these objects; any other use can only be regarded as one in which it functions as a disguised description.

At least part of Russell's reasoning about this can be reconstructed as follows: First, we define the notion of a logically proper name.

DEFINITION: LOGICALLY PROPER NAME
A logically proper name is a term the meaning of which is its referent.

Next, let us assume, for the sake of argument, that one cannot be mistaken about whether or not one means something by one's words. Often when I use an expression it seems that I can be certain that I mean something by it, even though I may not be certain that what I mean by it is the same as what others mean by it, and even though I may not be certain that the expression really **refers** to anything, when it is used with the meaning that I attach to it. In these cases, I can be certain that I **mean** something by an expression, even if I am not certain that the expression succeeds in referring to anything in the world. For example, I can be sure that I mean something when I use the words *the house I own in Princeton* even if I am not completely sure that this expression refers to anything, since it is at least possible that my house may have burned down since I left it. Similarly, Russell would say that just as I mean something when I use the ordinary name *Santa Claus*, even though it doesn't refer to anything, so I can be sure that I mean something when I use the name *Plato*, even if I am not completely sure that there really was such a man. Russell would have expressed this by saying (i) that the grammatically proper name *Santa Claus*, as used by me, has a meaning, even though it lacks a referent, and (ii) that I can know that the grammatically proper name *Plato*, as used by me, has a meaning, even if I don't know that it has a referent.

Suppose now that some expression N is used by me as a logically proper name—i.e., as an expression the meaning of which is its referent. Then, one might argue, whenever I sincerely use N to mean something, N, as used by me, both means and refers to something. This is guaranteed because whenever I sincerely use N to mean something, it does mean something, and what it means is what it refers to. Moreover, the thing which it both means and refers to is what I take it to mean and refer to. Thus, the only objects that can be referents of logically proper names are objects the existence of which I couldn't possibly be mistaken about in any situation in which I wanted to refer to them. Material objects and other human beings do not satisfy this condition, and so cannot be the referents of logically proper names. The only kinds of concrete objects which do satisfy the condition, and hence which can be the referents of logically proper names, are oneself, and one's own thoughts or momentary sense data. By reasoning in this way, Russell came to believe that whenever we think or talk about material objects or other people, the words we use **describe** them, rather than **naming** them directly. In addition, the propositions we believe never contain material objects or other people as constituents, but rather are always entirely made up of the properties and relations that are the meanings of descriptive terms we use, plus the abstract concepts that are the meanings of the logical words, and the relatively few concrete particulars that can be the referents of logically proper names. This was one of the central doctrines expressed in Russell's paper, "Knowledge by Acquaintance and Knowledge by Description," published in 1910.[10]

Russell's Rules for Determining the Logical Forms of Sentences Containing Descriptions

The Extent of Russell's Theory

So far we have considered only a small class of sentences—negative existentials. It is now time to extend Russell's theory of descriptions to

[10] See Russell, "Knowledge by Acquaintance and Knowledge by Description," *Proceedings of the Aristotelian Society* 11 (1910–11), reprinted in *Propositions and Attitudes*, N. Salmon and S. Soames, eds. (Oxford: Oxford University Press, 1988).

a wider class of cases. Consider a sentence α *is F*, where α is either a demonstrative like 'this', an ordinary proper name like 'Plato', or a singular definite description *the G*. Russell recognizes two possibilities regarding the analysis of α, and of the sentence α *is F*.[11]

(i) α is a logically proper name, in which case the logical form of the sentence is just *Fa*.

(ii) α is a definite description or a disguised definite description, in which case the logical form of the sentence is $\exists x \, \forall y \, [(Gy \leftrightarrow y = x) \, \& \, Fx]$.

In order to determine in any given case which of these possibilities prevail, Russell applies two tests:

T1. Can you understand the meaning of α *is F* without knowing which thing α refers to? If so, then α is not a logically proper name, but must be analyzed as a description.

T2. Would α *is F* be meaningful even if α had no referent? If so, then α is not a logically proper name but must be analyzed as a description.

Russell makes this second test explicit in the following passage from *Principia Mathematica*:

Whenever the grammatical subject of a proposition can be supposed not to exist without rendering the proposition meaningless it is plain that the grammatical subject is not a [logically] proper name ... in all such cases the proposition must be capable of being so analyzed that what was the grammatical subject shall have disappeared.[12]

When Russell applied these tests to sentences containing singular descriptive phrases of the sort *the so and so*, as well as to sentences containing ordinary proper names, like *Plato*, he came to the conclusion that they must be analyzed in accord with his theory of descriptions.

---

[11] I illustrate here using only the simplest sentences, consisting of a subject and a verb. Russell would extended this more broadly to include simple sentences of many different grammatical forms, including sentences with transitive verbs—α *v's* β. We do well, however, to exclude special cases like *The Greeks worshiped Zeus* and *Scientists seek the cure for cancer*.

[12] Russell and Alfred North Whitehead, *Principia Mathematica* (Cambridge: Cambridge University Press, 1950), vol. 1, chapter 3, p. 66.

Ambiguity and the Law of the Excluded Middle

Extending his analysis this far allowed him to provide solutions to a number of additional puzzles, over and above the problem of negative existentials that originally motivated his analysis. One of these puzzles involved the law of classical logic called *the law of the excluded middle*. Here is what Russell says about the puzzle in "On Denoting."

> By the law of excluded middle, either 'A is B' or 'A is not B' must be true. Hence either 'The present King of France is bald' or 'The present King of France is not bald' must be true. Yet if we enumerated the things that are bald and the things that are not bald, we should not find the present King of France in either list. Hegelians, who love a synthesis, will probably conclude that he wears a wig.[13]

Consider the sentences:

14a. The present king of France is bald.

  b. The present king of France is not bald.

In the passage, Russell seems to suggest that neither (14a) nor (14b) is true. But that seems to violate *the law of the excluded middle*—a general law of logic that tells us that for every sentence S, either S or ~S is true. Since Russell regarded the law as valid, he needed a way of defusing this apparent counterexample.

The key to doing this lies in his general rule R for determining the logical form of sentences containing definite descriptions.

R. $\Psi[\text{the } \Phi] \Rightarrow \exists x \, \forall y [\Phi y \leftrightarrow y = x) \, \& \, \Psi x]$

This rule for translating a sentence into its logical form says that if a definite description occurs in some sentence along with additional material Ψ, then it can be eliminated (bringing us closer to the logical form of the sentence) by replacing the description with a variable, and introducing quantifiers plus the uniqueness clause as indicated.

In the case of sentence (14a), Ψ corresponds to the phrase *is bald* and the description is *the present king of France*. Putting this in the form of the left-hand side of R, we have (14a').

14a'. B [the present king of France]

---

[13] Russell, "On Denoting," p. 48.

Applying R to this gives the logical form (lfa).

lfa. $\exists x\, \forall y[(Kyf \leftrightarrow y = x)\, \&\, Bx]$[14]

In giving rule R, Russell takes himself to be explaining the contribution that a definite description makes to **any** sentence that contains it. Thus R is intended to apply to all sentences, no matter how complex they may be. With this in mind, let us apply it to the slightly more complex example, (14b).

Russell would first express the sentence in a more convenient form.

14b'. ~B [the present king of France]

There are now two ways of applying R depending on what part of (b') we choose to play the role of Ψ. If we take Ψ in (14b') to be just what it was in (14a'), namely the predicate B, then we are viewing (14b') as (14b'1) and applying R inside the parentheses.

14b'1. ~ (B [the present king of France])

This gives us

lfb1. ~ $\exists x\, \forall y[(Kyf \leftrightarrow y = x)\, \&\, Bx]$

If, on the other hand, we take ~B in (14b') to play the role of Ψ, then we treat (14b') as (14b'2), and applying R will give us (lfb2).

14b'2. (~ B [the present king of France])

lfb2. $\exists x\, \forall y[(Kyf \leftrightarrow y = x)\, \&\, \sim Bx]$

Thus, Russell's rule R for relating English sentences to their logical forms yields the conclusion that negative sentences containing descriptions are ambiguous.

What is the difference between these two interpretations of (14b)—i.e., between (lfb1) and (lfb2)? The former may be paraphrased: *It is not the case that there is someone who is both bald and unique in being king of France*; the latter: *There is someone who is both not bald and unique in being king of France*. The latter logically entails that there is a king of France, whereas the former does not. Notice also that (lfa) is incompatible with both of the logical forms of (14b)—i.e., (lfa) and (lfb1) cannot be jointly true, and (lfa) and (lfb2) cannot be jointly true.

---

[14] Here 'B' abbreviates the predicate *is bald*, 'K' abbreviates the two-place predicate *is king of* and 'f' names France.

However, (lfa) and (lfb2) can be jointly untrue; both are untrue when there is no unique king of France. This does not violate the law of the excluded middle because (lfb2) is not the logical negation of (lfa). Rather, (lfb1) is the logical negation of (lfa); these two cannot both fail to be true. If one is untrue, then the other must be true, exactly as the law maintains.

We can now see how the theory of descriptions solved Russell's puzzle about the law of the excluded middle. That law applies to logical forms. When we look at the logical forms of (14a) and (14b), they provide no counterexample to the law. This is compatible with the observation that there is a way of understanding (14a) and (14b) in which neither is true. This is so because (14b) is ambiguous. On the interpretation of (14b) in which it is logically the negation of (14a), it is always true when (14a) isn't, and the law is upheld. On the interpretation of (14b) in which both (14a) and (14b) can be jointly untrue, (14b) isn't logically the negation of (14a), and we don't have an instance of the law. Hence the puzzle is solved.

The Scope of Descriptions

Our example of the interaction of negation and descriptions provides a convenient way of explaining some of Russell's terminology. When sentence (14b) is analyzed as (14b′1) and ultimately as having the logical form (lfb1), the description *the present king of France* is said to take **narrow scope,** and to have **secondary occurrence**, in the sentence or proposition. When (14b) is analyzed as (14b′2), and ultimately as having the logical form (lfb2), the description is said to take **wide scope** over the negation operator, and to have **primary occurrence** in the sentence or proposition.

Another example of the same sort is provided by (15), which may be conveniently represented as 15′, where 'F' is taken to express the property of being famous.

15. John believes that the person sitting over there is famous.

15′. John believes that F [the person sitting over there]

As in the case of a negative sentence, Russell's theory predicts that there are two interpretations of this sentence, and hence that it is ambiguous. On one interpretation the description *the person sitting over there* has narrow scope and secondary occurrence. On this interpretation,

R is applied within the subordinate clause by itself to give the logical form

1f1. John believes that
$(\exists x \, \forall y[(\text{Sitting over there } (y) \leftrightarrow y = x) \, \& \, Fx])$

When interpreted in this way, (15) tells us that John believes that there is just one person sitting over there and whoever that person may be, that person is famous. On this reading (15) may be true, even if no one is sitting over there; it may also be true if Mary is sitting there, but John doesn't know that she is, or think that she is famous—all that is required is that he believe that some famous person or other is sitting alone over there.

On the other interpretation of (15), the description *the person sitting over there* has wide scope over the belief predicate and primary occurrence in the sentence or proposition as a whole. On this reading, R is applied to 15″, with the underlined expressions playing the role of Ψ in the rule.

15″. <u>John believes F</u> [the person sitting over there]

This results in the logical form

1f2. $\exists x \, \forall y[(\text{Sitting over there } (y) \leftrightarrow y = x)$
$\& \text{ John believes that } Fx]$

When (15) is interpreted in this way, it tell us that there is one and only one person sitting over there and John believes that person to be famous. In order for this to be true, there really must be just one person sitting over there and John must believe that person to be famous; however, it is not necessary that John have any idea where that person is, or believe that anyone is sitting over there.

Scope, Propositional Attitudes, and the Puzzle about George IV and the Author of Waverley

Another logical puzzle to which Russell took his theory of descriptions to provide the answer involved constructions that have come to be known as *propositional attitude ascriptions* (sentences with verbs like *believe, know, assert, doubt, wonder,* etc., that report a relation between an agent and a proposition) and a law of logic often referred to as *the substitutivity of identity*. Here is Russell's statement of the puzzle in "On Denoting."

If *a* is identical with *b*, whatever is true of the one is true of the other, and either may be substituted for the other in any proposition without altering the truth or falsehood of that proposition. Now George IV wished to know whether Scott was the author of *Waverley*, and in fact Scott *was* the author of *Waverley*. Hence we may substitute *Scott* for *the author of 'Waverley'*, and thereby prove that George IV wished to know whether Scott was Scott. Yet an interest in the law of identity can hardly be attributed to the first gentleman of Europe.[15]

While far from a model of clarity—Russell here swings inconsistently back and forth between talking about expressions and talking about the individuals that the expressions designate, as well as between talking about sentences and talking about the propositions those sentences express—the problem posed by the passage is clear enough. Sentences P1 and P2 of the following argument appear to be true, even though the conclusion, C, appears to be false.

P1. George IV wondered whether Scott was the author of *Waverley*.

P2. Scott was the author of *Waverley*—i.e., Scott = the author of *Waverley*

C. George IV wondered whether Scott was Scott.

What makes this observation troubling is the apparent conflict created by the law of the substitutivity of identity, which may be stated as follows:

SI. When α and β are singular referring expressions, and the sentence $\boldsymbol{\alpha = \beta}$ is true, α and β refer to the same thing, and so substitution of one for the other in any true sentence will always yield a true sentence.

If P1 and P2 are true, and C follows by the rule SI, then C must also be true. The problem is that it appears not to be.

Later in "On Denoting," Russell claims that his theory of descriptions solves the problem.

The puzzle about George IV's curiosity is now seen to have a very simple solution. The proposition 'Scott was the author of *Waverley*',

---

[15] "On Denoting," pp. 47–48 in Marsh.

... [when written out in unabbreviated form] does not contain any constituent 'the author of *Waverley*' for which we could substitute 'Scott'. This does not interfere with the truth of inferences resulting from making what is *verbally* the substitution of 'Scott' for 'the author of *Waverley*', so long as 'the author of *Waverley*' has what I call a *primary* occurrence in the proposition considered.[16]

The second sentence of the passage contains the key idea. Since 'the author of *Waverley*' is a singular definite description, it is not, logically, a singular referring expression, and so it does not figure in applications of the rule SI. (In discussing this example, Russell treats *Scott* as if it were a logically proper name.) This rule, like every logical rule, applies only to logical forms of sentences. Thus, to evaluate the argument, P1 and P2 have to be replaced with their logical forms.

Since P1 is a compound sentence containing a definite description, it is ambiguous—having one reading in which the description has primary occurrence, and one reading in which the description has secondary occurrence. Thus, there are two reconstructions of the argument— one corresponding to each of these readings of P1.[17]

ARGUMENT 1: PRIMARY OCCURRENCE
OF THE DESCRIPTION IN P1

$P1_p$. $\exists x \, \forall y \, [(y \text{ Wrote } Waverley \leftrightarrow y = x) \, \& \text{ George IV wondered whether Scott} = x]$

There was one and only one person who wrote *Waverley* and George wondered whether he was Scott.

P2. $\exists x \, \forall y \, [(y \text{ Wrote } Waverley \leftrightarrow y = x) \, \& \text{ Scott} = x]$

There was one and only one person who wrote *Waverley* and he was Scott.

C. George IV wondered whether Scott = Scott.

ARGUMENT 2: SECONDARY OCCURRENCE
OF THE DESCRIPTION IN P1

$P1_s$. George IV wondered whether $\exists x \, \forall y \, [(y \text{ Wrote } Waverley \leftrightarrow y = x) \, \& \text{ Scott} = x]$

George IV wondered whether (there was one and only one person who wrote *Waverley* and he was Scott)

---

[16] Pp. 51–52.
[17] In discussing this argument, I ignore tense.

P2. $\exists x \, \forall y \, [(y \text{ Wrote } \textit{Waverley} \leftrightarrow y = x) \, \& \, \text{Scott} = x]$
There was one and only one person who wrote *Waverley* and
he was Scott.

C. George IV wondered whether Scott = Scott.

Russell takes the reading on which the description has secondary
occurrence as the most natural one. With this in mind, let us evaluate
Argument 2. Suppose that $P1_s$ and P2 are true. Then George wondered whether a certain proposition—the one expressed by P2—was
true that, in fact, was true. However, since P2 is not a simple identity
statement $\alpha = \beta$, and there is no singular referring expression in $P1_s$ to
be substituted for 'Scott', we cannot use the rule SI to derive C from
$P1_s$ and P2. So far so good.

It is important to note that this cannot be the whole story. For in
the last sentence of the passage Russell says: "This does not interfere
with the truth of inferences resulting from making what is *verbally* the
substitution of 'Scott' for 'the author of *Waverley*', so long as 'the
author of *Waverley*' has what I call a *primary* occurrence in the proposition considered." His point is that when the description is interpreted as having primary occurrence in P1, the truth of the premises
$P1_p$ and P2 **does** guarantee the truth of the conclusion C. But, according to the theory of descriptions, SI no more applies in Argument 1
than it did in Argument 2. Hence one cannot explain the difference
between the two arguments, and the invalidity of Argument 2, by noting
that the theory of descriptions does not allow one to apply SI by substituting 'Scott' for 'the author of *Waverley*'.

To understand what is responsible for the difference in these arguments, it is best to begin by verifying that the step from premises to
conclusion in Argument 1 is truth preserving. If $P1_p$ is true, then there
is one and only one individual who wrote *Waverley*, and the sen-
tence—(i) *George IV wondered whether Scott* = $\underline{x}$—is true when '$\underline{x}$' is
taken as a logically proper name of that individual. This in turn will be
true just in case George IV wondered whether a certain proposition
p—namely, the one expressed by the sentence (ii) *Scott* = $\underline{x}$—was
true, again taking '$\underline{x}$' to be a logically proper name of the unique individual who wrote *Waverley*. If P2 is true, then this individual is none
other than Scott, in which case '$\underline{x}$' and 'Scott' are logically proper names
for the same person. (Recall that in discussing this example Russell
treats 'Scott' as if it were a logically proper name.) Since they are logically proper names, their having the same reference guarantees that

they mean the same thing, and hence that substitution of one for the other in any sentence doesn't change the proposition expressed. From this we conclude that *Scott = Scott* expresses the same proposition p as (ii) *Scott = x*. Since we have already established that George IV wondered whether p was true, it follows that C is also true. Thus the inference from P1$_p$ and P2 to C is guaranteed to be truth preserving, in Argument 1.

Next consider Argument 2. If P1$_s$ is true, then George IV wondered whether a certain proposition q was true—where q is the proposition that a single person wrote *Waverley*, and that person was Scott. If P2 is true then q is, in fact, true. However, this tells us nothing about whether George IV wondered whether the proposition p, that Scott is Scott, was true. Since it is clearly possible to wonder whether q is true without wondering whether p is true, it is possible for the premises of Argument 2 to be true, while the conclusion is false. Hence the argument is not valid.

The Clash between Russell's Epistemology and His Theory of Descriptions

The moral of the story up to now is that Russell's theory of descriptions does explain why, on a natural interpretation of premise 1, the argument about George IV turns out to be invalid; as a bonus it provides a further explanation of how, if premise 1 is understood in a different way, the argument is valid. There is, however, a problem with this otherwise successful application of the theory. Russell, it seems clear, would have regarded it as absurd to suppose that anyone might doubt whether the proposition that Scott was Scott was true.[18] Hence, he would have had no choice but to regard P1 as false, when it is analyzed as P1$_p$, and 'the author of *Waverley*' has primary occurrence. However, this is counterintuitive, since it seems that the sentence *the individual who wrote Waverley was such that George IV wondered whether he was Scott* might easily be true. As the following passage from "On Denoting" indicates, it would seem that Russell himself agreed.

> [W]hen we say 'George IV wished to know whether Scott was the author of *Waverley*', we normally mean 'George IV wished to

[18] For contemporary modifications of Russellianism that allow for such doubt, see, Nathan Salmon, *Frege's Puzzle* (Cambridge MA: MIT Press, 1986); Scott Soames, *Beyond Rigidity* (New York: Oxford University Press, 2002); and the introduction to Salmon and Scott Soames, eds., *Propositions and Attitudes* (Oxford: Oxford University Press, 1988).

know whether one and only one man wrote *Waverley* and Scott was that man', but we *may* also mean: 'One and only one man wrote *Waverley*, and George IV wished to know whether Scott was that man'. In the latter, 'the author of *Waverley*' has a *primary* occurrence; in the former, a *secondary*. The latter might be expressed by 'George IV wished to know, concerning the man who in fact wrote *Waverley*, whether he was Scott'. **This would be true, for example, if George IV had seen Scott at a distance, and had asked 'Is that Scott?'**[19]

This is puzzling. How, if George IV didn't wonder whether Scott was Scott, could P1 have been true on the interpretation in which 'the author of *Waverley*' has primary occurrence? One natural answer is that in taking the sentence to be true in the type of situation he describes, Russell may have been implicitly interpreting the ordinary proper name 'Scott' as a disguised description (with secondary occurrence in the sentence), rather than as a logically proper name. Though Russell did not emphasize the status of such ordinary names in "On Denoting," in later work he explicitly maintained that they were to be understood in this way. Such a view may, implicitly, have been at work in the passage.

Nevertheless, important problems remain. First, the view that ordinary proper names mean the same as descriptions associated with them by speakers, though it flourished for many decades after Russell's pioneering work, was ultimately shown to be deeply problematic by Saul Kripke in *Naming and Necessity*.[20] We will examine the descriptive analysis of proper names in detail in volume 2; for now it is enough to note that such a view is a weak foundation on which to rest an explanation of how P1 could be true in the type of situation Russell describes, when 'the author of *Waverley*' is taken to have primary occurrence.[21] The second problem with Russell's account of descriptions that take wide scope in propositional attitude ascriptions bypasses controversies about the analysis of ordinary proper names. For example, consider (16).

16. Mary wondered whether the author of *Waverley* wrote *Waverley*.

---

[19] "On Denoting," p. 52, my boldface emphasis.
[20] Saul Kripke, *Naming and Necessity* (Cambridge, MA: Harvard University Press, 1980); originally published in *Semantics of Natural Languages*, D. Davidson and G. Harman, eds. (Dordrecht: Reidel, 1972), pp. 253–355. Citations will be to the 1980 edition.
[21] See the works of Salmon and Soames for contemporary Russellian explanations of this.

The most natural interpretation of this sentence is one in which the description has primary occurrence—one and only one person wrote *Waverley* and Mary wondered whether that person wrote *Waverley*. A speaker who assertively uttered (16), intending this interpretation, might know precisely who the author of *Waverley* was, and have overhead Mary say "Did he write *Waverley*?," pointing at the man in question. It seems clear that if (16) were used in this way, it would express a truth.

Although Russell's theory of descriptions would seem to be ideally suited to capture this fact, the natural application of the theory to this case collides with important epistemological doctrines mentioned above in the section on logically proper names. As previously indicated, in his paper "Knowledge by Acquaintance and Knowledge by Description," published in 1910, Russell took the position that the only objects that can be referents of logically proper names are objects about the existence of which one couldn't possibly be mistaken. Since material objects and other human beings do not satisfy this condition, he held that they cannot be the referents of logically proper names. What he didn't seem to recognize was that this creates a problem for the interpretation, 16_p, of an example like (16) in which the description is given wide scope.

16_p. $\exists x \, \forall y \, [(y \text{ Wrote } \textit{Waverley} \leftrightarrow y = x) \, \& \, \text{Mary wondered whether x wrote } \textit{Waverley}]$

As we have seen, on Russell's account this is true iff a single person wrote *Waverley* and the sentence *Mary wondered whether x̲ wrote Waverley* is true when 'x̲' is treated as a logically proper name of that person.[22] If we are now told that there can be no logically proper names of other people, this account will no longer suffice.

In fact, the problem is worse. Russell's restrictive epistemological doctrine about the possible referents of logically proper names was coupled with a similarly restrictive doctrine about the propositions that an agent is capable of entertaining, believing, doubting, asserting, and the like. As Russell put it:

The fundamental epistemological principle in the analysis of propositions containing descriptions is this: *Every proposition*

[22] To treat a variable as a logically proper name of an object o can be thought of either as replacing the variable with a new logically proper name of o (obtained by underlining the variable), or as evaluating formulas in which the variable has a free occurrence relative to an assignment of o to the variable.

*which we can understand must be composed wholly of constituents
with which we are acquainted.*[23]

Since, according to Russell, the only things that one is acquainted with
are oneself and one's own momentary thoughts and sensations, plus
abstract properties and relations (called *universals*), it follows that one
cannot believe or entertain any propositions that contain other agents,
or other concrete objects, as constituents. The only sense in which we
can believe or entertain a proposition about such an object o is by believing or entertaining a proposition that states that some (unique) object has certain properties, which in fact o turns out to have. To know
some proposition that bears this relation to o is, in Russell's terminology, to *know o by description*. It is a central doctrine of "Knowledge by
Acquaintance and Knowledge by Description" that all our knowledge
of other people and other objects is knowledge by description. Russell
sums up his view as follows:

> To sum up our whole discussion: We began by distinguishing two
> sorts of knowledge of objects, namely, knowledge by *acquain-
> tance* and knowledge by *description*. Of these it is only the former
> that brings the object itself before the mind. We have acquaintance
> with sense-data, with many universals, and possibly with ourselves,
> but not with physical objects or other minds. We have *descriptive*
> knowledge of an object when we know that it is *the* object having
> some property or properties with which we are acquainted; that is
> to say, when we know that the property or properties in question
> belong to one object, and no more, we are said to have knowledge
> of that one object by description, whether or not we are acquainted
> with the object. Our knowledge of physical objects and of other
> minds is only knowledge by description, the descriptions involved
> being usually such as involve sense-data. All propositions intelligible
> to us, whether or not they primarily concern things only known
> to us by description, are composed wholly of constituents with
> which we are acquainted, for a constituent with which we are not
> acquainted is unintelligible to us.[24]

Thus, Russell came to believe that whenever we think or talk about
material objects or other people, the words we use **describe** them,

---

[23] "Knowledge by Acquaintance and Knowledge by Description," p. 23 in *Propositions and
Attitudes.*
[24] Ibid., p. 31.

rather than **naming** them directly. In addition, the propositions we believe or entertain never contain material objects or other people as constituents, but rather are always entirely made up of properties and relations that are the meanings of descriptive terms we use, plus the abstract concepts that are the meanings of the logical words, and the relatively few concrete particulars that can be the referents of genuine logically proper names. Whatever else may be true of this doctrine, it had disastrous consequences (never squarely addressed by Russell) for the application of his theory of descriptions to propositional attitude ascriptions (17a) and (17b), in which v is a verb like *believe, doubt, assert,* or *wonder* that relates an agent to a proposition, and the complement sentence S contains a description *the D* that can be interpreted as having a primary occurrence in the sentence as a whole.

17a. A v's that S(the D)

b. A v's whether S(the D)

When these sentences are interpreted in this way, Russell's theory of descriptions tells us that (17a) is true iff $(17a_p)$ is true, and (17b) is true iff $(17b_p)$ is true.

$17a_p$. $\exists x \, \forall y \, [(Dy \leftrightarrow y = x) \, \& \, A \, v's \, that \, S(x)]$

$17b_p$. $\exists x \, \forall y \, [(Dy \leftrightarrow y = x) \, \& \, A \, v's \, whether \, S(x)]$

These in turn can be true only if the agent bears the cognitive relation (belief, doubt, assertion, wondering-about-the-truth-of) expressed by v to the proposition expressed by $S(\underline{x})$, when '$\underline{x}$' is taken to be a logically proper name for the one and only object that has the property expressed by D. The central epistemological doctrine of "Knowledge by Acquaintance and Knowledge by Description" is that agents **cannot** bear any such cognitive relation to that proposition when the object in question is a physical object or another human being. Hence, this doctrine has the consequence that all examples of the form $(17a_p)$ and $(17b_p)$ involving such objects are false. In this way, Russell's chief epistemological doctrine in "Knowledge by Acquaintance and Knowledge by Description" came to threaten one of the most impressive applications of his theory of descriptions, including his famous treatment in "On Denoting" of the crucial motivating example of George IV's curiosity about Scott and the author of *Waverley*. Although this conflict indicates that there is clearly something wrong with Russell's overall view, he never solved the problem, or dealt with it in any systematic way.

Linguistic Analysis and the Practice of Metaphysics

Nevertheless, the Russellian logical analysis of language was a great success, combining with Moore's insistence on common sense as the starting point in philosophy to create a style of philosophical analysis that proved remarkably potent. This may be illustrated by applying it to a doctrine of the absolute idealist predecessors of Moore and Russell. As I mentioned at the beginning of this chapter, these philosophers held that all of reality is spiritual, and that the whole of reality is a single unified object—either a divine mind or (depending on the idealist) an integrated system of interdependent minds. As further mentioned, one idea that contributed to this picture was an expansive version of *the doctrine of the reality of internal relations*. Roughly put, this version of the doctrine held that the nature and existence of each object is so dependent on that of every other object that, had any entity lacked even a single property that it actually possesses, neither the universe itself, nor any part of it, would have existed.

This remarkably counterintuitive claim was the product of two more basic ideas. The first was that among the properties of any object are properties of standing in relations to other objects, which in turn have certain properties. For example, I have the property of residing on Harrison Street in Princeton. Thus, you have the property of reading something written by someone who resides on Harrison Street in Princeton. Obviously, examples like this could be multiplied indefinitely. We can even generalize the point as follows: For any object o and property P possessed by o, there are relational properties PS—of being like o in possessing P—and PD—of being unlike o in not possessing P. Since o itself has P, every other object that has P also has PS, and every object that lacks P has PD. Moreover, if o were to come to lack P, then every object that now possesses PS would come to lack PS, and every object that now has PD would come to lack PD. Hence any change in the properties of one object involves a change in the properties of all objects.[25]

Considering the broad conception of a property of an object used in this argument—namely, anything that may truly be predicated of the object—this conclusion is not very interesting in itself. However, it acquires punch when combined with a second doctrine typically held

[25] This argument is adapted from J.M.E. McTaggart, *The Nature of Existence*, vol. 1 (Cambridge: Cambridge University Press, 1921).

by the absolute idealists. This is the doctrine that every property of an object is essential to it—in the sense that the object could not have existed without having the property. This doctrine of Rampant Essentialism together with the observation that the properties of every object are interconnected with those of all other objects led to the expansive version of the doctrine of the reality of internal relations favored by many absolute idealists.

In 1919 Moore published a withering attack on this view, subjecting it to careful analysis and arguing that it was based on conceptual confusion.[26] Although we need not follow the twists and turns of his painstaking discussion, we can illustrate the basic point using Russell's distinction between logical form and grammatical form. To this end, consider the following generic argument for Rampant Essentialism.

S1. Necessarily, if a = b, then every property of a is a property of b.

S2. Hence, if a has property P, then, necessarily, if b does not have P, then b ≠ a.

S3. More generally, if a has P, then, necessarily, anything that doesn't have P isn't a.

S4. So, if a has P, then it is a necessary truth that anything that doesn't have P isn't a.

S5. If it is a necessary truth that anything that doesn't have P isn't a, then for every possible state of the world w (i.e., for every way w that the world could have been) and for any object o whatsoever, if o were to lack P, were the world in state w, then o wouldn't be a.

S6. Since a would always be a, no matter what possible state the world might be in (provided that a would exist were the world in that state), there is no possible state w such that, were the world in w, a would exist without having P.

S7. Since there is no way that the world could be such that if it were that way, a would exist without having P, a could not exist without having P.

[26] "External and Internal Relations," *Proceedings of the Aristotelian Society,* 1919–20, reprinted in G. E. Moore, *Philosophical Studies* (Totowa, NJ: Littlefield and Adams, 1968).

S8. Since the same argument can be given for any property of any object, every property of an object is an essential property of that object—in the sense that the object could not exist without having that property.

The first premise of this argument is obviously true, and each step has an air of plausibility; yet the conclusion is incredible. How can this be? Is our commonsense conviction that we ourselves, as well as the things around us, could have had at least slightly different histories so befuddled and insecure as to be refuted by this little argument? Surely not. The confusion is in the argument itself, and can be revealed by logical analysis.

As indicated, S1 is fine, as is the progression from S4 to S8. The problem lies in an ambiguity in some sentences containing the word *necessarily* that affects the inferences to steps 2, 3, and 4. The argument can be understood in such a way that all occurrences of this word express the property of being a necessary truth. Thus, S1 can be understood as having the logical form LS1:

LS1. It is a necessary truth that [if a = b, then every property of a is a property of b]

Here, the property of being a necessary truth is attributed to the proposition expressed by the sentence in brackets—i.e., the proposition that if a is the very same thing as b, then every property of a is a property of b. By contrast, S2 is ambiguous, due to different possible scopes of the necessity operator. Here we have an example of the pervasiveness of scope ambiguities in English; just as some sentences containing descriptions are ambiguous due to different possible scopes of the descriptions, so some are ambiguous due to different possible scopes of necessity operators.

On one interpretation the logical form of S2 is LS2a, and on another it is LS2b.

LS2a. It is a necessary truth that [if a has property P, then (if b does not have P, then b ≠ a)]

LS2b. If a has property P, then it is a necessary truth that [if b does not have P, then b ≠ a]

LS2a follows from LS1. Since the bracketed sentence of LS2a is a logical consequence of the bracketed sentence in LS1, if the one expresses a necessary truth, the other must do so as well. However, LS2b does

not follow logically from LS1. LS1 tells us that there is no possible state w such that if the world were in w, a would be the very same object as b, while nevertheless not having the same properties as b. LS2 tells us something quite different: namely that if the world is **actually** in a state in which a has a certain property P, then there is **no possible** state which is such that if the world were in it, an object b that didn't have P would be the very same object as a. In order to draw this conclusion on the basis of LS1, one would have to add a further assumption: namely, that if the world is actually in a state in which a has P, then there is no possible state w, such that if the world were in w, a would lack P. However, since this is what the argument is designed to **prove**, to introduce it as an assumption would be to render the argument circular. Thus, if the argument is to have any chance of serving its purpose, S2 must be interpreted as having the logical form LS2a.

Similar reasoning establishes that if S3 is to follow from LS2a, it must have the logical form LS3a.

> LS3a. It is a necessary truth that [for any object o, if a has property
> P, then (if o does not have P, then o ≠ a)]

However, now there is no way to get to S4, the logical form of which is, unambiguously, LS4.

> LS4. If a has P, then it is a necessary truth that [for any object o,
> if o does not have P, then o ≠ a]

Just as before, there is no way of validly inferring LS4 from LS3a, short of assuming that which is supposed to be proved. Of course, since S3 is ambiguous, it has another interpretation in which S4 does follow from it, namely an interpretation in which S3 has the same logical form as S4. However, on that interpretation S3 doesn't follow from LS2a.

To sum up, logical analysis of the argument for Rampant Essentialism reveals that it rests on a hidden ambiguity. Certain key sentences in it have more than one logical form. The fact that each step has an interpretation on which it follows logically and non-circularly from previous steps gives the argument its air of plausibility. However, there is no consistent way of interpreting the ambiguous sentences so that every step follows validly and non-circularly from the others. Because of this, the argument does nothing to rebut the commonsense conviction that we ourselves, and the objects around us, could have had slightly different histories. In short, the idealists have done nothing to rebut the rational presumption in favor of this conviction, and nothing to establish their grand metaphysical theses. For us, this result serves as a useful illustration of the power, in philosophical argument, of the conception of analysis that emerged from the early work of Moore and Russell.

CHAPTER 6

LOGIC AND MATHEMATICS:
THE LOGICIST REDUCTION

Introduction to the Logicist Program

In developing his theory of descriptions, Russell distinguished logical form from grammatical form and used this distinction to solve
philosophical puzzles arising from problematic views about meaning.
His theory of descriptions was taken to be a paradigm of analysis,
and the success of the theory gave strong impetus to the view that
logical and conceptual analysis was the road to progress in philosophy. That view was given powerful additional support by his next
major achievement—the completion of the logicist project of reducing mathematics to logic presented in his great work, *Principia
Mathematica*, coauthored with Alfred North Whitehead and pub-

lished in 1910.[1] The logicist project can be divided into two parts—
the reduction of higher mathematics to arithmetic, and the reduction
of arithmetic to logic. Russell's major contribution was to this second reduction. When both reductions were completed, the end result, roughly put, was the reduction of essentially all classical theorems of both elementary and higher mathematics to a system that
was plausibly regarded by many as a theory of pure logic.

In order to understand this program, it is necessary to understand
what a mathematical or logical theory is, and what it means to reduce
one such theory to another. One can think of a *theory* as a set of sentences, each of which is a logical consequence of some specified set of
axioms. The axioms express propositions that the theorist takes as
given, and accepts without proof. The *theorems* of the theory constitute the totality of statements that can be proven from the axioms.
Since they follow logically from the axioms, they must be true, if the
axioms are.

The axioms contain the *primitive vocabulary* of the theory. These
are words or symbols that express concepts with which we are familiar
without definition. Just as the axioms themselves are the primitive
sentences of the theory that are accepted without proof, so the vocabulary used in the axioms are the primitive symbols the meanings of
which we take ourselves to know without definition. Sometimes, in
addition to axioms of a theory, we also have a class of sentences called
definitions of the theory. These define new terminology that does not
appear in the axioms in terms of the primitive symbols that do appear
there.

For example, in many theories there is no primitive symbol for the
definite article *the* that is used in forming singular definite descriptions. Nevertheless, it is convenient to have the ability to form such descriptions when working with the theory, often as a means of keeping the
sentences of the theory from getting too long and hard to process psychologically. Thus, the description operator is sometimes introduced
by a definition such as the following:

---

[1] Vol. 1 of *Principia Mathematica* was published in 1910, vol. 2 in 1912, and vol. 3 in 1913,
all by Cambridge University Press. Russell's work on logicism was preceded and much influenced by the pioneering work of the great philosopher and mathematician Gottlob Frege, in
his groundbreaking work, *Grundgesetze der Arithmetik* (The Basic Laws of Arithmetic), the
first volume of which was published in 1893, the second in 1903.

Where Ψ is any (simple) atomic predicate, and Φ is any formula,

$$\Psi \text{ the } x: \Phi x \equiv \exists x \, \forall y \, [(\Phi y \leftrightarrow y = x) \, \& \, \Psi x]$$

When the definite description operator is introduced in this way, it will turn out that some theorems of the theory contain definite descriptions, even though the axioms do not. In this sort of case, the theorems of the theory are taken to be logical consequences of the axioms **plus** the definitions of the theory. In general, we will take a theory to involve a set of axioms that are accepted without proof, plus, in some cases, a set of stipulative definitions that define new terminology in terms of the theory's primitive vocabulary. Theorems are logical consequences of the axioms plus the definitions.

We now turn to the notion of theoretical reduction. Suppose we have two theories, T1 and T2. To reduce T2 to T1 is to do two things. First, one formulates a set of stipulative definitions that define the primitive vocabulary of T2 in terms of the vocabulary of T1. That is, one takes those terms that appear in the axioms of T2, the meanings of which are simply assumed or taken for granted from the perspective of T2, and one provides those terms with definitions drawn from the vocabulary of T1. Second, one shows how the axioms of T2 can be proved from the axioms of T1 together with the stipulative definitions one has adopted. The end result is that the concepts of T2 are analyzed in terms of the concepts of T1, and the axioms which had been accepted without proof are now given rigorous justifications by proving them from still more basic assumptions. In effect, theory 2 comes to be seen as an elaboration of what was already implicitly present in T1.

With this in mind, we can gain some appreciation of the scope of the enterprise Russell was engaged in. Prior to Russell, two significant achievements had occurred that were directly relevant to his project. First, the theory of the arithmetic of the natural numbers had been formalized. A set of axioms had been formulated, using the three primitive arithmetical concepts of zero, successor, and natural number; a further set of definitions had been adopted defining the arithmetical operations of addition and multiplication in terms of these primitives; and all previously established results of classical arithmetic had been shown to be derivable from these axioms and definitions. Second, prior to Russell it had been shown that theories in advanced mathematics could be reduced, in the sense just explained, to arithmetic. For our purposes we may take it that all traditional results of mathematics could be so reduced.

This meant that arithmetic could be viewed as the foundation of all mathematical knowledge. Given some branch of higher mathematics, with its own axioms and primitive concepts, one could always formulate definitions of those concepts in terms of arithmetical concepts, and prove the axioms of the higher branch from the axioms of arithmetic plus stipulative definitions adopted for the reduction. Typically, these proofs and definitions ended up being long and complicated. Thus, someone engaged in higher mathematics would certainly not want to pursue his field by rewriting everything in arithmetical terms; such a translation would typically be so cumbersome and difficult to work with that following this path would hinder, if not halt, mathematical progress. Nevertheless, the reductions were thought to be theoretically important, in the sense that they showed that the entire epistemological weight of mathematics could be made to rest on arithmetic. If anyone wanted to **justify** the results of higher mathematics in terms of something more basic, arithmetic was always there to do the job. Consequently, if one could show that arithmetic should be accepted, then the acceptability of the rest would follow.

But what about arithmetic? Could one define its primitive concepts and prove its axioms from something even more basic? That is the primary question with which Russell, and before him the German philosopher, Gottlob Frege, were concerned. Their task was to show that arithmetic could be reduced to pure logic, and hence that mathematics in general was simply an elaboration of logic. Part of the motivation for this task was straightforwardly mathematical. It was a significant mathematical problem to determine whether the same sort of reduction that had been performed in the other cases could be performed here. However, this project also attracted philosophical interest.

Philosophical logicists had three main motivations for trying to show that arithmetic, and hence mathematics in general, could be reduced to logic. In discussing these, I will discuss pure, or generic, versions of these motivations, without going into the complications arising from different variations on these motivations, and different emphases favored by different logicists. Even Russell himself held different views about the philosophical significance of the logicist reduction at different times, and he by no means always shared the classical generic motivations that I will sketch. Taken together, these motivations characterize a composite, hypothetical philosopher—the classical logicist—rather than the views of any one person.

The first and most obvious motivation for the logicist reduction involved the epistemological aim of justification. In the case of empirical theories, we formulate hypotheses and test them against experimental data. To the extent that the predictions made by the hypotheses are borne out by observational tests, the hypotheses are confirmed. To the extent that they are not, they are disconfirmed. By contrast, in mathematics there are no experiments or observations. Theorems are standardly accepted on the basis of their derivations from the axioms. But how can the axioms themselves be justified? An attractive idea was that by showing that mathematics is reducible to logic, one could justify mathematical axioms as being nothing more than logical consequences of purely logical principles. Since, presumably, everyone has to accept logic, the problem of justification would be solved.[2]

This is closely related to the second main philosophical motivation of the classical logicist. Mathematical truths seem to be knowable apriori, independent of experience. How is such knowledge possible? On the one hand, it is natural to think that all of our knowledge arises in some way from sense experience. On the other hand, it is hard to see how sense perception could ground or provide the justification for our apriori knowledge of the necessary truths of mathematics; after all, we don't have to go out and make observations to confirm arithmetical equations. Different philosophers have reacted differently to this problem. Some have posited innate ideas as the source of such knowledge; some have claimed that there is an abstract but genuine realm of real mathematical objects revealed to us by a special perception-like faculty of intellectual intuition; still others have claimed that the necessity and apriori character of mathematics somehow results from the operations and categories that our mind imposes on experience. Logicists were not satisfied with any of these answers.

One historically important strand of logicist thinking saw the possibility of a different kind of answer. On this view, mathematics is reducible to logic, which itself has a linguistic foundation. The principles of logic are thought to be true simply in virtue of the meanings of the logical words like *all, some, and, or*, and *not* that they contain. Thus, the explanation of how we can have apriori knowledge of mathematics is seen as

---

[2] This is a highly simplified and elementary sketch of the logicists' view of the relevance of his project to the question of justification. By the time that Russell saw clearly how the logicist reduction was to proceed, his views about justification were considerably more complicated and nuanced. See for example his 1907 paper, "The Regressive Method of Discovering the Principles of Mathematics," reprinted in Bertrand Russell, *Essays in Analysis*, edited by Douglas Lackey (New York: George Braziller, 1973).

similar to the explanation of how we can have apriori knowledge that bachelors are unmarried. How do we know this trivial truth about bachelors? We simply **decide** to use the words *bachelor* and *unmarried* in a certain way, with certain meanings. The truth of sentences like *Bachelors are unmarried* is supposed somehow to follow from these decisions. The idea was that we can know that certain sentences, and the propositions they express, are true simply by knowing how we have decided to use certain words. Thus, on one important version of logicism, the reduction of mathematics to logic was taken to show that the truths of mathematics are analytic, and hence knowable in the same way that trivial truths like our example about bachelors are (allegedly) known.[3]

The third significant philosophical motivation that logicists found in the reduction of mathematics to logic was ontological. If we think about the ontology of various parts of mathematics it might seem that we are forced to posit the existence of a variety of different things—natural numbers, negative numbers, rational numbers, irrational numbers, and so on. But do we really have to posit the existence of many different kinds of mathematical objects in order to accept the results of mathematics? The reduction of higher mathematics to arithmetic was taken to indicate that we do not. Different types of numbers can be reduced to different constructions of natural numbers. The reduction of arithmetic to logic was taken to show that natural numbers could themselves be reduced to sets of certain types. Thus, we have what can be seen as a kind of depopulating of the philosophical universe. The process that began with Russell's use of his theory of descriptions to eliminate nonexistent objects of thought (like carnivorous cows and the round square) is now extended to natural numbers and other mathematical objects.

A System of Arithmetic

We are now ready to begin looking at some of the details of Russell's reduction of arithmetic to logic. We begin with a specification of his arithmetical theory. There are three primitive terms used in the theory: 'N', which we take to stand for the set of natural numbers; '0', which stands for the first number in the series of natural numbers; and the

---

[3] A good exposition of this version of logicism can be found in Carl Hempel, "On the Nature of Mathematical Truth," *American Mathematical Monthly*, 52 (1945): 543–56; reprinted in *The Philosophy of Mathematics*, 2nd edition, P. Benacerraf and H. Putnam, eds. (Cambridge: Cambridge University Press, 1983).

apostrophe—'—which stands for the successor function—i.e., the function which, when applied to any natural number, gives us the next number in the series. These three terms appear in the arithmetical axioms, and are taken to be understood without definition. In effect, in giving the arithmetical theory, we take it that we know what a natural number is, that we know what zero is, and that we know what it means to go from one number to the next.

In addition to the arithmetical primitives, the axioms contain logical vocabulary that is common to all sorts of theories—quantifiers, variables, and truth functional connectives. There are also two further symbols to notice— '=' and 'ε'. The first of these is the identity predicate, which holds between an object and itself. The second stands for the set membership relation—a relation that holds between the members of a set and the set they are members of. Russell regarded these as logical primitives, and hence not special to arithmetic.

We are now ready to state the arithmetical axioms. For each axiom I will first give the formal statement, and then specify in English what the axiom says.

A1. $0 \in N$
   Zero is a natural number.

A2. $\forall x \, (x \in N \rightarrow x' \in N)$
   The successor of any natural number is a natural number.

A3. $\sim\exists x \, (0 = x')$
   Zero is not the successor of anything.

A4. $\forall x \, \forall y \, [(x \in N \,\&\, y \in N \,\&\, x' = y') \rightarrow x = y]$
   No two (different) natural numbers have the same successor.

In addition to these four axioms we have an axiom schema, A5, which stands for the infinite set of axioms obtainable from the schema A5 by substituting for 'F' any formula in the language of arithmetic which contains free occurrences of the variable 'x' and only the variable 'x'.

A5. $[F(0) \,\&\, \forall x \, (x \in N \rightarrow (Fx \rightarrow Fx'))] \rightarrow \forall x \, (x \in N \rightarrow Fx)$
   Here $F(0)$ is the result of replacing all free occurrences of 'x' in the formula replacing 'F' with occurrences of '0'. Informally, $F(0)$ says that zero "is F." Thus, each instance of A5 says that if zero "is F" and if whenever a natural number "is F" then its successor also "is F," then every natural number "is F." Instances of A5 are often called *induction axioms*.

Next we have a pair of definitions that define the notions of addition and multiplication in terms of the arithmetical primitives. First the definition of '+'.

D1. $\forall x\, \forall y\, [(x \in N \,\&\, y \in N) \rightarrow ((x + 0) = x \,\&\, (x + y') = (x + y)')]$

> For any natural numbers x and y, the result of adding zero to x is x, and the result of adding the successor of y to x is the successor of the result of adding y to x.

In using the definition, we first note what it is to add zero to x. We then use this result, together with the second conjunct of the consequent of the definition, to figure out what it is to add the successor of zero, 1, to x; the definition tells us that the sum of x and 1 is the successor of x + 0, which is the successor of x, namely x'. Next we apply the definition again to determine that the sum of x and 2 is x''. The process can be repeated to determine, for each number y, the result of adding y to x. Since x can be any number, D1 completely determines the sum of every pair of numbers, even though it does not have the familiar form of an explicit definition.

This is illustrated by the following example.

Illustration: 3 + 2 = 5

(i) $(0''' + 0'') = (0''' + 0')'$ From D1 plus A1 and A2, which guarantee that $0'''$ and $0''$ are natural numbers

(ii) $(0''' + 0') = (0''' + 0)'$ From D1, A1, and A2

(iii) $(0''' + 0'') = (0''' + 0)''$ From substitution in (i) of equals for equals on the basis of (ii)

(iv) $(0''' + 0) = 0'''$ D1

(v) $(0''' + 0'') = 0'''''$ From substitution in (iii) on the basis of (iv)

Finally, we define multiplication in terms of addition. (We use '*' as the symbol for multiplication.)

D2. $\forall x\, \forall y\, [(x \in N \,\&\, y \in N) \rightarrow ((x * 0) = 0 \,\&\, (x * y') = (x * y) + x)]$

> For any natural numbers x and y, the result of multiplying x
> times zero is zero, and the result of multiplying x times the
> successor of y is the sum of x and the result of multiplying x
> times y.

D2 works in the same way as D1. Thus, multiplication is defined in terms of repeated addition, which in turn is defined in terms of repeated application of the successor function. As you can imagine, proofs of elementary facts about multiplication get quite long. However, the usual results can all be proved in the system of arithmetic consisting of A1–A5 plus D1 and D2. This is the theory to which higher branches of mathematics can be reduced, and which Russell reduces to his system of logic.

Russell's System of Logic

Next we turn to the system to which Russell reduced this system of arithmetic. I will not specify in detail the usual logical principles that allow one to prove straightforward logical truths like $Pv\sim P$, $\forall x\, Fx \rightarrow Fa$, $\forall x\, \forall y\, (x = y \rightarrow (Fx \leftrightarrow Fy))$, and so on. We will just take it for granted that Russell's system contains logical apparatus sufficient for this task. However, we will take note of certain special features of Russell's logic that figure prominently in his reduction. One of these is a new primitive symbol, 'ϵ', standing for set membership (i.e. for the relation that we attribute to x and y when y is a set and we say that x is a member of y). The other special feature consists of axioms governing the use of this primitive, plus an axiom guaranteeing the existence of a sufficient number of logical objects.

The first set of new axioms governing the use of this symbol for set membership consists of all instances of L_1, which is known as *the axiom schema of comprehension*.

L_1. $\exists y\, \forall x\, (Fx \leftrightarrow x \in y)$

> Here the variable 'y' ranges over sets and *Fx* may be replaced
> by any formula containing free occurrences of the variable 'x'
> (and no free occurrences of any other variable). Different
> choices of formulas to play the role of *Fx* result in different
> instances of the schema. Each such instance asserts the exist-
> ence of a set of all and only those things that satisfy (have the
> property expressed by) the formula.

The idea behind this axiom schema is that for every open formula in the language containing one variable free—intuitively, for every formula in the language that expresses a property of objects—there is a set of precisely those things that satisfy the formula (have the property expressed). To think of this as a logical principle is, in effect, to think that talk about an individual x's being so and so is interchangeable with talk about x's being in the set of things that are so and so.

Examples of sets asserted to exist by instances of L_1 are as follows:

(i) where the formula replacing *Fx* is any formula having the meaning *is a natural number < 29*, the existence of the set of natural numbers less than 29 is asserted;

(ii) where the formula $x \in N \& x = x$ replaces *Fx*, the existence of the set of all natural numbers is asserted;

(iii) where the formula $x \neq x$ replaces *Fx*, the existence of the empty set, i.e., the set with no members, is asserted;

(iv) where the formula $\forall z\ (z \in x \leftrightarrow z \neq z)$ replaces *Fx*, the existence of the set whose only member is the empty set is asserted. ('x' here ranges over sets.)

According to the axiom schema of comprehension, for every formula $\Phi(x)$ there will be a set of all and only those things that satisfy $\Phi(x)$.

The next axiom governing Russell's primitive, '$\in$', for set membership is L_2, which is known as *the axiom of extensionality*.

L_2. $\forall a\ \forall b\ [\ \forall x\ (x \in a \leftrightarrow x \in b) \rightarrow a = b]$

If a and b are sets with the same members, then $a = b$—i.e., no two sets have the same members. ('a' and 'b' are variables that range over sets.)

The final axiom, L_3, that is special to Russell's logical system is called *the axiom of infinity*. The purpose of the axiom is to ensure the existence of an infinite number of logical objects that are needed for the reduction of arithmetic to logic. The reason why this axiom is needed, and the reason why it is stated in the peculiar way that it is, will become clear only after we have gotten a good way into the reduction itself.

L_3. $\emptyset \notin N$

The empty set is not a member of the set of natural numbers.

Before turning to the reduction, I need to say a word about Russell's logical system, as I have described it so far. The system I have described is close to the system that Russell actually used in giving the reduction. However, it differs from it in certain respects. The most important of these involves the axiom schema of comprehension. I have stated this schema in a completely general and unrestricted way. One of Russell's discoveries was that when the axiom schema is stated in this way, it leads to a contradiction, now known as *Russell's paradox*, which we will examine in due course. The paradox shows that L_1 cannot be accepted as presently stated. Fortunately, however, there turn out to be ways of restricting it that block the contradiction, while allowing the reduction of arithmetic to logic to go through more or less unchanged. Our strategy will be to use the system as I have now stated it to sketch the reduction. Once the leading ideas become clear, I will present Russell's paradox and explain briefly how he handled it with his theory of types, while leaving the reduction basically intact. Once all of this is done, we will discuss the philosophical significance of Russell's reduction.

One final preliminary: we will introduce certain defined terms into Russell's system of logic. These will serve as convenient abbreviations for various concepts we will make use of in the reduction.

CONVENIENT ABBREVIATIONS
(in what follows, 'x', 'y', and 's' range over sets)

(i) Definite Descriptions

Ψ the z: Φz $\exists z \, \forall w \, [(\Phi w \leftrightarrow w = z) \, \& \, \Psi z]$

(ii) The Empty Set

$\varnothing$:   the x: $(\forall z \, (z \notin x))$

(iii) The set the only member of which is w

{w}:   the x: $[\forall z \, (z \in x \leftrightarrow z = w)]$

(iv) The set of all and only the things that "are F" (have the property expressed by F)

$\uparrow$z Fz: the y: $[\forall z \, (Fz \leftrightarrow z \in y)]$

(v) The intersection of the sets x and y—i.e., the set of things that are members of both

x $\cap$ y :   the s: $[\forall w \, (w \in s \leftrightarrow (w \in x \, \& \, w \in y)]$

(vi) The union of the sets x and y—i.e., the set of things that are members either of x or of y (the total contents of x and y taken together)

x ∪ y: the s: [∀w (w ∈ s ↔ (w ∈ x ∨ w ∈ y)]

(vii) The complement of a set x—the set of all things not in x

Comp(x):   the y: [∀z (z ∈ y ↔ z ∉ x)]

The Reduction of Arithmetic to Logic

In order to reduce our system of arithmetic to Russell's logical system, one must first define the arithmetical primitives using terms of Russell's logical system, and then derive all the axioms of the arithmetical system from those definitions, plus the axioms of Russell's logic. In this way, all arithmetical theorems become theorems of the system of logic. As one might imagine, the trick is coming up with the right definitions.

Definitions of Arithmetical Primitives

We begin with definitions of three the arithmetical primitives—zero, successor, and natural number. The first two definitions are as follows:[4]

THE DEFINITION OF ZERO

$0 = \{\varnothing\}$

Zero is the set the only member of which is the empty set.

THE DEFINITION OF SUCCESSOR

The successor of a set x is the set of all those sets y that contain a member z which, when eliminated from y, leaves one with a member of x.

$x' = ↑y[\exists z \ (z \in y \ \& \ [\ (y \cap Comp(\{z\})) \in x])]$

---

[4] Those who already know about Russell's paradox may wonder about the definition of successor given here, which assumes the existence of a set that contains everything except z. One of the lessons of the paradox is that there is no such set, if by everything one means absolutely *everything* in the universe, including all sets. Not to worry. Once the theory of types is introduced, *Comp({ z })* in the definition of *successor* will be understood as denoting the set of all and only those things at the level z except z (i.e., the set of all individuals except z)—and there will always be such a set.

The successor of a set x = the set of all sets y which contain a member z such that the intersection of y with the complement of the set the only member of which is z—i.e., with the set containing everything except z—is a member of x.

These definitions interact with one another in the following manner:

$$0' = \uparrow y[\exists z \, (z \in y \, \& \, [\, (y \cap \text{Comp}(\{z\})) \in \{\varnothing\}])]$$

The successor of zero [i.e., the number 1] is the set of all sets y that contain a member z which when eliminated from y leaves one with the empty set—the set with no members at all. In other words, the successor of zero is the set of all 1-membered sets, the successor of the successor of zero (i.e., the number 2) is the set of all two-membered sets, and so on.

There are three things to notice about this procedure. First, it is **not** circular. The number 2 turns out to be the set of all two-membered sets. However, we didn't **define** the number 2 using the notion *two-membered set* (or *set with two members*). Rather, we may define 2 as the successor of 1, which in turn may be defined as the successor of zero. The fundamental notions here—namely *zero* and *successor*—are themselves defined without any arithmetical concepts. Hence there is no circle.

Second, you should be able to see from our procedure that, intuitively, no two natural numbers m and n—reached via this chain of successors—can share a member in common. If n consists of all and only n-membered sets, while m consists of all and only m-membered sets, then no set can be a member of both m and n, provided that m and n are different numbers. Another way of putting the point is that if n and m are natural numbers according to the Russellian definition, and if they have a member in common, then n and m must be the same number. Although we haven't given a proof of this here, it turns out to be formally provable from the axioms of Russell's system of logic. We will return to this later in the reduction, since it plays a role in the proof of one of the arithmetical axioms.

The third thing you should appreciate about this procedure for defining the individual numbers is how natural it is. Russell speaks to this point at the beginning of chapter 2 of *Introduction to Mathematical Philosophy*.

In seeking a definition of number, the first thing to be clear about is what we may call the grammar of our inquiry. Many philosophers, when attempting to define number, are really setting to work to define plurality, which is quite a different thing. *Number* is what is characteristic of numbers, as *man* is what is characteristic of men. A plurality is not an instance of number, but of some particular number. A trio of men, for example, is an instance of the number 3, and the number 3 is an instance of number; but the trio is not an instance of number. This point may seem elementary and scarcely worth mentioning; yet it has proved too subtle for the philosophers, with few exceptions.

A particular number is not identical with any collection of terms having that number: the number 3 is not identical with the trio consisting of Brown, Jones, and Robinson. The number 3 is something which all trios have in common, and which distinguishes them from other collections. A number is something that characterizes certain collections, namely, those that have that number.[5]

We can illustrate Russell's point by noting that the property of being red is not identical with any red thing. Rather, it is something all red things have in common. Similarly, the number 3 is not identical with any set of three things; rather it is something that all sets of three things have in common. We could say that the number 3 is the property of being a set with three members. However, in Russell's system talk of properties is dropped in favor of talk of sets. Thus, for him the number 3 becomes the set which contains all sets with three members. What does every trio have in common? Membership in the number 3.

We are now ready to define the final arithmetical primitive—'N'— which we took to stand for the set of natural numbers. Since we already have zero and successor, it might seem that we could define the class of natural numbers as the class of those sets each of which can be reached by starting with zero and applying successor finitely many times. However, that presupposes that the notion of a **finite number** is one of our logical primitives, which it is not. Rather, it is an arithmetical concept which needs definition. In fact, as used in the proposed definition, it is the very concept we are trying to define, since to apply successor a finite number of times is just to apply it n times, for some natural number n. So we need to think again.

[5] Bertrand Russell, *Introduction to Mathematical Philosophy*, 2nd edition, 1920 (London: Allen and Unwin; New York: Macmillan); reprinted in 1993 (New York: Dover), pp. 11–12.

Suppose we tried the following:

> N = the set which contains zero, and which is closed
> under successor—i.e., which contains the successor
> of each of its members

Initially it might seem that everything we would want to call a natural number would fall under this definition. However, this is an illusion. The definition is unacceptable because there is no such thing as **the** set satisfying the condition. For example, each of the following sets satisfies the condition *set which contains zero, and which is closed under successor.*

Set 1   {0, 0′, 0″, 0‴, . . .}

Set 2   {0, 0′, 0″, 0‴, . . . {{Bill}}, the set of all sets that contain Bill plus something else, ...}

Set 3   {0, 0′, 0″, 0‴, . . . {{Bill}, {Mary, Ron}}, the union of the successor of {{Bill}} and the set of all triples containing Mary and Ron, . . .}

Given this result, we need some way of enriching the condition used to define 'N' that eliminates all but set 1. We can do this as follows:

THE DEFINITION OF NATURAL NUMBER

The set of natural numbers = the smallest set containing zero and closed under successor

$$N = \uparrow x \, [\forall y \, ((0 \in y \, \& \, \forall z \, (z \in y \to z' \in y)) \to x \in y)]$$
('x' and 'y' range over sets)

The set of natural numbers is the set of all and only those sets x which are members of every set y which contains zero and is closed under successor.

This concludes the definition of arithmetical concepts in terms of the concepts in Russell's logical system. All that remains to complete the reduction of arithmetic to logic is to show that the arithmetical axioms are provable from Russell's logical axioms with the help of these definitions.

Proofs of the Arithmetical Axioms

The first two axioms follow trivially from the definitions we have adopted.

A1. $0 \in N$
     Zero is a natural number.

Using the definition of 'N', we see that this says that zero is a member of the smallest set containing zero and closed under successor. Thus, it is trivially true.

A2. $\forall x \, (x \in N \rightarrow x' \in N)$
The successor of any natural number is a natural number.

Again using the definition of 'N', we see that this says that *if x is a member of the smallest set containing zero and closed under successor, then the successor of x is a member of that set too.* This also is trivial—from what it means for a set to be *closed under successor.*

Next consider A3, which says that zero isn't the successor of anything.

A3. $\sim \exists x \, (0 = x')$

This can be proved by *reductio ad absurdum*:

(i) Suppose that for some x, zero is the successor of x.

(ii) By the definition of 0, this means that $\{\varnothing\} = x'$.

(iii) By the definition of successor, we have: for any member y of $\{\varnothing\}$, there is a member z of y which is such that dropping z out of y leaves one with a member of x.

(iv) From this it follows that there is a member z of $\varnothing$.

(v) But that is impossible, since $\varnothing$ has no members.

(vi) Thus, (i) is false; zero is not the successor of anything. This establishes A3.

We now skip to axiom schema A5.

A5. $[F(0) \, \& \, \forall x \, (x \in N \rightarrow (Fx \rightarrow Fx'))] \rightarrow \forall x \, (x \in N \rightarrow Fx)$
Here *F(0)* is the result of replacing all free occurrences of 'x' in the formula that replaces 'F' with occurrences of '0'. Informally, *F(0)* says that zero "is F." Thus, each instance of A5 says that if zero "is F" and if whenever a natural number "is F" then its successor also "is F," then every natural number "is F."

We will prove this for an arbitrary instance of the schema. To prove the instance we assume the antecedent and try to prove the consequent. The antecedent says that (i) zero is F and (ii) whenever a natural number is F, then its successor is too. We must show that if this is true then the consequent must also true—i.e., it must be true that (iii) every natural number is F. We begin by considering **the class which consists of all and only those natural numbers which are F**. The axiom schema, L_1, of comprehension guarantees that there is such a set. The two clauses (i) and (ii) of the antecedent tell us that this set contains zero and is closed under successor. Recall that we defined the natural numbers to be those things that are members of **every** set that contains zero and is closed under successor. Since we have just seen that **the class of natural numbers which are F** is one of those sets, we know that every natural number must be a member of it. Thus (iii) is true—every natural number is F. In this way we can prove each instance of axiom schema A5.

In order to complete the reduction, all that needs to be proved is A4.

A4. $\forall x \, \forall y \, [(x \in N \;\&\; y \in N \;\&\; x' = y') \to x = y]$
      No two (different) natural numbers have the same successor.

To prove this we assume

   (i) x and y are natural numbers; and

   (ii) $x' = y'$

and then show that (iii) follows.

   (iii) x = y

In showing that (iii) follows, we will consider two possibilities that may at first seem a little strange, but which will become clear as the proof progresses.

   <u>Possibility 1</u>
   $x' = y' \neq \varnothing$ (i.e. x', y' is a set with members)

   <u>Possibility 2</u>
   $x' = y' = \varnothing$

First consider possibility 1. (a) For any member w of x' (i.e., of y'), eliminating one of its members z gives us a member s of x (from the definition of successor). (b) Similarly, for any member w of y' (i.e., x'), eliminating one of its members z* gives us a member s* of y (from the definition of successor). (c) Since x' (y') is a number, s is a member of x and y, as is s*. (This follows from the fact that when n' is a number, it doesn't matter which member of a member w of n' that one eliminates;

the result will always be a member of n. Thus, regardless of which member (z or z*) of a member of x′ (i.e., y′) one eliminates, the set one ends up with must be a member of both x and y.)[6] (iv) Thus, x and y are numbers that have a member in common. From our construction of the numbers, we can see that this guarantees that x = y.[7] This is sufficient to prove A4, provided we can exclude possibility 2.

It is now time to turn to that possibility. How could ∅ be the successor of anything? Well, suppose there were only 10 existing objects that could be used in the construction of numbers. On Russell's definition, 10 = the set of all 10-membered sets. Now consider the successor of 10. By definition, it is the set of all those sets y that contain a member z which, when eliminated from y, leaves one with a 10-membered set. In other words, 10′ = the set of all 11-membered sets. But if there were only 10 things in the universe to be used in the construction of numbers, then there would be no 11-membered sets. In that case the set of all 11-membered sets would be the empty set, ∅. In this eventuality the successor of 10, 10′, would be the empty set, ∅.

Next consider the successor of 10′—i.e., 10″. It is, by definition, the set of all sets y which contain a member z which, when eliminated from y, leaves one with a member of ∅. Since ∅ has no members, no y is such that eliminating one of its members leaves one with a member of ∅. Thus, in the bizarre scenario we are considering, 10″ = ∅. This means that we have 10′ = ∅ = 11′ (i.e., 10″). But still, 10 ≠ 11, since 11 = ∅, while 10 = the set of all ten-membered sets, which, by hypothesis, is not empty. But this would falsify A4—since we would have x′ = y′, but not x = y. Thus, if the universe had only ten objects —or indeed if it had only a finite number of objects—to be used in the construction of Russellian numbers, then A4 would fail.

---

[6] This point is a little tricky. When applied to an **arbitrary** set x, the definition of successor does **not** say that no matter which member z of a member w of x′ one eliminates from w, one will always be left with a member of x. It only says that for every member w of x′, there is at least one element z that can be removed from w, leaving one with a member of x. Thus, if we applied the definition of successor to **arbitrary** sets x′ and y′ such that x′ = y′, then the definition would not preclude the possibility that (i) eliminating a certain z from a member w of x′ (y′) might give us a member of x but not a member of y; while (ii) eliminating a different z* from w might give us a member of y that was not a member of x. These possibilities **are** precluded when x′ (i.e., y′) is a natural number, as is assumed in A4. Although it is fairly easy to see this intuitively, it is something that has to be proved in a fully rigorous and formal proof. Although it can be, we won't go into the details here.

[7] Again, although this can be proved formally, we won't go into the details.

It was the need to avoid this result that prompted Russell to posit the Axiom of Infinity, in the initially strange seeming formulation

$$L_3. \quad \varnothing \notin N,$$

as one of the postulates of his system of logic. Note that in the context of Russell's system, this axiom has the effect of guaranteeing the existence of infinitely many objects, without having to make use of the notions *finitely many* or *infinitely many* as primitives. With L_3 in place, possibility 2 is characterized as impossible, and A4 is provable from the system of logic. This completes the reduction.

Russell's Paradox and the Theory of Types

Having seen how Russell reduced arithmetic to logic, we are now ready to scrutinize two of the special axioms of his logical system—the unrestricted axiom schema of comprehension

$$\exists y \, \forall x \, (Fx \leftrightarrow x \in y)$$

and the axiom of infinity

$$\varnothing \notin N.$$

In the case of the axiom of infinity, one might doubt that the question of how many objects there are really is a matter of logic alone, and hence one might doubt that the axiom of infinity should be regarded as a genuine **logical** axiom. Russell gave this matter some thought, and at least initially believed that the worry could be put to rest. For example, if sets are regarded as objects, it would seem that one could generate them indefinitely—$\varnothing$, $\{\varnothing\}$, $\{\{\varnothing\}\}$, and so on. It doesn't seem worrisome to suppose that there are infinitely many things, if pure sets such as these count as things. Or again, suppose for the sake of argument that there are only finitely many concrete particulars. Let n be the number of such particulars. Then there are 2^n sets of such particulars, 2 to the 2^n sets of such sets, and so on. Continuing this process indefinitely and collecting all these together in a single set would clearly give us an infinite set. Again, if all the members of this set count as things, then it would seem that the axiom of infinity wouldn't be problematic.

Although Russell was initially convinced by such arguments, he soon discovered a serious problem that, among other things, undercuts this way of persuading oneself that the axiom of infinity is nothing to worry about.[8] The problem was Russell's paradox, and his solution to it was his *theory of logical types*. The paradox arises from the unrestricted axiom schema of comprehension.

$$\exists y\ \forall x\ (Fx \leftrightarrow x \in y)$$

Instances of this axiom schema arise from replacing *Fx* with any formula of the logical language containing only the variable 'x' free. The idea was that whatever the formula replacing *Fx* turns out to be, there must surely be a set of all and only those things that satisfy the formula— the set of things that "are F." In some cases, this may be the empty set. But that is all right; the empty set is a set.

Suppose, however, that we replace *Fx* with the formula

$$\sim x \in x$$

Doing this gives us (1) as an axiom of Russell's system of logic.

1. $\exists y\ \forall x\ (\sim x \in x \leftrightarrow x \in y)$

   There is a set of all and only those things that are not members of themselves. Let us introduce a new symbol, '$\underline{y}$', as a name for this supposed set. With this definition of '$\underline{y}$', (2) must be true, if (1) is.

2. $\forall x\ (\sim x \in x \leftrightarrow x \in \underline{y})$

   Everything is such that it is a member of $\underline{y}$ iff it is not a member of itself.

But now, since everything includes **every** single thing, the claim made by (2) must include $\underline{y}$ itself. Thus, (3) must be true, if (2) is.

3. $(\sim \underline{y} \in \underline{y} \leftrightarrow \underline{y} \in \underline{y})$

   $\underline{y}$ is a member of itself iff $\underline{y}$ is not a member of itself.

But (3) is a contradiction, and so cannot be true. Since (3) is a logical consequence of (1), which in turn is an instance of the axiom schema of comprehension, it follows that Russell's system of logic is contradictory. That is Russell's paradox.

The existence of this paradox required Russell to modify the system so that it would no longer generate the contradiction. The modification grew out of a diagnosis of how the problem arose. It arose from two aspects of the axiom schema of comprehension: (i) the ability to

---

[8] See chapter 13 of his *Introduction to Mathematical Philosophy*, pp. 134–43.

replace Fx in the schema with **any formula** of the logical language and (ii) the interpretation of the universal quantifier $\forall x$ as ranging over **everything**. Since these two aspects of the axiom schema combine to produce the contradictory result, avoiding the result requires changing one or both. Russell's theory of logical types was a way of changing both aspects simultaneously.

I will now give a very brief and simplified sketch of this theory. We begin with a hierarchical conception of the universe. At the initial, most basic, level we have individuals—i.e., concrete particulars of all kinds—including people, material objects, and so on. At the next level we have all the sets that can be formed using the individuals at the previous level as members. At the following level the process is repeated, so that we have sets members of which are sets of individuals. The hierarchy continues with each level being followed by a level encompassing all sets of things at the previous level. (You may notice that on this way of doing things we never get sets the members of which come from different levels. That is a limitation that can be transcended. However, since we never need such sets in the construction of numbers, we will stick with the simple scheme.)

Corresponding to the hierarchical universe is a hierarchical logical language. This language is our original logical language with two modifications. (i) Variables and names are given **subscripts** to indicate the level of the thing they name, or the things they range over. For example, we have $x_i, x_{ii}, x_{iii}, \ldots$, and similarly in the case of names. (ii) These subscripts are used to put restrictions on what formulas are meaningful and what formulas are not. The restrictions of interest to us are illustrated by the formulas $x_n \in y_{ni}$ and $x_n = y_n$.[9] In the case of atomic formulas containing the two-place predicate $\in$, the restriction requires that singular term that appears to its right to be indexed for the level immediately above the level for which the singular term that appears to its left is indexed. In the case of atomic formulas containing the identity predicate, '$=$', the singular terms flanking the predicate are required to be indexed for the same level. Formulas that violate these restrictions—e.g., $x_n \in y_n$ and $x_{ni} = y_n$, are claimed to be meaningless.

The reason for imposing these restrictions is that they allow us to restate the axiom schema of comprehension in a way that blocks the contradiction.

---

[9] I use x_n as a convenient abbreviation for x subscripted by n 'i's.

$$\exists y_{ni} \, \forall x_n \, (Fx_n \leftrightarrow x_n \in y_{ni})$$

Instances are obtained by replacing Fx_n with any formula of level n in which the only variable that occurs free is x_n. (A formula of level n is one containing a subscripted term of level n, but no higher level.)

Intuitively, this axiom schema tells us that for any condition stated on things at any arbitrary level n, there is a set at the next level of all and only those things at level n that satisfy the condition. Note, the formulas $\sim x \in x$ and $\sim x_n \in x_n$ **cannot** be substituted for Fx_n, but rather are regarded as meaningless. Nor can the formula $\sim x_n \in y_{ni}$ be substituted for Fx_n. Although this formula is meaningful, it is not a formula of level n, and, in addition, it does not contain only the variable x_n free. Thus, it cannot be substituted into the schema to obtain an instance. To get such an instance one must use a formula that states a condition on things of level, or type, n, and no higher. Moreover, no matter what formula of level n we substitute for Fx_n, we will never obtain an instance in which any set at the next level comes into the range of the quantifier.

If we have a genuine instance of the schema, it will assert the existence of a set at the next level above n of all and only those things of level n that satisfy a certain condition. Let us call this set $\underline{y_{ni}}$. Given any such instance, we know that something of the form

$$\forall x_n \, (Fx_n \leftrightarrow x_n \in \underline{y_{ni}})$$

is true. When we derive consequences from this by erasing the universal quantifier and substituting the name of any arbitrary object of level n for the occurrences of the variable x_n, we are barred from using any name for an object at the next level; hence we cannot select $\underline{y_{ni}}$. Thus, there is no way that a contradiction of the sort originally derived from the unrestricted axiom schema of comprehension could be derived in the new system of logical types. This is an important virtue of the new system.

Another thing that might be said on its behalf is that it has a certain amount of naturalness. It could be argued that when we think of a set, we first think of its members, and then we think of the set as a sort of grouping together of those members. It is as if the members were conceptually prior to the set, in some sense. If that really is how we think of sets, then to say that a set might be a member of itself should be absurd. And if it is absurd, then it is understandable why someone might take it to be meaningless.

This is, of course, a very brief and sketchy introduction to Russell's theory of logical types, which is itself an extremely complicated subject. Fortunately, we can ignore most of the complications. For our purposes, there are three elementary points to emphasize. The first point involves a certain assumed parallel between language and reality. Just as it is impossible for a set to be a member of itself, so, Russell thought, it is **meaningless**, not just false, to say that a set is a member of itself. Just as it is impossible for a constituent at one level of the hierarchy to be identical with something at another level, so Russell regarded it is **meaningless** to say that something at one level is, or is not, identical with something at another level. You can look at this either as the structure of the world imposing constraints on what is meaningful in language, or as the range of possible meanings in language as limiting our conception of the world. Probably, giving priority either to the world or to language would be misleading. The most accurate thing to say, on Russell's view, may simply be that there is this parallel, and to try to say anything more about what is responsible for it is futile. As we will see later, this idea of there being an important parallel between language and the world received further development and articulation in later work by Russell and Wittgenstein, in their systems of logical atomism.

The second point to notice about the theory of types is how restrictive it is. Several times during my informal presentation of it, I either said, or was tempted to say, things like *no constituent of one level is identical with any constituent at another level*, and *no set is a member of itself*, and *it is impossible for a set to be a member of itself*. But if the theory of types is correct, then all of those statements are meaningless. To say that no set is identical with any of its members seems **true**. However, if Russell's theory of types is correct, then it cannot meaningfully be said. In general, when explaining the theory of types, one finds it virtually irresistible to say things which, once one has the theory, are claimed to be meaningless.

One response to this perplexity might be to claim that the system of subscripts adopted in the theory somehow **expresses** or **shows** that which one futilely tries to **say** or **assert** when one utters the words *No set is identical with any of its members*. The system shows this simply because the formation rules for '=' require identical subscripts, whereas those for 'ϵ' prohibit them. As we will see, this idea that a symbol system might show something that cannot meaningfully be said is another idea that was developed later—particularly by Wittgenstein (though not in connection with the theory of types).

The third point to be noticed about the theory of types, and the most important for the business of this chapter, is how it affects the reduction of arithmetic to logic. With the theory in place, the reduction is carried out over four levels of the hierarchy. Although any four succeeding levels will do, the most intuitive are the first four.

LOGICAL TYPES INVOLVED IN THE
REDUCTION OF ARITHMETIC TO LOGIC

Type i   (concrete) individuals

Type ii   sets of individuals

Type iii   sets of sets of individuals (Numbers are at this level.)

Type iiii   sets of (sets of sets of individuals) (The set of
              natural numbers appears here.)

The definitions of zero, successor, and natural number are now restated as follows:

THE DEFINITION OF ZERO

$$0_{iii} = \{\varnothing_{ii}\}$$

Zero is the iii-level set the only member of which is the ii-level set that has no members.

THE DEFINITION OF SUCCESSOR

The successor of a iii-level set x_{iii} is the set of all those ii-level sets y_{ii} that contain an individual z_i which, when eliminated from y_{ii}, leaves one with a member of x_{iii}.

$$x_{iii}{}' = \uparrow y_{ii}[\exists z_i\,(z_i \in y_{ii}\ \&\ [\,(y_{ii} \cap \text{Comp}(\{z_i\})\,)\,) \in x_{iii}])]$$

The successor of a iii-level set x_{iii} = the set of all ii-level sets y_{ii} which contain an individual z_i such that the intersection of y_{ii} with the complement of the ii-level set the only member of which is z_i—i.e., with the ii-level set containing every individual except z_i—is a member of x_{iii}.

THE DEFINITION OF NATURAL NUMBER

The set of natural numbers = the smallest iiii-level set that contains zero (the iii-level set the only member of which is the ii-level empty set) and is closed under successor.

$$N_{iiii} = \uparrow x_{iiii}[\forall y_{iiii} ((0_{iii} \in y_{iiii} \And \forall z_{iii} (z_{iii} \in y_{iiii} \to z_{iii}' \in y_{iiii}))$$
$$\to x_{iii} \in y_{iiii})]$$

The set of natural numbers is the iiii-level set of all and only those iii-level sets which are members of every iiii-level set which contains the iii-level set zero and is closed under successor.

With this in mind, let us revisit the role played by the axiom of infinity in proving A4 of the arithmetical system. A4 states that no two different natural numbers have the same successor. To prove this we needed to assume that the iii-level set with no members is never the successor of any natural number. This is guaranteed by the axiom of infinity, which is now stated as follows:

$$\sim (\varnothing_{iii} \in N_{iiii}).$$

To postulate this is to assume that there will always be enough i-level things—concrete particulars, say—to make ii-level sets of any finite size. For if there weren't, if there were only, say, 10 individuals at the i-level, then the number 10 would be the iii-level set the only member of which was the ii-level set containing all 10 i-level individuals. Applying the definition of successor to this, we would find that there is no ii-level set containing an individual which, when you removed it, left you with the set of all 10 i-level individuals. This would mean that the successor of 10 was the iii-level empty set. The axiom of infinity rules this out. In like fashion it rules out the possibility that we will ever run out of i-level individuals to be used in the construction of numbers. Thus, in assuming the axiom of infinity, we are assuming the existence of infinitely many concrete particulars—of infinitely many things that are **not** sets.

Would it help to move up higher in the hierarchy, and perform the reduction of arithmetic to logic at a higher level? No. If there were only a finite number of i-level individuals, there would be only a finite number of ii-level sets of individuals, only a finite number of iii-level sets of ii-level sets, and so on for each level of the hierarchy. Since we are always going to need an axiom of infinity in the Russellian reduction, we are always going to need to assume that there are infinitely many non-sets. Is this assumption reasonable? Well, perhaps. Perhaps matter and/or regions of space are infinitely divisible, thus providing infinitely many non-sets. However, whether or not this is so is far from being completely clear. Certainly, it is hard to see how the existence of infinitely many such things could be a matter of pure logic alone.

I should say that there are ways of reducing arithmetic to claims about sets that do not require an axiom of infinity for concrete individuals, or for non-sets generally. Often, however, these ways of doing the reduction dispense with Russell's theory of types, and they handle his paradox by giving up the axiom schema of comprehension entirely, and replacing it with quite different axioms. When you do things in one of these alternative ways, you can still reduce arithmetic to your system of set theory. But these systems of set theory look more like separate mathematical theories with their own subject matter than systems of pure logic.

This points up one way in which Russell's reduction of arithmetic to logic was unsuccessful. One can reduce arithmetic to a formalized system of set theory, which may be, as Russell would say, in some sense more basic. However, it looks as if one **cannot** reduce arithmetic to anything that deserves the name *pure logic*. If this is right, then the original grand philosophical plan of reducing mathematics to logic must be regarded as having failed.

The final nail in the coffin, sealing this result, came two decades after *Principia Mathematica* in the form of Kurt Gödel's proof of the incompleteness of arithmetic. Roughly put, Gödel proved that any consistent first-order theory of arithmetic (like the one we have employed in discussing Russell's reduction) must leave some arithmetical truths unprovable. At best, any formalized theory of arithmetic allowing the proof of arithmetical theorems from a decidable set of arithmetical axioms will have the result that every provable theorem is true; however, it is impossible for any system to prove all and only the arithmetical truths. In short, arithmetical truth itself is not fully formalizable. Since Gödel's result implies that no set of axioms can suffice to derive all and only the arithmetical truths, it shows, *a fortiori*, that no set of **logical** axioms, whether pure or not, can do so.

The Philosophical Significance of Logicism

Having examined Russell's reduction of arithmetic to his system of logic, let us return to the philosophical motivations associated with the logicist project. How well did Russell's technical achievement live up to these motivations? Recall that one of the motivations of the classical logicist was to use logic to **justify** arithmetic, and thereby to justify all of classical mathematics. A related motivation was to **explain** how apriori knowledge of mathematics is possible. The classical logicist tied these together by viewing the twofold reduction of mathematics to arithmetic, and arithmetic to logic, as showing that all the results of classical mathematics are analytic.

A clear statement of this position is given by Carl Hempel, in "On the Nature of Mathematical Truth," written in 1945.[10] Addressing the issue of justification, Hempel writes:

> If therefore mathematics is to be a correct theory of the mathematical concepts in their intended meaning, it is not sufficient for its validation to have shown that the entire system is derivable from the Peano postulates [i.e., the axiomatized system of arithmetic used in Russell's reduction] plus suitable definitions; **rather, we have to inquire further whether the Peano postulates are actually true** when the primitives are understood in their customary meaning. This question, of course, can be answered only after the customary meaning of the terms "0," "natural number," and "successor" have been clearly defined.[11]

In this passage Hempel indicates that he takes the problem of justifying or validating the arithmetical axioms to require defining the primitive arithmetical terms that appear in them. After saying this, he immediately turns to the logicist, indeed to the Russellian, definitions, which he accepts as giving "the customary meaning" of the terms '0', 'natural number', and 'successor', and he stresses the fact that using these definitions plus the postulates of Russell's system of logic, one can **prove** the arithmetical axioms to be true.[12] This, according to Hempel, solves the problem of justification.

Summing up the classical logicist position, he says:

> Mathematics is a branch of logic. It can be derived from logic in the following sense:

---

[10] Carl Hempel, "On the Nature of Mathematical Truth," *American Mathematical Monthly* 52 (1945): 543–56; reprinted in *The Philosophy of Mathematics*, Benacerraf and Putnam, eds. Citations will be to this volume.

[11] P. 374, my boldface emphasis.

[12] In fn. 9, p. 375, Hempel indicates that by the "customary meaning" of the relevant terms he has in mind what he calls "the logical sense of 'meaning'" rather than "the psychological sense." The issues raised by this distinction, only very briefly sketched by Hempel, will be discussed below.

a. All the concepts of mathematics, i.e., of arithmetic, algebra, and analysis, can be defined in terms of four concepts of pure logic.

b. All the theorems of mathematics can be deduced from those definitions by means of the principles of logic (including the axioms of infinity and choice).

In this sense it can be said that the propositions of the system of mathematics as here delimited are true by virtue of the definitions of the mathematical concepts involved, or that they make explicit certain characteristics with which we have endowed our mathematical concepts by definition. **The propositions of mathematics have, therefore, the same unquestionable certainty which is typical of such propositions as "All bachelors are unmarried,"** but they also share the complete lack of empirical content which is associated with that certainty: The propositions of mathematics are devoid of all factual content; they convey no information whatever on any empirical subject matter.[13]

Not only are mathematical propositions supposed to have the property of being "unquestionably certain" because they are analytic, the explanation of how they can be known to be true apriori is supposed to be essentially the same as the explanation of how we can know trivialities like *All bachelors are unmarried* to be true. We can know them to be true because they are true in virtue of meaning, and we can know what they mean. In short, according to the classical logicist, the truths of traditional mathematics are analytic because the logicist reduction has shown that they are, essentially, truths of logic, which are themselves analytic, or true in virtue of meaning.

It is worth noting that Russell himself did not fully or explicitly embrace this picture. Initially, he did seem to think of the logicist reduction as potentially responsive to the demand for a justification of the arithmetical axioms. Very early on, however, he came to appreciate a crucial problem with this view. In the case of the axioms of arithmetic, we are more certain of them, pretheoretically, than we are of axioms of any so-called system of logic to which they might be reduced. For example, it seems clear that Russell's axioms of comprehension and infinity, as modified by his theory of logical types, raise far more questions, and are subject to a greater degree of rational doubt, than the

---

[13] P. 378, my boldface emphasis.

system of arithmetical axioms that the logicist uses them to derive. We may put this by saying that Russell's logical axioms are themselves more in need of justification than the arithmetical axioms that he reduced to them. This being so, if there really was a problem of justifying the arithmetical axioms in the first place, it is **not** solved by reducing them to an even more problematic axiom system—whether or not one attaches the word *logic* to that system.

Indeed, Russell came to believe that a substantial part of the justification for his logical premises lies in the fact that they can be used to derive the intrinsically more obvious axioms of arithmetic.[14] To a certain extent, then, he came to see the direction of justification as being reversed. Still, he thought, the reduction was theoretically important for three reasons. First, showing that the arithmetical axioms, and through them, the theorems of the rest of classical mathematics, are derivable from a system of logical axioms, indicates how our system of mathematical knowledge is organized, and how the different parts of that system are related to one another. Second, showing ordinary arithmetic to follow from underlying logical and set-theoretic principles can lead to useful extensions and unifications of mathematical knowledge, such as the extension of the arithmetic of the natural numbers to the theory of transfinite arithmetic. Third, Russell claimed that by illuminating the logical nature of mathematics, one might throw light on the philosophical question of what mathematical knowledge amounts to, and how it is achieved.[15]

I am not sure precisely what he had in mind by this last point. However, having indicated that logicism does **not** solve the problem of justifying arithmetic, we still have the task of evaluating the contribution of logicism to the problem of explaining how our knowledge of mathematics is possible. Let us put aside, for a moment, the question of whether the truths of mathematics are justified. Let us also put aside any question about whether we know them to be true. Of course they are justified, and of course we know them to be true. At any rate, we know very many arithmetical truths. Moreover, we seem to know them not by observation and experience, but apriori. The question at issue is whether the logicist reduction of arithmetic to logic provides an analysis of the arithmetical statements that we know apriori to be true which reveals how this knowledge is possible.

[14] See "The Regressive Method of Discovering the Premises of Mathematics," 1905, in Bertrand Russell, *Essays in Analysis,* Douglas Lackey, ed. (New York: George Braziller, 1973).
[15] Ibid., pp. 282–83.

There is an analogy here with Moore's response to the radical skeptic. Confronted with the skeptic's challenge, Moore would insist that, of course, we know that there are things external to our minds. That doesn't stand in need of further justification. The fundamental task of philosophical analysis is to articulate a conception of knowledge, and a conception of what is known when one knows of the existence of some external object, that will allow us to explain how we know what we most obviously do. The question we are asking now, about the content of our apriori knowledge of mathematics, is analogous to the question Moore asks about the content of our knowledge of the external world.

Does the logicist reduction provide an analysis of the content of the arithmetical claims that we know apriori to be true that explains how this knowledge is possible? In attempting to answer this question, let us grant, for the sake of argument, what might otherwise seem to be a questionable point. Let us grant that we know apriori the basic principles of Russell's logical system, and that this knowledge is itself readily explainable. Given this, we know that if arithmetical sentences really do mean the same as the logical sentences into which Russell translates them in doing the reduction, then our ability to acquire knowledge of the truth of the propositions expressed by those sentences will be readily explainable.

But do arithmetical sentences express the very same propositions as the logical sentences into which Russell translates them? This may seem like a strange question. Didn't Russell simply **define** arithmetical concepts in terms of logical ones? Yes, he did. But then isn't it obvious that, in virtue of those definitions, arithmetical sentences must express the same propositions as logical ones? Well, yes and no.

Yes, you can, if you like, simply **stipulate** that what you are going to mean by various arithmetical symbols is just that which is expressed by their logical translations in the Russellian system of logic. If you do stipulate this, then arithmetical sentences will express the same propositions as logical sentences, for you. However, suppose we ask a different question. What propositions did arithmetical sentences express before Russell came up with his reduction? Prior to Russell, mathematicians, philosophers, and ordinary people were all familiar with arithmetic. They used arithmetical sentences, and performed arithmetical calculations. Presumably, the arithmetical sentences they used had meanings and expressed propositions that many knew to be true. Even after Russell's discovery, many people haven't heard of his, or any other, attempt to reduce arithmetic to logic. Despite this, these people know plenty of arithmetic. What is it that they know when they know that (3 times 3) plus (4 times 4) = (5 times 5)? Is the proposition that they know the same as the proposition expressed by the enormously complicated logical sentence into which Russell would translate that simple arithmetical sentence?

There are two arguments that point to the conclusion that it isn't. (i) Russell's proposition is too complicated and unfamiliar to attribute knowledge of it to all people we would ordinarily take to know that (3 times 3) plus (4 times 4) = (5 times 5). Many people who know this arithmetical truth wouldn't understand a Russellian translation of it, even if it was explained to them. This makes it implausible to say that what they have known all along is something it took a genius like Russell (or Frege) to discover. (ii) After Russell completed his reduction, it became clear that there are many different ways of achieving more or less the same result. One doesn't have to take zero to be the set the only member of which is the empty set, and one doesn't have to define successor exactly as Russell did. There are substantially different ways of defining arithmetical concepts in terms of logical or set-theoretical concepts. Given two such ways, there will be two substantially different translations of an arithmetical sentence like *(3 times 3) plus (4 times 4) = (5 times 5)*. When the details are spelled out it becomes highly plausible that the two alternate logical translations express different propositions. Thus, they can't both express **the** proposition that (3 times 3) plus (4 times 4) = (5 times 5). But there seems to be no more reason to say that one of them does, than that the other does. Rather, it would seem that the most reasonable thing to say is that neither expresses the very same proposition as the arithmetical sentence, though both express propositions that are, in a certain sense, equivalent to that proposition.

However, if we do say this, we must face a difficulty. Imagine some pre-Russellian mathematician, or some intelligent fourth grader, or indeed anyone who has not heard of Russell, or the reduction of arithmetic to logic, but who nevertheless knows that (3 times 3) plus (4 times 4) = (5 times 5). If the proposition that this person knows is not the very same proposition as the corresponding logical proposition in Russell's reduction, then how can Russell's proposition be said to be an **analysis** of the proposition that (3 times 3) plus (4 times 4) = (5 times 5)? Further, and most crucially, how can an explanation of how Russell's proposition is knowable apriori provide any explanation at all of how the ordinary person's proposition—that

(3 times 3) plus (4 times 4) = (5 times 5)—is known, or is knowable, apriori? If they are not the same proposition, then explaining how one is, or could be, known would seem to be quite different from explaining how the other one is, or could be, known.

The problem we are confronted with here is an instance of a recurring problem, a sort of paradox, that tended to crop up when philosophers tried to solve really substantial philosophical problems by offering surprising and far-reaching analyses of the concepts involved in stating the problem. One starts off with some philosophically troubling questions about certain commonsense propositions—propositions like *I know that there are material objects, I know that I have a hand*, or *I know that (3 times 3) plus (4 times 4) equals (5 times 5)*. One might feel, like Moore and Russell, that one really does know these things. But as a philosopher one wants to understand how this knowledge is possible. In the case of material-object statements, one may want to know how knowledge of one's own sensations, which make up one's basic data, can give rise to knowledge about material objects, which goes far beyond one's own sense data. In the case of mathematics, one may want to know how one can have *apriori* knowledge of mathematical propositions that is independent of experience.

The method pursued by Moore and Russell was one of analyzing the commonsense propositions one knows into their supposedly more basic constituents, thereby arriving at results that are less philosophically troublesome. But here is where the problem arises. If one comes up with an analysis that is strong enough to answer the initial philosophical questions that prompted one's inquiry, then it is likely to be complicated enough, and far enough removed from our ordinary understanding of the sentences being analyzed, that it becomes difficult to justify the claim that what one is doing is just revealing the content of the sentences as they were understood all along. On the other hand, if one's analysis sticks close to one's ordinary, pre-philosophical understanding, then it is likely not to produce anything substantial enough to resolve one's initial philosophical worries. In short, either one's analysis won't go beyond what one is analyzing, in which case one's philosophical worries won't go away; or one's analysis will show how one might resolve one's philosophical worries, but only by **replacing** that which one was analyzing with something new.

In general, adherents of the Moore-Russell method of analysis followed one or the other of two strategies for dealing with this problem. Strategy 1 involved trying to argue that the complicated, philosophically revealing analyses really gave the contents of the propositions that have been expressed by commonsense sentences, and known by ordinary people, all along—despite the unfamiliarity of the analyses. Someone who adopted this strategy, and who viewed Russell's reduction as providing a genuine analysis of arithmetical expressions, would maintain that anyone who has ever known that (3 times 3) plus (4 times 4) equals (5 times 5) has known the very proposition that Russell's reduction associates with this sentence. On this view, explaining how knowledge of the Russellian proposition is possible **is** explaining how knowledge of the ordinary arithmetical truth is possible.

Strategy 2 is to argue that **strictly speaking** the ordinary person doesn't, and never did, know that (3 times 3) plus (4 times 4) equals (5 times 5)—as we now come to understand that proposition in light of Russell's reduction. To be sure, the ordinary person was vaguely and imprecisely getting at, or approximating, something that is knowable, and indeed knowable apriori—namely Russell's proposition. However, since the ordinary person didn't have that very proposition in mind, we can't say, strictly speaking, that he, or she, knew anything apriori. Proponents of this way of looking at things sometimes referred to their analyses as *explications.* The point of the explication was to provide philosophically uncontentious concepts that could **replace** potentially problematic ordinary concepts. In the case of Russell's reduction, one who followed this strategy would point out that any intellectual task that could be accomplished using numbers in the ordinary sense could, in principle, be accomplished using Russell's set-theoretic construction; one doesn't need sets **and** numbers. Therefore we simplify our conception of the universe by renouncing numbers in the old sense, and replacing them with sets—thereby hoping to gain something philosophically.

Often, adherents of the Moore-Russell method of analysis were not really clear about which, if either, of these alternatives they wanted to adopt. They knew there was a sort of **paradox of analysis**, and they felt that there must be some answer to it. However, they often seemed unsure precisely what the answer was. However, they didn't let their uncertainty on this point slow down their search for analyses, or undermine their confidence that somehow the process of analysis would provide answers to their philosophical questions.

CHAPTER 7

LOGICAL CONSTRUCTIONS
AND THE EXTERNAL WORLD

Logical Constructions

Up to now in our discussion of Russell, we have examined two quite different examples of logical or linguistic analysis—the theory of descriptions and the reduction of arithmetic to logic. Both were motivated in substantial part by philosophical considerations. The theory of descriptions allowed Russell to rid himself of his previous commitment to supposedly real, but nonexistent, objects such as Santa Claus and the round square. The reduction of arithmetic to logic was seen as indicating that one doesn't need to posit the existence of any platonic, mathematical objects over and above sets, and as showing how our mathematical knowledge can be justified and explained.

The next step in Russell's development of the idea of philosophy as logical and linguistic analysis involved applying his methods to Moore's problem of the external world. According to Moore, we know that there are material objects, and the evidence upon which this knowledge is based comes from perception. However, Moore recognized a gap between this evidence and the knowledge that arises from it. The material objects that we know about are public in the sense that they may be perceived by different people, and they are independent of us in the sense that they may exist unperceived. Our sensory impressions, on the other hand, were thought by Moore to be conceptually private to us, and to exist only when they were being perceived. The problem was to explain how to bridge this gap.

In *Our Knowledge of the External World*,[1] Russell made a proposal for doing this. His main idea may be summed up in the slogan: *Material objects are logical constructions out of sense data*. Although this might sound like a doctrine about how material objects are constructed or constituted, it really is not. Rather, it is a linguistic doctrine about the meanings of sentences of a certain kind. According to the doctrine, sentences that appear to be about material objects are really about sense data and nothing more.

Before we attempt to spell out what this means, it is best to look at simpler paradigmatic cases of the type of analysis that Russell had in mind. Among the simplest such cases are statements about "the average child." Consider, for example, sentence 1.

1. The average child between the ages of 6 and 18 has had 4.7 cavities.

Looking just at the grammatical structure of this sentence, it would seem to be about some one person, the average child between the ages 6 and 18, and it would seem to say that this child has had 4.7 cavities. However, we all know that this is not what the sentence really means. Rather, it means something roughly along the lines of (2).

2. The number of children between the ages of 6 and 18 multiplied by 4.7 equals the number of cavities they have had.

Sentence (2) talks about the cavities of individual children, but it doesn't single any one of them out as the average child (between 6 and 18) and attribute to that child the property of having had 4.7 cavities. Philosophers in the period we are studying expressed this point by saying that the average child is a **logical construction** out of individual children. What this means is that all statements which might, on the basis of their grammatical structure, appear to be about the average child are really statements with complex logical forms that are about individual children. Thus, if we were to count all the things in the universe, we would have to count each individual child. But once we finished counting them, there would be no other "average child" remaining to be counted.

---

[1] Originally published in 1914, by Allen and Unwin; reprinted in 2000 (New York and London: Routledge).

A less obvious example of what some philosophers would take to involve the same thing is provided by statements about nations.

3. Mexico devalued the peso.

Here we have a sentence which, by its grammatical form, looks to be about a certain nation—Mexico. But now, one might ask, what exactly is a nation? Someone might answer that a nation consists of a group of people who live in a certain place and who engage in certain patterns of thought and behavior, some of which involve conformity to a certain set of laws, including those that constitute a monetary system. Is there anything more to a nation than this? If one were counting the entities in the universe, one would have to count people, places, physical objects, and perhaps even thoughts, actions and laws. But when one had finished with these, would there be any further entities—nations—left over to count? Some philosophers would say *no*; and some of these philosophers would further say that when we talk about nations we are really just talking about people, places, physical objects, and the complex patterns of thought and behavior they engage in. For example, these philosophers might say, what appear to be statements about Mexico are just rough, shorthand ways of making statements about the thoughts and activities of a group of people living just north of Central America and south of the Rio Grande. On this view, the meaning of each sentence that appears on the surface to be about "the country Mexico" is given by a set of more complex sentences about the people living in a certain place. Philosophers who take this position would say that nations are logical constructions out of people and places.

There is, of course, a significant difference between sentences "about the average child" and sentences "about nations." Since, typically, it is relatively clear what statement or statements about individual children a statement about the average child is shorthand for, such statements have more or less transparent analyses. This is certainly not true of statements about nations. For example, no one is prepared to offer a precise analysis of what sentences like (3) or (4) are supposed to mean, solely in terms of people and places.

4. Mexico wants to play a leading role in Latin America.

Despite the fact that analyses of statements about nations in terms of statements about people and places are far from transparent, at one time many philosophers felt that nations must be logical constructions out of people and places, because there is nothing other than people and places for nation statements to be about.

Material Objects and Sense Data

With this in mind, we now turn to Russell's doctrine that statements "about material objects" are really statements about sense data and nothing more. According to the view he advocated in *Our Knowledge of the External World*, physical objects are logical constructions out of sense data. Thus, if we were counting the entities in the world, we would have to count each individual sense datum, and each perceiver. However, after these had been counted, there would be no physical objects left over to count. This doesn't mean that when we use a material object statement, or, so to speak, "talk about material objects," we are invariably saying something false. Rather, it means that the truths we assert that seem to be about material objects are in reality nothing more than truths about sense data.

Suppose, for example, that I walk around the table, and say that I see that there is a table here that presents slightly different appearances depending on my different positions. What, according to Russell, is the real meaning or content of my statement?

A table viewed from one place presents a different appearance from that which it presents from another place. This is the language of common sense, but this language already assumes that there is a real table of which we see the appearances. Let us try to state what is known in terms of sensible objects alone, without any element of hypothesis. We find that as we walk round the table, we perceive a series of gradually changing visible objects. But in speaking of "walking round the table," we have still retained the hypothesis that there is a single table connected with all the appearances. What we ought to say is that, while we have those muscular and other sensations which make us say we are walking, our visual sensations change in a continuous way, so that, for example, a striking patch of colour is not suddenly replaced by something wholly different, but is replaced by an insensible gradation of slightly different colours with slightly different shapes. This is what we really know by experience, when we have freed our mind from the assumption of permanent "things" with changing appearances. What is really known is a correlation of muscular and other bodily sensations with changes in visual sensations.[2]

In this passage, Russell lays the groundwork for a striking doctrine, but does so in an equivocal way. The striking doctrine is that material objects are logical constructions out of sense data—that is, statements which appear to be about the one are to be understood as being statements that are entirely about the other. The groundwork for this doctrine consists in (i) the conviction that we do know "material object statements" to be true on the basis of perception, plus (ii) the view, outlined by Russell above, that what we know on the basis of perception is that certain types of sense data are correlated with other types of sense data. The equivocation is over whether the doctrine that material objects are logical constructions out of sense data is supposed to be an accurate reflection of what statements about material objects really mean, in ordinary language, or whether it is what we, as philosophers, should mean by them. Russell is understandably wary of making such a strong, unqualified claim about ordinary meaning. However, he is ready to claim that insofar as ordinary sentences about material objects make statements that are capable of being **known** by us to be true, the statements they make are nothing more than statements about sense data—and that is striking enough.

What, then, is the analysis of what is known when I say I know (5)?

5. I see a table.

Part of the analysis is certainly something of the sort indicated by (5a).

5a. I see a certain sort of table-like sense datum (with such and such shape and structure).

Obviously, this is far too vague. What does a visual sense datum have to be like to count as table-like? However, even apart from this vagueness, (5a) cannot be the whole of the analysis. After all, we must distinguish seeing a table from dreaming or hallucinating that one sees a table, as well as from merely seeing an image of a table. If (5a) were

[2] Bertrand Russell, *Our Knowledge of the External World*, pp. 84–85.

the whole meaning of (5), then it would be impossible to make these distinctions. Thus, the analysis of (5) must also include clauses of the sort indicated by (5b) and (5c).

5b. If I were to have the sensations that are called "walking toward the table"—i.e., if I were to have the "muscular" sensations that are called "walking" at the same time that I had a sequence of gradually changing and steadily larger visual "table-like" sense data—then, ultimately, I would experience tactile sensations of pressure and hardness.

5c. If I were to have the sensations called "walking around the table," then my visual sense data would gradually change in a certain continuous way . . .

That is not all. Roughly speaking, for every sense experience that would contribute to verifying (5), Russell would include a clause representing that possible experience in the analysis of (5). Thus, according to this analysis, what looks on the surface like a very simple, unproblematic statement of English is taken to have an enormously long and complex analysis.

Before going further, let me make a comment about my exposition of Russell regarding the analysis of material object statements like (5.) In giving the analysis I have made use of what are called *counterfactual conditionals*—statements of the sort *if such and such were to occur, then so and so would occur*. (5b) and (5c) are counterfactual statements about sense data. Sometimes, in giving his analyses, Russell uses counterfactuals of essentially this sort.[3] However, at other times he speaks of a system of private perspectives, or points of view. Each such perspective consists of a set of appearances, or sense data—essentially the appearances an observer **would** experience if he occupied that perspective. (Note the counterfactual location.) Material objects are then said to be *logical constructions* out of certain similar, or related, appearances (sense data) given in different perspectives.[4] For our

---

[3] See, for example, his discussion of the blue spectacles on p. 88, where he says, "If now we find a blue patch moving in this way in sight-space, when we have no sensible experience of an intervening tangible object, we nevertheless infer that, if we put our hand at a certain place in touch-space, we **should** experience a certain touch-sensation," my boldface emphasis.

[4] See, in particular, pp. 94–100.

purposes, the details of this construction are not important. What is important is that the analysis of material object statements I have given in terms of categorical statements about sense data like (5a) plus counterfactual statements about sense data like (5b) and (5c) is in all essential respects equivalent to the analysis of material object statements in terms of statements about the sense data found in perspectives occupied by actual observers plus statements about the sense data found in perspectives that no one actually occupies (at least at the moment), but which **could** be occupied if certain conditions were fulfilled. Since the two styles of analysis are equivalent, I will stick with analyses like (5a–c) that are formulated using explicitly counterfactual language.

It should be emphasized that Russell never thought that he had arrived at a complete analysis of any particular material object statement. He knew that no matter how many clauses like (5a), (5b), and (5c) he might produce, there would always be many more that would have an equal claim to being part of a complete analysis of the physical object statement. He also knew that clauses like (5a–c) are themselves sketchy and not fully specified. These clauses continually talk of sense data "of a certain sort," without spelling out precisely what these different sorts are. However, this did not deter Russell, or later philosophers who were influenced by him. They adopted for material object statements a rather extreme version of the attitude I mentioned earlier about nation statements. In the case of nation statements we noted that it is not at all evident how to give precise translations of them into equivalent statements about people and places. Nevertheless, some philosophers have felt that talk about nations must somehow reduce to talk about people and places, because there are no other entities for nation statements to be about. In the case of material object statements, the situation is similar. Here it is, for all practical purposes, impossible to give even approximate translations of material object statements into equivalent statements about sense data. Nevertheless, Russell felt that talk about physical objects must reduce to talk about sense data. We need to understand why.

The following passage gives a good indication of what was driving his analysis.

I think it may be laid down quite generally that, *in so far* as physics or common sense is verifiable, it must be capable of interpretation in terms of actual sense-data alone. The reason for this is simple.

Verification consists always in the occurrence of an expected sense-datum . . . Now if an expected sense-datum constitutes a verification, what was asserted must have been about sense-data; or, at any rate, if part of what was asserted was not about sense-data, then only the other part has been verified.[5]

If we ignore Russell's final qualification for a moment (he doesn't make serious use of it), then the content of the passage may be expressed by the following principles.

6. Verification always consists in the occurrence of sense data.

7. If the occurrence of sense data constitutes verification of a statement S, then S must be about sense data.

Together, (6) and (7) constitute a historical precursor to a famous philosophical principle—the "Verifiability Criterion of Meaning"—that we will discuss at length later in our investigation of Logical Positivism. For now, we will look only at Russell's use of these ideas.

Russell's reasoning can, I think, be reconstructed more or less as follows: From (6) and (7) it follows that insofar as ordinary statements of common sense, and also statements about physics, are verifiable, they must be about sense data. Since we know these statements to be true, they must be verifiable; indeed, it is by verifying them that we come to know them. Thus, the statements of both physics and common sense must be about sense data.

This, I think, is how Russell arrives at his conclusion. But is his reasoning persuasive? The first thing to notice is that at least one of his major premises—namely (7)—is not obviously correct. To see this, consider a premise which differs from (7) only in being more general.

8. If occurrences of x verify a statement S, then S must be about x's.

Forget about Russell's philosophy for a moment, and consider certain examples that might be used to test (8). One example involves theoretical statements in physics—for example, statements about subatomic particles such as protons and electrons. We do not directly observe these things. Rather, we posit their existence because they allow us to explain various phenomena that we do observe. Many of the observations that we are interested in are recorded by complex measuring in-

---

[5] *Our Knowledge of the External World*, pp. 88–89.

struments. Thus, for some statements about electrons and protons, the way we verify them is by taking readings from complicated instruments. But note what this means. If (8) is accepted, then we must conclude that when we make statements about subatomic particles such as protons and electrons, what we are really talking about are instrument readings. The fact that this doesn't seem to be what we are talking about constitutes prima facie evidence against (8).

Or consider a different example. Suppose we are trying to figure out whether in the distant past a certain person x murdered another person y. Suppose that x and y are now both dead, and that to verify the hypothesis that x murdered y all we can do is consult presently surviving historical records. If (8) were correct, this would mean that the claim that x murdered y is itself a claim about observations of those historical records. But that doesn't seem right. The hypothesis seems to be about x and y themselves; the fact that they are now long gone and no longer available to us does not seem to be relevant.

Considerations like these may induce one to doubt, or even reject, principle (8), and to hold instead that **what a statement is about** is not necessarily the same thing as **the observations one might make in attempting to verify it**. But then, if one rejects, or doubts, (8), one may well want to reject, or at least doubt, (7), which is just a special case of (8). Since (7) is crucial to Russell's argument, one may then come to doubt its soundness, in which case Russell's conclusion, that material object statements are really nothing more than abbreviations for complex statements about sense data, will be threatened.

Of course, as is often the case in philosophy, the argument might be run in the other direction. If, like Russell, you are convinced that (7) is correct, then you might accept (8) as well, together with the corollary that statements about subatomic particles are really just abbreviations for complex statements about instrument readings, and other observations, and the related corollary that statements about the past are really just abbreviations for statements about observations we make of presently existing historical records. The point I am trying to make now is **not** that (7) is definitely incorrect (though I believe it is), but only that it is not an obvious or self-evident principle. Hence Russell cannot legitimately expect that an argument that appeals to it will be convincing unless he can give a good reason to accept it.

Why, then, did Russell accept the premise? Although he doesn't say, it may well be connected with his general conception of how knowledge arises. The picture seems to include the following:

(i) The foundation of all empirical knowledge (i.e. knowledge about the world) consists of sense data statements—e.g., *I am now seeing a circular red patch.* These are the statements of which we can be most certain. Provided that we have the right sorts of experiences, it would be pathological to doubt the truth of such statements.

(ii) All other empirical knowledge is built up from, and justified by, these foundational statements in certain fixed ways. Two main ways are deduction and simple enumerative induction (*this A is B, that A is B, . . . all A's are B's*).

Note that induction or deduction from sense data statements will always leave one with sense data statements; hence, sense data statements along with deduction and enumerative induction will never be enough to deliver material object statements. In addition, Russell would, I think, admit that there is a third way of building up empirical knowledge—something that we might call *the method of hypothesis.* This consists of formulating a hypothesis and deducing consequences from it (together, perhaps, with further observational statements). If the observable consequences one derives are true in enough cases, we may say that the hypothesis has been confirmed. Perhaps if the confirmation is strong and systematic enough, we may, in this way, come to know that the hypothesis is true.

This method of arriving at knowledge is familiar from the sciences. However, Russell implicitly added a restriction to it that limited its power. He seems to have thought that if the observable consequences one deduces from the hypothesis (perhaps together with further, independent observational claims) are sense data statements, then the hypothesis itself must be a sense data statement. Actually, there are two possibilities. Either the hypothesis is solely about sense data, in which case Russell would say that it is verifiable, and hence a possible object of knowledge; or the hypothesis is partially about sense data and partially about something else, in which case Russell would hold that the part about something else must be unverifiable and unknowable.

With this Russellian restriction, it is clear that the only knowledge that the method of hypothesis can provide is knowledge of sense data. Since the only other ways of obtaining empirical knowledge that he seems to recognize are induction and deduction from sense data statements, the only knowledge one can have of the world that he recognizes is knowledge of sense data. Since he agrees with Moore that we do know various material object statements to be true, he thinks that material object statements **must** really be analyzable into sense data statements; material objects must be logical constructions out of sense data.

One of the questionable aspects of this reasoning is the claim that if one can **deduce** observational consequences about observable objects from a hypothesis H, then H must be about those observable objects. What conception of deduction would justify this claim? Well, one might think of deduction as **logical deduction** in a purely formal system of symbolic logic. On this conception of deduction, if P is a substantive, non-contradictory premise containing certain non-logical vocabulary, and Q is a substantive, non-necessary conclusion containing only non-logical vocabulary that does not appear in P—e.g., if Q is made up of observational predicates that are applied to observable objects on the basis of ordinary perceptual experience, whereas P contains no such predicates—then Q will **not** be deducible from P, without appealing to definitions of at least some of the vocabulary of P in terms of the vocabulary of Q.

Think of Russell's mathematical model here. We can deduce claims about sets from claims about numbers because numbers are definable in terms of sets. With this model in mind, one might well think that a hypothesis H from which one could deduce an observational claim $(O_1 \supset O_2)$ must itself either contain the observational vocabulary of O_1 and O_2, or contain vocabulary that is definable in terms of that observational vocabulary. Either way, if this were so, then H might truly be said to be about observational objects.

The problem is that this conception of deduction is very narrow. As we saw in discussing Moore's problematic use of the concepts *analyticity, entailment*, and *logical consequence* in attempting to establish his startling claims about goodness, there may be conceptual relations between concepts, even when those concepts are not definable in terms of one another.[6] Because of this, there are cases in which Q is deducible from P in the sense that it is both apriori knowable and obvious that if P is true then Q must be true, even though P is non-contradictory, Q is contingent, the non-logical vocabulary of Q

---

[6] The conception of deduction alluded to in the preceding paragraph is essentially *analytic consequence* in the narrow sense, discussed in connection with Moore—Q is an analytic consequence of P iff Q' is a strict logical consequence of P', where P' and Q' differ from P and Q at most in substitution of synonyms (and definitions are taken to provide synonyms).

differs completely from that of P, and the two are unrelated by any definitions. With this conception of deduction, there is no reason why a hypothesis H from which one can deduce observational consequences must itself contain observational vocabulary, or be about observable objects in any direct sense.

Beyond this, there is still a further problem with the reasoning behind Russell's restriction of verifiable statements to those that are solely about sense data. A hypothesis may consist of a complex statement with many clauses, or even a set of statements. In such cases, the observational consequences deducible from the hypothesis can often be derived only by appeal to many or even all parts of the hypothesis, whether they be clauses or separate statements. In such cases—when it takes many or all parts of the hypothesis working together, so to speak, to entail certain observational predictions—there may be no way to divide up those predictions and assign each to one part of the hypothesis as opposed to others. Since, in this sort of case, many or all parts of the hypothesis are needed to entail the predictions, if those predictions are discovered by observation to be true, they may be taken to confirm or verify the **whole** hypothesis—or at least all the parts, observational and non-observational, that together conspire to generate the predictions. Thus, Russell's restriction, which tacitly assumes that the observational predictions of a hypothesis can always be traced solely to its observational parts, cannot be supported. These two problems undermine his argument that material object statements—insofar as they are knowable—must be analyzable into sense data statements.

The Problem Posed by Knowledge of Other Minds

At the time he wrote *Our Knowledge of the External World*, Russell saw the view that material objects are logical constructions out of sense data as providing an answer, perhaps the only possible answer, to the question *Granted that we know that there are material objects, how is this knowledge possible?* If material objects are simply logical constructions out of sense data, then knowledge of material objects is nothing more than knowledge of categorical and hypothetical statements about sense data. Since such knowledge seemed to be relatively unproblematic, Russell saw his view as a solution to the philosophical problem regarding knowledge of the external world.

However, there was a serious difficulty, of which Russell was fully aware, with this basic strategy. Our knowledge of the external world includes not only knowledge of material objects, but also knowledge of other people. But, Russell was **not** willing to say that other people are merely logical constructions out of sense data. To say this would be to claim that when I say that you exist, all I am really saying is something about my own sense data. To his credit, this is something that Russell was sensible enough not accept.

> When we see our friend drop a weight upon his toe, and hear him say—what we should say in similar circumstances, the phenomena *can* no doubt be explained without assuming that he is anything but a series of shapes and noises seen and heard by us, but practically no man is so infected with philosophy as not to be quite certain that his friend has felt the same kind of pain as he himself would feel.[7]

Here Russell indicates that he will not attempt to analyze statements about other people in terms of statements about his own sense data. But then, how can he explain our knowledge of other people? Obviously, the same answer cannot be given as was given for material objects.

Russell briefly considers one traditional philosophical argument— the argument from analogy. The argument goes more or less as follows: (i) I notice that there is a correlation between things that happen to my body and certain experiences I have. For example, if I prick my finger with a needle, I feel pain. (ii) Next, I notice that there are other bodies like mine, and that some of the same things that happen to my body happen to those other bodies. (iii) When a finger of another body is pricked with a needle, I don't feel any pain. But since I have observed a correlation between my body and my experiences, I postulate that the same correlation holds for other bodies. (iv) Consequently, I conclude that when a finger of another body is pricked with a needle, that event is accompanied by an experience of pain by someone else. But to say that someone else has experiences of this sort is to say that other people, or other minds, as we might put it, exist. (v) Moreover, I know that other minds exist because I know that the correlation between bodily events and mental events holds in my own case, and I know, on the basis of the argument from analogy, that it holds for other people too.

[7] *Our Knowledge of the External World*, p. 90.

Although Russell considered this argument, he was not very happy with it, and he didn't think that one could place much weight on it. Two difficulties are worth noting. First, at best the argument is a matter of induction from a single case. One finds an instance of a correlation— between events involving one's body and one's feeling of pain. One then observes thousands of other bodies, and on the basis of one observed correlation posits that the same correlation holds for all of those other cases. But why is this any more reasonable than thinking either that since one doesn't feel pain oneself in cases involving other bodies, there really is no pain in those cases, or that, since one has no way of knowing whether there are other minds that feel pain in those cases, one simply has no basis for determining whether the correlation holds in those cases? Nothing in the argument from analogy provides an answer to this question. Since this question is just another way of expressing the original difficulty, *How does one know that there are other people?*, the argument can hardly be regarded as successful.

The second objection to the argument, in the context of Russell's project, is that in its usual form it takes it for granted that there really are material objects—in particular, human bodies. But if one takes bodies to be logical constructions out of sense data, then the argument from analogy takes a bizarre twist. I can more or less understand what it would be for the same correlation to exist between **other bodies** and **their experience** as exists between **my body** and **my experience**— **provided that bodies are taken for granted and not analyzed away**. But if they are not taken for granted, but rather analyzed in terms of sense data, then the argument becomes very problematic. If all bodies are logical constructions out of sense data, then they must be logical constructions out of **someone's** sense data. Since at this stage of the argument Russell is trying to establish the existence of other minds, he cannot assume other minds in the analysis of material objects statements. With this in mind, imagine that I am trying to employ Russell's argument myself. My only recourse would seem to be to regard material objects as logical constructions out of **my** sense data. But then the argument from analogy would have me saying that the same correlation that exists between **my experiences** and certain of **my** sense data (namely those used to analyze statements about my body) also exists between the experiences of **other minds**, and certain other sense data of **mine** (namely those that I use to analyze statements about other bodies). That is strange. How can one really suppose that I am connected with my sense data in the same way that other minds are connected with **my** sense data? In short, if we eliminate from the argument from analogy the assumption that there really are other bodies, and try to state it making use of the doctrine that material objects are logical constructions out of sense data, then the argument becomes even more unreasonable than before.

At any rate, Russell doesn't put much credence in it.

> The hypothesis that other people have minds must, I think, be allowed to be not susceptible of any very strong support from the analogical argument. At the same time, it is a hypothesis which systematizes a vast body of facts and never leads to any consequences which there is reason to think false. There is therefore nothing to be said against its truth, and good reason to use it as a working hypothesis. When once it is admitted, it enables us to extend our knowledge of the sensible world by testimony, and thus leads to the system of private worlds which we assumed in our hypothetical construction. In actual fact, whatever we may try to think as philosophers, we cannot help believing in the minds of other people, so that the question whether our belief is justified has a merely speculative interest. And if it is justified, then there is no further difficulty of principle in that vast extension of our knowledge, beyond our own private data, which we find in science and common sense.[8]

In this passage Russell indicates that we should accept the claim that there are other people as a "working hypothesis." He seems to be thinking along the following lines: We begin with the problem of explaining how we know there are material objects and other people. He admits that he can't satisfactorily explain or justify our knowledge of other people. But he seems to suppose that if we grant that other people exist, then we can explain and justify our knowledge of material objects; Russell's explanation is that we can know that there are material objects because they are logical constructions out of sense data, and we can know about sense data. Presumably, Russell would say that this represents progress. It is progress in that we have solved half the problem of our knowledge of the external world—namely, the problem of explaining how we know of material objects. Although our knowledge of other people has not been shown to be on a firm foun-

[8] Ibid., pp. 103–4.

dation, it is better to have explained some firmly grounded knowledge than none at all.

So Russell seems to have thought. However, such a position can't be correct. On the contrary, Russell's inability to explain knowledge of other people undermines his analysis of material objects. The reason for this can be seen by considering the analysis of a simple material object statement.

9. There is a table in the classroom.

Presumably the analysis of this statement cannot be given solely in terms of my sense data. This is shown by the fact that if I assertively utter (9), and you here and now assertively utter (10),

10. There is no table in the classroom.

then what you say is logically incompatible with what I say; it is logically impossible for what I say and what you say to be jointly true. However, if you were to make a statement solely about your sense data, it would not be logically incompatible with any statement that was solely about my sense data. Thus, the statements that you and I make when we utter sentences like (9) and (10) cannot both be analyzed into statements that are solely about our own private sense data. And if they both can't be analyzed in that way, then surely neither one can be so analyzed.

I think that Russell implicitly recognizes this. However, it is not clear that he recognizes its implications for his position. What we have seen is that if material objects are to be logical constructions out of sense data, then they must be logical constructions out of everyone's sense data. On this view, (9) is analyzed into a series of statement of the sort illustrated by (9a) and (9b).

9a. Anyone "in the classroom" and looking "in the right place" (at this time) would have visual sense data of such and such type.

9b. Anyone "walking into the room" and proceeding "in a certain direction" would end up having tactile sensations of hardness and pressure.

But surely, if Russell can't explain how we know that other people exist, then he can't explain how we are supposed to know what everyone else's sense data would be like under every imaginable contingency. Thus, analyzing material objects as logical constructions out of everyone's sense data will not solve the problem it was designed to solve. It will not explain our knowledge of material objects.

If anything, such an analysis makes the problem worse. At least I can be sure, outside of philosophy, in everyday life, that I do know that there are material objects. But I don't feel at all sure that I know what everyone else's private sense experiences would be like under all imaginable conditions. To try to analyze knowledge of material objects in terms of alleged knowledge of other people's sense experience is not to reduce a complicated type of knowledge to something simpler and easier to explain. Rather, it is to replace one philosophical problem with an even more difficult one. Since this is not a promising strategy, the most reasonable alternative is to reject the analysis of material objects as logical constructions out of sense data.

That, at least, is my view. It is not how Russell, or some philosophers who followed him, saw the matter. Despite serious difficulties with the view that material objects are logical constructions out of sense data, it continued to exercise a strong influence on philosophers for two decades or more. We will see a good example of this when we discuss the logical positivists. For now, however, we will leave the topic, and turn our attention to a different subject—namely the system of philosophy called *logical atomism*, which was developed by Russell and Wittgenstein in the four years after Russell delivered *Our Knowledge of the External World* as lectures at Harvard in March of 1914.

CHAPTER 8

RUSSELL'S LOGICAL ATOMISM

CHAPTER OUTLINE

1. *The aim of constructing a comprehensive philosophical system*

2. *The ideal language, and the parallel between language and the world*

   Linguistic simples and metaphysical simples
   > Russell's problematic basis for positing a parallel between logically proper names and metaphysically simple objects

   Atomic and molecular sentences, and the facts corresponding to them
   General sentences and general facts
   Nonextensional sentences and facts

3. *Russell's Imagined System*

The Aim of Constructing a Comprehensive Philosophical System

Up to now, we have talked about three main elements of Russell's philosophy—his theory of descriptions, his reduction of arithmetic to logic, and his doctrine of logical constructions, in which his reductionist techniques are extended to the problem of knowledge of the external world. In 1918, he gathered these elements together in the sketch of a comprehensive philosophical system, which he presented in a series of eight lectures in London that were published under the title *The Philosophy of Logical Atomism*.[1] Unlike the earlier work we have examined, which was aimed at the resolution of specific philosophical problems (ontological commitment and the problem of negative existentials, the justification of mathematics and the explanation of our mathematical knowledge, and the problems posed by our knowledge of the external world), *The Philosophy of Logical Atomism* does not attack and attempt to resolve any one specific and familiar philosophical problem, or cluster of problems. Instead, it sketches the outlines of an

---

[1] Bertrand Russell, *The Philosophy of Logical Atomism* (La Salle, IL: Open Court, 1985); originally published in *The Monist*, 1918.

ambitious philosophical system that posits a thoroughgoing parallelism between language and the world, a parallelism that allows one to use the techniques of linguistic and logical analysis to reveal the ultimate structure of reality. Before, Russell had offered logical and linguistic analyses in a piecemeal fashion—to provide solutions to different philosophical problems as they came up. Now he sought to develop a systematic framework for doing philosophy in general, a system in which philosophy simply is logical and linguistic analysis. The heart of the system was a theory of language and its relation to the world.

Russell's student, Ludwig Wittgenstein, was working on a similar system at the same time. Although the work of Wittgenstein and Russell was largely independent (at least after Wittgenstein's five semesters at Cambridge in 1912 and 1913), they did influence each other to a significant degree. Russell—with his characteristic intellectual generosity and eagerness to appreciate the contributions of others—says at the beginning of *The Philosophy of Logical Atomism* that he was heavily influenced by Wittgenstein's ideas. He added (this was in 1918) that he hadn't had the opportunity to communicate with Wittgenstein since August of 1914, so his development of some of Wittgenstein's ideas had proceeded independently. (Wittgenstein spent the First World War in the Austrian army.) My plan is to sketch Russell's system in this chapter, and then to turn, in part 3, to the great classical system of logical atomism presented by Wittgenstein in his *Tractatus Logico-Philosophicus*, which first appeared in German in 1921, and was translated into English in the following year.[2] There I will begin by comparing the main features of Russell's version of atomism to the system developed in the *Tractatus*, introducing modifications in Russell that bring us closer to the views of Wittgenstein. This way of presenting things does not claim to be faithful to the history of how the two systems developed. At least from 1914 on, Wittgenstein worked independently. He didn't arrive at his system by starting with Russell's and then changing certain fundamental principles, though he certainly was influenced by Russell's earlier work in a variety of ways. However, our way of proceeding has its advantages. In addition to highlighting the differences between the two views, as well as their similarities, this

---

[2] Ludwig Wittgenstein, *Tractatus Logico-Philosophicus*, translated by C. K. Ogden (Mineola, NY: Dover, 1999); originally published in English in 1922 by Routledge. Another useful translation was done by Pears and McGuinness (London: Routledge, 1974).

approach has the advantage of starting with a position that is relatively easy to comprehend—Russell's—and moving by comprehensible steps to Wittgenstein's position, which is much less readily accessible.

Russell's version of logical atomism starts from a conception of a **logically perfect language** that would be an ideal tool for describing reality. Given such a language, the philosopher's central task would be to dispose of philosophical problems by translating natural language sentences that express those problems into the sentences of the logically perfect language, where they could be either solved or dissolved and shown to be pseudo-problems. However, before this can be done, we first must understand the logical language. What is this logically perfect language? Essentially, it is the language we have been using up to now in presenting Russell's theory of descriptions and his reduction of arithmetic to logic. However, there are some new twists and additions, so it won't hurt to review the language.

The Ideal Language, and the Parallel between Language and the World

Linguistic Simples and Metaphysical Simples

The simplest sentences of the language are called *atomic sentences.* Each such sentence consists of a predicate followed by one or more logically proper names—e.g., *Ra* (a is red), or *Lab* (a is to the left of b). The predicates are supposed to stand for universals—i.e., abstract properties and relations. The names are supposed to stand for the ultimate atoms, or metaphysically simple objects, that make up the universe. Note the parallel. Linguistically simple elements—predicates and logically proper names—are taken to stand for the most basic constituents of reality—universals and metaphysically simple objects. Why this parallel should exist, and what justifies us in believing that it does, are fundamental questions to which Russell was able to give only partial, and not very persuasive, answers.

Certainly, it is natural, even if not inevitable, to assume, as he did, that there are simple elements of language—expressions the meanings of which consist simply in the things they stand for, independent of the meanings of other expressions. But even granting this, why must one assume (a) that all objects are decomposable into metaphysically simples—i.e., basic particulars that cannot further be broken down into simpler constituents—or (b) that, if there are such simples, they, and only they, can be named by logically proper names? Russell does, of course, have his epistemological doctrine from "Knowledge by Acquaintance and Knowledge by Description" to rely on. According to it, the only propositions we are capable of entertaining, and hence the only thoughts we are capable of having, are those the constituents of which we are directly acquainted with in a way that precludes significant error. One corollary of this doctrine is that we can't be mistaken about what we mean by an expression, or, therefore, about what a genuine logically proper name means, as used by us. As we saw in chapter 5, this view, together with Russell's stipulation that the meaning of a logically proper name is its referent, leads to the conclusion that the only objects named by the logically proper names in one's language are one's own sense data, one's ideas, and oneself. Though not inevitable, it is, perhaps, understandable how Russell could have taken these things to be metaphysically simple.

Nevertheless, we are already getting into trouble. First, as we saw at the end of chapter 5, these epistemological conclusions threaten applications of Russell's theory of descriptions to such central cases as George IV's questioning of whether Scott was the author of *Waverley*. This suggests that if the theory of descriptions is to do all the work that Russell envisioned for it, the epistemological doctrines of "Knowledge by Acquaintance and Knowledge by Description" may have to be modified. Second, Russell's epistemological restrictions do not, by themselves, exclude the possibility that there may be many objects that we can think about by apprehending descriptions that apply to them, even though they can't be constituents of our thoughts, or referents of our logically proper names, because we are not directly acquainted with them in his epistemologically privileged sense. Thus, the possibility remains open that reality may contain a domain of objects, unrelated to the metaphysical simples named by logically proper names, which are not themselves metaphysically simple, and which may not, as far as we know, even be composed of metaphysical simples.

Genuine material objects are a case in point. Of course, one might wonder how, from a Russellian perspective, one could ever know of, or be justified in believing in, the existence of such objects. As we saw in chapter 7, Russell tried to circumvent these questions by defending the doctrine that material objects are logical constructions out of sense data. Had his defense been successful, material objects would have been, essentially, eliminated and replaced by sense data. Such a result would have added to the coherence and plausibility of his emerging philosophy of logical atomism by removing from consideration a class of objects which are neither themselves metaphysically simple, nor knowable apriori to be composed out of metaphysical simples. However, as we have seen, Russell's defense of his logical constructions doctrine was not successful, and the doctrine itself is indefensible. As a result, the central tenet of logical atomism that posits a systematic parallel between linguistically simple expressions—logically proper names—and metaphysically simple objects can only be regarded as an unsubstantiated and implausible postulate.

So it appears to us, with the benefit of hindsight. The same cannot be said for Russell and his contemporaries. Presuming the essential correctness of his earlier views, he, quite understandably, regarded the fundamental parallel between language and the world posited in his philosophy of logical atomism to be the natural next step in the evolution of a coherent and unified picture. It was a natural step; but the basis from which it was taken was already flawed.

Atomic and Molecular Sentences, and the Facts Corresponding to Them

Nevertheless, there is much of interest in the system, and much that is historically illuminating. Pursuing the parallel between language and the world, we move from the correlation between linguistically simple expressions and metaphysically simple constituents of reality to the parallel between simple—i.e., atomic—sentences and the facts to which they correspond. As already indicated, an atomic sentence consists of a predicate followed by one or more logically proper names; the predicate stands for a universal—an abstract property or relation—and the names stand for metaphysical simples. Such a sentence is supposed to be true just in case it corresponds to an atomic fact, which was taken by Russell to be a complex entity consisting of the universal designated by the predicate together with the objects named by the names. For example, the sentence Ra is supposed to be true just in case there is in the world an actually existing fact consisting of the object a's being red, and the sentence Lab is supposed to be true just in case there is in the world an existing fact consisting of the object a's bearing the relation to-the-left-of to the object b.

The ideal language also contains sentences obtained by performing truth-functional operations on simpler sentences. For example, if S is a

sentence of the language, so is the negation, ~*S*, of S; and if S and R
are sentences of the language, so is their conjunction, *S & R*, their disjunction, *(S v R)*, the conditional, *(S → R)*, the antecedent of which is
S and the consequent of which is R, and the biconditional, *(S ↔ R)*.
Russell calls these *molecular sentences*. What should we say about the
relationship between these sentences and facts? In the case of atomic
sentences, Russell accepts a version of the correspondence theory of
truth: a true atomic sentence is one that corresponds to an atomic fact.
So now we must ask, are there disjunctive facts in the world for true
disjunctive sentences to correspond to, conjunctive facts for true
conjunctions to correspond to, negative facts for true negations to
correspond to, and so on? Are conjunction, disjunction, and negation
somehow "in the world"?

Russell's answer to this question was a little more complex than one
might first imagine. In the case of conjunction, he held that *(S & R)* is
true just in case it corresponds both to the fact that makes S true and
to the fact that makes R true. Here we don't need any complex conjunctive fact because the correspondence to the two constitutive facts is
enough to explain the truth of the conjunction. Thus, '&' doesn't stand
for anything in the world. A similar point holds for disjunctions. *(R v S)*
is true just in case there is a fact that makes R true or a fact that makes
S true. We don't need any disjunctive fact for true disjunctions to correspond to, since the truth of any disjunction can be seen as resulting
from its correspondence to one, or both, of the relevant constituent
facts. Like '&', 'v' doesn't stand for anything in the world.

However, Russell thought that negation was another story. One
principle he seems to have taken to be obvious was the following:

THE CORRESPONDENCE PRINCIPLE
For any true sentence S, there is a set F of facts such that
correspondence of S to one or more of the members of F is
responsible for the truth of S.

Although this principle is compatible with the lack of conjunctive and
disjunctive facts, it is arguable that it requires negative facts. Suppose
that ~*S* is true. Then its truth can't be due to correspondence with a
fact that makes S true, for there is no such fact. What other fact could
it correspond to? Russell could see no plausible alternative to admitting
negative facts. ~*S* is true because it corresponds to a fact in which an
abstract constituent designated by '~' combines with a non-linguistic
complex represented by the sentence S. In this way, we are led to the

surprising conclusion that the negation symbol stands for something in the world.

Russell realizes that this is apt to sound strange. In discussing negative facts in lecture III of *The Philosophy of Logical Atomism* he says:

> When I was lecturing on this subject at Harvard, I argued that there are negative facts, and it nearly produced a riot; the class would not hear of there being negative facts at all. But I am still inclined to think that there are.[3]

The reason he thinks this seems to be his commitment to the Correspondence Principle. If this principle is accepted, then his argument that there is no very good alternative to the view that there are negative facts is rather persuasive. Also persuasive is his argument that no other true molecular sentences in the logically perfect language require molecular facts.

General Sentences and General Facts

This brings us to general, or quantificational, sentences of the sort *At least one A is B* and *Every A is B*—i.e., $\exists x \, (Ax \, \& \, Bx)$, $\forall x \, (Ax \rightarrow Bx)$. Russell thought that there had to be general facts to which true sentences of this sort correspond. He gives his reason for thinking this in the following passage.

> We have such propositions as *All men are mortal* and *Some men are Greeks*. But you have not only such *propositions;* you have also such *facts,* and that, of course, is where you get back to the inventory of the world: that, in addition to particular facts, which I have been talking about in previous lectures, there are also general facts and existence-facts, that is to say, there are not merely *propositions* of that sort but also *facts* of that sort. That is rather an important point to realize. You cannot ever arrive at a general fact by inference from particular facts, however numerous. . . . Suppose, for example, that you wish to prove in that way that *All men are mortal,* you are supposed to proceed by complete induction, and say *A is a man that is mortal, B is a man that is mortal, C is a man that is mortal,* and so on until you finish. You will not be able, in that way, to arrive at the proposition *All men are mortal,* unless

[3] P. 74.

you know when you have finished. That is to say that, in order to arrive by this road at the general proposition *All men are mortal*, you must already have the general proposition *All men are among those I have enumerated*. You never can arrive at a general proposition by inference from particular propositions alone. You will always have to have at least one general proposition in your premises.[4]

There are several points suggested by this passage. In the discussion immediately following the quoted material, Russell draws a conclusion about knowledge. Taking it for granted that we do know some general truths, he concludes that there must be knowledge of general propositions that is not based on logical, deductive inference from non-general propositions. This conclusion in turn is based on the elementary logical point that no universal generalization, $\forall x\ (Ax \rightarrow Bx)$, is ever a logical consequence of any set I of sentences, *x is an A that is a B, y is an A that is a B, z is an A that is a B*, . . . , that are instances of the generalization. No matter how large the set I may be—no matter even if it happens to contain, for each actual thing x that A is really true of, and for no other things, a sentence *n is an A that is a B*, where n refers to x—it will still be **logically possible** for there to be more things that A is true of. Since it is logically possible that B might **not** be true of some of these things, it is logically possible for all the sentences in I to be true, while the universal generalization $\forall x\ (Ax \rightarrow Bx)$ is false. Thus the universal generalization is **not** a logical consequence of the set I of individual sentences.

Corresponding to this logical point is a metaphysical, or ontological, point. Suppose that for each thing x that A is actually true of, and for only such things, there is a sentence *n is an A that is also a B* in I, where n refers to x. Suppose further that all these sentences are true, and that corresponding to them is a set of facts F_I. If, as we have seen, it is still **logically possible** for there to be more things that A is true of, then it is natural to think that there **could have been** more things that A is true of than there actually are. Supposing that B could have failed to be true of some of these things, we get the result that there is a possible state of the world—a way the universe could have been—in which all the facts in F_I continue to exist and obtain, yet *All A's are B's* is untrue, and fails to correspond to any fact.

[4] P. 101.

Russell took this possibility to show that there must be general facts that are not reducible to particular facts. This conclusion makes sense, provided we add the following corollary to his Correspondence Principle.

> COROLLARY TO THE CORRESPONDENCE PRINCIPLE
> Correspondence to members in F is responsible for the truth of S only if it would be impossible for the members of F to exist without S being true.

Given all of this, one is forced to posit general facts, along with atomic and negative facts.[5]

Nonextensional Sentences and Facts

There is still one further type of fact that Russell requires—non extensional, or as they are sometimes called, *intensional* facts. In this connection we will mention two kinds of sentences—propositional attitude ascriptions and counterfactual conditionals.

> PROPOSITIONAL ATTITUDE ASCRIPTIONS
> x believes / knows / expects / hopes . . . that S.

> COUNTERFACTUAL CONDITIONALS
> If it were the case that S, then it would be the case that R.

These sentences have something in common with the truth-functional compounds we looked at earlier. Like those sentences, they contain full sentences as constituents. However, they differ from the truth-functional sentences in that the truth or falsity of these sentences is not determined by the truth values of their sentential constituents.

---

[5] Although Russell gives no explicit argument for it, he claims that there are also existence facts corresponding to existential generalizations such as $\exists x\ (Ax\ \&\ Bx)$. One might try to argue for this (taking for granted both the Correspondence Principle and the Corollary) by first arguing for the existence of negative facts corresponding to true sentences like $\sim\exists x\ (Cx\ \&\ Dx)$. (The argument for this parallels the argument for facts corresponding to true universal generalizations.) Next, one might observe that such facts must consist of something designated by '$\sim$' plus some non-linguistic complexes represented by $\exists x\ (Cx\ \&\ Dx)$. But then, one might maintain, if such complexes must exist anyway, they may qualify as facts in cases in which $\exists x\ (Cx\ \&\ Dx)$ is true. Needless to say, this argument is rather problematic, and it is unclear whether Russell would, or could, have accepted it. Thus, it is unclear what the basis was for his claim that there are existence facts. He could, of course, simply have defined $\exists x\ (Cx\ \&\ Dx)$ as $\sim\forall x\sim(Cx\ \&\ Dx)$, and identified the "existence fact" corresponding to the former with the "negative fact" corresponding to the latter.

This can be seen by noting certain elementary results involving substitution. If we start with a truth-functional sentence like *(A v B)*, and substitute for A any sentence C with the same truth value as A—i.e., any truth if A is true or any falsehood if A is false—then the resulting sentence *(C v B)* will always agree in truth value with the original—i.e., it will be true just in case *(A v B)* was true, and false just in case *(A v B)* was false. This is not the case with nonextensional (i.e. intensional) sentences. For example, if (1a) is true, and we substitute any true sentence S for the true sentence *2 + 2 = 4*, it does not follow that (1b) must be true.

1a. John believes that *2 + 2 = 4.*

b. John believes that S.

Someone who believes one truth doesn't necessarily believe them all; whether or not someone believes something doesn't depend on the truth value of that thing. Thus, belief sentences are **not** truth functions of their complement clauses, and there is no hope of explaining their truth in terms of facts corresponding to those clauses. For this reason, Russell needed a new category of fact corresponding to true belief sentences, and to true propositional attitude ascriptions generally. I will not present Russell's analysis of these sentences, and the facts corresponding to them. Although it is quite interesting, it is also complicated. Russell himself had doubts about it, and never really completed his line of thought. For our purposes it is enough to note that some special account of these sentences is needed.

The other intensional sentences needed in Russell's ideal language are counterfactual conditionals like (2).

2. If it had been the case that *I dropped this chalk*, then it would have been the case that *this chalk fell to the floor.*

As it happens, both italicized clauses of (2) are false—I didn't drop the chalk, and it didn't fall to the floor. Nevertheless, the entire counterfactual conditional is true. Note, however, that if I substituted another false sentence for *I dropped the chalk*, the entire compound might turn out to be false, as is the case with (3).

3. If it had been the case that *I put this chalk in my pocket*, it would have been the case that *this chalk fell to the floor.*

Thus, counterfactual conditionals are **not** truth functional. Hence Russell has reason to include special intensional facts corresponding to true counterfactual conditionals.

I say this despite the fact that he doesn't mention counterfactual sentences or facts in *The Philosophy of Logical Atomism*. On the contrary, in one place in the lectures he has disparaging comments to make about closely related notions—necessity, possibility, and impossibility—which suggests that he might not have been willing to countenance counterfactual conditionals in his logically perfect language at all.[6] Nevertheless, I have included them in our picture of the Russellian ideal language for the simple reason that I don't see how it would possible for him to maintain his doctrine that physical objects are logical constructions out of sense data without them. As we saw in chapter 8, according to that doctrine a material object statement like *I see a table* is analyzed into a set of categorical and hypothetical statements about sense data. Since these hypothetical statements are supposed to tell us what sense data we **would** have if various conditions were fulfilled, they must be counterfactual conditionals. Thus, Russell needs this class of sentences, and the facts corresponding to them, so long as he wishes to maintain his doctrine that material objects are logical constructions out of sense data.

Russell's Imagined System

This completes our discussion of Russell. It is evident that his sketch of the basic principles of logical atomism was nothing more than a bare-bones outline of an imagined philosophical system. The system he envisioned was one in which the development of a logically perfect language would provide philosophers with an ideal tool for describing

---

[6] Pp. 96–97. Russell's professed skepticism on this point is quite remarkable for someone whose text is laced with claims about what is possible or impossible, what could be and what could not be. On p. 96 he claims that necessity is the property possessed by a propositional function that is, as he puts it, "always true," possibility is the property of propositional functions of being "sometimes true," and impossibility is the property of being "never true." He goes on to say, "Much false philosophy has arisen out of confusing propositional functions and propositions. There is a great deal in ordinary traditional philosophy which consists simply in attributing to propositions the predicates which only apply to propositional functions, and, still worse, sometimes in attributing to individuals predicates which merely apply to propositional functions. This case of *necessary, possible, impossible*, is a case in point. In all traditional philosophy there comes a heading of 'modality', which discusses *necessary, possible,* and *impossible* as properties of propositions, whereas in fact they are properties of propositional functions. Propositions are only true or false." Yet, if one looks at Russell's text one finds him repeatedly using these modal notions in more or less their traditional sense, as opposed to the sense that he officially assigns to them here.

reality. Using this tool, the job of the philosopher would be to solve or dissolve philosophical problems by explaining philosophically significant parts of natural language in terms of this ideal language. In effect, the philosopher would show us how to translate from the natural to the ideal.

Russell himself never took this vision much further. He never worked systematically within the rigid confines of the framework that he sketched; nor, one suspects, could he have done so. The powerful, creative, and restless mind that gave us the theory of descriptions, the distinction between logical and grammatical form, the logicist reduction of arithmetic to logic, and the theory of types was not well-suited to the defense of any confining philosophical orthodoxy—even one of his own making. However, the vision of logical atomism that he so cursorily sketched was destined to be given a much grander, more compelling, and more powerful elaboration by his former student, Ludwig Wittgenstein, whose *Tractatus Logico-Philosophicus* presented what may be the most unified, ambitious, and fascinating philosophical system of the twentieth century. It is to it that we turn in Part 3.[7]

---

[7] I am indebted to Jeff Speaks for valuable advice about the organization and some of the topics covered in this chapter and the next.

SUGGESTED FURTHER READING
FOR PART TWO

Main Primary Sources Discussed

Russell, Bertrand. *Introduction to Mathematical Philosophy*. London: Allen & Unwin, and New York: Macmillan, 1919; reprinted New York: Dover, 1993.

———. "Knowledge by Acquaintance and Knowledge by Description." *Proceedings of the Aristotelian Society* 11 (1910–11); reprinted in N. Salmon and S. Soames, eds., *Propositions and Attitudes* (Oxford: Oxford University Press, 1988).

———. "On Denoting." *Mind* 14 (1905); reprinted in R. C. Marsh, ed., *Logic and Knowledge* (New York: Capricorn Books, 1956).

———. *Our Knowledge of the External World*. London: Allen and Unwin, 1914; reprinted London and New York: Routledge, 2000.

———. *The Philosophy of Logical Atomism*. La Salle, IL: Open Court, 1985; originally published in *The Monist*, 1918.

Additional Primary Sources

Hempel, Carl. "On the Nature of Mathematical Truth." *American Mathematical Monthly* 52 (1945): 543–56; reprinted in P. Benacerraf and H. Putnam, eds., *The Philosophy of Mathematics*, 2nd edition (Cambridge: Cambridge University Press, 1983).

Moore, G. E. "External and Internal Relations." *Proceedings of the Aristotelian Society*, 1919–20, reprinted in G. E. Moore, *Philosophical Studies* (Totowa, NJ: Littlefield and Adams, 1968).

Russell, Bertrand. "The Regressive Method of Discovering the Premises of Mathematics," 1905. In Russell, *Essays in Analysis*, edited by Douglas Lackey (New York: George Braziller, 1973).

Additional Recommended Reading

Nathan Salmon, "Existence." In J. Tomberlin, ed., *Philosophical Perspectives*, vol. 1: *Metaphysics* (Atascadero, CA: Ridgeview, 1987).

———. "Nonexistence." *Noûs* 32 (1998).

PART THREE

LUDWIG WITTGENSTEIN'S *TRACTATUS*

CHAPTER 9

THE METAPHYSICS OF THE *TRACTATUS*

Comparison with Russell

We now turn to Wittgenstein's celebrated development of logical atomism. In general, all atomist views can be seen as having a two-part structure. The first part, or atomic level, consists of doctrines about atomic facts and the metaphysical simples that make them up, together with theories about the relationship between these simple constituents of reality and the basic elements of language—atomic sentences and the linguistically simple expression that make them up. The second part of an atomist view consists of doctrines about non-atomic sentences and their relation both to atomic sentences and to non-linguistic reality.

We saw that for Russell the basic metaphysical simples that make up reality are minds and sense data, plus properties of, and relations among, these elements. We can lay out Russell's view graphically as follows:

	Language	Reality
Atomic Level	Logically proper names	Minds and sense data (particulars)
	predicates	properties and relations (universals)
	atomic sentences	atomic facts
	Pa . . . n	combinations of particulars and universals
2nd Level	Truth-functionally compound sentences	
	$\sim$S	negative facts
	(S&R)	———
	(SvR)	———
	Sentences expressing generality	
	$\forall$x Fx	general facts
	$\exists$x Fx	existence facts
	Nonextensional sentences	Nonextensional (or intensional) facts
	propositional attitude ascriptions (belief)	facts about the attitudes
	counterfactual conditionals	unspecified intensional facts

The thrust of Russell's logical atomism was that all empirical reality and everything that can meaningfully be said can be incorporated in this framework.

Wittgenstein's version of logical atomism had a similar two-level structure, and a similar emphasis on the parallel between language and the world. However, the content of his system ended up being very different from that of Russell's. Whereas Russell thought that sense data and minds were basic metaphysical simples (named by logically proper names), Wittgenstein made no such claim, and seemed to think that genuine metaphysical simples were objects of quite a different sort. Whereas Russell thought that there were negative and general facts corresponding to certain logically complex compound sentences, Wittgenstein did not. Instead he thought that the truth or falsity of all such compounds could be explained in terms of conditions on atomic facts alone. Whereas Russell seemed to require the existence of non-extensional sentences and facts, Wittgenstein thought that all meaningful sentences are truth-functional compounds of atomic sentences, and all facts are atomic facts.

Another fundamental difference between Russell and Wittgenstein concerned the differing philosophical visions motivating their systems. For Russell the basic metaphysical simples were minds, sense data, and Platonic universals. His motivation for taking these to be basic was largely epistemological. He thought that if these were the basic elements of reality, then we would have a good chance of being able to explain how knowledge of the world is possible. Wittgenstein did not share Russell's empiricist epistemological motivations; indeed, he says very little about how we come to know the truth or falsity of the basic atomic statements on which all else rests in his system. At one point, he does try to justify his commitment to the claim that there must be metaphysical simples of some sort, which he assumes to be the referents of logically proper names. But this justification is quite different from what Russell might have offered; rather than basing his atomism on explicitly epistemological concerns, Wittgenstein seems to have thought that certain atomist theses follow from the fact that we are able to represent the world in language. As we shall see, however, the motivation he sketches is unpersuasive, and, in the end, it does little to justify his basic commitment to an atomist metaphysics.

The relevant passage from the *Tractatus* is the following:[1]

2.02   The object is simple.

2.0201   Every statement about complexes can be analyzed into a statement about their constituent parts, and into those propositions which completely describe the complexes.

2.021   Objects form the substance of the world. Therefore they cannot be compound.

2.0211   If the world had no substance, then whether a proposition had sense would depend on whether another proposition was true.

---

[1] Ludwig Wittgenstein, *Tractatus Logico-Philosophicus*, translated by C. K. Ogden (Mineola, NY: Dover, 1999); originally published in English in 1922 by Routledge.

2.0212   It would then be impossible to form a picture of the
world (true or false).

Section 2.02 tells us that there are metaphysically simple objects
(which Wittgenstein takes to be referents of logically proper names).
Section 2.0201 is a compressed statement of his commitment to the
fundamental parallel between language and the world. Since simple
sentences consist of predicates and logically proper names, they report
the relations that metaphysical simples bear to one another; thus, sentences that talk about complex objects must themselves be complex.
Since all complex sentences are ultimately to be explained in terms of
the atomic sentences that they are logically dependent upon, statements about complex objects are ultimately analyzable in terms of
sentences about the simple objects that make them up. Section 2.021
reminds us that this process of analysis, of moving from the more complex to the less complex, must come to an end—in metaphysically simple objects, on the side of the world (and in logically proper names and
atomic sentences composed of them, on the side of language).

   So far these doctrines are simply asserted without argument.
Sections 2.0211 and 2.0212 are meant to provide an argument for this
last claim—i.e., for the claim that the process of decomposition and
analysis must terminate in the metaphysically simple. What, precisely,
that argument is supposed to be is not made fully explicit. However,
given other assumptions of the *Tractatus*, one can make an educated
guess. As I see it, the most likely argument is the following: (i) suppose
there were no metaphysical simples; (ii) then the simplest elements in
language—logically proper names—would refer to composite objects;
for example, the logically proper name n might refer to an object o,
made up of a, b, and c composed in a certain way; (iii) in that case,
whether or not o existed, and, hence, whether or not n referred to
anything, would depend on whether or not it was true that a, b, and c
were composed in the requisite way; (iv) since the meaning of n is simply its referent, it would follow that whether or not n had a meaning at
all, and hence whether or not any atomic sentence containing n had a
meaning, would depend on the truth of the proposition that a, b, and
c are composed in the requisite way; (v) moreover, if there were no metaphysical simples, then this process could be repeated for a, b, and c—
i.e., whether or not it was even meaningful that a, b, and c were related
in the requisite way would depend on the truth of still further propo-

sitions—and so on without end; (vi) the process could also be repeated for every name and every atomic sentence; (vii) finally, the result extends to all logically complex sentences, since (as we shall see) it is a central doctrine of the *Tractatus* that the meanings of all complex sentences are dependent on the meanings of atomic sentences; (viii) thus, if there were no metaphysically simple objects, then whether or not any sentence whatsoever had a meaning would depend on the truth, and hence meaningfulness, of still further statements, the meaningfulness would depend on yet further statements, and so on. Since Wittgenstein regarded this scenario as absurd, he concluded that there really must be metaphysically simple objects.

There are two main points to notice about this argument. First, it is replete with assumptions about language—i.e., about logically proper names, atomic sentences, and the relationship between atomic and non-atomic sentences. Although Wittgenstein introduces these assumptions later in the *Tractatus*, they are neither obvious in themselves, nor given persuasive independent justifications. Thus, on this interpretation, the argument for metaphysical simples rests on a linguistic foundation which itself raises serious questions. Second, even if one relies on Wittgenstein's linguistic assumptions, one must do more to show that the resulting *reductio ad absurdum* really reaches an absurdity—as Wittgenstein takes it to. Why is it absurd that the meaning of some, perhaps even all, sentences should depend on the truth of further propositions (sentences)?[2]

In answering this question it is crucial to clarify what one means by saying that the meaning of one sentence, P, depends on the truth of another sentence, or proposition, Q. Suppose what one means is that in order to determine, or come to know, that P is meaningful one must **first** determine, or come to know, that Q is true. On this interpretation, what is said in the argument is that in order to determine, or come to know, that any sentence has a meaning, one has **first** to determine, or come to know, that other sentences are both true and meaningful, and so on, *ad infinitum*. That really is absurd, since it leads to the result that we can never determine, or come to know, that any sentence has a meaning.

---

[2] One of the problems with the argument is that it trades on a certain sloppiness involving the difference between sentences and propositions. Since this is a vexed topic for Wittgenstein, and since the argument can be untangled without making an issue of it, I will not here dwell on the distinction.

But the argument does not establish that this absurdity follows (in the presence of Wittgenstein's other assumptions about language) from the supposition that there are no metaphysical simples, since, on this interpretation, steps (iii) and (iv) do not follow from step (ii). To see this, suppose I were to use the word *this* as a logically proper name to refer to the chair I am sitting on. In order for this particular use of the word to have a meaning, the chair I intend to use it to refer to must exist. Suppose now that my chair is made up of a huge collection of molecules configured in a certain way. Since my chair is made up of these molecules in this configuration, it may be necessary in order for my chair to exist, and, hence, in order for my use of the word *this* on the present occasion to have both a referent and a meaning, that these molecules be configured in the right way. But this is **not** something I have to know about, in order to know that the chair exists, or that my utterance meant what I took it to mean.

We can even imagine a group of people with no conception of molecular structure, who speak a language L with precisely the logical structure that Wittgenstein imagines, where the logically proper names are restricted to referring to people and ordinary middle-sized objects of their acquaintance. Even if none of the names, atomic sentences, or non-atomic sentences of L would have meanings were it not for the fact that certain molecular configurations existed, speakers of L could know their words to have the meanings they do without knowing any of this. It is a defect of the Tractarian argument for metaphysical simples that it doesn't rule out the possibility that our language might be like L in never referring to metaphysical simples. Hence, it does not establish that there are metaphysical simples.

One could, of course, repair the argument so that steps (iii) and (iv) really did follow from step (ii). However, in order to do this, one would have to stipulate that for the meaningfulness of a sentence S to **depend** on the truth of the claim that so and so is simply for it to be the case that were it not a fact that so and so, then S would not be meaningful. However, with this interpretation of dependence, the conclusion derived from the supposition that there are no metaphysical simples is no longer absurd. Why shouldn't it be the case that for any sentence S, S wouldn't have a meaning were it not a fact that so and so, which, in turn, would not have been a fact had not it also been a fact that such and such, and so on, *ad infinitum*? Perhaps there is some good reason for thinking that this really is impossible, or absurd. If so, however, Wittgenstein didn't give it.

Thus, like Russell, he failed to establish either that there are metaphysically simple objects, or that, if there are, they, and only they, can be the referents of logically proper names. For this reason, it is better, I think, to view these doctrines as basic postulates of the Tractarian system, than as theorems forced on Wittgenstein by other more basic assumptions. As I see it, he had a certain conception of language, and a certain parallel conception of reality. Although the two fit together quite elegantly, neither can simply be derived from the other; and neither can be demonstrated from clearly acceptable, or self-evident, starting points. Rather, the system may be judged to stand or fall as a whole. Regarding Wittgenstein's metaphysical vision, it seems to have been a radically logicized version of traditional metaphysical atomism.[3]

Wittgenstein's Logicized Version of Metaphysical Atomism

Traditional atomism held that there are certain simple, indivisible bits of matter called 'atoms' which are the building blocks out of which everything in the universe is made up. All change in the universe is held to be the result of old combinations of atoms breaking down and new combinations being formed to take their place. Moreover, even though atoms are the source of all change, they are themselves eternal and unchanging. Wittgenstein took over this traditional picture and recast it in a new form. The traditional statements of atomism had the look of very general empirical hypotheses that might eventually be confirmed, refuted, partially supported, or partially undermined by continuing progress in science. Wittgenstein's version of atomism was not of this type. His statements couldn't be confirmed or refuted by science, but rather were supposed to be prior to science. In addition, the simples that Wittgenstein talked about were not only the eternal unchanging source of all change; they were also the source of all conceptual or logical possibility. Just as all change—all variation over time—is the result of the combination and recombination of unchanging simples, so all variation in what one might call *logical space* between one possible state of affairs and another is nothing more

---

[3] This point is emphasized in Robert Fogelin's *Wittgenstein*, 2nd edition (London and New York: Routledge, 1987).

than variations in the way that the same metaphysical simples are combined.

Wittgenstein expresses this idea in different places, in a variety of ways. For example in sections 2.027, 2.0271, and 2.0272, we get the idea that the metaphysically simple objects are the unchanging source of all change.[4]

2.027   The fixed, the existent and the object are one.

(Objects, the unalterable, and the subsistent are one and the same.)

2.0271   The object is the fixed, the existent; the configuration is the changing, the variable.

(Objects are what is unalterable and subsistent; their configuration is what is changing and unstable.)

2.0272   The configuration of the objects forms the atomic fact.

Wittgenstein also makes it clear that the metaphysically simple objects of the world exist in all possible states of the world, and are the source of all logical possibility. On this view, to say that something isn't the case, but could have been, is to say that although the basic objects are not combined in a certain way, they could have been so combined. Sample passages indicating this view include the following:

2   What is the case, the fact, is the existence of atomic facts.

2.01   An atomic fact is a combination of objects (entities, things).

2.011   It is essential to a thing that it can be a constituent part of an atomic fact.

2.012   In logic nothing is accidental: if a thing *can* occur in an atomic fact the possibility of that atomic fact must already be prejudged in the thing.

---

[4] Wittgenstein, *Tractatus*, translated by Ogden. Parenthesized material is an alternate translation by David Francis Pears and Brain McGuinness (London: Routledge, 1974). In what follows, unless otherwise indicated, unparenthesized material is from the Ogden translation; Pears and McGuinness translations will appear in parentheses.

2.0122   The thing is independent, in so far as it can occur in all *possible* circumstances, but this form of independence is a form of connection with the atomic fact, a form of dependence. . . .

2.0123   If I know an object, then I also know all the possibilities of its occurrence in atomic facts.

2.0124   If all objects are given, then thereby are all *possible* atomic facts also given.

2.013   Every thing is, as it were, in a space of possible atomic facts. . . .

2.014   Objects contain the possibility of all states of affairs.

2.0141   The possibility of its occurrence in atomic facts is the form of the object.

2.02   The object is simple.

2.0201   Every statement about complexes can be analyzed into a statement about their constituent parts, and into those propositions which completely describe the complexes.

2.021   Objects form the substance of the world. Therefore they cannot be compound.

2.022   It is clear that however different from the real one an imagined world may be, it must have something—a form—in common with the real world.

2.023   This fixed form consists of the objects.

According to the *Tractatus*, simple objects are fixed and unchanging. All possibility and all change are understood in terms of the combinations and recombinations of the same simple objects. Just as the simples are eternal and exist throughout all time, so their existence is necessary and they exist in every possible state that the world could be in. In the *Tractatus*, all possibility—all variation in logical space—is nothing more than variation in the way that the same metaphysical simples are combined. But what are these objects like? From what we have said so far, one might think that they are something like the tiny billiard-ball bits of matter envisioned in traditional versions of atomism. However, this is not what Wittgenstein had in mind.

The Hiddenness of the Metaphysically Simple

According to Wittgenstein, objects are simple. They are shapeless, colorless, and in general have none of the familiar properties exemplified by ordinary medium-sized things we encounter in everyday life. Not only do the basic metaphysical simples not have those familiar properties; they are what, so to speak, make or constitute such properties. One might say that the familiar properties of everyday life "come into existence" only with the configuration of simple objects. For this reason, we have no way of describing such objects, though, supposedly, we can name them.

In this connection, Wittgenstein makes an illuminating comment about shape in the notebooks he kept while working on the *Tractatus*. He says:

> Let us suppose we were to see a circular patch: is the circular form its property? Certainly not. It seems to be a structural 'property'. And if I notice that a spot is round, am I not noticing an infinitely complicated structural property?[5]

The point here, I think, is something like the following: when we say that something we perceive is circular what we are really saying is that the metaphysically simple objects that make it up bear certain structural (in this case, spatial) relations to one another. If this is right, then the logical form of the sentence *The so and so is circular* is, or at least includes, a complex statement of the sort, *a is related to b in such and such way, which in turn is related to c in a certain way, which in turn is related to d* . . . (and so on). Here, 'a', 'b', 'c', and 'd' are logically proper names for metaphysical simples that make up the complex thing denoted by the subject of the original sentence. This means that all talk about circularity can be analyzed into talk about how multitudes of simples are related to one another. If we now ask whether the metaphysical simples are themselves circular, we are asking a nonsensical question. To say that something is circular, or indeed that it has any shape, is to presuppose that it is a complex, the parts of which stand in certain relations to one another. Since, by definition, simples have no parts, they have no shape. On Wittgenstein's view, shape

[5] Wittgenstein, *Notebooks 1914–1916* (Oxford: Basil Blackwell, 1961), p. 18.

is a property that arises only at the level of combinations of objects; it is nonsensical to suppose that metaphysically simple objects are of any shape.

What applies to shape also applies to other familiar properties encountered in everyday life. Whenever we say of anything that it has one of these properties, what we are saying is that the simples that make it up are arranged in a certain way. Since all these properties arise only at the level of combinations of simples, it is nonsensical to ascribe them to the simples themselves. We can, in principle, name the simples with logically proper names, and say something about how they are arranged, but we cannot say what they are like in themselves.

The hiddenness of the metaphysical simples, and our inability to give a positive characterization of what they are like, are, for Wittgenstein, not the result of any remediable ignorance on our part. Rather, the mystery in which they are shrouded is somehow essential to them, and is closely connected with central doctrines of the *Tractatus*.

2.021   Objects form the substance of the world. Therefore they cannot be compound.

2.0231   The substance of the world *can* only determine a form and not any material properties. For these are first presented by the propositions—first formed by the configuration of the objects.

(The substance of the world *can* only determine a form, and not any material properties. For it is only by means of propositions that material properties are represented—only by the configuration of objects that they are produced.)

2.0232   Roughly speaking: objects are colorless.

2.0233   Two objects of the same logical form are—apart from their external properties—only differentiated from one another in that they are different.

The first of these passages identifies objects with the substance of the world. The second tells us that the substance of the world—the metaphysically simple objects—can only determine a form; that is, they only have possibilities of entering into different configurations. In saying that they do not determine "material properties," Wittgenstein is, I take it, saying that they do not themselves exhibit or possess specific properties like shape or color, nor do the objects by themselves determine which things actually instantiate such properties. Rather, we are told that these properties are represented only by propositions, and they come into being with "the configuration" of objects. In other words, such properties are to be analyzed in terms of the relations among the simples. In the third passage we are given an example. Colors are among the "material properties" that Wittgenstein is talking about. Since being a certain color—say red—is simply a matter of being made up of simples that stand in a certain configuration, the simples themselves cannot be colored. Thus, we are told that they are colorless. Finally, in the fourth passage, we are told that two metaphysical simples of the same logical form—that is two simples which have the same **possibilities** of combining with other objects—have no **intrinsic** properties that differentiate them. They may have different external or **relational** properties; they may, as a matter of actual fact, happen to be combined with different objects, and hence bear different relational properties. However, apart from that there are no intrinsic properties to differentiate one from the other. One of them, a, simply has the property of being non-identical with b, whereas the other, b, has the property of being non-identical with a.

In light of this, it seems evident that Wittgenstein thinks that the only thing we can say about simple objects is how they combine. He explicitly draws this conclusion at 3.221.

3.221   Objects I can only *name*. Signs represent them. I can only speak *of* them. I cannot *assert them*. A proposition can only say *how* a thing is, not *what it is*.

(Objects can only be *named*. Signs are their representatives. I can only speak *about* them: I cannot *put them into words*. Propositions can only say *how* things are, not *what* they are.)

Although we cannot say what metaphysical simples are like, we are supposed to be able to specify how they combine. However, there is a real question about how far we can succeed in doing even this. Other doctrines of the *Tractatus* place very severe constraints on the relational statements about metaphysically simple objects that we can intelligibly make. These doctrines go to the heart of the *Tractatus*, and concern the nature of necessity and possibility.

The Logical Independence of Atomic Sentences and Atomic Facts

The relevant doctrines about necessity and possibility are expressed in several places in the text. At 6.375 we are told that the only necessity is **logical** necessity and the only possibility is **logical** possibility. At 5.13, 5.131, and 4.1211 we are told that whenever propositions stand in any logical relation to one another, this is due to their structure (and hence will be shown on an analysis that reveals their logical forms).

5.13   That the truth of one proposition follows from the truth of other propositions, we perceive from the structure of the propositions.

5.131   If the truth of one proposition follows from the truth of others, this expresses itself in relations in which the forms of these propositions stand to one another, . . .

4.1211   . . . If two propositions contradict one another, this is shown by their structure; similarly if one follows from one another, etc.

Two corollaries of these views are: (i) that one atomic sentence never is a necessary consequence of another—i.e., the truth of one atomic sentence never follows necessarily from the truth of another, and (ii) that atomic sentences are never incompatible with one another. The first corollary is made explicit at 5.134.

5.134   From an elementary proposition no other can be inferred.

(One elementary proposition cannot be deduced from another.)

The second of these corollaries is explicitly endorsed at 6.3751.

6.3751   . . . It is clear that the logical product of two elementary propositions can neither be a tautology nor a contradiction.

Elementary propositions (sentences) are atomic propositions (sentences).[6] The logical product of two propositions is their conjunction.

---

[6] In the *Tractatus* a proposition is, roughly, a sentence together with its interpretation.

If the conjunction of two atomic propositions can never be a contra-diction, then the two propositions cannot be incompatible.

The idea behind these corollaries is clear. If an atomic proposition *Ha* logically entailed, or was logically incompatible with, another atomic proposition *Gb*, then the logical relation between the two would **not** be a matter of the structural relations between these two propositions, but rather would be about their subject matters, or con-tents. This cannot be, because logic has no specific subject matter. Rather, the logical relationships holding among different sentences is always a purely formal matter; for Wittgenstein, it is always discover-able from an examination of their structure.

Since logic has no subject matter of its own, it has no method of finding out which atomic sentences are true and which are not. A cen-tral task of logic is to find sentences—logical truths, or tautologies—that are guaranteed to be true no matter how truth values are assigned to the atomic sentences; another task is to find sentences—contradic-tions—that are guaranteed to be false no matter how truth values are assigned to atomic sentences. Related to these tasks, logic will tell us when the truth of one sentence, or one set of sentences, guarantees the truth of another sentence (no matter which atomic sentences are true or false), as well as when a set of sentences cannot jointly be true. If to this conception of logic one adds the Tractarian doctrine that all necessity is logical necessity and all impossibility is logical impossibility, one gets the result that every necessary truth is a logical truth, or tautology, and every necessary falsehood is a logical falsehood or con-tradiction. One also gets the result that whenever the truth of one proposition necessitates the truth, or the falsity, of another, the second proposition is either a **logical** consequence of the first, or **logically** in-compatible with the first.

Suppose for the moment that Wittgenstein is right: if p and q are atomic propositions, then the truth, or the falsity, of p is always com-patible with the truth, or the falsity, of q; it is possible for both to be true, both to be false, or for either one to be true while the other is false. In short, the two are independent. Since the *Tractatus* posits a parallel between atomic propositions and atomic facts, the same sort of result holds for atomic facts. Thus, just after being told at 5.134 that one elementary proposition can never be logically deduced, or in-ferred, from another, we are told at 5.135 that "in no way can an inference be made from the existence of one state of affairs to the existence of another entirely different from it."[7] Similarly, at 2.061 and 2.062 we get the following:

2.061   Atomic facts are independent of one another.

2.062   From the existence or non-existence of an atomic fact we cannot infer the existence or non-existence of another.

These doctrines about the independence of atomic sentences and facts can be used to throw light on what atomic sentences really say about metaphysical simples, and what atomic facts really are possible. At 6.3751, Wittgenstein himself provides an example of the kind of argument we can use.

6.3751   For two colors, e.g., to be at one place in the visual field, is impossible, logically impossible, for it is excluded by the logical structure of color. . . .

[It is clear that the logical product of two elementary propositions can neither be a tautology nor a contradiction. The assertion that a point in the visual field has two different colors at the same time, is a contradiction.][8]

It follows from these remarks that there can be no meaningful atomic sentence *a is red* that says of some particular object that it is red. The reason that there can be no such atomic sentence is that if there were, its truth would be **incompatible** with the truth of the atomic sentence *a is green*. Thus, these sentences—*a is red* and *a is green*—cannot be atomic. Likewise, there is no possible atomic state of affairs that a is red, since this state of affairs would not be independent of the possible state of affairs that a is green.

Now, this might not seem surprising, since we have already determined that, according to Wittgenstein, objects cannot have color, or indeed any other material properties. However, the point is much more far-reaching than this. For example, consider the following relational statements.

1a. a is to the right of b.

b. b is to the right of a.

[7] Ogden translation.
[8] These are Wittgenstein's brackets in the Ogden translation.

c. a is to the right of a.

2a. a is heavier than b.

b. b is heavier than a.

c. a is heavier than a.

3a. a is exactly two inches away from b.

b. a is exactly one inch away from b.

c. a is exactly one inch away from a.

4a. a is touching b.

b. b is touching a.

In each case, the (a) and (b) statements are not independent of each other. In the first three cases they are incompatible with one another—i.e., it is impossible for both to be true. In the fourth case they are necessary consequences of one another—if one is true, then the other must be true. Similarly, sentence (c) in the first three cases is necessarily false. These observations together with Tractarian doctrines about atomic propositions entail that the sentences in each example cannot all be atomic. Since in each example there is every reason to think that if one is atomic they all are, it follows from the fact that they are not logically independent that none qualify as atomic sentences, or propositions, in the sense of the *Tractatus*. Moreover, we could produce the same sort of argument for virtually any statement involving spatial relations, temporal relations, relations involving measurement, or relations of relative size or degree. It follow from this that no statements of these types can be atomic propositions in the sense postulated by the *Tractatus*. This means that atomic propositions cannot attribute ordinary properties to metaphysical simples, nor can they attribute familiar relations involving space, time, measurement, or degree to these objects.

This leaves little or nothing we can imagine that atomic sentences can say. This is a truly incredible result. According to Wittgenstein, atomic sentences are the building blocks out of which all meaning is constructed. But if his doctrines are correct, we can scarcely conceive of any atomic sentences, or the specific contents they might have. In the end, Wittgenstein seems to be forced into saying that all our talk about the world reduces to talk about simple objects that have no properties and cannot be combined in any ways that we can imagine, but nevertheless do combine in ways we cannot explain or comprehend. It is hard enough to understand what this really amounts to, let alone why anyone should believe it. It is, I think, fair to say that few, if any, philosophers really did. Wittgenstein's views about metaphysical simples and the way they combine to form atomic facts are among the darkest and most implausible aspects of the *Tractatus*. However, there are other aspects of the *Tractatus* that were much more interesting and influential. Particularly important were the doctrines about the nature of meaning, the nature of logic, and the notions of necessity and possibility, as well as Wittgenstein's doctrines about the relationship between logically complex sentences and atomic sentences. These are the aspects of the *Tractatus* which we will examine in the next chapter.

CHAPTER 10

MEANING, TRUTH, AND LOGIC
IN THE *TRACTATUS*

Truth, Meaning, and the Picture Theory

In the previous chapter we discussed Wittgenstein's conception of
metaphysical simples, and the way they combine to form atomic facts.
We now turn to his views on truth, meaning, necessity, possibility, con-
ceivability, and logic. As before, we begin with atomic sentences. These,
we are told, are combinations of logically proper names that **picture** or
represent possible states of affairs. In the Tractarian system, each name
names exactly one object, which is its meaning, and each object is named
by exactly one name. The way names are put together in an atomic sen-

tence represents a way in which the objects named could be combined. Atomic sentences (which Wittgenstein also calls *atomic propositions*) are said to **picture** possible facts or states of affairs, which can be taken to be their meanings. There are two things to notice here—the picture analogy and Wittgenstein's conception of meaning.

First, the picture analogy. This can be illustrated by a pair of well-known examples. The first is a courtroom model of a traffic accident in which toy cars stand for real cars. In the model, putting the toy cars in a certain spatial arrangement represents real cars being in that arrangement. In this example the spatial properties and relations of the model allow it to picture or represent spatial properties or relations of the real cars. The second example is a representational painting of a barn. In this case, by making a certain portion of the canvass red, one represents the barn one is painting as red.

What about language? We don't use different colored inks to represent the different colors of the referents of various words. Nor do we normally place words in spatial relationships that correspond in direct, point-by-point ways to the spatial relationships existing among the items we are talking about. Still, Wittgenstein thought, an atomic sentence has the ability to represent a possible fact, or state of affairs, only in virtue of the sentence and the state of affairs sharing a common form. This common form cannot, in general, be a spatial one, as in the traffic model, or a material one involving properties like color, as in the case of the painting of the barn. Thus, Wittgenstein says that the form shared by an atomic sentence and the state of affairs it pictures or represents must be an abstract **logical form**.[1]

Although this doctrine sounds rather grand, it is, I think, pretty simple. According to Wittgenstein, an atomic sentence is a **linguistic fact**—a certain structured combination of names—while a state of affairs is a possible **non-linguistic fact**—a certain structured combination of objects. In order for the linguistic fact to picture or represent the possible state of affairs, something about the way the names are combined in the sentence must correspond to how the objects are combined in the state of affairs. There is not much that can be said, in a general way, about what this something is. It is simply a matter of linguistic convention that certain ways of combining names—i.e., certain ways of putting names in specific relations to one another to form a sentence—represent possible states of affairs in which the objects referred to by

---

[1] See chapter 2 of Robert Fogelin, *Wittgenstein*, for further discussion of the picture theory.

the names stand in certain relations. For example, in the sentence *Nab* (meaning that a is to the north of b) the name *a* stands in the relation to the name *b* of **occurring-immediately-before-it-and-after-the-symbol-N**. Combining the two names in this relation represents the object named by *a* standing in the relation **to-the-north-of** to the object named by *b*. In setting up a language, one adopts linguistic conventions specifying which objects different proper names refer to, and which non-linguistic relations holding among the objects different linguistic relations holding among the names in a sentence stand for. When Wittgenstein says that an atomic sentence and the possible atomic fact it represents share a logical form, all he means, I think, is that just as the possible atomic fact is a combination in which objects stand in a certain relation R_o, so the atomic sentence is a combination in which names stand in a certain relation R_n, and some linguistic convention has been adopted according to which placing the names in the relation R_n represents the objects named as bearing the relation R_o to one another in the possible fact.[2]

To recap, according to the picture theory, in order for one fact to represent another fact, the two facts must share a common form. Sometimes, as in the case of the traffic model and the representational painting of the barn, that form involves certain material properties and relations—colors or spatial relations—being common to the representing fact and the fact represented. In other cases, as with language, the common form is simply an abstract logical form, in the sense just indicated.

We now turn to a different point suggested by the picture theory. Consider representational paintings. What makes a painting representational is not the existence of any actual thing that it represents; a painting of a unicorn can be representational, even though there are no unicorns. In light of this, one might think that what makes a painting representational is that it presents an object or situation which could, or might imaginably, exist, even if in fact it does not exist. Next, consider atomic sentences. We might ask, *what makes an atomic sentence representational—i.e., meaningful?* Some philosophers might answer that the meaningfulness of an atomic sentence consists in the fact that it stands for, or expresses, something—some entity, which is its meaning. One such philosopher was the early Russell, who thought of propositions as abstract objects expressed by sentences that are capable of being believed or asserted by agents. However, this is not Wittgenstein's con-

---

[2] Thanks to Boris Kment for his insights on this and related matters.

ception of what makes an atomic sentence meaningful, or what its meaningfulness consists in. According to him, an atomic sentence is meaningful, or representational, just in case it is possible for the objects named in the atomic sentence to be arranged in a manner corresponding to the way in which the names in the sentence are arranged. In his view, we may express this by saying that the meaning of an atomic sentence is a **possible** fact or state of affairs.

However, he would add that if we do express ourselves in this way, we must be careful not to give the wrong impression. Wittgenstein did **not** think that in addition to **actual** facts or states of affairs, there are some further entities—merely **possible** facts or states of affairs—that have a kind of being that falls short of full-fledged existence or actuality. Considered as genuine entities, there are no merely possible facts or states of affairs. On this view, when we say that some state of affairs is merely possible, what we mean is that things could have been different in a certain way from the way they actually are. We don't mean that there is some combination of objects that in the actual world has a weak kind of being, but which could have had a stronger kind of being.[3]

The upshot of this is that there are no such things as meanings of false atomic sentences. Such sentences are meaningful, but what it is for such a sentence to be meaningful is not for it to stand for, or express, any entity which is its meaning. Rather, an atomic sentence is meaningful if and only if objects in the world could have been arranged in a way corresponding to the way that the names in the sentences are arranged. To know the meaning of an atomic sentence is not to be acquainted with some abstract entity—a meaning, a proposition, or a possible state of affairs. Rather, it is to know what the world would have to be like if the sentence were to be true. This idea—that a theory of meaning does not require meanings as entities, and that to understand a sentence is to know the conditions under which it is true—was, in time, to become an enormously influential idea for philosophers and theorists of language. It is noteworthy that it seems to have been given its first systematic development in the *Tractatus*.

This brings us to Wittgenstein's views about truth. An atomic sen-

---

[3] This manner of speaking seems to commit one to "ways things (e.g., the universe) could have been," and "ways objects could have been combined," which, arguably, are themselves entities of a kind—possible states of the world (sometimes misleadingly called "possible worlds"), and possible states of affairs ("possible facts"). Although this point tends to undercut Wittgenstein's seeming denial that there really are such things, he does not pursue it. Instead, he seems to have preferred to speak this way without recognizing its apparent ontological commitments.

tence is true if and only if it corresponds to an atomic fact. This will be so just in case the objects named in the sentence really are combined in the way they are represented as combining by the way the names in the sentences are combined. In short, an atomic sentence is true if and only if objects in the world really are as the sentence says they are; otherwise the sentence is false. What about non-atomic sentences? For Wittgenstein, the truth or falsity of non-atomic sentences is always determined by the truth or falsity of atomic sentences. Thus, he sees no need to posit non-atomic facts. For example, consider negation. Let us take as an illustration the atomic sentence *Lab* (which, for the sake of argument, we may imagine says that a is to the left of b). The negation, ~*Lab*, of this sentence is true iff the original sentence, *Lab*, is not true—i.e., iff there is **no fact** consisting of a being to the left of b. In order to explain the truth of the negative sentence, you don't need to say that there is a fact in the world to which it corresponds. Rather, its truth consists in its **not** corresponding to any facts.

In effect, Wittgenstein adopts a two-stage theory of meaning and truth. At stage 1, atomic sentences are said to stand for possible states of affairs the actual existence of which would make them true.[4] At stage 2, the truth and meaning of non-atomic sentences is explained in terms of the truth and meaning of atomic sentences. There is no possible state of affairs that a truth-functionally compound sentence stands for, the actual existence of which would make it true. To know the meaning of a negative sentence ~S is to know the meaning of S, and to know what it is to apply the negation operation to a sentence. The negation operator doesn't name an object in the world, and ~S doesn't picture or correspond to a fact, when it is true. To know the meaning of ~S is not to correlate **it** with a possible state of affairs. Rather, it is to correlate it with S in a certain specific way, where S, in turn, is correlated with a possible state of affairs (if S is atomic). A similar story can be told for other truth-functionally compound sentences.

The general picture developed in the *Tractatus* is one in which atomic facts are all the facts there are. Different combinations of possible atomic facts constitute different possible worlds (ways the universe could be). There is nothing in any possible world over and above the atomic facts that exist in that world. We can spell out what this means a little more precisely by looking at things from the perspective of lan-

[4] Are there or are there not such merely possible states of affairs. Here we have an example, discussed in the previous footnote, of the Wittgensteinian tendency to want to have it both ways.

guage. Let A be the set of all atomic sentences, and let f be an assignment of truth values to members of A. For each sentence S in A, f assigns S either truth or falsity. The set of sentences in A to which f assigns truth represents one complete possible world. If we had a different assignment, f′, the set of sentences to which f′ assigned truth would represent a different possible world. Finally, consider every possible assignment of truth values to members of A—i.e., every possible way of distributing truth and falsehood among the atomic sentences. One of these ways will assign truth to every atomic sentence, one will assign falsity to every atomic sentence, and for every possible combination between these two extremes, there will be an assignment that gives that combination of truth values to the sentences in A. The doctrines of the *Tractatus* maintain (i) that each possible assignment represents a genuine possible world (a way the universe really could be, or could have been) and (ii) that each possible world is represented by one possible assignment.

With this in mind, suppose that S is some non-atomic sentence. Since we know that there are no non-atomic facts, we know that S's truth or falsity cannot consist in its correspondence, or lack of correspondence, with a non-atomic fact. Rather, S's truth or falsity must be determined by which atomic facts exist; or to put it another way, S's truth or falsity must be determined by which atomic sentences are true, and which are false. Wittgenstein expressed this by enunciating the startlingly strong and far-reaching doctrine that **every proposition (meaningful sentence) is a truth function of atomic propositions**. According to this doctrine, any assignment of truth values to all the members of the set A of meaningful atomic sentences (propositions) automatically determines the truth values of every genuine proposition (meaningful sentence). Moreover, Wittgenstein seemed to think that to know the meaning of any logically complex sentence is to know how its truth or falsity is determined from atomic sentences.[5]

[5] Two pitfalls to be avoided by anyone who adopts this approach are worth noting. First, if understanding meaning is to be explained by knowledge of truth conditions, then the notion of truth must not itself presuppose meaning, and the claim made by '*S*' *is true* cannot be taken to be identical with, or trivially or obviously equivalent to, the claim made by S itself; otherwise one gets the absurd result that knowing that snow is white iff snow is white is sufficient for knowing that 'snow is white' is true iff snow is white, and hence for knowing the truth conditions, and thereby the meaning, of 'snow is white'. Second, the truth functional connectives cannot themselves be defined in terms of truth and falsity, since any such definition—e.g., ~*S* is true iff S is not true—will end up presupposing one or more of the connectives to be defined. Thus, at least some truth-functional connectives must be primitives. It is not at all clear that Wittgenstein himself avoided these errors.

That is the general picture. I will next say a word about how Wittgenstein filled in the details of how complex sentences are analyzed in terms of atomic sentences. Here it is helpful to begin with a brief review of Russell's approach, so we can contrast it with Wittgenstein's.

Wittgenstein's System of Logic

In Russellian logic, we start with atomic formulas—e.g., *Fa* and *Fx*. Complex formulas are constructed out of simpler formulas in two ways: (i) we can apply truth-functional operators—$\sim$, &, v, $\to$, $\leftrightarrow$—to get formulas like *(Ga & Hab) v $\sim$ (Px $\to$ Qy)*; and (ii) we can apply the operations of existential and universal quantification to get sentences like $\exists x\ Fx$ and $\forall x\ Fx$. In Russell's logic some formulas involve both sorts of complexity—e.g., $\forall x\ (Fx \to Gx)$. This sentence is constructed from the atomic formulas *Fx* and *Gx*, by **first** using the truth-functional operator '$\to$' and **then** adding the universal quantifier. The order in which these operations take place makes a difference. If we reversed the order, by first applying universal generalization to the atomic sentences and then connecting these with the truth-functional operator '$\to$' for conditionals, we would get a different and non-equivalent formula, *($\forall x\ Fx \to \forall x\ Gx$)*. So, for Russell, complex formulas are built up from atomic formulas by finitely many applications of truth-functional—$\sim$, &, v, $\to$, $\leftrightarrow$—and quantificational—$\forall x$, $\exists x$—operators. Some compound sentences involve both kinds of operators, and the order in which the operators are applied in constructing a sentence makes a difference to what it says.

Wittgenstein's logic was designed with an eye to getting essentially the same results as Russell, but by different means. First, Wittgenstein generalized the notion of a truth-functional operator. Whereas Russell had $\sim$, &, v, $\to$, $\leftrightarrow$, Wittgenstein had a single operator, *N*, for joint negation. Unlike Russell's truth-functional operators, which always applied either to a single formula—as in *$\sim$S*—or to a pair of formulas—as in *(A&B)*—Wittgenstein's operator *N* can be applied to any number of formulas—*N(A), N(A,B), N(A,B,C)* . . . —to produce a complex formula that is true iff all the formulas it is applied to are false. Second, Wittgenstein adopted a system of quantification different from Russell's. Whereas Russell's logic had quantifiers—$\forall x$, $\exists x$—which are not themselves truth-functional operators, Wittgenstein's logic eliminated quantifiers as separate operators. His idea was that the work of quantifiers could be taken over by further generalizing the operator N so that, in principle, it could be applied even to infinite collections of formulas. For example, in Wittgenstein's system, $N(Fx)$ is a sentence that is true just in case every sentence $N(Fa)$, $N(Fb)$, $N(Fc)$, . . . that results from replacing the variable x with a name of an object (one sentence for each object) is true. In short, Wittgenstein tried to develop a system in which every genuine proposition could be constructed by starting with simple atomic propositions (sentences) and applying the single truth-functional operator N.

In laying out this system in the *Tractatus*, Wittgenstein did not fully specify all the details needed to get the result he desired. However, his idea can be carried through by supplementing his explicit remarks with certain additions.[6] What follows is a brief sketch of how this is done.

THE LANGUAGE

1. Atomic formulas are n place predicates followed by n names or variables.

2a. If $F_1, \ldots, F_n$ are formulas, $(F_1, \ldots, F_n)$ is a set representative.

  b. If G is a formula in which the variable v has a free occurrence, then $(v[G])$ is a set representative.

  c. Nothing else is a set representative.

3. If S is a set representative, NS is a formula. (Nothing else is a formula.)

4. A sentence is a formula in which all occurrences of variables are bound. (When a variable v is used to form a set representative in the manner of (2b), it binds all free occurrences of v within G. Occurrences not bound in this way are free.)

TRUTH CONDITIONS

1. An atomic **sentence** is true iff its predicate applies to the objects named by its logically proper names. (Note that in order for an atomic formula to be a sentence, it cannot contain any variables.)

---

[6] This is shown in S. Soames, "Generality, Truth Functions, and Expressive Capacity in the *Tractatus*," *Philosophical Review* 92:4 (1983), 573–89.

2. A sentence *NS* is true iff all **sentences** corresponding to the set representative S are false.

3a. If S = *(v[G])*, then a sentence corresponds to S iff it arises from G by substituting occurrences of a single name for all free occurrences of v in G.

b. If S = $(F_1, \ldots, F_n)$, then a **sentence** corresponds to S iff it is one of the F_i's.

EXAMPLES OF RUSSELLIAN SENTENCES
AND THEIR TRACTARIAN EQUIVALENTS

~P	N(P)
~P & ~Q	N(P, Q)
P & Q	N(N(P), N(Q))
P v Q	N(N(P, Q))
P & ~Q	N(N(P), Q)
~(P & ~Q)	N(N(N(P), Q))
P → Q	N(N(N(P), Q))
~P v Q	N(N(N(P), Q))
~∃x Fx	N(x[Fx])
∃x Fx	N(N(x[Fx]))
~∃x~Fx	N(x[N(Fx)])
∀x Fx	N(x[N(Fx)])
~∃x (Fx & Gx)	N(x[N(N(Fx), N(Gx))])
∃x (Fx & Gx)	N(N(x[N(N(Fx), N(Gx))]))
∃x (Fx & ~Gx)	N(N(x[N(N(Fx), Gx)]))
~∃x (Fx & ~Gx)	N(x[N(N(Fx), Gx)])
~∃x~(Fx → Gx)	N(x[N(N(Fx), Gx)])
∀x (Fx → Gx)	N(x[N(N(Fx), Gx)])
∀y ∃x(Rxy)	N(y[N(x[Rxy])])

Sample Explanation:

'N(y[N(x[Rxy])])' is true iff each of the following is false: (i) 'N(x[Rxa])', (ii) 'N(x[Rxb])', (iii) 'N(x[Rxc])', and so on, one sentence for each object. That will be the case iff (i) '~∃x Rxa' is false, (ii) '~∃x Rxb' is false, (iii) '~∃x Rxc' is false, and so on, one of these statements for each object. That in turn will be the case iff (i) '∃x Rxa' is true, (ii) '∃x Rxb' is true, (iii) '∃x Rxc' is true, and so on, one such statement for each object. But that is the case iff for every object y it is true that ∃x Rxy—i.e., iff '∀y ∃x(Rxy)' is true.[7]

Wittgenstein's General Logical Doctrines

After this brief technical excursus, we can now return to our discussion of Wittgenstein's general logical doctrines. Earlier I mentioned that according to the *Tractatus*, all genuine propositions—i.e., all genuinely meaningful sentences—are truth functions of atomic sentences (propositions). If this is so, then any assignment of truth values to all the atomic propositions will automatically determine the truth values of all other propositions. The specific way in which this is supposed to be achieved involves repeated applications of the generalized truth-functional operator *N*, in accordance with the rules of Wittgenstein's system.[8] For our purposes, the details of how the construction is supposed to proceed in particular cases usually won't matter. The general doctrines are what are most important.

With this in mind, we define three elementary logical notions.

- A proposition S is a *tautology* (logical truth) iff every assignment of truth values to atomic propositions makes S true. (We will say that a proposition is *logically necessary* iff it is a tautology.)

---

[7] It should be noted that the Russellian quantificational sentences and their Wittgensteinian counterparts are logically equivalent in the sense of having the same truth values in every domain. However, there are differences between the two systems in that whereas Russellian logic defines logical notions like *logical truth* and *logical consequence* in terms of truth in all possible domains, no matter what the size; the system of the *Tractatus* presupposes a fixed domain. This leads to important differences that we will explore later.

[8] For more on this see "Generality, Truth Functions, and Expressive Capacity in the *Tractatus*," pp. 585–88.

- A proposition S is a *contradiction* iff every assignment of truth values to atomic propositions makes S false. (We will say that a proposition is *logically impossible* iff it is a contradiction.)

- A proposition S is *logically contingent* iff S is neither a tautology nor a contradiction.

Using these notions, we now pose a series of questions. What is the relation between necessity and logical necessity? What is the relation between impossibility and logical impossibility? What is the relation between contingency and logical contingency?

We can answer these questions by recalling certain basic assumptions that Wittgenstein makes about the relation between atomic propositions and possible worlds (i.e., ways the universe could be, or could have been).

A1. Atomic propositions are contingent (true in some possible worlds and false in others).

A2. Each atomic proposition is independent of all other atomic propositions; it is possible for it to be true (or to be false) no matter what truth values the others have.

A3. A possible world is nothing over and above a collection of possible atomic facts.

It follows from these assumptions that every assignment of truth values to atomic propositions determines a possible world, and that every possible world corresponds to some assignment of truth values to atomic propositions. In fact, there is a one-to-one correspondence between assignments of truth values to members of the set of atomic propositions, on the one hand, and genuine possible worlds—i.e., ways the universe really could be, or could have been—on the other. This provides us with answers to our previous questions.

- A proposition S is necessary—i.e., S is true in all possible worlds in the sense that S would have been true no matter which possible state the universe had been in—iff S is logically necessary (and hence a tautology).

- A proposition S is impossible—i.e., S is false in all possible worlds in the sense that S would have been false no matter which possible state the universe had been in—iff S is logically impossible (and hence a contradiction).

- A proposition is contingent—i.e., S is true in some possible worlds and false in others in the sense that had the universe been in certain possible states, S would have been true, while had the universe been in different possible states, S would have been false—iff S is logically contingent.

According to Wittgenstein, logically necessary propositions and logically impossible propositions are in a certain sense degenerate propositions. We can see what this means by looking more closely at tautologies. Since these sentences are true in all possible worlds, they don't give us any information about the actual state of the world that distinguishes it from any other possible state of the world. Thus, in a certain sense, they don't give us any information about how things **are**, as opposed to how they could be. This leads Wittgenstein to claim that they don't **say** anything. Tautologies are simply the result of having a symbol system that includes truth-functional operators. You need the truth functions in order to say things like *The world is not so and so*, and *The world is either such and such or so and so.* But once you have truth-functional operators, tautologies will result from combining them in certain admissible ways.

According to Wittgenstein, the truth of tautologies is not due to the existence of necessary facts. There are no necessary facts in the world for tautologies to correspond to. Tautologies are nothing more than artifacts of our symbol system. When you recognize, for example, that *(A v ~ A)* and *((A & (A → B)) → B)* are tautologies, you are not grasping metaphysically necessary facts; you are just seeing something about how the truth-functional operators work. In the case of the second of these two tautologies, one might put this by saying that when you grasp the tautology, you see that our symbolism is such that B follows from A, and *(A → B)*. Of course, the tautology doesn't say that; it doesn't say "our symbol system is such that B follows from the formulas A and *(A → B)*." According to Wittgenstein, the tautology itself doesn't **say** anything. However, its status as a tautology is due to what it **shows** about how the symbols for truth functions work.[9]

---

[9] Here I use the psychologically simpler Russellian, rather than Tractarian, symbolism to illustrate Wittgenstein's general logical points. I will continue to do so except when some point of significance depends on Wittgenstein's special symbolism.

Since tautologies are products of the symbolism, it would seem desirable if one could always tell whether or not a proposition was a tautology just be looking at how it is symbolized. Wittgenstein thought that one could always do this. This brings us to the Tractarian doctrine that logical necessity is always determinable by form alone. In order to understand this doctrine, we need to consider more carefully what Wittgenstein meant by it.

One thing he may have meant by it is that there is a purely mechanical **decision procedure** which, when applied to any proposition, will always tell us (after a finite number of steps) whether or not it is a tautology. Now, in fact, the logical system that Wittgenstein used as his initial model—namely the propositional calculus—has precisely this property. It is a logical system in which every proposition is either atomic, or the result of **finitely** many applications of truth-functional operators to **finitely** many atomic propositions. There are no quantifiers or any other means of expressing generality in the propositional calculus. Rather all formulas are either single sentence letters (the atomic propositions) or constructed from finitely many such formulas by finitely many applications of truth-functional operations. For example, the sentence $((A \mathrel{\&} (A \to B)) \to B)$ is constructed from two atomic propositions A and B by three applications of truth-functional operators. All the propositions of the calculus are like this.

The simplest and most natural decision procedure that will tell us whether this, or any other proposition of the propositional calculus, is a tautology is called *the truth-table method*. It is illustrated by the following truth table.

A	B	((A	&	(A	→	B))	→	B)
T	T	T	*T*	T	*T*	T	T	T
T	F	T	*F*	T	*F*	F	T	F
F	T	F	*F*	F	*T*	T	T	T
F	F	F	*F*	F	*T*	F	T	F

Each row in the table represents a possible assignment of truth values to the two atomic propositions in the formula. Since there are four such assignments, the table has four rows. Each truth value on a row is the truth value of a sub-formula of the entire formula, given the assignment to A and B at the left of the row. Truth values of truth-functionally compound formulas are listed under the truth-functional connective used in constructing that formula out of its parts. The **main** truth-functional connective of the formula is the second occurrence of the '→'. (The formula as a whole is a conditional the consequent of which is B, and the antecedent of which is $(A \& (A \to B))$.) The boldface truth value under that main connective on each row gives the truth value of the whole formula determined by the assignment to the atomic formulas at the left of the row. Since the truth value under the main connective is **T** on every row, the entire formula is true on every possible assignment to the atomic propositions it contains. Thus, it is a tautology. Its truth is a matter of logic, since no matter how truth values are assigned to its atomic parts, the formula as a whole comes out true. This method works for all propositions of the propositional calculus. To employ it for any given sentence S, one just writes out the truth table for S. When one is finished, one looks to see if one has *T's* in every line under the main connective. If one does, then S is a tautology. If one doesn't, then it isn't.

The logical system in the *Tractatus* is like the propositional calculus in some ways, and unlike it in others. It is like the propositional calculus in that every proposition is (in a certain sense) a truth function of atomic propositions. It is **unlike** the propositional calculus in two respects. First, in the propositional calculus, each sentence is a truth function of finitely many atomic propositions. In the *Tractatus*, some sentences—indeed, any that contain variables—are truth functions of a potential **infinity** of atomic propositions. Second, in the propositional calculus, each sentence is constructed by applying at most finitely many truth-functional operations to other sentences in the system. However, in the Tractarian system, some sentences, e.g., $N(y[N(x[Rxy])])$ and $N(x[N(N(Fx), N(Gx))])$, involve a potential **infinity** of applications of the truth-functional operator N to other sentences. For example, consider the first of these sentences, $N(y[N(x[Rxy])])$. It arises from applying N to each of the potential infinity of sentences: (i) '$N(x[Rxa])$', (ii) '$N(x[Rxb])$', (iii) '$N(x[Rxc])$', and so on until we have one sentence of this sort for each of the potential infinity of objects a, b, c, d, e, ... Moreover, the same is true for each member of this series. For example, (i) '$N(x[Rxa])$' arises from applying N to each of the potential infinity of statements 'Raa', 'Rba', 'Rca', 'Rda', and so on. Thus, the original sentence $N(y[N(x[Rxy])])$ arises from applying N to a potential infinity of propositions each of which arises from applying N to a potential infinity of propositions. Obviously, there is no way of writing down a truth table for such a sentence.

Because of this, the truth-table method cannot always be applied to the sentences in the Tractarian system. Nevertheless, Wittgenstein appears to have thought that his system was similar enough to the propositional calculus that it should be possible to construct a decision procedure for it. That is, he appears to have thought that whether or not a sentence was a tautology in his system was in principle decidable by mechanical means. If so, however, he was wrong. A little over a decade after the *Tractatus* was written, the mathematician and philosopher Alonzo Church proved that no formal decision procedure for determining logical truth is possible for standard systems of Russellian logic, or indeed for any system in which one moves beyond the propositional calculus by adding the full power of quantifiers, multiple variables, and 2-place predicates or higher to the system, as in Russellian logic, or, equivalently, by allowing sentences to be the result of infinitely many applications of truth-functional operations to infinitely many atomic sentences, as in the system of logic in the *Tractatus*. So if what Wittgenstein had in mind by his doctrine that all logical necessity is determinable by form alone was that there is a formal decision procedure for determining whether an arbitrary sentence of his ideal logical language is logically true, then he was pretty clearly mistaken.[10]

There is, however, a weaker interpretation of the doctrine that all logical necessity is determinable by form alone that is worth examining in its own right. This interpretation is based on another mathematical theorem about standard Russellian logic that was proven by Kurt

[10] There is a debate about this which is complicated by the fact that although Wittgenstein seems to have intended to sketch a system with the full power of standard Russellian logic, the details concerning variables and generality explicitly provided in the *Tractatus* are sufficient only for a system that is expressively much weaker than standard Russellian systems. There have been two main responses to this. One, championed by Robert Fogelin in chapter 6 of the 2nd edition of *Wittgenstein*, interprets him as committed only to the weaker system, which allows a formal decision procedure for logical truth. The other, advocated independently by Peter Geach (in "Wittgenstein's Operator 'N'," *Analysis* 41 [1981], and "More on Wittgenstein's Operator 'N'," *Analysis* 42 [1982] and by me (in "Generality, Truth Functions, and Expressive Capacity in the *Tractatus*"; see in particular sections III and IV), argues that Wittgenstein should be seen as advancing a system with the power of the one presented in the text above. Despite the fact that he didn't fill in all the details, Wittgenstein's descriptions of generality and the operator 'N' are consistent with the treatment given here, which, I believe, is needed to overcome what would otherwise be absurd restrictions on expressive power—especially when one remembers that the system was intended to express all meaningful propositions. (E.g., without filling in such details, one cannot express such simple sentences as $\forall y \, \exists x(Rxy)$, $\exists x(Fx \,\&\, Gx)$ or even $\exists x \neg Fx$ in the Tractarian system.) Although this interpretation makes Wittgenstein vulnerable to the criticism that he wrongly took his system to be decidable, his error is understandable, since Church's theorem had not yet been proven, and was revolutionary, from the perspective of the time that he was writing the *Tractatus*.

Gödel about a decade after the *Tractatus*. The doctrine may be stated as follows: **There is a sound, complete, effective positive test for logical truth in standard Russellian systems**. That is, there is a purely mechanical test which has the following characteristics: (i) whenever you give it a sentence that is a logical truth, it will correctly tell you that it is a logical truth after a finite number of steps; (ii) whenever you give it a sentence that isn't a logical truth, it will either correctly tell you that it isn't a logical truth or it will work forever without telling you anything. Another way to put this is as follows: Every Russellian logical truth can be **proven** in a finite number of steps on the basis of its logical form alone. However, if you are trying to prove a sentence and haven't yet succeeded, then there is no general way of knowing whether you will later be able to prove it, or whether it is not provable at all.

Since we have shown how Russell's truth-functional and quantificational operators can be correlated with those in Wittgenstein's system, it might seem natural to suppose that this important logical result would carry over to Wittgenstein's system. Although there is a sense in which that is right, there is also a hitch worth noticing. Standard Russellian logical truth and Wittgensteinian logical truth are defined in somewhat different ways.

> A sentence is a **Russellian logical truth** iff it comes out true no matter what its names refer to, no matter what its predicates apply to, and no matter what objects are chosen for its quantifiers to range over.
>
> A sentence is a **logical truth in the system of the *Tractatus*** iff it comes out true in all possible Tractarian states of affairs—that is, in all states of affairs in which the basic metaphysical simples have been combined in any arbitrary way. This is equivalent to the claim that a sentence is a logical truth in the system of the *Tractatus* iff it comes out true no matter what combinations of metaphysical simples its predicates apply to, and no matter which metaphysical simples its logically proper names refer to, so long as every name refers to a simple, and every simple has a name. (We also follow Wittgenstein in assuming that there is no predicate for identity in the language. More on this below.)

This definition of Tractarian logical truth is isomorphic to the definition of Russellian logical truth except for one significant feature. In the

Tractarian system we have a fixed domain of objects—the metaphysical simples—that are present throughout all possible Tractarian states of affairs. In the Russellian system we don't have this. Russellian logical truths must come out true no matter what domain of objects is chosen for the quantifiers to range over. By contrast, Wittgensteinian logical truths must come out true in every interpretation involving a fixed domain of objects—namely, the class of actual metaphysical simples, no matter what they turn out to be.

It follows from this that all Russellian logical truths are Tractarian logical truths. However, strictly speaking, there might be Tractarian logical truths that are not Russellian logical truths—sentences true in all interpretations in which the domain of quantification consists of all actually existing objects, but not true in some interpretations with other domains. Thus, for all we know, it might turn out that all Russellian logical truths are provable on the basis of their form alone, even though not all Tractarian logical truths are provable on the basis of their form alone.

In fact, there is some reason to think that this possibility is borne out. For each number n, we can construct a sentence that is true in all interpretations that have at least n objects.

L. $\exists x\, \exists y\, (x \neq y)$, $\exists x\, \exists y\, \exists z\, (x \neq y\; \&\; x \neq z\; \&\; y \neq z)$, ...

Since, in the Russellian system, the domain of quantification can be of **any size**, none of the sentences in this list are Russellian logical truths. However, since in the Wittgensteinian system, all the domains contain the same metaphysical simples, and so have the same size, there is a danger that many of these sentences might end up being classified as Tractarian logical truths. To see this, we reason as follows: Suppose there are at least two basic metaphysical simples. Then these simples will exist in all possible Tractarian states of affairs. The first sentence on the list will be true in all such states of affairs, since it says that there are at least two objects. Thus, it will qualify as a Tractarian tautology, or truth of logic. Similarly, suppose that there are at least three basic metaphysical simples. Then they will exist in all possible Tractarian states of affairs, and hence the first **two** sentences on the list will qualify as Tractarian logical truths. The same reasoning can be produced for every n. Thus, whatever the number of actual metaphysical simples turns out to be, all sentences in the list up to and including the one corresponding to that number will turn out to be Tractarian tautologies. But surely, there is no **interesting** sense in which their truth is determinable by examining their form alone.[11]

Thus, we have a *prima facie* problem for this interpretation of Wittgenstein's doctrine that all necessity is logical necessity, which, in turn, is always determinable by form alone. However, there is a mitigating factor here that might, at first, seem to prevent the problem from arising. At the time he wrote the *Tractatus*, Wittgenstein held that identity should **not** be expressed as a predicate. Instead, he adopted the convention that different variables should stand for different objects, as should different names. Although the topic involves some complications that we need not go into, the following passage gives the general idea.

5.53   Identity of the object I express by identity of the sign and not by means of a sign of identity. Difference of the objects by difference of the signs.

5.5301   That identity is not a relation between objects is obvious. . . .

5.5303   Roughly speaking: to say of *two* things that they are identical is nonsense, and to say of *one* thing that it is identical with itself is to say nothing.

5.531   I write therefore not "F(a,b) & a = b", but "F(a,a)" (or "F(b,b)"). And not "F(a,b) &~ a = b", but "F(a,b)".

5.532   And analogously: not "(∃x,y)[F(x,y) &x = y]", but "(∃x)F(x,x)"; and not "(∃x,y)[F(x,y) &~x = y]", but "(∃x,y) F(x,y)".

5.5321   Instead of "∀x(Fx → x = a)" we therefore write e.g., "[(∃x)Fx → Fa & ~ (∃x,y)(Fx & Fy))]". And the proposition "*only* one x satisfies "F( )" reads: "[(∃x)Fx &~ (∃x,y) (Fx & Fy)]".

5.533   The identity sign is therefore not an essential constituent of logical notation.

[11] Of course there could be an oracle that was built into the sound, complete, effective positive test for tautology that simply specified the number of objects, but such an oracle would be epistemologically useless to us, since we have no way of distinguishing truth-telling oracles from those that tell falsehoods.

5.534 And we see that apparent propositions like: "a = a",
       "(a = b & b = c) → a = c", "∀x(x = x)", "∃x(x = a)",
       etc. cannot be written in a correct logical notation at all.

5.535 So all problems disappear which are connected with such
       pseudo-propositions. . . .

By barring the identity predicate, Wittgenstein bars the sentences listed
in L, each one of which says something of the sort *There are at least n
objects*. It might seem that in doing this, he saves his doctrine that all
logical necessity is determinable by form alone (on the interpretation
we are considering).[12] Certainly, if these sentences **were** allowed in the
language, then many of them **would** turn out to be Tractarian tautologies, even though there is no reasonable sense in which this fact about
them would be determinable from their form alone.

But this impression appears to be mistaken. Given Wittgenstein's
doctrine that different names, and different variables, stand for different objects, one can construct sentences in the Tractarian system that
pose the same problem for his doctrine as the sentences listed in L. For
example, consider the new list L*, where the sentences are understood
to be in accord with Wittgenstein's dictum that different variables in a
sentence are to stand for different objects.[13]

L*. $\exists x \, \exists y \, (R_2xy \, v \sim R_2xy)$, $\exists x \, \exists y \, \exists z \, (R_3xyz \, v \sim R_3xyz)$, ...

The first sentence on this list is true in all Tractarian worlds in which at
least two simples exist. The second sentence is true in all Tractarian
worlds in which at least three simples exist, and so on, just as in L.
Because of this, it seems that Wittgenstein's doctrine that all necessary
truth is logical truth, and all logical truth is determinable from form
alone, cannot be sustained in anything like the sense in which he intended. In fact, what we see here appears to be a conflict between

---

[12] In so doing he was also saving the doctrine from being counterexemplified by truths of
the form $a = b$ and $b \neq c$, since the doctrines of the *Tractatus* can plausibly be taken to have
the result that if these are true, then they are necessarily true—even though their truth is not
discoverable from their form alone. In this connection it is worth noting that $a = b$, $b = c$,
$a = c$, do not in any case satisfy the Tractarian constraints on atomic propositions, since the
falsity of the final proposition is not compatible with the truth of the first two. As we have
seen, it is a doctrine of the *Tractatus* that the truth or falsity of any atomic proposition is
compatible with the truth or falsity of any other atomic propositions. Hence, these cannot all
be atomic; and if one of them isn't, then surely none is.

[13] A similar result could be gotten from the list $\exists x \, \exists y \, [(Ax \, v \sim Ax) \, \& \, (Ay \, v \sim Ay)]$, $\exists x \, \exists y \, \exists z$
$[(Ax \, v \sim Ax) \, \& \, (Ay \, v \sim Ay) \, \& \, (Az \, v \sim Az)]$, ...

Wittgenstein's doctrines of metaphysical atomism and his doctrines about the logical and linguistic source of all necessary truth.

This is significant because it threatens what many philosophers took to be the striking simplicity and plausibility of Wittgenstein's conception of the relationship between metaphysical notions of necessity and possibility, on the one hand, and the logical notions of tautology (logical necessity) and consistency (logical possibility) on the other. This conception is summed up in three important Tractarian doctrines:

(i) All necessity is linguistic necessity, in the sense that it is the result of our system of representing the world, rather than the world itself. There are sentences or propositions that are necessarily true, but there are no necessary facts for them to correspond to. Rather their necessity is due to the meanings of words (and is therefore knowable apriori).

(ii) All linguistic necessity is logical necessity.

(iii) All logical necessity is determinable by form alone.

The first of these doctrines, that all necessity is linguistic necessity, dominated philosophical thought on this topic for roughly the next fifty years, and was important to the conception of philosophy as linguistic analysis that flourished during that period. The second and third doctrines, while not without influence, were recognized to be potentially problematic much sooner.

CHAPTER 11

THE TRACTARIAN TEST OF INTELLIGIBILITY
AND ITS CONSEQUENCES

The Intelligibility Test

At the end of the last chapter, we uncovered a problem with Wittgenstein's identification of all necessity with logical necessity, discoverable by an examination of logical form alone. As we will see, this problem points to something deeper, involving the philosophically ambitious manner in which Wittgenstein used his doctrines about meaning. According to the *Tractatus*, every meaningful statement S falls into one or the other of two categories: either (i) S is contingent (true in some possible worlds and false in others), in which case S is both a truth function of atomic propositions and something that can be known to be true or false only by empirical investigation, or (ii) S is a tautology or contradiction that can be known to be such by purely formal calculations. The paradigmatic cases of meaningful sentences for Wittgenstein are those in the first category. The sentences in the second category are included as meaningful because they are the inevitable product of the rules governing the logical vocabulary used in constructing the sentences of the first category. For Wittgenstein, tautologies and contradictions don't state anything, or give any information about the world. However, their truth or falsity can be calculated, and understanding them reveals something about our symbol system. Thus, they can be regarded as meaningful in an extended sense.

However, many sentences do not fit neatly into either category—for example, the most fundamental claims of ethics, aesthetics, and traditional philosophy. Since typically these sentences purport to be necessary truths, and since they don't seem to be capable of being known on the basis of empirical observation, they appear not to fit into Wittgenstein's first category. Since they don't seem to be logical tautologies or contradictions, the truth or falsity of which can be determined simply by examining their form, they appear not to fit into his second category either. Given that Wittgenstein's doctrine purports to state the conditions that must be fulfilled in order for a sentence to be meaningful at all, he has little choice but to conclude that the sentences of ethics, aesthetics, and indeed all of traditional philosophy are, strictly speaking, meaningless.

What we have here appears to be a very powerful test, one that consigns huge masses of apparently genuine statements into the category of meaningless sentences. However, before we go too far in drawing radical consequences from the intelligibility test, it is worth noting certain difficulties inherent in applying it in particular cases. Two difficulties stand out immediately. First, Wittgenstein never gives any examples of either metaphysical simples or atomic propositions about them. As we have seen, this is no accident. Central doctrines of the *Tractatus* make it all but impossible to give examples of either, even though those doctrines maintain that metaphysical simples and atomic propositions not only exist, but must exist in order for any of our talk to make sense. This poses a problem when applying the intelligibility test. In the absence of any specification of what the metaphysical simples and atomic propositions are, it is unclear how we are supposed to be able to tell whether propositions drawn from science and ordinary language really are contingent truth functions of atomic propositions. How are we supposed to decide whether propositions like *Uranium atoms are unstable, Space is curved, Heat is molecular motion,* and *Other minds exist* are contingent truth functions of atomic propositions, if we don't know which propositions are atomic?

The second difficulty involved in applying the *Tractatus* test for intelligibility is that we can't reliably apply the test to a sentence unless we know its logical form. However, according to Wittgenstein, the logical forms of the sentences of ordinary language are hidden, and are revealed only on analysis. This is indicated at 4.002, where he elaborates on the hiddenness of logical form, and the difficulty of providing analyses.[1]

    4.002 Man possesses the ability to construct languages capable of expressing every sense, without having any idea how each word has meaning or what its meaning is—just as people speak without knowing how the individual sounds are produced.

        Everyday language is part of the human organism and is no less complicated than it.

        It is not humanly possible to gather immediately from it what the logic of language is.

        Language disguises thought. So much so, that from the outward form of the clothing it is impossible to infer the form of the thought beneath it, because the outward form of the clothing is not designed to reveal the form of the body, but for entirely different purposes.

        The tacit conventions on which the understanding of everyday language depends are enormously complicated.

This doctrine of hiddenness has a central impact on attempts to apply the intelligibility test. If the logical form of a sentence in everyday language is hidden, then, when confronted with a sentence that one suspects must be necessary, if meaningful at all, one may not know how to find out whether its necessity **is** discoverable from its logical form alone. We know from the test that if the sentence is not contingent, but there is no way to determine its necessity from its form alone, then it must be meaningless. However, since its logical form is hidden, or disguised, we may not be able to apply the test. This difficulty may not arise in every case, but it certainly does arise in some, and it is always in the background. Thus, Wittgenstein's test for intelligibility is **not** a definite and unequivocal one.

    Let's try to apply the test to a few examples. First consider the sentence

    1a. If a thing is red (all over), then it isn't green (all over).

---

[1] I here use the Pears and McGuinness translation.

This seems to be a necessary truth, something that couldn't be false. Thus, we may ask, is its necessity determinable from its logical form alone? At first glance, it would seem not to be, since the form of (1a) would seem to be something like (1b) (in Russellian notation), or (1c) (in Tractarian notation); and we certainly can't determine truth from those forms.

1b. $\forall x \, (Rx \rightarrow \sim Gx)$

c. $N(x[N(N(Rx), N(Gx))])$

However, if we say that it is not the case that the necessity of (1a) is the result of its form alone, then Wittgenstein's test will require us to say that it is either meaningless, or merely contingent. Neither result seems correct.

Wittgenstein was aware of this problem, which he discusses at 6.3751. We will concentrate first on the beginning and ending of that section, and then return to the comments he makes in the middle.[2]

> 6.3751 For two colors, e.g., to be at one place in the visual field is impossible, logically impossible, for it is excluded by the logical structure of color.
>
> Let us consider how this contradiction presents itself in physics. Somewhat as follows: that a particle cannot at the same time have two velocities; i.e., that at the same time it cannot be in two places; i.e., that particles that are in different places at the same time cannot be identical.
>
> (It is clear that the logical product of two elementary propositions can neither be a tautology nor a contradiction. The assertion that a point in the visual field has two different colors at the same time, is a contradiction.)

It seems evident from the comments at the beginning and end of this section that Wittgenstein would not want to call a sentence like (1a) either meaningless or contingent. It is just too obvious that it is genuinely necessary, and hence meaningful in his extended sense. This requires him to deny that the statements *x is red* and *x is green* are elementary propositions, and that either (1b) or (1c) represent the real logical form of (1a). In effect, he conveniently invokes the doctrine of hidden logical form, and implicitly suggests that, at the level of hidden logical form, the necessity of (1a) **is** a matter of its form alone.

---

[2] This is from the Ogden translation.

This would be less worrisome if he had given us some hint regarding what the real logical form of (1a) is supposed to be. Some might think that the middle paragraph of 6.3751 provides such a hint: the hint being, I suppose, that the analysis of statements about color is given by the physical theory of color. But whether or not Wittgenstein thought this, it doesn't help with the problem at hand. That problem is to explain color incompatibility in terms of formal, logical impossibility. At most the middle paragraph might be taken to suggest that ordinary color incompatibility can be assimilated to physical impossibility—i.e., the impossibility of (2a).

> 2a. x is at place p at time t and x is also at an entirely different place p′ at time t.

But the apparent logical form of (2a) is just (2b), which is **not** formally contradictory.

> 2b. Lxpt & Lxp′t

Thus, the problem of color incompatibility remains.[3]

This is just one example of a vast and pervasive problem. As (2a) illustrates, ordinary language is full of conceptual incompatibilities or necessities that are not in any obvious way determinable from the manifest linguistic form of the sentences themselves. To solve this problem, Wittgenstein would have to provide analyses in which the purely formal or structural properties of the logical forms of these sentences invariably revealed the conceptual incompatibilities and necessities holding among them. However, he does not give such analyses, and provides few clues about how to come up with them.

Wittgenstein clearly had some inkling of this, as the color incompatibility problem continued to trouble him in the years after he wrote the *Tractatus*. He worked on it more in the late 1920s and in the early 1930s, and in the end he came to believe that it was a counterexample to the doctrines of the *Tractatus* that simply could not be resolved in the Tractarian framework.[4] However, at the time he wrote the *Tractatus*, he was so confident that his general principles must be correct that he thought that problems like the color incompatibility problem must be resolvable. Since (1a) is so obviously both meaningful (in

---

[3] See pp. 91 and 92 of Fogelin, *Wittgenstein*, for further discussion.
[4] See "Some Remarks on Logical Form," *Proceedings of the Aristotelian Society*, supplementary vol. 9 (1929), 162–71.

his extended sense) and necessary, he thought that it must have a logical form that showed it to be a tautology. We can see from this how the Tractarian doctrine of the hiddenness of logical form can be used to protect the test for intelligibility from having undesirable consequences. Of course, this is a weakness of the test, since it leaves a great deal of room for dispute about how it should be applied. Nevertheless, at one time Wittgenstein and others thought that the test could be used to draw powerful philosophical conclusions.

However, the color problem was not the only problem for the Tractarian test of intelligibility, and related doctrines. Another interesting and revealing problem was posed by propositional attitude ascriptions like (3a).

3a. John believes (says/hopes/has proved) that the earth is round.

This sentence has another sentence, *The earth is round*, as one of its constituent parts. According to the *Tractatus*, the only way for a sentence S to have another sentence R as one of its parts, is for S to be a truth function either of R by itself, or of R together with other sentences. It is a central doctrine of the *Tractatus* that all meaningful sentences are constructed by applying **truth-functional** operations to other sentences, and ultimately to atomic sentences. See, e.g., 5.54:[5]

5.54 In the general propositional form propositions occur in a proposition only as bases of the truth-operations.

Since, in the *Tractatus*, the general propositional form is something that tells us how all meaningful propositions are constructed, Wittgenstein is here claiming that the only way for a meaningful sentence S to have another sentence R as a constituent is for R to be one of the propositions to which truth-functional operators are applied in constructing S.

Sentences like (3a) pose a threat to this doctrine. If the doctrine is correct, and if (3a) is genuinely meaningful, then the only way that the sentence *The earth is round* could occur as a constituent of (3a) would be for *The earth is round* to be among the bases of the truth-functional operations used to construct (3a). However, that could be so only if

---

[5] From the Ogden translation. The Pears and McGuinness translation reads: "In the general propositional form propositions occur in other propositions only as bases of truth-operations."

replacing *the earth is round* in (3a) with any other truth would always preserve the truth of (3a). This means that, according to the *Tractatus*, *The earth is round* can be a constituent of the meaningful (3a) only if the result of replacing it with, say, the true sentence *Classical arithmetic is reducible to set theory* preserves the truth of the whole—i.e., only if the truth of (3a) (3b), and (3c) logically guarantees the truth of (3d).

    3b. The earth is round.

      c. Classical arithmetic is reducible to set theory.

      d. John believes (says/hopes/has proved) that classical arithmetic is reducible to set theory.

Since, obviously, the truth of (3d) is **not** logically guaranteed by the truth of (3a–c), the doctrines of the *Tractatus* lead to the result that either (3a) is meaningless, or (3a) is meaningful, but the sentence *The earth is round* is not one of its constituent parts.

    Another way to put the problem is this: (3a) is not an atomic proposition. So, according to the *Tractatus*, it must either be meaningless or a truth-functional compound of other propositions. But it is **not** a truth-functional compound of *The earth is round*, either by itself or together with other propositions. Since it is hard to imagine (3a) being a truth-functional compound of anything else, the doctrines of the *Tractatus* seem to lead to the conclusion that it is meaningless.

    As in the case of color, Wittgenstein was aware of this problem—which he addresses at 5.541 and 5.542. In the immediately preceding section, he has just said, *"In the general propositional form propositions occur in a proposition only as bases of the truth-operations."* He now adds:[6]

    5.541 At first sight it looks as if it were also possible for one proposition to occur in another in a different way.

          Particularly with certain forms of proposition in psychology, such as *A believes that p is the case* and *A has the thought p*, etc.

          For if these are considered superficially, it looks as if the proposition p stood in some kind of relation to an object A.

---

[6] This is from the Pears and McGuinness translation.

(And in modern theory of knowledge (Russell, Moore, etc.) these propositions have actually been construed in this way.)

5.542 It is clear, however, that *A believes that p, A has the thought p*, and *A says p* are of the form *"p" says p*: and this does not involve a correlation of a fact with an object, but rather the correlation of facts by means of the correlation of their objects.

In these passages, Wittgenstein claims that the real logical form of a sentence like (3a) is different from what it first appears to be. In reality, the logical form of any sentence of this sort is something the form (4).

4. "p" says (that) p.

Presumably, this means that the logical form of the specific sentence (3a) is (5).

5. "the earth is round" says (that) the earth is round.

Despite the fact that in the passage Wittgenstein assures us that this *is clear*, his reasoning at this point seems quite obscure. Nevertheless, we may be able to make something of it.[7]

He may have had in mind something like the following: When a person believes something, he constructs a mental picture of a possible state of affairs—some representation of it. The representation is a fact, and the state of affairs represented is a possible fact. Since the one is a representation of the other, the elements in the facts are correlated with one another. In the case of the belief sentence (3a), the expressions in the linguistic fact—i.e., in the sentence "The earth is round"—are correlated with the things in the world that make up the non-linguistic fact of the earth's being round. That, in effect, is what (5) tells us.

Now, Wittgenstein says that (5) is the logical form of (3a). However, it is hard to see how he could have literally meant this—since (5) would remain the same no matter who the believer in (3a) was. In addition, (5) would seem to remain the same even if the agent in (3a) was not described as **believing** that the earth is round, but only as **asserting** that the earth is round, or **wondering** whether the earth is round. Since (5) leaves out both the agent of (3a) and the particular

---

[7] See also chapter 5, section 7, of Fogelin for an illuminating discussion.

attitude—belief—that the agent bears to the representation in (3a), it is hard to see (5) as specifying the total content of (3a). Still, someone might take (5) to be part of the logical form of (3a). For example, one might understand (3a) as saying the agent John has formulated and adopted the attitude of accepting some representation that says that the earth is round; and one might think that the logical form of this claim may contain something like (5) as a part. At any rate, if one did think that, it would be sufficient for some of the points that Wittgenstein was interested in making.

What points are those? At this stage of the discussion, it may seem that we haven't made much progress. It may seem that being told that (5) either is, or is part of, the logical form of (3a) doesn't help with our original problem. After all, the sentence *The earth is round* that occurs in (5) does **not** do so as a truth-functional component. If it did, then we should be able to replace **one** of its occurrences with any other true sentence, without changing the truth value of (5). But if we try this, say by replacing the final occurrence of *the earth is round* in (5) with the sentence *2 + 2 = 4*, we end up with (6), which is false.

6. "the earth is round" says (that) $2 + 2 = 4$.

Since substitution has not preserved truth value, it might be argued that we have the same trouble making the doctrines of the *Tractatus* compatible with the meaningfulness of (5) as we had making them compatible with the meaningfulness of (3a). At a minimum, we haven't been shown how, according to the *Tractatus*, either one can be genuinely meaningful.

So what is Wittgenstein's position? Although the text is open to interpretation, I incline to the view that he accepts the conclusion that propositional attitude ascriptions like (3a) and statements about meaning like (5) are **not** meaningful after all. As I read him, he would claim that a sentence like (5)—which is supposed to be at least part of the analysis of (3a)—attempts to **state** something about the relationship between language and the world. But the relationship between language and the world is something that, according to the *Tractatus*, **cannot** be meaningfully described, or stated, in language; it can only be shown.

In this connection, I draw your attention to 4.12–4.1211.[8]

---

[8] Pears and McGuinness translation.

4.12   Propositions can represent the whole of reality, but they cannot represent what they must have in common with reality in order to be able to represent it—logical form.

In order to be able to represent logical form, we should have to be able to station ourselves with propositions somewhere outside logic, that is to say outside the world.

4.121   Propositions cannot represent logical form: it is mirrored in them.

What finds its reflection in language, language cannot represent.

What expresses *itself* in language, *we* cannot express by means of language.

Propositions *show* the logical form of reality.

They display it.

4.1211   Thus one proposition '*fa*' shows that the object *a* occurs in its sense, two propositions '*fa*' and '*ga*' show that the same object is mentioned in both of them.

If two propositions contradict one another, then their structure shows it; the same is true if one of them follows from the other. And so on.

4.1212   What *can* be shown, *cannot* be said.

Wittgenstein's position in these passages seems to be that we cannot use language to state or describe the relationship between language and the world that allows language to be meaningful, and that makes individual expressions mean what they do.

What should we think of this? Wittgenstein may very well be right in thinking that there is no room for statements about the relationship between language and the world in the rigid system of the *Tractatus*, but he doesn't attempt to give any independent reason to think that the view is plausible. Perhaps it might be suggested on his behalf that to use language you have to already grasp the relation between language and the world that allows your words to have meaning; but once you have grasped that relationship, there is nothing left to state. However, this is not very convincing. All that is established by the observation that in order to understand language one has to grasp the relationship between it and the world is that someone who didn't know any language couldn't learn to use language by being **told** what the relation between language and the world is. Such a person couldn't learn language that way because he couldn't understand the instructions. It is like saying you can't learn to read by reading a book that tells you how to read a book. There is nothing deep in this. Certainly, educational psychologists can discover the elements of the reading process, and write them down for others to read. It is hard to see why the same can't be said for language in general.

To take a simple example, the sentence

7. 'Firenze' names Florence.

seems perfectly meaningful—and true—even though it says something about the relation between language and the world. It is worth noting that if I use the sentence

8. Bill is tall.

to tell you about a certain man's height, then I use the fact that the word 'Bill' names Bill to say something about him. Of course, my remark doesn't **state** the fact that the word 'Bill' names Bill. Rather, Wittgenstein would say that (8) **shows** this. Fine. He might add that no sentence states **all** those facts about its own relation to the world that allow it to say what it does. All right. However, it does **not** follow that no sentence can state **any** of the facts about relations between its expressions and the world that allow it to say what it does. And it does **not** follow that no sentence can state a fact about the relationship between some expression and the world that allows **another** sentence to say what it does. For example, there is no reason to deny that (9) states a fact about the relationship between language and the world that is one of the facts that allows both (8) and (9) to say what they do.

9. 'Bill' refers to Bill.

The upshot of this is that the doctrines of the *Tractatus* lead Wittgenstein to deny that sentences like (3a), (5), (7), and (9) are meaningful, even though all these sentences appear to be perfectly acceptable. There are two ways to look at this: that it shows those sentences to be meaningless, or that it shows that the doctrines of the *Tractatus*, including its test for intelligibility, are seriously flawed. It is hard to believe that there is much to be said for the first of these positions.

The Limits of Intelligibility:
Value, the Meaning of Life, and Philosophy

Consider value statements like *Happiness is good, Friendship is good, Causing pain unnecessarily is wrong,* and *Michelangelo's Pietà is beautiful.* Wittgenstein rejects the view that these are contingent, empirical statements.[9]

6.4   All propositions are of equal value.

6.41   The sense of the world must lie outside the world. In the world everything is as it is, and everything happens as it does happen: *in* it no value exists—and if it did exist, it would have no value.

      If there is any value that does have value, it must lie outside the whole sphere of what happens and is the case. For all that happens and is the case is accidental.

      What makes it non-accidental cannot lie *within* the world, since if it did it would itself be accidental.

      It must lie outside the world.

Wittgenstein doesn't give much by way of reason for rejecting the view that value judgments are contingent. However, the rejection does seem plausible. Philosophers might disagree about the truth or falsity of many statements of value—statements like *Happiness alone is good, Taking an innocent life is always wrong,* and *All other things being equal, lying is wrong*—but it is hard to imagine these statements being true in some possible states of the world and false in others; it is also hard to imagine empirical observation and investigation being needed to find out whether the actual state of the universe is one that makes these statements true, or one that makes them false.[10] But if these value judgments are **not** contingent, they also appear **not** to be tautologies (or contradictions). For one thing, value judgments seem to have a kind of importance to us, to play a role guiding our actions, that tautologies (and contradictions) don't. For another thing, if value

[9] Pears and McGuinness translation.

[10] Of course, not all value statements are necessary and apriori, if true at all. Some, like *Your speeding through a red light was justifiable, since your passenger was hemorrhaging, and would have died, had you not gotten her to the hospital when you did,* are clearly contingent and aposteriori, if true at all. However, since statements like this are not viewed by Wittgenstein as either atomic or truth functions of atomic sentences, they too are regarded as meaningless.

judgments really were analyzable as tautologies (or contradictions), the truth (or falsity) of which must be discoverable by their form alone, then presumably evaluative words like *good, bad, right,* and *wrong* would have to be definable in terms of non-evaluative words. But by the time of the *Tractatus*, G. E. Moore had convinced most analytic philosophers that evaluative words were not definable.

The moral of the story is that in the *Tractatus* sentences containing evaluative words are characterized as being neither contingent, truth functions of atomic propositions, nor tautologies or contradictions. Thus, they are claimed to be, strictly speaking, meaningless. If one person says *Murder is always wrong* and the other says *Murder is sometimes right*, then neither has said anything true, and neither has said anything false. Wittgenstein's point is **not** that we can't find out which one is correct, and which incorrect. His point is also **not** that no one can **prove** his moral or evaluative beliefs to a skeptic. His point is much more radical: since moral and evaluative sentences are meaningless, they don't express propositions; since there are no moral or evaluative propositions for us to believe, we don't have any moral or evaluative beliefs.

> 6.42 So too it is impossible for there to be propositions of ethics.[11]

One can, of course, produce the **words** *Murder is always wrong,* but one will **not** thereby have **said** anything more than if one had produced the words *Procrastination drinks plentitude.*

According to the *Tractatus,* there are no moral statements; there are no moral beliefs, and there are no moral questions or problems. To think otherwise is to be confused about language. Once the workings of language have been laid bare, the traditional philosophical problems of value will not be solved; rather we will see that there never were any real problems there in the first place. From this a slogan was born: The philosophical analysis of language doesn't **solve** philosophical problems of value, it **dissolves** them.

It might seem that someone who characterizes all of ethics and aesthetics as meaningless talk would take the attitude that ethical and aesthetic concerns are insignificant, and unworthy of serious attention. You get the picture of someone who thinks that what is important is giving an accurate factual, or scientific, description of the world. Since values don't fit into that description, they have no importance. That

---

[11] Pears and McGuinness translation.

sort of picture is, I think, often associated with the next group of philosophers we will study, the logical positivists—though even in their case it is an exaggeration.

However, this picture is not associated with Wittgenstein at all, and for good reason. Although both he and the logical positivists thought of the realm of value as lacking in sense, Wittgenstein thought of it as very important non-sense. According to the *Tractatus*, all meaningful statements are either tautologies, contradictions, or contingent statements that describe the way objects in the world are, or at least could be, combined. Although such statements are meaningful, Wittgenstein claimed not to regard them as very interesting or important. What was important and interesting, he thought, was how one lived one's life, what attitude one took towards things, and how one acted. But, according to the *Tractatus*, these are matters about which it is impossible to say, or even to think, anything sensible.[12]

> 6.423 It is impossible to speak about the will in so far as it is the subject of ethical attributes.
>
> And the will as a phenomenon is of interest only to psychology.

> 6.43 If the good or bad exercise of the will does alter the world, it can alter only the limits of the world, not the facts—not what can be expressed by means of language.
>
> In short the effect must be that it becomes an altogether different world. It must, so to speak, wax and wane as a whole.
>
> The world of the happy man is a different one from that of the unhappy man.

Wittgenstein is clearly being metaphorical here. However, one gets some idea of what he is talking about. Consider the case of the happy man, H, and the unhappy man, U. According to Wittgenstein, they might not differ at all in what they know or believe. Both might know all there is to know about science, history, psychology, or any discipline that studies the world. They might believe all the same things about inanimate objects, animals, other people, and even each other. Of course in certain cases they will express their beliefs differ-

---

[12] Pears and McGuinness translation.

ently. When H believes that he is coming down with a cold, he will express this belief with the words *I am coming down with a cold*, whereas U will express that same belief about H using the words *You are coming down with a cold*. Although the words they use are different, their beliefs are the same. Still, H is happy and U is unhappy. H wakes up in the morning filled with anticipation and a sense of well-being. He delights in his surroundings and his activities, and he treats other people in an unfailingly kind and considerate way. U, on the other hand, feels and behaves in just the opposite way. The difference between the two is, as Wittgenstein might say, at the level of value. It has nothing to do with what they think, or believe, or what they know to be true.

The picture Wittgenstein draws is very much at odds with a certain old and venerable conception of philosophy. One traditional way of viewing philosophy has been to see it as a discipline that aspires to be at once the highest science and the deepest religion. As the highest science, its task is to discover the most important and fundamental truths about reality, and the place of human beings in it. As the deepest religion, its task is to discover what true excellence and happiness in human life consist in, and to show us how to achieve them. These goals—describing reality and learning how to live the best life—have been thought by many to be not only compatible, but complementary, and mutually reinforcing. An underlying presupposition of this view is that excellence in the art of living is the result of knowing important truths about reality, oneself, and others. Wittgenstein utterly rejects this thought. The truth about how to live is **not** a deep and difficult mystery for the philosopher, or anyone else, to discover; nor is it a simple matter that we somehow know in advance. Excellence in living is not a matter of truth, knowledge, or belief at all. It is a matter of one's attitude, or response, to life. What attitude one adopts may be the most important thing in life, but it is not a matter of learning any facts.

It is, I think, hard **not** to be sympathetic with this picture, or **not** to find important elements of it suggestive, insightful, and even true—even though that may sound paradoxical from a strictly Tractarian point of view. Much of the picture is distinctively, even uniquely, Wittgensteinian—especially his invitation to mysticism. But there is also something in this outlook that is not unique to Wittgenstein, but rather is quite characteristic of the whole period in analytic philosophy that we are studying. The gulf between (empirical) fact and value that we saw open up with Moore becomes even greater with Wittgenstein, as it does with the logical positivists, and still later non-cognitivists, who were to follow Wittgenstein. Philosophers during this period were **not** reluctant to make far-reaching methodological claims about ethics or other evaluative matters; they were **not** averse to telling us what ethical or evaluative language was, or was not, all about. But they were very reluctant to argue for substantive, controversial, or far-reaching normative theses of any kind, and they were often anxious to sharply distinguish what they thought could be achieved in philosophy from anything of that sort.

Why this attitude was so widely shared during this period is an interesting question. Undoubtedly part of the answer is purely internal to the tradition—a matter of which philosophers, and which doctrines, were the most compelling, and deservedly attracted the most attention. However, part of the answer may have to do with broader cultural currents—the rise of science, the decline of religion, the growth in wealth, the increase in urbanization, and the space for personal autonomy and freedom from traditional constraints that all this created. Whatever the ultimate causes, the absolute gulf between fact and value portrayed in the *Tractatus* was part of this current, including Wittgenstein's own extreme and idiosyncratic take on it all.

To repeat, Wittgenstein adopts the paradoxical view that (i) if a statement is meaningful, then it has nothing to do with value, and is not very significant to life, and (ii) if a statement is significant to the way we should live, then it is meaningless, and does not express anything that can even be thought. These views applied as much to religion, or to anything else connected to the meaning of life, as they did to ethical or other straightforwardly evaluative matters. Wittgenstein elaborates this at 6.5 to 6.521.[13]

> 6.5   When the answer cannot be put into words, neither can the question be put into words.
>
> *The riddle* does not exist.
>
> If a question can be framed at all, it is also *possible* to answer it.
>
> 6.51   Skepticism is *not* irrefutable, but obviously nonsensical, when it tries to raise doubts where no questions can be asked.

---

[13] Pears and McGuinness translation.

For doubt can exist only where a question exists, a question only where an answer exists, and an answer only where something *can be said*.

6.52 We feel that even when all *possible* scientific questions have been answered, the problems of life remain completely untouched. Of course there are then no questions left, and this itself is the answer.

6.521 The solution of the problem of life is seen in the vanishing of the problem.

(Is not this the reason why those who have found after a long period of doubt that the sense of life became clear to them have then been unable to say what constituted that sense?)

For Wittgenstein, ethics, religion, and talk about the meaning of life is relegated to the unsayable. What about philosophy itself? The *Tractatus* is uncompromising about this. Just as the most fundamental ethical claims are neither tautologies nor contingent statements about empirically knowable facts, so philosophical claims are, in general, neither tautological nor contingent statements about empirical facts. Thus, like ethical sentences, they are non-sense. Hence, there are no meaningful philosophical propositions; there are no genuine philosophical questions; and there are no philosophical problems for philosophers to solve. It is not that philosophical problems are so difficult that we can never be sure we have discovered the truth about them. There is no such thing as the truth about them, because there are no philosophical problems.

What then is responsible for the persistence of the discipline of philosophy, and for the illusion that it is concerned with real problems for which answers might be found? The answer, according to Wittgenstein, is linguistic confusion. As he saw it, all the endless disputes in philosophy are due to a single cause—confusion about how language works. If we could ever fully reveal the true workings of language, these confusions would die out, and then we would see the world correctly. And when we did, we would see that there is no place in it for philosophy, just as there is no place for ethics. However, that doesn't mean that there is nothing for philosophers to do now. Certainly there are no propositions the truth of which it is their job to discover. Philosophy cannot properly aim at discovering true propositions; but, it can aim at clarifying the propositions we already have. As we have already noted, Wittgenstein believed that everyday language disguises thought by concealing true logical form. The proper aim of philosophy is to strip away the disguise and illuminate that form.

In articulating these views, the *Tractatus* was a key document in what was later called by some *the linguistic turn in philosophy* (a temporary turn, but more on that later). Wittgenstein makes this clear at 4.11–4.112.[14]

4.11   The totality of true propositions is the whole of natural science (or the whole corpus of the natural sciences).

4.111 Philosophy is not one of the natural sciences.

(The word 'philosophy' must mean something whose place is above or below the natural sciences, not beside them.)

4.112 Philosophy aims at the logical clarification of thoughts.

Philosophy is not a body of doctrine but an activity.

A philosophical work consists essentially of elucidations.

Philosophy does not result in 'philosophical propositions', but rather in the clarification of propositions.

Without philosophy thoughts are, as it were, cloudy and indistinct: its task is to make them clear and to give them sharp boundaries.

According to the *Tractatus*, philosophy is linguistic analysis. Wittgenstein gives a clear statement of what he takes analysis to be in his first post-*Tractatus* paper.[15]

The idea is to express in an appropriate symbolism what in ordinary language leads to endless misunderstandings. That is to say, where ordinary language disguises logical structure, where it allows the formation of pseudo-propositions, where it uses one term in an infinity of different meanings, we must replace it by a symbolism which gives a clear picture of the logical structure, excludes pseudo-propositions, and uses its terms unambiguously.

---

[14] Pears and McGuinness translation .
[15] Wittgenstein, "Some Remarks on Logical Form," p. 163.

This conception of philosophy leads to a natural question about the status of the *Tractatus* itself. It is obvious that in writing the *Tractatus* Wittgenstein did not follow his own advice about philosophy. He did not produce a precise symbolism and then give actual analyses of ordinary language in that symbolism. He did not do philosophy by actually producing the kind of analyses that he thought philosophers ought to produce. Rather, in the *Tractatus*, he practiced a kind of philosophy that his own doctrines characterize as impossible. The *Tractatus* is filled with statements that purport to be neither empirical claims that describe contingent features of the world, nor tautologies the truth of which is determined by their formal structure alone. As a result, the statements of the *Tractatus* can only be judged meaningless by Wittgenstein's own criteria.

Wittgenstein, of course, realized this, as is indicated by the final three sections of the work.[16]

> 6.53 The correct method in philosophy would really be the following: to say nothing except what can be said, i.e., propositions of natural science—i.e., something that has nothing to do with philosophy—and then, whenever someone else wanted to say something metaphysical, to demonstrate to him that he had failed to give a meaning to certain signs in his propositions. Although it would not be satisfying to the other person—he would not have the feeling that we were teaching him philosophy—*this* method would be the only strictly correct one.

> 6.54 My propositions serve as elucidations in the following way: anyone who understands me eventually recognizes them as nonsensical, when he has used them—as steps—to climb up beyond them. (He must, so to speak, throw away the ladder after he has climbed up it.)

> 7 What we cannot speak about we must pass over in silence.

There are two ways of viewing Wittgenstein's final position. On one view, the *Tractatus* as a whole is self-defeating and/or self-contradictory, despite its illuminating insights on many points. Thus, the Tractarian system must be rejected, and we should strive to find ways of preserving its insights while avoiding its clear inadequacies. On another view,

---

[16] Pears and McGuinness translation.

the *Tractatus* is acceptable as it stands. In it, Wittgenstein has deliberately violated the rules of language in an attempt to show us what those rules really are; to get us to see what the rules of intelligible thought and language really are, he had to go beyond them. At the time he wrote the *Tractatus*, Wittgenstein adopted the second view. Later he had the good sense to change his mind.

In my opinion, the first view of the *Tractatus* is clearly correct. Despite its many important insights, it can be seen as an object lesson in the absurdity of going down certain paths all the way to the end. One of these paths involved the following Tractarian identifications:

(i) the identification of the metaphysically necessary (what could not have failed to be the case) with (a) that which is knowable apriori (if knowable at all), (b) that which is linguistically true (or true in virtue of meaning), (c) that which (on analysis) is logically true, and (d) that which can be logically proven to be true on the basis of its logical form alone,

(ii) the identification of the metaphysically impossible (what could not have been the case) with (a) that the negation of which is knowable apriori (if knowable at all), (b) that which is linguistically false (or false in virtue of meaning), (c) that which (on analysis) is logically false, and (d) that which can be logically proven to be false on the basis of its logical form alone,

(iii) the identification of the metaphysically contingent (that which is true, but could have been false) with (a) that which is knowable aposteriori (if at all), (b) that which is true, but not linguistically true (i.e., not true in virtue of meaning), (c) that which is true, but not (on analysis) logically true, (d) that which is true, but cannot be proven to be true on the basis of its logical form alone.

As we have seen, many of the central problems of the *Tractatus* are traceable to these identifications. Although it was not evident at the time, progress in philosophy would ultimately require rejecting them, as different analytic philosophers attempted to do in different ways for much of the next fifty years.

SUGGESTED FURTHER READING
FOR PART THREE

Main Primary Sources Discussed

Wittgenstein, Ludwig. *Tractatus Logico-Philosophicus*, translated by C. K. Ogden, Mineola, NY: Dover, 1999; originally published in English in 1922 by Routledge. See also the translation by Pears and McGuinness, London: Routledge, 1974.

Additional Primary Sources

Wittgenstein, Ludwig. *Notebooks 1914–1916*. Oxford: Basil Blackwell, 1961.
———. "Some Remarks on Logical Form." *Proceedings of the Aristotelian Society*, supplementary volume 9, 1929.

Additional Recommended Reading

Fogelin, Robert. *Wittgenstein*, 2nd edition. London and New York: Routledge, 1987.
Geach, Peter. "Wittgenstein's Operator 'N'." *Analysis* 41 (1981).
———. "More on Wittgenstein's Operator 'N'." *Analysis* 42 (1982).
Soames, Scott. "Generality, Truth Functions, and Expressive Capacity in the *Tractatus*." *Philosophical Review* 92:4 (1983).

PART FOUR

LOGICAL POSITIVISM AND EMOTIVISM

CHAPTER 12

THE LOGICAL POSITIVISTS ON NECESSITY
AND APRIORI KNOWLEDGE

CHAPTER OUTLINE

1. *Overview and historical antecedents*

   Introduction to logical positivism; comparison of Ayer's version
   of positivism with the views of Russell and the early
   Wittgenstein

2. *Analyticity, apriority, and necessity*

   Motivation of the positivists' identification of the necessary and
   the apriori, and their appeal to analyticity to explain both

3. *The linguistic explanation of apriori knowledge*

   Critique of the positivists' claim that apriori knowledge is always
   explainable in terms of knowledge of meaning

Overview and Historical Antecedents

In this chapter, we begin our discussion of logical positivism. This
movement in philosophy was unusual in that it became famous, even
infamous, far beyond the confines of the professional philosophical
community. One reason for this was that its proponents were effective
communicators with a kind of missionary zeal. Another reason was
their message, which featured shocking declarations about what was
meaningful, and what was not, as well as bold attempts to dissolve age-
old philosophical problems. In addition, logical positivism appealed to
the scientific temper of the times. Reading the positivists, one gets the
feeling that they thought that just as modern science had revolution-
ized our understanding of the natural world, and just as technology
was revolutionizing modern life, so a proper scientific outlook would
transform philosophy in particular, and intellectual culture in general.

Nevertheless, the actual doctrines of logical positivism were not a
radically new departure from the philosophical systems that immediately preceded them. Most of the groundwork can be found in Russell
and Wittgenstein. The positivists modified those views, combined
them in new ways, and made some important additions, but didn't

strike out in an entirely new direction. There were, of course, significant differences among the positivists. We will concentrate mostly on the version of positivism presented by A. J. Ayer in his well-known and influential book *Language, Truth, and Logic*, the first edition of which was published in 1936, and the second in 1946.[1] This version of positivism, though differing in some respects from other versions, was quite representative of the general tendencies of the movement.

One can get a feeling for the relationship between logical positivism and its roots in Russell and Wittgenstein by comparing some of the central tenets of Ayer's position with the doctrines of its two most important predecessors.

EARLY-TO-MIDDLE RUSSELL	AYER'S LOGICAL POSITIVISM
1. Mathematics is reducible to logic.	1. Truths of mathematics, along with all other necessary and apriori truths, are analytic.
2. Physical objects are logical constructions out of sense data.	2. Physical objects, other minds, and the self are logical constructions out of sense data.
3. The theory of descriptions is the paradigm of philosophical analysis.	3. All of philosophy is linguistic analysis.

EARLY WITTGENSTEIN	AYER'S LOGICAL POSITIVISM
1. Language is divided into atomic and non-atomic sentences.	1. Language is divided into observation and non-observation sentences.
2. All meaningful sentences are tautologous, contradictory, or contingent-empirical.	2. All meaningful sentences are analytic, contradictory, or contingent-empirical.

---

[1] A. J. Ayer, *Language, Truth, and Logic* (New York: Dover, 1952; reprinting of the 1946 2nd edition).

3. Meaningful empirical statements are truth functions of atomic statements.

4. An atomic statement is true iff it corresponds to an atomic fact.

5. The truth values of non-atomic statements are determined by the truth values of atomic statements.

6. Ethical and other philosophical statements are meaningless. They try to state what can only be shown.

3. Meaningful empirical statements are verifiable by (possible) observation.

4. An observation statement is true iff it can be established by observation.

5. The truth values of non-observation statements are tested by agreement or disagreement with observation statements.

6. Ethical statements are cognitively meaningless. They express, but do not describe, attitudes and emotions. Philosophical statements are analytic, if true, and so do not provide information about the world. By contrast, metaphysical claims are meaningless.

To put this comparison in a nutshell, we may say that logical positivism combined Wittgenstein's emphasis on an explicit test of meaningfulness with Russell's logical techniques and his emphasis on sense experience and observation. The result was an ambitious, logicized version of traditional empiricism, put forward as a theory about the scope and limits of meaning.

The central doctrine of logical positivism was its analysis of the meaning of empirical sentences in terms of verification. However, the positivists also held very important and highly influential doctrines about meaningful sentences not subject to the criterion—analytic truths and contradictions (analytic falsehoods). In this chapter, we will discuss the origins and significance of those doctrines, their development by the positivists, and the difficulties to which they give rise. This will prepare us for the next chapter, in which we will examine the empiricist, or verifiability, criterion of meaning, the philosophical implications its proponents attempted to extract from it, and the devastating problems that arose in attempting to make it precise.

Analyticity, Aprioricity, and Necessity

The first step in discussing the verifiability criterion of meaning is to draw a distinction between analytic sentences and statements, on the one hand, and synthetic sentences and statements, on the other.[2] We have seen how, in the *Tractatus*, Wittgenstein divided up the class of meaningful sentences, or statements, into three classes—analytic sentences (or, for him, *tautologies*), which were supposed to be true in virtue of meaning alone; contradictions, which were supposed to be false in virtue of meaning alone; and synthetic sentences, the truth or falsity of which was thought to depend both on what they mean and on the way the world is. The character of synthetic sentences is illustrated by the example *La Universidad de Princeton esta en Nuevo Jersey.* This sentence is true because (i) it **means** or says that Princeton University is in New Jersey, and because (ii) the part of the world that the sentence describes—Princeton University—**is** the way the sentence represents it to be. By contrast, Wittgenstein maintained that sentences like (1) and (2) tell us **nothing** about how the world actually is, or was.

1. If a man is a bachelor, then he is unmarried.

2. Either it rained in Oxford on May 1, 1935, or it didn't rain in Oxford on May 1, 1935.

---

[2] In general, the positivists tended to be rather vague and elusive about the relationship between sentences and statements. On the one hand, they did not want simply to identify the two; after all two people can make the same statement by uttering different sentences. On the other hand, they didn't want to say that statements are distinct from the sentences used to make them. On the whole, the positivists tended to be content to observe that just as statements are made using sentences, so the statement itself, that which is stated, is nothing more than a sentence used in a certain way. One difficulty here is that it is not clear what entity a sentence-used-in-a-certain-way is, if it is not the sentence itself. For other difficulties, see Richard Cartwright, "Propositions," in *Analytical Philosophy,* 1st series, edited by R. J. Butler (Oxford: Basil Blackwell, 1962), 81–103. In my discussion of the positivists, I will mostly overlook these difficulties—except when the distinction between sentences and statements (propositions) makes a crucial difference to the arguments.

Since these sentences tell us nothing about the world, Wittgenstein thought that their truth must be due to their meaning alone. Ayer, and other logical positivists, agreed.

Although traditionally many philosophers have distinguished between analytic and synthetic statements, not all of them have drawn the distinction in the way that Wittgenstein and the positivists did. One important feature of the way that Wittgenstein and the positivists made the distinction was that, for them, the analytic/synthetic distinction coincided exactly with the necessary/contingent distinction, and the apriori/aposteriori distinction. A necessary truth is a statement that is true, and could not have been otherwise. If S is necessary, then for any possible state w that the universe could be in, if the universe were (or had been) in state w, then S would be (or would have been) true. Traditional examples of such truths, beyond trivialities like (1) and (2), are the truths of logic and mathematics. Not only is the statement made by $2^5 = 32$ true, it could not have been false.

Wittgenstein and the positivists held that all necessary truths are analytic, and that meaning was the source of necessity. For Wittgenstein, the basis of this view lay in his contention that for a sentence to **say** anything, for it to provide any information, is for its truth to **exclude** certain possible states that the world could be in. Since necessary truths exclude nothing, they say nothing; and since they say nothing about the way the world is, the way the world is makes no contribution to their being true. Hence, their truth must be due to their meaning alone. The positivists, who found this conclusion welcome, emphasized a different line of reasoning. Being empiricists, they believed that all knowledge about the world is dependent on observation and sense experience. It follows that since apriori truths can be known independently of observation and sense experience, they must not be **about** the world; and if they don't tell us anything about the world, then the world must play no role in determining that they are true. Rather, their truth must be due to their meanings alone.

If one thinks about these motivations, one sees that, in effect, Wittgenstein's reasoning identified the necessary with the analytic, whereas the positivists' reasoning identified the apriori with the analytic.[3] Although in theory these certainly could have amounted to different identifications, in practice they didn't. There was no real dis-

---

[3] See chapter 4 of *Language, Truth, and Logic*, which is fittingly titled "The Apriori."

agreement between Wittgenstein and the positivists on this point, because both identified the necessary with the apriori. Thus, for these philosophers, the necessary, the apriori, and the analytic were one and the same.

In fact, one can go further. The positivists, in particular, were inclined to cite a kind of explanatory priority. The **reason**, they insisted, for the necessity or aprioricity of any sentence is to be found in its analyticity. On their view, there simply is no explaining what necessity is, how we can know any truth to be necessary, or how our knowledge of any necessary truth can be apriori, without appeal to the notion of truth by virtue of meaning. Consider, for example, our knowledge that certain truths are necessary. The positivists thought that without appeal to analyticity, one could make no sense of the notion of knowing something to be true, not only given the way the world actually is, but given any possible state that the world could be in. Surely, they would have insisted, we don't examine all possible world-states and compare the sentence with them one by one. If, on the other hand, the truth of a statement is guaranteed by its meaning, then in knowing its meaning we know, or are in a position to come to know, that it must be true, no matter what state the world happens to be in. Hence, knowledge of meaning explains knowledge of necessity.

The positivists made similar claims about the explanation of apriori knowledge. According to the them, if p is necessary, then p is knowable apriori, and hence knowable independent of any possible confirmation or disconfirmation by experience. But how, the positivists wondered, can any knowledge be independent of experience in this way? Ayer raises this question at the beginning of chapter 4 of *Language, Truth, and Logic*.

Having admitted that we are empiricists, we must now deal with the objection that is commonly brought against all forms of empiricism; the objection, namely, that it is impossible on empiricist principles to account for our knowledge of necessary truths. For, as Hume conclusively showed, no general proposition whose validity is subject to the test of actual experience can ever be logically certain. [Read *logically certain* as *apriori*.] No matter how often it is verified in practice, there still remains the possibility that it will be confuted on some future occasion. The fact that a law has been substantiated in n−1 cases affords no logical guarantee that it will be substantiated in the nth case also, no matter how large we take n to be. And this means that no general proposition **referring to a matter of fact** can ever be shown to be necessarily and universally true. [*Because if it were necessarily true, it would be apriori (logically certain) and so demonstrably true independent of any substantiation by experience.*] It can at best be a probable hypothesis. [*Ayer contrasts being probable with being certain, which he runs together with being knowable apriori.*] And this, we shall find, applies not only to general propositions, but to all propositions which have **factual content**. They can none of them ever be logically certain [*i.e., apriori, and hence necessary*].[4]

Ayer's point is that if p is necessary, then it is knowable apriori, and hence has no factual content. The implication here is that if p has no factual content, then the world makes no contribution to its truth, in which case its truth must be due to its meaning alone.

This is made clear a few pages further on.

There is no need to give further examples. Whatever instance we care to take, we shall always find that the situations in which a logical or mathematical principle might appear to be confuted are accounted for in such a way as to leave the principle unassailed. And this indicates that Mill was wrong in supposing that a situation could arise which would overthrow a mathematical truth. [*i.e. Mill was wrong in denying that the propositions of mathematics are apriori/necessary.*] The principles of logic and mathematics are true universally **simply because we never allow them to be anything else.** And the reason for this is that **we cannot abandon them without contradicting ourselves, without sinning against the rules which govern the use of language,** and so making our utterances self-stultifying. In other words, **the truths of logic and mathematics are analytic propositions or tautologies.**[5]

According to Ayer, necessary truths are true no matter what way the world is **because** they are true in virtue of meaning; similarly, they are knowable apriori, without appeal to empirical evidence for justification, **because** this knowledge is nothing more than knowledge of meaning. Certainly, there is no philosophical mystery in our being able

---

[4] P. 72, my boldface emphasis.
[5] P. 77, my boldface emphasis.

to know what we have decided our words are to mean. And surely, the positivists thought, there is no mystery in the idea that the truth of a sentence may follow, and be known by us to follow, entirely from our decisions about meaning. Putting these two ideas together, they thought that they had found a philosophical explanation of what otherwise would have been problematic—our apriori knowledge of necessary truths. For example, the statements that (1) if a man is bachelor, then he is unmarried, and (2) either it rained in Oxford on May 1, 1935 or it didn't rain in Oxford on May 1, 1935 are necessary truths which are knowable apriori. We know these things because we know what the words in (1) and (2) mean, and we know that the truth of these sentences follows from the meanings we have assigned to those words. The same holds for our apriori knowledge of any necessary truth—including all the truths of logic and mathematics.

Although this picture was, for decades, very attractive to many philosophers, it suffered from several problems that were not immediately apparent. First, the identification of necessary truths with truths that are knowable apriori is fraught with difficulties, as Saul Kripke would show nearly forty years later in *Naming and Necessity.*[6] Since this point will be discussed extensively in volume 2, we bypass it for now. Second, the positivists' claim that analyticity was conceptually prior to the notions of necessity and aprioricity, and could be used to give philosophically satisfying explanations of the latter, was shown by W. V. Quine to be fundamentally flawed, in his paper "Two Dogmas of Empiricism," published in 1951[7]—which we will scrutinize at the end of this volume. Third, the positivists seriously underestimated how hard it is to explain apriori knowledge by appeal to knowledge of meaning.

The Linguistic Explanation of Apriori Knowledge

As we have seen, their explanation rested on two bits of linguistic knowledge that they took to be unproblematic—(i) knowledge of what we have decided our words are to mean, and (ii) knowledge that the truth of certain sentences **follows from** our decisions about what the words they contain mean. However, there is a problem here, lo-

---

[6] Saul Kripke, *Naming and Necessity* (Cambridge, MA: Harvard University Press, 1980); originally published in Donald Davidson and Gilbert Harman, eds., *Semantics of Natural Language* (Dordrecht: Reidel, 1972).
[7] Quine, "Two Dogmas of Empiricism," *Philosophical Review* 60 (1951); reprinted in Quine, *From a Logical Point of View* (Cambridge, MA: Harvard University Press, 1953).

cated in the words *follows from*. Clearly we don't stipulate the meanings of all the necessary / apriori / analytic truths individually. Rather, it must be thought, we make some relatively small number of meaning stipulations, and then draw out the **consequences** of those stipulations for the truth of an indefinitely large class of sentences. What is meant here by *consequences*? Surely not wild guesses or arbitrary inferences, with no necessary connection to their premises. No, by *consequences* the positivists meant something like *logical consequences, knowable apriori to be true if their premises are true*. But now we have gone in a circle. According to the positivists, all apriori knowledge of necessary truths—including our apriori knowledge of the necessary truths of logic—arises from our linguistic knowledge of the basic conventions, or stipulations, that we have adopted to give meanings to our words. However, in order to derive this apriori knowledge from our linguistic knowledge, one has to appeal to an antecedent knowledge of logic itself. Either this logical knowledge is apriori or it isn't. If it is apriori, then some apriori knowledge is not explained linguistically; if it is not apriori, then our knowledge of logic isn't apriori. Either way, the positivist program fails.

This, in a nutshell, was one of the central arguments of Quine's paper, "Truth by Convention," published in 1936.[8] Although not fully appreciated right away, it eventually became a classic, and is now widely known for its powerful critique of the program of grounding apriori knowledge in knowledge of meaning. Since, in my opinion, the problems with this program are even more severe than is sometimes realized, it may help to illustrate them with a simple example.

3a. If x is a square, then x is a rectangle with four equal sides.

Let us suppose that the word *square* means the same as the phrase *rectangle with four equal sides*. Then sentence (3a) is synonymous with, and expresses the same proposition as, (3b).

3b. If x is a rectangle with four equal sides, then x is a rectangle with four equal sides.

---

[8] Quine, "Truth by Convention," first published in O. H. Lee, ed., *Philosophical Essays for A. N. Whitehead* (New York: Longmans, 1936); reprinted in H. Feigl and W. Sellars, eds., *Readings in Philosophical Analysis* (New York: Appleton, 1949); in Benacerraf and Putnam, eds., *Readings in the Philosophy of Mathematics* (Englewood, NJ: Prentice Hall, 1964); and Quine, *The Ways of Paradox* (New York: Random House, 1966).

Next we distinguish two questions.

Q1. How do we know that (3a) is a true sentence of English?

Q2. How do we know that if x is a square, then x is a rectangle with four equal sides?

These are different questions. The knowledge that Q2 asks about can be had by someone who knows nothing about the English language, whereas the knowledge that Q1 asks about is knowledge of a certain fact about English. Moreover, knowledge that (3a) is a true sentence of English is neither apriori, nor knowledge of a necessary truth. Rather, it is ordinary empirical knowledge of a contingent fact about our language—something one learns when one becomes a proficient speaker. By contrast, our knowledge that if something is square, then it is a rectangle with four equal sides is apriori knowledge of a genuinely necessary truth.

Next we ask how, if at all, knowledge of meaning plays a role in answering Q1 and Q2. First consider Q1. If someone knows that *square* means the same as *rectangle with four equal sides*, then we may suppose that he knows that (3a) means the same as (3b), and hence that (3a) is true, if (3b) is. But how does such a person determine that (3b) is true? Well, it might be argued, (3b) is of the form *if p, then p*, and, surely, anyone who knows the meaning of *if, then* knows that any sentence of this form is true. But what exactly is knowing the meaning of *if, then*, and how is this knowledge used in determining that all sentences of the form *if p, then p* are true? Here, our attempt to use our knowledge of meaning to answer Q1 bottoms out in the question of how, if at all, our knowledge of the meanings of the logical operators explains our knowledge of which sentences are logically guaranteed to be true.

Next consider Q2. We may take it that our assumptions about meaning give the result that the proposition that x is a square is identical with the proposition that x is a rectangle with four equal sides. Since to know that so and so is just to bear the knowledge relation to the proposition that so and so, it follows that our knowledge that if x is a square, then x is a rectangle with four equal sides is simply our knowledge that if x is a rectangle with four equal sides, then x is a rectangle with four equal sides. So how do we know that? Well, it might be argued, to know that is just to know the proposition expressed by a logical truth of the form *if p, then p*, and, surely, anyone who knows the meaning of *if, then*, plus the meaning of the sentence replacing 'p', will know that proposition to be true. Again we may ask, what is it exactly to know this meaning, and how is this knowledge put to use to secure the desired result? Here, our attempt to use knowledge of meaning to answer Q2 bottoms out in the question of how, if at all, knowledge of meanings of the logical operators explains our knowledge of the propositions expressed by logically true sentences.

Faced with these questions, the positivists' standard move was to claim (i) that logic is true by convention, and hence analytic, and (ii) that, therefore, knowledge of logical truth is nothing more than knowledge of meaning. (They would say essentially the same about knowledge that certain inferences are truth preserving.) However, these points are far from transparent, as can be seen by considering the following scenario. Suppose I were to introduce a simple logical language L by listing some familiar predicates and names used in forming atomic sentences, plus the logical constants '&', 'v', '→', '~', and '∀', and the variables 'x', 'y', etc. Imagine that you already understand the names and predicates, but that the logical symbols are new to you. I next go on to endow the logical symbols with meaning by making a complicated stipulation of the following sort: Let these logical symbols of L mean whatever they have to mean to make true every sentence of the forms:

$$(A \lor \sim A), (A \to A), [(A \& B) \to B], [A \to (A \lor B)],$$
$$[\sim(A \& B) \to (\sim A \lor \sim B)], [(A \& (A \to B)) \to B],$$
$$[\forall x\, Fx \to Fn], [(\forall x\, (Fx \to Gx) \& Fn) \to Gn], \text{ etc.}$$

The precise details of the stipulation are not important. The idea is to make a stipulation that can be satisfied only if '~', '&', '∀x' and all the other logical operators are assigned interpretations which assure that all and only those sentences of L that are standardly classified as logically true are guaranteed to be true by the meanings of the logical operators. Let us suppose, for the sake of argument, that this is possible. If some group or community decides to adopt such a stipulation as a linguistic convention governing their use of L, then it would be natural to characterize the logical truths of L as sentences that are *true by convention*, and thus, *analytic*.

So, at any rate, the positivists thought; and, so far, we have found nothing to object to in the thought. However, this isn't the end of the matter. What about (i) knowledge of which sentences of L are true by convention, and (ii) knowledge of the propositions expressed by those truths? Regarding (i), consider the sentence (3c) of L, which is a counterpart to the English (3b).

3c. ($\underline{x}$ is a rectangle with 4 equal sides → $\underline{x}$ is a rectangle with 4 equal sides)

To establish that this sentence is true by convention, one might reason as follows:

P1. All sentences of L of the form $(A \to A)$ are stipulated to be true, and so are true by convention.

P2. (3c) is a sentence of L of the form $(A \to A)$.

C. Therefore sentence (3c) is true by convention.

Similar arguments could be given for other logical truths of L.

Although there is nothing wrong with these arguments, each presupposes a certain logical fact. Each argument is of the form:

P1. All F's are G. (All sentences of such and such a form are true.)

P2. n is an F. (n is a sentence of such and such a form.)

C. Therefore, n is G. (Sentence n is true.)

In order for someone to recognize that the premises of the argument justify the conclusion that a certain sentence of L is true, he must recognize that if all F's are G's, and n is an F, then n is a G.[9] **This knowledge** isn't explained by knowledge of any stipulations about L; rather it is presupposed in using knowledge of the stipulations to arrive at knowledge of which sentences of L are true. Consequently, although (3c) can be regarded as a sentence of L that is true by convention, and although one can arrive at the knowledge that it is by learning the linguistic conventions of L, one can do so only if one has **prior** knowledge of the truth of propositions expressed by logical truths of the form *if all F's are G's, and n is an F, then n is a G*. This is precisely the kind of genuine, apriori knowledge of necessary truths

---

[9] The point here is, of course, not that in order to draw the conclusion he needs the claim that if all F's are G's and n is an F, then n is a G, as a further premise. (We know from Lewis Carroll that that isn't so.) The point is that (i) if he is to know the conclusion on the basis of knowing the premises, he must recognize the argument as justifying the conclusion, and (ii) recognizing this is tantamount to knowing that if all F's are G's and if n is an F, then n is a G.

for which the positivists promised an explanation. What we have seen is that in appealing to the linguistic conventions of L, they haven't succeeded in giving one.

The same point could be made by focusing on sentences of English that are logical truths, and the propositions they express. The only difference is that it now becomes even harder for the positivists to make their case. When introducing logical constants into the new language L by stipulation, I was free to express the stipulation using antecedently understood expressions of English, including logical terms like *every*. However, if we try to imagine all the logical terms in English getting their meanings by stipulation, we are at a loss to understand how such stipulations could be expressed. Thus, it is harder to understand in what sense the logical truths of English could be true by convention in the first place.

It may be that this last difficulty is not insuperable. For example, it may be that speakers have some beliefs and intentions independent of any ability to express them in language. It may even be that some of these language-independent beliefs and intentions are about the use of expressions, and the meanings that speakers intend to assign to them. Perhaps a case could be made for holding that these beliefs and intentions have the effect of meaning-giving stipulations, even though they are not publicly expressed in language. If so, then someone might argue that the logical words, for example, acquire their meanings by such unexpressed stipulations, in which case it might be maintained that the logical truths of English and other natural languages are true by convention, in some extended sense.

However, even if this were so, it would seem that speakers' knowledge that certain sentences are true (or true by stipulation) would still presuppose antecedent, apriori knowledge of logical facts—i.e., apriori knowledge of certain (necessarily true) propositions expressed by logically true sentences. Since this is precisely the sort of knowledge that the positivists were trying to explain, it is hard to see how their program could succeed. Putting this in terms of answers to our illustrative questions Q1 and Q2, we see that although the positivists were right in thinking that knowledge of meaning may play a role in answering Q1, they did not succeed in showing that such knowledge is sufficient by itself (without appeal to prior knowledge of logical facts) to answer Q1; nor were they able to show that it makes **any** contribution to answering Q2.

For all these reasons, the positivists' program of explaining apriori knowledge by appeal to analyticity and linguistic conventions did not succeed. However, despite Quine's arguments in "Truth by Convention," this was not widely recognized until he revisited the topic of analyticity many years later in "Two Dogmas of Empiricism." By this time, crippling difficulties with the positivists' central doctrine, the empiricist criterion of meaning, had made it clear to just about everyone that there were intractable difficulties at the center of their philosophical vision.

CHAPTER 13

THE RISE AND FALL OF THE EMPIRICIST
CRITERION OF MEANING

CHAPTER OUTLINE

1. *The idea behind the empiricist criterion of meaning and its philosophical significance*

2. *Observation statements*

   Problems delimiting the class; sense data statements and material object statements; the distinction between theoretical and observational statements

3. *Attempts to formulate the empiricist criterion of meaningfulness in terms of strong verification*

   Attempts based on conclusive verifiability and conclusive falsifiability; why they failed

4. *Attempts to formulate the empiricist criterion of meaningfulness in terms of weak verification*

   The idea that an empirical statement is meaningful if observation is relevant to determining its truth or falsity; why this idea is too weak; the refutations of Hempel and Church

5. *Empirical meaningfulness as translatability into an empiricist language*

   Carnap, Hempel, and the move toward holistic verificationism; "disposition terms" and theoretical terms

6. *Lessons of the positivists' failed attempt to vindicate verificationism*

   Moves toward linguistic holism and ordinary language philosophy; verificationism and Moorean methodology

The Idea behind the Empiricist Criterion of Meaning and Its Philosophical Significance

As we saw in the last chapter, analytic sentences were supposed by the positivists to express necessary truths that are knowable apriori simply by understanding and reflecting on the meanings of the sentences that express them. A sentence was regarded as contradictory if and only if it was analytically false—i.e., iff its negation was analytic. All other meaningful sentences were classified as synthetic, or empirical. The empiricist criterion of meaning focused on this last class of sentences.

The guiding idea behind the criterion may be put as follows:

THE BASIS OF VERIFICATIONISM

A non-analytic, non-contradictory sentence S is meaningful iff S bears relation R to statements the truth or falsity of which can be determined directly by simple observation.

The most important task facing the positivists was to give a precise definition of the relation R in this principle. It is obvious that, at the outset, positivists like Ayer had no idea how difficult an undertaking this would turn out to be. They were confident that they had hit upon a fundamental insight that would transform philosophy, and finally put it on a solid foundation. As they saw it, the cause of past philosophical confusion and the reason for the lack of more significant progress in the discipline was that philosophers hadn't realized that all meaningful statements have to be either analytic, contradictory, or empirically verifiable. Many of the statements of traditional philosophy—particularly in ethics and metaphysics—simply don't fall into these categories (as the positivists conceived of them).

Metaphysical statements are **not** analytic, because their truth or falsity is supposed to be something more than a conventional or linguistic matter. Since they purport to be **about** the world, their truth or falsity must be determined by whether or not they correctly **describe** the world. However, these statements have often been held to be both necessary and knowable independently of experience, in the sense that ordinary empirical observation has been deemed unnecessary to ascertaining their truth or falsity. The positivists insisted that this combination of characteristics was impossible. Any meaningful claim that purports to be about the world **must** be both contingent and capable of being verified or falsified by experience. Since metaphysical statements do not pass this test, the positivists rejected them as meaningless. In so doing, they also rejected the negations of all such claims. For example, in proclaiming that *God exists* is cognitively meaningless, they did not take themselves to be committed to the claim that God doesn't exist. On the contrary, they maintained that if *God exists* is meaningless, then *God doesn't exist* is also meaningless. According to the positivists, there simply are no genuine metaphysical problems to be addressed.

Similar points apply to ethics, as traditionally conceived. Often, the most general and fundamental claims of ethics have been regarded as necessary (and knowable apriori), if they are true at all; but they have also been thought **not** to be analytic, since accepting them seems to involve more than deciding how to use words. Though they have traditionally been taken to be descriptive claims, capable of being true or false, they have also been understood to play an important role in guiding our actions. The positivists insisted that no claims can be both necessary (or apriori) and non-analytic; and no claims can be both fact-stating descriptions and action-guiding admonitions. Thus, they maintained that ethical sentences are cognitively meaningless, in the sense that they are not used to make statements or express genuine beliefs. At best they are disguised imperatives used to make recommendations, and to give orders.

The fact that the positivists rejected entire domains of traditional philosophical inquiry didn't mean that they thought that all traditional philosophy was mistaken. Some of it they viewed as having successfully achieved important linguistic clarifications. For example, Hume's analysis of causation as constant conjunction, Locke's conception of all knowledge as arising from experience, Russell's theory of descriptions, his reduction of arithmetic to logic, and his theory of logical constructions, as well as Wittgenstein's attempt to trace the limits of the meaningful, all met with favor from the positivists. They didn't see themselves as starting philosophy again, completely anew. But they did see their contribution, the empiricist criterion of meaning, to be the cornerstone of all future philosophical progress.

In this chapter, we will examine the positivists' attempts to state an acceptable version of that criterion. Their first attempts were based on the notion of *strong verification*. The idea was that an empirical—i.e., non-analytic, non-contradictory—statement is meaningful iff its truth, or its falsity, could, in principle, be conclusively established by deductive inference from true observation statements alone. After showing these attempts to be too restrictive, in the sense of incorrectly characterizing certain clearly meaningful sentences as meaningless, we will chronicle later attempts by the positivists to construct a criterion of meaning based on a different approach, known as *weak verification*. According to this approach, an empirical statement S is meaningful iff observation statements are relevant to determining the truth or falsity of S, by virtue of the fact that they are logically entailed by S together with other statements of a theory which, as a whole, makes empirical predications. After showing that these attempts were far too liberal, in the sense of characterizing many meaningless sentences as meaningful, we will examine a final attempt designed to avoid the problems with both weak verification and strong verification. Finding serious problems with this attempt as well, we will close with a discussion of the reasons that the logical positivists' version of verificationism failed.

Observation Statements

The first step in trying to turn the idea behind verificationism into a precise criterion of meaning was to characterize the class of observation statements. Historically, this was a point of contention, with different positivists offering different characterizations at different times. One central dispute was over whether observation statements should be taken to be statements about one's own sense data (that one could not possibly be mistaken about), or whether ordinary (fallible) statements about perceivable, medium-sized, physical objects should count as observational.

Ayer himself, like several of the early positivists, was originally attracted to the first, and more radically empiricist, alternative. In *Language, Truth, and Logic*, he takes sense data to be the objects of perception, and compounds Russell's earlier error in *Our Knowledge of the External World* by declaring not only (i) that material objects are logical constructions out of sense data,[1] but also (ii) that other people are logical constructions out of material objects (statements about other minds are analyzable into statements about the behavior of other bodies)[2]—thereby saddling himself with the view (iii) that both material objects and other people are logical constructions out of sense data. Whose sense data, one might ask? Although Ayer doesn't explicitly raise and answer this question, the only way for him to avoid circular-

---

[1] *Language, Truth, and Logic*, pp. 63–68.
[2] Pp. 128–32. For example, on p. 130 Ayer says: "the distinction between a conscious man and an unconscious machine resolves itself into a distinction between different types of perceptible behavior. The only ground I can have for asserting that an object which appears to be a conscious being is not really a conscious being, but only a dummy or a machine, is that it fails to satisfy one of the empirical tests by which the presence or absence of consciousness is determined. If I know that an object behaves in every way as a conscious being must, by definition, behave, then I know that it is really conscious. . . . For when I assert that an object is conscious I am asserting no more than that it would, in response to any conceivable test, exhibit the empirical manifestations of consciousness."

ity is to maintain that material objects and other people are logical constructions out of **his own** sense data. The resulting doctrine then maintains that any statement one makes (as well as any thought one entertains) that might appear to be about material objects and other people is, in reality, a statement (or thought) about one's own sense data, **and nothing more**—i.e., about sense data one is experiencing, has experienced, or would experience if various (solipsistically characterized) conditions were fulfilled. This can only be regarded as a *reductio ad absurdum*.

The way out of this dead end is to give up the view that material objects are logical constructions out of sense data.[3] But if material objects are regarded as distinct from sense data, with only statements about the latter being regarded as observational, then verificationists will have trouble with material-object statements right from the start. Since these statements are not entailed by any finite set of sense data statements, they won't count as strongly verifiable, and the empiricist criterion of meaning will be threatened before it gets off the ground. Difficulties over these issues occupied the positivists in intense disputes among themselves throughout much of the '30s.[4] In time, however, these disputes faded in significance. When the real problems inherent in attempts to formulate the empiricist criterion of meaning began to be recognized, it became apparent that fundamental difficulties in defining the relationship that non-observation statements were supposed to bear to observation statements in order to count as empirically meaningful would remain, no matter how observation statements were characterized.

---

[3] One can't hold that material objects are logical constructions out of one's own sense data, since that would commit one to the false doctrine about meaning that when one person says *there is a table in the room* and another person in the very same situation says *no, there is no table in the room*, the two speakers do not contradict each other. One can't hold that material objects are logical constructions out of everyone's sense data, since that would commit one to the view that knowing the truth of any material object statement requires **prior** knowledge of the sense experiences of others—something we clearly don't have. See chapter 7 for a discussion of these points in the critique of Russell's views about logical constructions.

[4] For an illustrative sample of positions taken in this debate, see Otto Neurath, "Protocol Sentences", *Erkenntnis*, 3 (1932–33); Moritz Schlick, "The Foundation of Knowledge," *Erkenntnis*, 4 (1934); A. J. Ayer, "Verification and Experience," *Proceedings of the Aristotelian Society*, 37 (1936–67), all reprinted (in English) in Ayer's useful collection, *Logical Positivism* (New York: Free Press, 1959). See also section 3 of Ayer's introduction to the volume.

For this reason, we will be rather liberal and informal in our characterization of observation statements.[5]

OBSERVATION STATEMENTS

An observation statement is one that could be used to record the result of some possible observation. These statements assert that specifically mentioned observable objects have, or lack, specified observable characteristics—e.g., *The book is on the table, The chalkboard isn't green, The cup is empty and the glass is full.*

Among the potentially important questions we leave aside here are *Observable by whom?* and *Observable by what means?* Obviously, instances of ordinary, unaided observation by normal human beings count as possible observations that may be recorded in observation statements. Whether or not observations involving magnifying glasses, binoculars, telescopes, microscopes, radio telescopes, electron microscopes, and the like should be counted as observations for these purposes is something we will not stop to puzzle over. Certainly, the positivists wanted to exclude from the class of observation statements those the verification of which required both sense experience and substantial theoretical assumptions to interpret that experience. But what should be counted as substantial theoretical assumptions was up for grabs, as was the troubling issue of whether there is a single, principled way of drawing the distinction between observation and theory once and for all, or whether, instead, there are many different, context-sensitive ways of drawing the line in different situations, for different scientific or philosophical purposes. These are serious questions, which would have to be answered if it were possible to find acceptable versions of the verifiability criterion of meaning that were unproblematic apart from worries about observation. However, there are formidable obstacles facing attempts to formulate **any** adequate versions of the criterion, no matter how observation statements are precisely defined. Since exploring these obstacles will be our central concern, we will

---

[5] This definition of *observation statement* allows for sentences of different logical forms to be observation statements—e.g., simple atomic sentences, negations, conjunctions, and even (in certain special cases) universal generalizations. In what follows, when I contrast observation statements with, say, universal generalizations, the contrast will be between observation statements and universal generalizations that are not themselves observation statements.

simply proceed as if there were some principled distinction between observational and non-observational claims, without worrying too much about how or where, precisely, the line is to be drawn.

Attempts to Formulate the Empiricist Criterion of Meaningfulness in Terms of Strong Verification

We begin by defining *conclusive verifiability* and *conclusive falsifiability*.

CONCLUSIVE VERIFIABILITY

A statement S is conclusively verifiable iff there is some finite, consistent set O of observation statements such that O logically entails S.

CONCLUSIVE FALSIFIABILITY

A statement S is conclusively falsifiable iff there is some finite, consistent set O of observation statements such that O logically entails the negation of S.

Note that conclusively verifiable statements are not invariably true, and conclusively falsifiable statements are not invariably false. A conclusively verifiable statement is one that is such that it is in principle **possible** that it could be conclusively shown to be true by virtue of the fact that it follows logically from a set O of observation statements that could themselves jointly be true. A similar point holds for conclusive falsifiability. A conclusively falsifiable statement is one that could, in principle, be conclusively shown to be false by virtue of the fact that its negation follows logically from a set O of observation statements that could all be true. The requirement that the set O be consistent is meant to ensure that it is possible for the members of O to be jointly true.[6] The requirement that O be finite is meant to guarantee that it is in principle possible for us to perform the observations needed to show that all its members are true.

We now consider two attempts to base empirical meaning—the meaning of non-analytic and non-contradictory statements—on conclusive verifiability and conclusive falsifiability.

---

[6] Here, the positivists were equating logical consistency with our ordinary notion of possibility. Although this identification is now recognized to be problematic, at the time it was second nature. We will let it pass.

ATTEMPT I

A non-analytic, non-contradictory sentence S is empirically meaningful iff S expresses a statement that is conclusively verifiable.

ATTEMPT 2

A non-analytic, non-contradictory sentence S is empirically meaningful iff S expresses a statement that is conclusively falsifiable.

These two attempts come to grief over the following facts.

FACT 1: UNIVERSAL GENERALIZATIONS (AND NEGATIONS OF EXISTENTIAL GENERALIZATIONS) ARE NOT CONCLUSIVELY VERIFIABLE.

(i) All moving bodies not acted upon by external forces continue in a state of uniform motion in a straight line.

(ii) All solid bodies expand when heated.

(iii) All swans are white.

These examples are of the form (iv).

(iv) $\forall x \, (Ax \rightarrow Bx)$ All A's are B's.

Although these sentences are clearly meaningful, the statements they express are not logically entailed by any finite, consistent set of observation statements, or, indeed, by any consistent set of statements *An, Bn,* . . . , no matter what size. Since sentences of the form (iv) are logically equivalent to those of the form (v), the same is true of negations of existential generalizations.

(v) $\sim \exists x \, (Ax \, \& \, \sim Bx)$ It is not the case that there is something which is A but not B.

FACT 2: UNIVERSAL GENERALIZATIONS (AND NEGATIONS OF EXISTENTIAL GENERALIZATIONS) ARE CONCLUSIVELY FALSIFIABLE.

The negation of an example of the form (iv) has the form (vi).

(vi) $\sim \forall x \, (Ax \rightarrow Bx)$ Not all A's are B's.

Sentences of this form are logically equivalent to those of the form (vii).

(vii) $\exists x \, (Ax \, \& \, \sim Bx)$ At least one A is not a B.

If A and B represent observable characteristics, then (vi) and (vii) are logically entailed by the set of observation sentences (viii).

(viii) An, ~Bn

Thus, the corresponding universal generalizations of the form (iv), and negations (of the form (v)) of existential generalizations, are conclusively falsifiable.

FACT 3: EXISTENTIAL GENERALIZATIONS (AND THE NEGATIONS OF UNIVERSAL GENERALIZATIONS) ARE NOT CONCLUSIVELY FALSIFIABLE.

A statement is conclusively falsifiable iff its negation is conclusively verifiable. Since the negation, (v), of the existential generalization, (vii), is **not** conclusively verifiable, it follows that the existential generalization (vii) is **not** conclusively falsifiable. Similarly, since the universal generalization (iv) is **not** conclusively verifiable, it follows that its negation, (vi), is **not** conclusively falsifiable.

It follows from these facts that Attempts 1 and 2 both exclude large classes of clearly meaningful sentences. Attempt 1 wrongly characterizes many meaningful universal generalizations, and many meaningful negations of existential generalizations, as meaningless. Attempt 2 wrongly characterizes many meaningful existential generalizations, and many meaningful negations of universal generalizations, as meaningless. In addition, both attempts characterize certain sentences as meaningful, while denying that their negations are. This result conflicts with two principles that were widely held by the positivists.

P1. A sentence is (cognitively) meaningful iff it expresses a statement that is either true or false.

P2. ~ S is true (false) iff S is false (true).

For all these reasons, Attempts 1 and 2 had to be rejected.

This brings us to the third attempt to formulate the verifiability criterion of meaning.

ATTEMPT 3

A non-analytic, non-contradictory sentence S is empirically meaningful iff S expresses a statement that is either conclusively verifiable or conclusively falsifiable.

When A and B stand for observable characteristics, this formulation handles universal generalizations *All A's are B's* because they express statements that are conclusively falsifiable, and it handles existential generalizations, *At least one A is a B*, because they express statements that are conclusively verifiable. Thus, both types of generalization can be correctly characterized as meaningful by Attempt 3. However, at least three other problems remain.

The first concerns mixed quantification—sentences that contain both a universal and an existential quantifier. Two examples are (3) and (4),

3. For every substance, there is a solvent. $\forall x \, (Sx \rightarrow \exists y \, Dxy)$

4. For every man, there is a woman who loves him.
   $\forall x \, (Mx \rightarrow \exists y \, (Wy \, \& \, Lyx))$

Since these are universal generalizations, they are not conclusively verifiable. So if they are meaningful at all, then, according to Attempt 3, they must be conclusively falsifiable. In order for (3) to be false, at least one of its instances—given in (3-Ia)—must be false; or, what is saying the same thing, at least one of the statements in (3-Ib) must be true.[7] (Here we assume that we can generate names for each object and that the lists may be infinite.)

3-Ia. $Sa \rightarrow \exists y \, Day, \quad Sb \rightarrow \exists y \, Dby, \quad Sc \rightarrow \exists y \, Dcy, \ldots$

3-Ib. $Sa \, \& \, \forall y \, {\sim}Day, \quad Sb \, \& \, \forall y \, {\sim}Dby, \quad Sc \, \& \, \forall y \, {\sim}Dcy, \ldots$

But since each of the conjunctions in (3-Ib) has a conjunct which is a universal generalization, **none** of these conjunctions is logically entailed by any finite, consistent set of observation statements. Moreover, since each of the conjunctions in (3-Ib) is logically independent of the others, no finite, consistent set of observation statements logically entails that at least one member of any pair of these conjunctions is true, that at least one member of any triple is true, or even that at least one instance in the whole list (3-Ib) is true. Thus, no finite, consistent set of observation statements logically entails that at least one of the statements in (3-Ia) is false. We may express this even more strongly by noting that since no finite, consistent set of observation statements logically entails that any instance of (3) is false, no such set entails that (3) is false—which means that (3) is not conclu-

---

[7] For $Sa \rightarrow \exists y \, Day$ to be false is for $Sa \, \& \, {\sim}\exists y \, Day$ to be true. ${\sim}\exists y \, Day$ is logically equivalent to $\forall y \, {\sim}Day$.

sively falsifiable. Since (3) is also not conclusively verifiable, Attempt 3 classifies sentence (3) as meaningless, despite the fact that it is obviously meaningful.[8] The same reasoning applies to sentence (4).

The second problem with Attempt 3 involves other kinds of quantification, for example quantifications of the sort illustrated in (5) and (6).

5. There are more A's in the universe than B's.

6. Most A's are B's.

It is evident that no finite, consistent set of observation statements of the sort illustrated in (7) logically entails (5) or (6).

7. Aa, Ab, Ac, . . . Bn, Bo, Bp, . . .

In order for such an entailment to exist, one would have to add to (7) some claim to the effect that the A's and B's enumerated there are all that there are.[9] But that statement would not be regarded by the positivists as an observation statement. Thus, statements made by sentences like (5) and (6) do not qualify as conclusively verifiable; analogous reasoning can be used to show that they are also not conclusively falsifiable. Since such statements are obviously meaningful, Attempt 3 wrongly characterizes meaningful sentences of this type as meaningless.

The third difficulty with Attempt 3 also plagued all attempts by the positivists to formulate a criterion of empirical meaning in terms of what they called *strong verifiability*. As we have seen, the basic idea behind all such attempts was that of being able to use simple sensory observations to establish absolutely conclusively that a non-observational statement was true, or that it was false. Criteria of meaning built on this idea maintained that a non-analytic, non-contradictory sentence is meaningful only if its truth or falsity could be established by logical deduction from some finite, consistent set of observation statements. But this is far too restrictive—so restrictive, in fact, that it excludes large parts of natural science.

---

[8] Note that we here rely on a Moorean confidence in the meaningfulness of these sentences (as well as their ubiquity in science) that exceeds our confidence in any philosophical thesis about meaning that may conflict with it. To the positivists' credit, they usually followed suit when problematic cases like these were pointed out.

[9] One would also have to include claims asserting the non-identity of the objects mentioned.

For example, consider (8).

8. The surface is being bombarded with electrons.

The scientists who developed the atomic theory did not directly observe electrons. Nor did they start with a finite, consistent set of observation statements, and go to their logic books to deduce (8) from that set. Notice that appealing to simple, enumerative induction, as well as deduction, won't do the job either. We don't start with observations and then deduce, or induce, (8) from them. Rather, scientists posit the existence of electrons as a way of explaining and predicting observable events.

Roughly speaking, the process works as follows: Statements like (8), together with the rest of one's scientific theory (including, in some cases, certain true observation statements describing experimental conditions), entail further observational statements as consequences. If all these observational consequences turn out to be true, then the theory is, to that extent, confirmed. If some turn out to be false, then the theory is incorrect in some way, and must be modified. The positivists introduced the term *weak verifiability* to describe the relationship that theoretical hypotheses like (8) stand to observational events that may confirm or disconfirm them, and the theories of which they are parts. How are such statements assessed for truth or falsity? By itself, (8) doesn't logically entail any observation statements. To get observational consequences, one must combine (8) with other statements of one's theory. Positivists like Ayer wanted to say that (8) is empirically meaningful because it, together with other statements, allows us to make empirical predictions that we would not be in a position to make without it. Thus, they needed a new formulation of the verifiability criterion of meaning that would capture this idea.

Attempts to Formulate the Empiricist Criterion of Meaningfulness in Terms of Weak Verification

The new attempt represented a different strategy from those that preceded it; the idea was that what makes an empirical sentence meaningful is not that it expresses a statement that can be **proven** to be true, or **proven** to be false, by some set of observations that we could possibly make. Instead, the idea was that a sentence is empirically meaningful if and only if it expresses a statement for which empirical observation is **relevant** to determining its truth or falsity. Positivists like Ayer thought that if a statement S was embedded in an empirical theory T from which one could deduce observational predictions that couldn't be deduced if S were removed from T, then the truth of those observational predictions would support the hypothesis that S is true (even if it didn't conclusively establish S), while the falsity of the observational predictions would tend to disconfirm the hypothesis that S is true (even if it didn't conclusively refute S). Since the positivists viewed scientific hypotheses that are confirmed or disconfirmed in this way as paradigmatic examples of meaningful empirical sentences, they needed a criterion of meaning that would count such sentences as meaningful.

Here is Ayer's discussion of the matter in chapter 1 of *Language, Truth, and Logic*.

> Accordingly, we fall back on the weaker sense of verification. We say that the question that must be asked about any putative statement of fact is not, *Would any observations make its truth or falsehood logically certain?* but simply, *Would any observations be relevant to the determination of its truth or falsehood?* And it is only if a negative answer is given to this second question that we conclude that the statement under consideration is nonsensical.
>
> To make our position clearer, we may formulate it in another way. Let us call a proposition which records an actual or possible observation an experiential proposition. Then we may say that it is the mark of a genuine factual proposition, not that it should be equivalent to an experiential proposition, or any finite number of experiential propositions, but simply that some experiential propositions can be deduced from it in conjunction with certain other premises without being deducible from those other premises alone.[10]

This gives us Attempt 4.

ATTEMPT 4

A non-analytic, non-contradictory sentence S is meaningful iff S, by itself, or in conjunction with certain further premises P, Q, R, . . . , logically entails some observation statement O that is not entailed by P, Q, R, . . . alone.

Note that if O were entailed by P, Q, R . . . alone, then S would play no role in the entailment, and hence S would not have been shown to have any connection with experience. That is the reason for the final,

[10] Pp. 38–39.

qualifying clause. Ayer's idea was that a statement that can play a role in explaining or predicting observations must be meaningful. He apparently thought that traditional metaphysical statements could not meet this test, and thus that his new formulation would count such statements as meaningless.

However, as he indicates in the introduction to the second edition of *Language, Truth, and Logic,* he later changed his mind, and came to realize that Attempt 4 was far too liberal.

> I say [in chapter 1 of the first edition] of this criterion that it "seems liberal enough," but in fact it is far too liberal, since it allows meaning to any statement whatsoever. For, given any statement "S" and an observation statement "O", "O" follows from "S" and "if S then O" without following from "if S then O" alone. Thus, the statements "the Absolute is lazy" and "if the Absolute is lazy, this is white" jointly entail the observation-statement "this is white," and since "this is white" does not follow from either of these premises, taken by itself, both of them satisfy my criterion of meaning. Furthermore, this would hold good for any other piece of nonsense that one cared to put, as an example, in place of "the Absolute is Lazy," provided only that it had the grammatical form of an indicative sentence. But a criterion of meaning that allows such latitude as this is evidently unacceptable.[11]

The problem is that Attempt 4 does not put any restrictions on the supplementary premises P, Q, R, that one can appeal to in testing the meaningfulness of an arbitrary sentence S. For this reason, Ayer concludes, it doesn't succeed in ruling anything out. Since any sentence S can always be combined with the supplementary premise $(S \to O)$ to entail O, Ayer concludes that Attempt 4 will always characterize S as meaningful. And that's right, provided that $(S \to O)$ does not entail O by itself. But can one always assume this? Is it the case that for any sentence S, one can always find a supplementary premise $(S \to O)$ which does not entail O by itself, and hence which can be used in Attempt 4 to generate the conclusion that S is meaningful?

In giving his argument, Ayer simply took it for granted that the answer to this question is *yes,* and for all intents and purposes it is. A more precise statement of the fact is this: For any non-analytic statement

---

[11] Pp. 11–12. Ayer credits the point in the passage to Isaiah Berlin, "Verifiability in Principle," *Proceedings of the Aristotelian Society* 39.

S, one can find an observation statement O and a supplementary premise $(S \to O)$ such that O follows logically from S and $(S \to O)$ without following from the supplementary premise itself. To see this, consider a pair of conflicting observation statements:

O1. The light is on.

O2. The light is not on (i.e., is off).

The conjunction of O1 and O2 is inconsistent. Suppose now that $(S \to O1)$ and $(S \to O2)$ logically entailed O1 and O2, respectively. If this were so, then $(\sim S \ v \ O1)$ and $(\sim S \ v \ O2)$ would entail O1 and O2, respectively.[12] But that would mean that $\sim S$ logically entailed both O1 and O2.[13] Since these two statements are inconsistent, this could be the case only if $\sim S$ were a contradiction, and S was analytic. Thus, for any **non-analytic** statement S, either S is judged to be meaningful by Attempt 4 because O1 is entailed by S together with $(S \to O1)$, without being entailed by $(S \to O1)$ itself, or S is judged to be meaningful by Attempt 4 because O2 is entailed by S together with $(S \to O2)$, without being entailed by $(S \to O2)$ itself. Since analytic sentences are automatically meaningful, this means that Attempt 4 leads to the absurd result that all sentences are meaningful.

Although Ayer freely admitted this in the introduction to the second edition of his book, he still thought that the idea behind Attempt 4 was basically right. In his view, the problem with the attempt was that it placed no restrictions on what supplementary principles one could appeal to in testing whether an arbitrary sentence S was meaningful. In particular, the problem seemed to arise from the fact that the supplementary premise $(S \to O)$, chosen to combine with an arbitrarily selected sentence S, could not **itself** be shown to be meaningful, without independently establishing the meaningfulness of the very sentence S that was being tested. What seemed to be required was a modification of Attempt 4 that restricted the use of supplementary premises to those that had already been established to be meaningful, **prior** to their use in testing the meaningfulness of any other sentences.

With this in mind, Ayer advanced Attempt 5 as his final criterion of meaning.[14]

---

[12] Since $(A \to B)$ is logically equivalent to $(\sim A \ v \ B)$.

[13] An individual disjunct entails any disjunction of which it is a part. Thus it entails everything the disjunction does.

[14] See p. 13 of the second edition.

ATTEMPT 5

S is **directly verifiable** iff (a) S is an observation statement; or (b) S by itself, or in conjunction with one or more *observation statements* P, Q, R, . . . , logically entails an observation statement that is not entailed by P, Q, R, . . . alone.

S is **indirectly verifiable** iff (a) S by itself, or in conjunction with other premises P, Q, R, . . . , logically entails a *directly verifiable* statement D that is not entailed by P, Q, R, . . . alone; and (b) the other premises P, Q, R, ... , are all either *analytic, directly verifiable,* or can be shown independently to be *indirectly verifiable.*

A non-analytic, non-contradictory sentence S is empirically **meaningful** iff S expresses a statement that is either directly or indirectly verifiable. (Analytic and contradictory sentences are also counted as meaningful.)

To understand this criterion of meaning, one must recognize the definition of *indirect verifiability* as working in stages. At the first stage, we select a sentence and test whether it is possible to combine it with some directly verifiable (or analytic) statements P, Q, R, etc. to entail some different directly verifiable statement that is not entailed by P, Q, R, etc. themselves. Any sentence that passes this test we may call a *stage-1-indirectly-verifiable-statement.* At stage 2 we select some new sentence S that is neither directly verifiable nor indirectly verifiable at stage 1. We test S to see whether it is possible to combine it with some statements P, Q, R, etc., that are either directly verifiable, stage-1-indirectly-verifiable, or analytic, with the result that S, P, Q, R, etc. together entail some directly verifiable statement not entailed by P, Q, R, etc. alone. Any sentence that passes this test we call a *stage-2-indirectly-verifiable-statement.* We repeat the process at stage 3, using statements shown to be indirectly verifiable at stage 2 as supplementary premises to arrive at a class of *stage-3-indirectly-verifiable-statements.* This process can then be repeated indefinitely. Any sentence that passes the test of indirect verifiability at any stage whatsoever is counted as indirectly verifiable, and hence meaningful. However, the only way a sentence can be classified as meaningful is by drawing out logical consequences of it in combination with sentences the meaningfulness of which has already been shown, independently, to be in accord with the criterion. Because of this, Ayer thought that he had completely avoided the problem that led to the collapse of Attempt 4.

In order to illustrate how the proposal works, and to establish a few elementary facts about it, we will work through some simple examples. For this purpose we let O_1a and O_2a be observation statements, neither of which entails the other. (Here a is a singular term that appears in both statements, and O_1x and O_2x are formulas arising from the two statements by replacing a with the variable 'x'.) Then, by clause (b) of the definition of direct verifiability, (1) and (2) are directly verifiable.

1. $(O_1a \rightarrow O_2a)$ e.g.,   If I drop this book, it will fall.

2. $\forall x\, (O_1x \rightarrow O_2x)$ e.g.,   If I drop any book, it will fall.

If O_3 is such that its conjunction with O_1a is logically independent of O_2a, then (3) will also be directly verifiable.

3. $(O_3 \rightarrow \forall x\, (O_1x \rightarrow O_2\,x))$ e.g.,   If I flip the switch, then every light will go on.

Notice that (3) is of the form (4).

4. $(O \rightarrow D.V.)$

We can easily show that where O is **any** observation statement and D.V. is **any** directly verifiable statement, the corresponding sentence of the form (4) is always characterized as meaningful. Proof: (4) plus O logically entails D.V. If O by itself doesn't logically entail D.V., then (4) is indirectly verifiable. If O does logically entail D.V., then (4) is a tautology (logically true), and hence analytic. In either case (4) is characterized as meaningful.

We can also show that the negation of a directly verifiable statement is always characterized as meaningful. Proof: Let D.V. be any directly verifiable statement, and let O be any observation statement the negation of which is an observation statement that is not logically entailed by D.V.—i.e., both O and $\sim O$ are observation statements, and D.V. does not entail $\sim O$. (For any directly verifiable statement D.V., there will always be such an observation statement O. Directly verifiable statements are non-contradictory. Thus if S and $\sim S$ are observation statements, at least one of them won't be entailed by D.V. Whichever one it turns out to be may be used to play the role of $\sim O$ in the following argument.) We have just established that (4) – $(O \rightarrow D.V.)$—is always either indirectly verifiable or analytic. $\sim D.V.$ plus (4) logically entails the observation statement $\sim O$. Since (by hypothesis) $\sim O$ isn't entailed by D.V. alone, $\sim O$ isn't entailed by $(\sim O\, v\, D.V.)$. (Anything entailed by a disjunction is entailed by both disjuncts.) Since *(~O v D.V.)* is logically equivalent to (4), this means that *~O* isn't entailed by (4) alone. Thus, *~D.V.* is indirectly verifiable, and hence is characterized as meaningful.

On the face of it, this is a good result. In general, we want to characterize *~S* as meaningful whenever we characterize S as meaningful. What we have just shown is that when S is a directly verifiable statement, Ayer's final criterion—Attempt 5—does this. Nevertheless, the criterion is demonstrably inadequate, as is shown by three problems— one due to Carl Hempel, one to Alonzo Church, and one inspired by Church.[15]

Here is Hempel's problem. We let S be any non-analytic, meaningful sentence that expresses a truth, and we let N be some sentence that is supposed to be nonsense. Next consider the conjunction of the two, *(S &N)*. The criterion of meaning given to us in Attempt 5 classifies the conjunction as meaningful, since whether S is directly or indirectly verifiable, the conjunction will be the same. However, Ayer also holds that every (cognitively) meaningful sentence is either true or false. Thus, he must hold that the conjunction *(S &N)* is true, or it is false. Either choice is problematic. If it is true, then N must also be true, since it is logically entailed by the truth, *(S &N)*. But no sentence that is meaningless can also be true. Suppose, then, that the conjunction is false. In that case its negation *~(S &N)* must be true, in which case *~N* must be true because it is entailed by the truths S and *~(S &N)*. Thus, *~N* must be meaningful. But that cannot be, since, by hypothesis, N is meaningless.

This problem is really a *reductio ad absurdum* of the conjunction of Attempt 5 with the subsidiary principles P1 and P2.

P1. A sentence is (cognitively) meaningful iff it expresses a statement that is either true or false.

P2. *~S* is true (false) iff S is false (true).

Whether or not Hempel's problem is a conclusive objection to Attempt 5 depends on whether or not proponents of that proposal might see their way clear to rejecting either P1 or P2, or both.

[15] Carl Hempel, "The Empiricist Criterion of Meaning," *Revue Internationale de Philosophie* 4 (1950), reprinted in *Logical Positivism*, A. J. Ayer (New York: Free Press), 1959. Alonzo Church, "Review of *Language, Truth, and Logic*: Second Edition", *Journal of Symbolic Logic*, 14 (1949): 52–53.

Conceivably, Ayer might have been willing to give up P1 by treating *(S & N)* as meaningful because it entails something meaningful, while denying it a truth value on the grounds that it contains N, which lacks one. However, whether or not such a move is feasible is moot, since Church's problem is enough to refute Attempt 5 by itself.

In his review of the second edition of *Language, Truth, and Logic,* Alonzo Church showed that Ayer's final formulation of the verifiability criterion of meaning—Attempt 5—has the consequence that for every sentence S, either S or its negation is meaningful. Church's argument can easily be strengthened in the following way to show that Ayer's criterion classifies every sentence as meaningful.[16] Here is the argument:

S1. Let P, Q, R be observation sentences none of which logically entail the others.

S2. Let S be any sentence.

S3. Let (a) be the following sentence: *(~P & Q) v (R & ~S)*.

S4. R is logically entailed by (a) plus P. Since (by hypothesis) R isn't logically entailed by P alone, (a) is directly verifiable.

S5. Q is logically entailed by (a) plus S.

S6. If Q is not logically entailed by (a) alone, then S is indirectly verifiable, and hence meaningful.

S7. If Q is logically entailed by (a) alone, then Q is also logically entailed by its right-hand disjunct (b): *(R & ~S)*.

If (b) does logically entail Q, then the combination of *~S* plus R logically entails an observation sentence Q that is not logically entailed by R alone—in which case *~S* is directly verifiable.

Thus, if Q is logically entailed by (a) alone, then *~S* is directly verifiable.

S8. We have already shown in our discussion of Attempt 5 that the negation of a directly verifiable statement is always

---

[16] This strengthening of Church's result makes implicit use, at step 8, of an assumption not employed by him—namely that in the case of at least some observation sentences, the negations of those sentences are also observation sentences. If by *an observation sentence* we mean one the truth or falsity of which can be determined by simple observation, this assumption seems innocuous—think of *this is red* and *~ this is red*.

indirectly verifiable, and hence meaningful. Thus, if ~S is directly verifiable, then both ~S and S are meaningful.

S9. From (S7) and (S8) it follows that if Q is logically entailed by (a) alone, then S is meaningful.

S10. From (S6) and (S9) it follows that if Q either is, or is not, logically entailed by (a) alone, then S is meaningful.

S11. Since Q is always either logically entailed by (a) alone, or not logically entailed by (a) alone, it follows that no matter which S we choose, Ayer's final criterion will characterize S as meaningful.

The final problem with Attempt 5 is just a variant of Church's original argument put in a more revealing form. Recall the problem with Attempt 4 that motivated Attempt 5. We saw that for any non-analytic sentence S, we can find an observation statement O, such that the combination of S with $(S \rightarrow O)$ logically entails O, even though $(S \rightarrow O)$ does not logically entail O by itself. This was enough to classify S as meaningful according to Attempt 4. This problem can be re-created in a nearly identical form for Attempt 5. In particular, we can show that for any non-analytic sentence S, we can find a pair of observations sentences O and R, such that the combination of S with $((S \lor R) \rightarrow O)$ logically entails O, and either (i) S is classified as meaningful because $((S \lor R) \rightarrow O)$ does not itself entail O, or (ii) S is classified as meaningful because the entailment of O by $((S \lor R) \rightarrow O)$ guarantees that ~S is directly verifiable. In effect, all the extra complexity of Attempt 5 over Attempt 4 is rendered useless when one appeals to the supplementary premise $((S \lor R) \rightarrow O)$ rather than $(S \rightarrow O)$.

Here is the demonstration.

S1. Let S be any sentence.

S2. Let R and ~R be incompatible observation sentences neither of which logically entails the observation sentence O.

S3. The combination of S with $((S \lor R) \rightarrow O)$ logically entails O.

S4. The conditional $((S \lor R) \rightarrow O)$ is directly verifiable, since the combination of it together with R logically entails the observation sentence O, which is not entailed by R itself.

S5. From S3 and S4 it follows that if O is not logically entailed by $((S \lor R) \rightarrow O)$ alone, then S is meaningful.

S6. If O is logically entailed by *((SvR) → O)* alone, then O is logically entailed by *~(SvR) v O* (which is logically equivalent to *((SvR) → O)*), in which case O is logically entailed by *~(SvR)*, and hence by *(~S&~R)* (which is logically equivalent to *~(SvR)*). But that means that *~S* is directly verifiable, since it, together with the observation sentence *~R*, logically entails the observation sentence O, which is not entailed by *~R* alone. Thus, if O is logically entailed by *((SvR) → O)* alone, then *~S* is directly verifiable.

S7. We have already shown in our discussion of Attempt 5 that the negation of a directly verifiable statement is always indirectly verifiable, and hence meaningful. Thus, if *~S* is directly verifiable, then both *~S* and S are meaningful.

S8. From (S6) and (S7) it follows that if O is logically entailed by *((SvR) → O)* alone, then S is meaningful.

S9. From (S5) and (S8) it follows that if O either is, or is not, logically entailed by *((SvR) → O)* alone, then S is meaningful.

S10. Since no matter how we choose S, it will always be the case that either O is, or is not, logically entailed by *((SvR) → O)* alone, it follows that Ayer's final criterion, Attempt 5, will always characterize S as meaningful.

For all intents and purposes, the collapse of Ayer's final formulation signaled the end of attempts to formulate the empiricist criterion of meaning in terms of either strong or weak verifiability. A few attempts were made to reformulate Ayer's criterion to save it from objections like the ones just considered. However, none proved successful. Either obviously meaningful sentences of science were wrongly characterized as meaningless, or obviously meaningless sentences were classified as meaningful. In this situation, it seemed clear that another approach was needed.

Empirical Meaningfulness as Translatability into an Empiricist Language

By the late '40s (after Church's review had appeared) there were still a number of philosophers who thought that there was something valuable in the positivists' original idea of somehow linking empirical meaning to empirical observation. Carl Hempel, who was also one of the chief critics of standard formulations of the verifiability criterion of meaning, was one of those philosophers. In his article, "The Empiricist Criterion of Meaning," first published in 1950, he catalogs the failures of the positivists to come up with successful formulations of their criterion in terms of either strong, or weak, verifiability. He then considers a different approach, which might be called *the translatability criterion of meaning.*

THE TRANSLATABILITY CRITERION OF MEANING

A sentence is empirically meaningful iff it can be translated into an empiricist language—i.e., if and only if it can be translated into a version of Russell's logical language of *Principia Mathematica* in which the only predicates allowed are those that stand for observable characteristics, plus those that are completely definable using predicates standing for such characteristics, together with the truth-functional operators and quantifiers of Russell's logical language.

Neither this criterion of meaning, nor the others he discusses, were original with Hempel; each is found, explicitly or implicitly, in the work of other positivists. The translatability criterion was drawn from Rudolf Carnap's 1936 essay, "Testability and Meaning."[17]

Although Hempel himself does not endorse this criterion, he does cite four of its virtues. First, it makes explicit provision for universal and existential quantifications. Since the Russellian logical language includes quantifiers of both types, sentences containing them are not excluded on principle from the realm of the meaningful, as they were by criteria based on conclusive verifiability and conclusive falsifiability. Second, Hempel assumes, quite plausibly, that sentences like *The absolute is perfect* cannot be translated into an empiricist language. Thus, the new criterion does not, as Ayer's later criteria did, end up attributing meaning to all sentences. Third, since *The absolute is perfect* cannot be translated into an empiricist language, there can be no meaningful conjunctions or disjunctions that contain it as a constituent. Fourth, the translatability criterion has the consequence that if S is meaningful, then its negation is too—since if the translation of S is P, then the translation of the negation of S will be $\sim P$.

[17] Rudolf Carnap, "Testability and Meaning," *Philosophy of Science*, 3, 4 (1936–37).

In addition to these virtues of the translatability criterion, Hempel noted two serious problems with it. The first involved what he called *disposition terms*, which he characterized as "terms which reflect the disposition of one or more objects to react in a determinate way under specified conditions."[18] As examples of such terms, he cites *temperature, electrically charged, magnetic, intelligent,* and *electrical resistance*. This list is surprising and controversial in certain ways. A clear example of a disposition term is *fragile*, which means something like *is disposed to break when struck*. However, it hardly seems that Hempel's example, *temperature*, means *is disposed to v*, for any choice of 'v'. Nevertheless, what Hempel had in mind is clear enough. Consider some statement of the form *The temperature of x is 90 degrees Fahrenheit*. Hempel does not regard this as a simple observation statement—presumably because ordinary observation, unaided by any special instruments or measuring devices, and unmediated by any background theory containing non-observational terms, is not enough to determine its truth. Thus, he thinks, it will be translatable into an empiricist language only if the relational two-place predicate *the temperature of x = y* can be completely defined in terms that are purely observational.

With this in mind, consider the following attempted definitions:

D1. For any object x and number y, the temperature of x = y degrees Fahrenheit iff x is in contact with a thermometer and the thermometer measures y degrees Fahrenheit on its scale.

D2. For any object x and number y, the temperature of x = y degrees Fahrenheit iff (x is in contact with a thermometer → the thermometer measures y degrees Fahrenheit on its scale).

D1 is obviously inadequate as a definition because it wrongly characterizes any object that is not in contact with a thermometer as not having any temperature. D2 is similarly inadequate because it wrongly characterizes any object that is not in contact with a thermometer as having every temperature. (The conditional statement on the right-hand side of D2 is a material condition, and hence is logically equivalent to *Either x is not in contact with a thermometer, or the thermometer it is in contact with measures y degrees Fahrenheit on its scale*.) Hempel

---

[18] P. 119 in the version reprinted in *Logical Positivism*.

notes that we might have more success in formulating a definition if we allowed ourselves the use of counterfactual conditionals, as in D3.

D3. For any object x and number y, the temperature of x = y degrees Fahrenheit iff (if it were the case that x was in contact with a thermometer then it would be the case that the thermometer measured y degrees Fahrenheit on its scale).

However, since counterfactual conditionals are **not** truth functional, and since they are **not** part of Russell's logical language, any language into which D3 could be translated would not qualify as an empiricist language. Thus, D3 is of no help to the proponent of the translatability criterion of meaning.

One might, of course, suggest that the criterion be liberalized by expanding the original definition of an empiricist language to include counterfactual conditionals, thereby allowing definitions like D3. Hempel considers this possibility, and says "*This suggestion would provide an answer to the problem of defining disposition terms if it were not for the fact that no entirely satisfactory account of the exact meaning of counterfactual conditionals seems to be available at present.*"[19] Although this comment about the lack of a satisfactory account of the meaning of counterfactuals was true at the time Hempel wrote, it was not to remain so forever. By the late '60s and early '70s, a number of philosophers, including most prominently Robert Stalnaker[20] and David Lewis,[21] had adapted the framework of possible worlds semantics developed by Rudolf Carnap,[22] Saul Kripke,[23] Richard Montague,[24] and others to the study of counterfactual constructions. Roughly put, the idea was that *If A had been the case, then B would have been the case* is true, when evaluated at a possible state of the world w iff among all the

---

[19] P. 120.
[20] Robert Stalnaker, "A Theory of Conditionals," *Studies in Logical Theory, American Philosophical Quarterly*, Monograph Series, no. 2 (Oxford: Basil Blackwell, 1968); and "Indicative Conditionals," *Philosophia*, 5, (1975).
[21] David Lewis, *Counterfactuals* (Cambridge MA: Harvard University Press, 1973).
[22] Rudolf Carnap, *Meaning and Necessity* (Chicago: University of Chicago Press, 1947).
[23] Saul Kripke, "A Completeness Theorem in Modal Logic," *Journal of Symbolic Logic*, 24:1 (1959); "Semantical Analysis of Modal Logic," *Zeitschrift für Mathematische Logik und Grundlagen der Mathematik*, 9 (1963); "Semantical Considerations on Modal Logic," *Acta Philosophica Fennica*, 16 (1963).
[24] Richard Montague, *Formal Philosophy: Selected Papers of Richard Montague* (New Haven: Yale University Press, 1974).

possible world-states at which A is true, B is true at those that are most similar to w. More informally, *If A had been the case, then B would have been the case* is true just in case a world-state differing from the actual world-state in the minimum amount needed to make A true is a world-state in which B is true. This approach is now widely accepted, and has proven fruitful in developing systematic logics for counterfactuals.

Since this development renders Hempel's critical comment outdated, one might naturally ask whether allowing definitions like D3 into empiricist languages would solve the problems posed for the translatability criterion of meaning by notions like *temperature*. There are two reasons to think that it would not. First, the semantic apparatus drawn from possible worlds semantics to explain counterfactuals contains elements that would have been regarded with suspicion by positivist proponents of that criterion. The notion of a possible state of the world—as used in the possible worlds framework—is most naturally understood as involving a **metaphysical** notion of possibility that is not reducible to, or explainable in terms of, purely linguistic conceptions of possibility, necessity, or analyticity. Hence, allowing it to be used to characterize an empiricist language might naturally be viewed by the positivists as importing a substantial amount of metaphysics into a criterion of meaning designed to exclude metaphysics as meaningless. To put the matter more dramatically, the semantic developments that gave us a logic of counterfactuals cannot naturally be used to save logical positivism, because those developments were based on the presupposition that the positivists were wrong about meaning in general, and possibility in particular.

The second reason for thinking that definitions like D3 don't solve the problems posed by terms like *temperature* for the translatability criterion of meaning is more prosaic. If definitions like this are non-circular, then they won't cover all the cases, and so will fail as definitions. To illustrate this, it suffices to remember that the temperature of some things is very high; for example, the temperature of the sun is so high that if a thermometer were to be put up against it, it would melt, or explode, and not give any reading. Nevertheless, the sun has a temperature. Since D3 does not allow for this, it is not an adequate definition.

What if someone were to object to this criticism by saying that D3 is incorrect only if we take the word *thermometer* in the definition to mean the sort of ordinary existing thermometers that we are all familiar with? Surely, the objector might continue, we can **imagine** thermometers that wouldn't melt or explode, even on the sun; and if we understand the word *thermometer* in D3 as talking about these imaginable thermometers, then the counterexample disappears. Very well, let us use the word *thermometer* in D3 to cover these non-existent but conceivable measuring devices. What, then, are we taking *thermometer* to mean? A natural thought, I suppose, is that by *thermometer* we mean *a device (however constructed) for accurately measuring temperature*. If that is what we mean, then perhaps it is true that if n is the temperature of the sun, and if a thermometer—i.e., an accurate device for measuring the temperature of the sun—were placed on the sun, then that device would read n on its scale. But the cost of making D3 come out true has been to define *thermometer* in terms of the antecedently understood notion of *temperature*, rather than the other way around. If that is how D3 is understood, then it is no definition of temperature, and we still have not succeeded in rendering statements about temperature translatable into an empiricist language. Thus, the problem for the translatability criterion of meaning remains.

The second defect with the criterion mentioned by Hempel involves what he calls *theoretical constructs*, examples of which include the terms *electron*, *gravitational potential*, and *electric field*. As Hempel defined an empiricist language, the only predicates allowed are observation predicates, and predicates that can be defined in terms of observation predicates plus Russell's logical apparatus. Hempel notes that a predicate like *is an electron* is neither an observation predicate, nor definable in strictly observational terms. Since this means that such predicates would be excluded from an empiricist language, the translatability criterion of meaning wrongly characterizes statements about electrons and other theoretical entities as meaningless.

Hempel's reaction to this problem was very important. He took it to show that empiricists must shift the focus of their criteria of meaning away from individual sentences, and toward whole systems of sentences. According to him, what makes sentences about theoretical entities meaningful is that they are embedded in a network of hypotheses and observational statements that can be used to make testable predictions. These predictions are the product of all the different aspects of the system working together. As a result, if one is given a set of observational predictions made by a theoretical system, one cannot, generally, match up each prediction with a single isolated hypothesis in the system. Hempel suggests that this is the crucial fact that makes it impossible to define theoretical terms in isolation. If it were the case that for each statement S involving a theoretical term, we could isolate a set of predictions made by S alone, and if these predictions exhausted the contribution made by S to the predictions made by the theory as a whole, then we could simply define S in terms of those predictions. However, the interdependence of S with other sentences in the system makes this impossible. Thus, what we have to look for is not the empirical content of each individual statement taken in isolation, but rather the role of each statement in an articulated system which, as a whole, has empirical content.

Lessons of the Positivists' Failed Attempt to Vindicate Verificationism

What, then, is left of the empiricist criterion of meaning? In effect, it has evolved into the claim that a non-analytic, non-contradictory sentence is meaningful when it plays a functional role in some system which makes observational predictions. There is much about this idea that is vague and open-ended. What counts as a theoretical system? What is the empirical meaning or content of such a system? What role must an individual sentence play in the system in order to be counted as meaningful in virtue of its contribution to the meaning of the whole? Are only systems that are actually used capable of conferring meaning on a sentence, or may a sentence be meaningful because it is **conceivable** that it should play an appropriate role in some merely possible systems? None of these questions are seriously addressed by Hempel, let alone answered. Still, the shift in emphasis away from the individual sentence to the system or theory as a whole is significant. The key notion is that the system as a whole is the thing that has observational consequences. Thus, if meaning is still to be analyzed in terms of such consequences, the natural units of meaning—the things to which empirical criteria of meaningfulness apply—should be entire theories or systems, rather than sentences taken individually.

This move towards *linguistic holism* was one of two major responses that grew out of the history of failed attempts to formulate a verificationist theory of meaning for individual sentences. The chief proponent of this response was Willard Van Orman Quine, whose philosophy we will take up at the end of this volume. The leading idea behind Quine's approach was that meaning really is explainable in terms of verification on the basis of observational consequences, but since these consequences can't be portioned out over sentences taken individually, but rather are derived from entire theories or conceptual schemes, it is such theories and conceptual schemes that are the primary bearers of meaning, or content. The other main historical reaction to the failure of positivism rejected the idea that meaning can be understood, or analyzed, in terms of verification, and attempted to find some other way of understanding meaning. Following the later Wittgenstein, many British philosophers in the post-positivist period—John L. Austin, Gilbert Ryle, Peter Strawson, Richard M. Hare, and others—attempted to explain meaning by appealing to the many different ways in which expressions are used in ordinary language, and to draw philosophical lessons from this approach. The development of these ideas will be examined in volume 2.

Before we leave the history of unsuccessful attempts to formulate an acceptable version of the empiricist criterion of meaning, there is one further philosophical lesson to be drawn from the positivists' failure. The lesson is one that may be seen as broadly Moorean in spirit. In discussing G. E. Moore's response to skepticism, we talked about one of his important methodological points. Suppose we are considering a general philosophical theory of what conditions must be satisfied in order for something to count as knowledge. No matter how attractive that theory might initially appear to be, when considered on its own and in the abstract, it can never be more securely supported than the great mass of our most confident commonsense judgments about what we know, and what we don't. Thus, if any general philosophical theory of knowledge can be shown to conflict with most of what we ordinarily take ourselves to know, then the philosophical theory—rather than the commonsense judgments—must be rejected as incorrect. The same point can be made in other areas of philosophy, the theory of meaning being no exception. Even though the positivists had an initially attractive and somewhat plausible theory about what empirical meaning must be, the fact that different formulations of the theory repeatedly conflicted with our most confident pre-theoretic judgments about which sentences are meaningful, and which are not, was, quite correctly, taken to show that the philosophical theory of meaning was wrong, rather than the other way around.

The general point goes well beyond the particular theories developed by the logical positivists. Any theory of meaning we might construct, any theory of the form

S is meaningful iff . . . ,

must be answerable—at least to some considerable extent—to our ordinary, pre-philosophical judgments of what is meaningful and what isn't. This is true no matter whether the theory is aimed exclusively at **describing** our ordinary concept of meaning, or is at least partially **revisionary**, in that it seeks to modify and refine our ordinary concept by purging it of obscure or problematic elements in a way that solves theoretical problems. Verificationist theories of meaning were consciously **reformist** in motivation. The positivists thought it was a virtue of their theories that they were not completely faithful to every confident judgment about meaning that ordinary people make. What we have seen is that even theorists whose aim is one of substantial conceptual reform cannot afford to stray too far from our ordinary, pre-philosophical judgments. The further one goes down the reformist path, the more implausible the consequences of one's theory are likely to become, until at some point the implausibility of the consequences comes to outweigh the initial attractiveness of the theory. This is not to say that no philosophical revisions of our ordinary judgments, or of our ordinary pre-philosophical concepts, can ever be justified. In some cases, they can. However, it is to say that our ordinary pre-philosophical judgments substantially constrain even the most philosophically well-motivated theories.

CHAPTER 14

EMOTIVISM AND ITS CRITICS

Emotivist Doctrines and the Arguments for Them

The emotivist theory of value is a well-known and influential philosophical view which, although an important part of logical positivism, was

also conceptually detachable from it. It was part of logical positivism because several of its main tenets were supported by the verifiability criterion of meaning. It was detachable from positivism because it had other sources of support as well. As a result, it was able to survive, in one form or another, after classical verificationism had fallen by the wayside. Two leading emotivists that we will consider are A. J. Ayer, who presented his views in chapter 6 of *Language, Truth, and Logic*, and Charles L. Stevenson, whose views are presented in his seminal paper, "The Emotive Meaning of Ethical Terms."[1]

We begin with four central claims made by Ayer.[2]

E1. No evaluative judgment (sentence/statement) is equivalent to any non-evaluative judgment (sentence/statement).

E2. No non-evaluative judgment (sentence/statement) entails any evaluative judgment (sentence/statement).

E3. No evaluative judgment (sentence/statement) entails any non-evaluative judgment (sentence/statement).

E4. Evaluative judgments (sentences/statements) are neither true nor false. They do not state facts. Rather, their meaning is entirely emotive.

There were three main argumentative routes that led Ayer and other positivists to these theses. The first was verificationist. Since ethical and other evaluative statements seemed not to be verifiable in any reasonable sense by ordinary empirical observation, the positivists regarded them as cognitively meaningless. They were therefore regarded as incapable of expressing statements that are either true or false, or as bearing logical relations to such statements. Thus, if they were to have any function at all, it seemed that their function must be non-cognitive, or emotional.

The second argumentative route to emotivism began with G. E. Moore. The emotivists accepted Moore's critique of ethical naturalism. According to Moore, the central evaluative notion, *good*, is indefinable. Thus the word *good* cannot stand for any complex property.

---

[1] Charles L. Stevenson, "The Emotive Meaning of Ethical Terms," *Mind* 46 (1937).

[2] Ayer especially, but some other positivists as well, tended to be quite breezy and undiscriminating when writing about sentences, statements, and judgments—their "meanings," their "entailments," or lack of such. In order to achieve reasonable fidelity to the texts I will, for the most part, follow this regrettable tendency in reporting their views, except where more precise reformulation is absolutely required.

Nor, Moore thought, could it stand for any simple natural property the presence or absence of which could be settled by observation. The emotivists accepted all this and agreed with Moore that *good* cannot stand for any natural property whatsoever. However, whereas Moore concluded that it must stand for a non-natural property, the positivists rejected the idea of a non-natural property as nothing more than a mysterious we-know-not-what, and concluded that *good* doesn't express any property at all. Its function, they thought, must not be to make statements or to describe facts, but to express emotions.

The third argumentative route to emotivism rested on the action-guiding character of evaluative language, something strongly emphasized by Stevenson. The emotivists thought that to sincerely judge that something is good or right is to have a positive emotional attitude toward it that is capable of providing motivation for action. To judge an act to be right is to recognize a positive motivation for performing it. The emotivists thought that it is part of what we mean by words like *good* and *right* that anyone who is indifferent to x, or has no positive feelings toward x, **cannot** sincerely judge x to be good or right. We may summarize this view by saying, *if one sincerely judges x to be good or right, then x cannot leave one cold.*

This view of the action-guiding character of evaluative concepts fit the emotivist theory that to call something good or right is nothing more than to express one's positive attitude toward it. It also was used argumentatively as a weapon against many descriptive theories of goodness or rightness. The emotivists pointed out that it is possible for a person to sincerely judge an action to be one that (i) produces the greatest happiness for the greatest number, (ii) promotes human survival, (iii) is approved of by most people, or (iv) is what God wants us to perform, without having any positive feelings about the action, or recognizing any motivation to perform it. Since, according to the emotivists, it is impossible for a person to sincerely judge an action to be good or right without having such feelings and recognizing such motivations, judging an action to be good or right cannot be the same as judging it to be one that satisfies any of the descriptions (i–iv). And that means that *good* and *right* cannot mean the same as *action that produces the greatest happiness for the greatest number, action that promotes human survival, action that is approved of by most people,* or *action that God wants us to perform.* Since it was common to think of ethical theories as theories about the meanings of evaluative terms, the emotivists thought that, in this way, they could refute most competing descriptive analyses of these evaluative notions.[3]

Emotivism, Egoism, and Ethical Disagreements

Still, there is at least one kind of descriptive theory of evaluative terms that cannot be refuted in this way—namely, an egoistic theory. According to (meta)ethical egoism, an evaluative claim like *telling the truth is right* means the same as a certain corresponding claim about the preferences of the speaker—something like *I prefer for people to tell the truth*. Since it would be incoherent to sincerely assert the second of these claims—the claim about what one prefers—and then go on to add, *but telling the truth leaves me cold; I am completely indifferent about it*, egoism, as a theory of value, is compatible with the positivists' observation that evaluative judgments are emotive and action guiding.

However, egoism is not compatible with emotivism. According to egoism, evaluative claims are psychological claims about what one prefers. Since these may be true or false, egoism holds that evaluative claims may be true or false. This conflicts with the emotivist doctrine that evaluative claims do not state facts, and cannot be true or false. The situation then is this. One can see how the emotivists would have thought that the principle that evaluative judgments are invariably expressions of emotion and motivation, may, if true, provide an argument against many versions of descriptivism in ethics. However, even if that principle is true, it provides no argument against egoism. In order to reject that theory, the emotivists had to find another argument.

C. L. Stevenson did this in "The Emotive Meaning of Ethical Terms," where he uses a version of Moore's old argument about disagreement to refute egoism.[4] Imagine the following dialog between A and B.

---

[3] This argument shows, at most, that *good* and *right* are not strictly synonymous with any descriptive phrase *D* that does not carry with it, as part of its meaning, an intrinsic connection with motivation. In itself, this result is very weak, and directly analogous to Moore's conclusion that goodness cannot be descriptively defined. To turn the emotivists' conclusion into something stronger, one needs the bundle of Moore's flawed assumptions about *synonymy, definition, analyticity, logical consequence,* and *entailment*. Although these assumptions were congenial to the positivists—with their one-dimensional conception of the modalities—they cease to be available to non-cognitivists when the link between non-cognitivism and its positivist origins is severed.

[4] See chapter 4.

A: Fighting terrorists is the right thing to do.

B: That's not so. Fighting terrorists is not right. We should try to understand them.

According to egoism, this dialog is equivalent to:

A': I prefer that we fight terrorists.

B': That's not so. I prefer that we not fight terrorists. We should try to understand them.

This analysis of the dialog seems wrong. On the egoist's analysis, B's response is bizarre. In saying "that's not so," it would seem that his intention is to **contradict** what A said. But if the egoist is right, he doesn't do this at all. Rather, he makes a statement describing his own feelings that is perfectly compatible with the egoists' analysis of A's statement.[5]

It is hard not to agree with Moore and Stevenson that the egoist's analysis of the disagreement between A and B leaves something to be desired. However, one might wonder whether the emotivist is capable of doing any better. Surely, if his analysis does nothing more than note the emotions of each speaker, it is hard to see how he can succeed in explaining the disagreement between the two. There is, however, more to emotivism than simple displays of raw emotion. According to Stevenson, many uses of evaluative language are better analyzed as **recommendations** put forward by the speaker, than as statements that are true or false. On this view, the original dialog between A and B is analyzed along the following lines:

A*: Let's all support the fight against the terrorists.

B*: On the contrary, let's not support the fight against them. Instead, let's try to understand them.

When the dialog is analyzed in this way, what we have is not a pair of conflicting statements, but a pair of conflicting recommendations.

---

[5] Ayer (p. 110 of *Language, Truth, and Logic*) takes a slightly different view of Moore's argument. Stevenson grants that there is an intuitive sense of disagreement in which A and B clearly disagree, and which is shown by Moore's argument not to be captured by egoism. According to Stevenson, this sense of disagreement—which he goes on to articulate and calls *a disagreement in interest*—is not what Moore would have taken it to be, namely a disagreement about facts. Ayer, on the other hand, builds into Moore's argument against egoism not only the assumption that there is a genuine disagreement of some sort between A and B, but also the assumption that the disagreement is a factual one. Thus, Ayer maintains that Moore's argument incorporates a false assumption. In making use of the argument above, I have separated the two assumptions, and have taken the argument to incorporate only the first.

Two **statements** conflict when the truth of one would conceptually or necessarily preclude the truth of the other. Two **recommendations** conflict when following one would conceptually or necessarily preclude following the other. According to the emotivists, the disagreement expressed in the dialog is of this latter type. It is not explicitly a disagreement in belief; rather it is what Stevenson calls *a disagreement in interest*.

How, then, are disagreements in interest to be resolved? According to the emotivists, many disagreements in interest arise not because people have fundamentally different values or preferences, but rather because they have different factual beliefs. The way to resolve these evaluative disagreements is to achieve agreement on the relevant facts. For example, the disagreement between A and B might be caused by an underlying factual disagreement about (i) the causes that led the terrorists to perpetrate their attacks, (ii) their ultimate goals and motivations, (iii) the prospects for, and costs of, defeating the terrorists and their allies militarily, (iv) the likelihood that future terrorism can be deterred by swift and strong military action, and (v) the likelihood that restraining the military and compromising with the terrorists would encourage others to launch similarly violent attacks in the future to advance their political agendas. All of these are factual matters that could, in principle, be argued and investigated in a rational way. Thus, emotivism does make room for rational debate to resolve evaluative disagreements.

However, this appeal to rationality to resolve evaluative disagreements will work only when the disagreements really are based on different beliefs about a factual matter. If A and B have fundamentally different values—fundamentally different preferences about certain kinds of conduct, various forms of social organization, or other fundamental matters—then emotivism maintains that there can be **no** rational resolution of their differences. Let me take one minor example. Suppose that A values punishing and even putting to death those who have murdered thousands of innocent people, not simply because doing so will deter others, but also because our sense of justice demands it. Suppose, on the other hand, that B abhors revenge and violence in any form, and would not favor retributive violence or capital punishment under any circumstances. If these different attitudes of A and B are **not** based on different factual beliefs, then emotivism tells us that a rational resolution of the evaluative differences between them is **conceptually impossible**.

Here, it is important to realize that the emotivists were not making a psychological or sociological point. It is not just that A and B might never in fact come to agree about capital punishment, for example. Nor is the point that, alas, human nature being what it is, one can never expect people to be rational about the things they hold dear. The emotivists' point goes far beyond this; it is that when A says, in the situation we have described, *Capital punishment of mass murderers is right* and B says *It is wrong*, there is no factual issue, there is no genuine belief whatsoever, separating the two parties. Since there is no belief on which they differ, **there is nothing separating them about which it is even possible to reason**. Their difference is entirely a difference in interest.

Criticisms of Emotivism

Having explained what emotivism is, and why the emotivists believed it to be true, I now turn to criticisms of the view.

The Problem of Evaluative Entailments

We begin by recalling three of the claims made by Ayer and other emotivists.

E1. No evaluative judgment (sentence/statement) is equivalent to any non-evaluative judgment (sentence/statement).

E2. No non-evaluative judgment (sentence/statement) entails any evaluative judgment (sentence/statement).

E3. No evaluative judgment (sentence/statement) entails any non-evaluative judgment (sentence/statement).

The key point is that these theses talk in terms of an **exhaustive dichotomy**. Every statement is either evaluative or non-evaluative. With this in mind, consider the following:

1. You stole that money.

2. You acted wrongly in stealing that money.

3. Stealing money is wrong.

Here (3) is clearly evaluative and (1) is apparently non-evaluative. But what about (2)? It would seem to be evaluative. But note that (2) entails (1), which is non-evaluative, which contradicts thesis E3.

Ayer discusses these examples on page 107 of *Language, Truth, and Logic.*

> The presence of an ethical symbol in a proposition adds nothing to its factual content. Thus if I say to someone, "You acted wrongly in stealing that money," I am not stating anything more than if I had simply said, "You stole that money." In adding that this action is wrong I am not making any further statement about it. I am simply evincing my moral disapproval of it. It is as if I had said it with the addition of some special exclamation marks. The tone, or the exclamation marks, adds nothing to the literal meaning of the sentence. It merely serves to show that the expression of it is attended by certain feelings in the speaker.

One of the things that Ayer seems to be saying is that (1) and (2) have the same literal content or meaning. But that would suggest that they are logically equivalent, which would contradict thesis E1.

To save Ayer from this problem, we might suggest that in reality (2) is a **complex** sentence including an **evaluative** part and an **empirical** part. On this view, the logical form of (2) is something like

2′. You stole that money, and stealing money is wrong (or that was wrong).

Here, the left-hand conjunct is an **empirical** sentence, and the right-hand conjunct is a purely **evaluative** sentence. What about the compound as a whole? We don't want to call it *evaluative*, because it entails the left-hand conjunct, which is empirical. We don't want to call it *empirical*, because it entails the right-hand conjunct, and that is evaluative. Rather we could just say that (2) and (2′) are **mixed** sentences. Thus, we end up recognizing three kinds of sentence—**evaluative, empirical,** and **mixed**.

We could then restate theses E1–E3 as follows:

E1′. No evaluative judgment (sentence/statement) is logically equivalent to any empirical judgment (sentence/statement).

E2′. No empirical judgment (sentence/statement) entails any evaluative judgment (sentence/statement).

E3′. No evaluative judgment (sentence/statement) entails any empirical judgment (sentence/statement).

In addition to these three theses, the emotivist should be thought of as continuing to hold that evaluative sentences are neither true nor false. They do not state facts; rather their meaning is entirely non-cognitive, or emotive.

So far, so good. Since example (2) is no longer covered by the emended theses, it is not a counterexample to them. However, we are still not out of the woods. According to standard definitions of entailment, the things that stand in this relation to one another are things that are capable of being true or false—statements, propositions, or sentences used to make statements or express propositions. We don't say that a cheer, a grunt, a smile, an exclamation—*Wow!*—or even a command **entails** anything, certainly not any statement.

With this in mind, consider again the observation that (2) entails (1). This might seem to be all right, in view of the fact that (2) is a mixed sentence, having the logical form (2'). But how is (2') to be understood? Since its right-hand conjunct is evaluative, it would seem that, according to at least some prominent emotivist analyses, (2') ought to be understood along the lines of (2").

2". You stole that money and don't steal money!

But does it really make sense to say that (2"), as a whole, is the sort of thing that can have a truth value? If not, then the emotivist cannot contend that (2) has a truth value, and so cannot admit what seems to be an obvious fact—namely, that (2) entails (1).

In fact, we can put the objection more strongly. (3) is an example of a **purely** evaluative sentence, which, according to the emotivist, ought to have a logical form along the lines of (3').

3'. Don't steal money!

However, it seems clear, pre-theoretically, that (3) entails the conditional the antecedent of which is sentence (1), and the consequent of which is sentence (2). In other words, (3), *Stealing money is wrong*, entails *If you stole that money, then you acted wrongly in stealing that money.* But whatever one says about (2) having a truth value, the emotivist **must** claim that (3) is incapable of being either true or false. Thus, it is not clear that the emotivist can capture our strong pre-theoretic conviction that (3) enters into genuine entailment relations, as is shown by the fact that (3) entails the conditional constructed by taking (1) as antecedent and (2) as consequent.

This is a serious problem for emotivism, though perhaps not an insoluble one. The problem is that evaluative sentences do enter into logical relations of some sort with various types of sentences. Emotivists can't explain this by appealing to the traditional notion of logical entailment. Hence, they must attempt to explain it some other way. This requires two things. First, the emotivists need to be more specific and precise about how evaluative uses of language are to be understood. Are they exclamations, are they equivalent to utterances of imperatives, are they performances of some sort—e.g., commands or recommendations? Second, having hit on a precise and explicit analysis, the emotivists need to characterize logical relations different from, but analogous to, the logical entailment that evaluative sentences enter into. Certain steps in this direction—for example, attempts to develop a logic of imperatives—were taken by descendants of the original emotivists.[6] Just how successful these steps were, or weren't, is something we won't examine here.

The Emotivists' Performative Fallacy

This brings us to another very serious problem for emotivism. As we have seen, emotivism was put forward as a theory of the meaning of evaluative words like *good, bad, right, wrong, just, unjust, should, ought,* and so on. The theory attempted to specify the meanings of these terms by specifying the meanings of certain simple sentences used with the intention of calling something good, bad, right, wrong, just, unjust, and the like—sentences like those in (4).

4a. That book is good.

  b. Stealing is wrong.

  c. The government is unjust.

The emotivists analyzed the meanings of these sentences in terms of the kinds of linguistic acts that speakers performed when they uttered them. Prominent among these linguistic acts were those of giving commands, issuing orders, and making recommendations. So, according to the emotivists, the meaning of the sentence *Stealing is wrong,* or *One ought not to steal,* was supposed to be roughly *Don't steal!* Similarly, the meaning of *That is good* was supposed to be something

---

[6] See R. M. Hare, *The Language of Morals* (New York: Oxford University Press, 1964), and *Freedom and Reason* (New York: Oxford University Press, 1965). Hare's work will be discussed in volume 2.

on the order of *Let's support x*, or *I recommend x*, where my utterance of *I recommend x* was taken **not** as an attempt to **describe** an act of recommending x, but rather as the very performance of the act of recommending itself.

That was the structure of the emotivist view. However, there was a fundamental flaw in this whole line of analysis. If what one is doing is giving a theory of meaning of evaluative words, phrases, and sentences, then one cannot restrict oneself to a limited range of linguistic environments; in particular, one cannot restrict oneself to simple sentences the utterance of which is used to perform acts of recommending, commanding, and the like. Rather, one's theory of the meanings of evaluative expressions must apply to all the different kinds of sentences in which those expressions may occur.

To my knowledge, the first critic of emotivism to make this point was Sir David Ross in his book *The Foundations of Ethics*, published in 1939.

> The theory that all judgements with the predicate 'right' or 'good' are commands has evidently very little plausibility. The only moral judgements of which it could with any plausibility be maintained that they are commands are those in which one person says to another 'you ought to do so-and-so'. A command is an attempt to induce some one to behave as one wishes him to behave, either by the mere use of authoritative or vehement language, or by this coupled with the intimation that disobedience will be punished. And there is no doubt that such words as 'you ought to do so-and-so' may be used as one's means of so inducing a person to behave a certain way. But if we are to do justice to the meaning of 'right' or 'ought', we must take account also of such modes of speech as 'he ought to do so-and-so', 'you ought to have done so-and-so', 'if this and that had been the case, you ought to have done so-and-so', 'if this and that were the case, you ought to do so-and-so', 'I ought to do so-and-so.' Where the judgement of obligation has reference either to a third person, not the person addressed, or to the past, or to an unfulfilled past condition, or to a future treated as merely possible, or to the speaker himself, there is no plausibility in describing the judgement as a command. But it is easy to see that 'ought' means the same in all these cases, and that if in some of them it does not express a command, it does not do so in any. And if the form of

words 'you ought to do so-and-so' may be used as a way of inducing the person addressed to behave in a particular way, that does not in the least imply that the apparent statement is not really a statement, but a command. What distinguishes its meaning from that of the genuine 'do so-and-so' is that one is suggesting to the person addressed a *reason* for doing so-and-so, viz., that it is right. The attempt to induce the person addressed to behave in a particular way is a separable accompaniment of the thought that the act is right, and cannot for a moment be accepted as the meaning of the words 'you ought to do so-and-so.[7]

Much later, this point was developed further by others—most notably Peter Geach and John Searle. The following criticism of emotivism is an elaboration of this general line of argument.[8]

Taking our cue from these philosophers, we recognize that in giving the meaning of evaluative words, phrases, and sentences, we cannot restrict ourselves to simple sentences like (4a–c), which are used to perform acts of recommending, commanding, and the like. Rather, our theory of the meanings of evaluative expressions must apply to all the different kinds of sentences in which those expressions may occur—including the sentences in (5).

5a. George Bush Sr. should have finished off Saddam Hussein in 1991.

b. I wonder whether I ought to work harder.

c. If western-style democracies are just, then they will win the allegiance of their citizens.

d. Bill hopes that that electric blanket is a good one.

It is hard to analyze these sentences in terms of imperatives, commands, orders, or recommendations. Certainly, they do not mean the same thing as the bizarre examples in (6).

---

[7] Sir W. David Ross, *Foundations of Ethics* (Oxford: Clarendon Press, 1939), pp. 33–34.

[8] For some reason, Ross's original objection seems not to have attracted much attention, or to have had much impact on the debate. Much later, in "Ascriptivism," (*Philosophical Review*, 69 [1960]), Peter Geach revived and elaborated the objection (without making reference to Ross), which he directed at proponents of the ordinary language school at Oxford in the '50s. Still later, John Searle, in "Meaning and Speech Acts" (*Philosophical Review*, 71 [1962]), elaborated the objection further, without reference to either Geach or Ross. Searle does, however, cite the discussion of Paul Ziff, *Semantic Analysis* (Ithaca: Cornell University Press, 1960), section 227 and following, where a similar line of argument is developed.

6a. George Bush Sr., listen up, finish off Saddam Hussein in 1991!

George Bush Sr., I order you to finish off Saddam Hussein in 1991.

George Bush Sr., I recommend that you finish off Saddam Hussein in 1991.

George Bush Sr., please, finish off Saddam Hussein in 1991.

b. I wonder whether: work harder!

I wonder whether I order myself to work harder.

I wonder whether I recommend that I work harder.

c. If: support western-style democracies!, then they will win the allegiance of their citizens.

If I order you to support western-style democracies, then they will win the allegiance of their citizens.

If I recommend western-style democracies, then they will win the allegiance of the citizens.

d. Bill hopes: I recommend that electric blanket!

Bill hopes that I recommend that electric blanket.

Bill hopes that he recommends that electric blanket.

Bill hopes: buy that electric blanket, if you are in the market for one!

The general point goes beyond amusing or bizarre examples like these. Evaluative expressions occur in a wide variety of sentences. Any theory of what these words mean must explain their contributions to the meanings of all sentences in which they occur. The problem with emotivism is that only a small number of sentences containing evaluative expressions can plausibly be analyzed as involving imperatives, commands, orders, recommendations, and the like.

As a result, emotivism misses the meanings of evaluative expressions when they occur in sentences like those in (5), which go beyond the restricted range of cases in which speakers use evaluative sentences to make straightforward recommendations, or to issue clear commands or orders. More strongly, there is reason to believe that this failure indicates that emotivism has not correctly specified the meanings even of simple evaluative sentences, like those in (4). After all, it doesn't seem plausible that evaluative expressions **change** their meaning from one linguistic environment to another. For example, when we consider the conditional sentence (5c), it seems clear that it is intended to be descriptive in some way. In order for it to be so, the evaluative clause that is its antecedent, *western-style democracies are just*, must be taken to be descriptive as well—rather than as an imperative, or a sentence used to make a recommendation. Presumably we don't want to say that the sentence *Western-style democracies are just* has a purely evaluative meaning—to be given solely in terms of imperatives or recommendations—when it is used all by itself, while having a different, descriptive, meaning when it occurs as the antecedent of a conditional (or the complement of a propositional attitude verb like *believe, hope,* or *wonder*). For if it did switch its meaning in this way, then the pattern of reasoning in (7) would be a simple piece of equivocation, rather than the deductively valid argument that we recognize it to be.

7a. Western-style democracies are just.

b. If western-style democracies are just, then they will win the support of their citizens.

c. Therefore, western-style democracies will win the support of their citizens.

The moral of this story is that evaluative expressions **don't** have the kinds of meanings that the emotivist theory of evaluative language claimed that they have. This doesn't mean that the emotivists were wrong when they noted that evaluative words are often used in simple sentences like those in (4) to make recommendations, to issue commands, or to exhort hearers to certain courses of action. These sentences **are** often used in these ways. But the **meanings** of these sentences are **not** given by specifying the actions of this sort that they are often used to perform. Perhaps an analogy will help. If I say, in a letter of recommendation, that a certain student is brilliant, I am performing the linguistic acts of praising and recommending the student. But that doesn't show that the word *brilliant* has a special, non-descriptive, performative meaning. What it shows is that the words *praise* and *recommendation* are understood in such a way that to say that a student has one of the characteristics, such as brilliance, that we find desirable in students is to praise or recommend her.[9] By the same token, to say that something is good is often to recommend it, but that doesn't show that the word *good* has some special performative meaning. Rather, it shows

---

[9] Another good example is *dangerous*. To say that something, or some person, is dangerous is, normally, to warn someone. Nevertheless, it is still a descriptive term.

that the word *recommend* is understood in such a way that one way to recommend something is to predicate goodness of it.

In this connection, it is worth noting that some words of English really do have non-descriptive, performative meanings that can be given by specifying the linguistic acts that they are used to perform. Among these are the words *hello, ditto, please,* and *yes.* To understand the word *hello* is to understand that to say "Hello" is to greet someone. To understand *ditto* is to know that to utter it is to signal agreement with a previous remark. To understand the word *yes* is, roughly, to understand that uttering it in response to a question like *Are you comfortable?* is to give a **positive** response, which in this case is equivalent to asserting that you are comfortable. To understand *please* is to understand that adding it to sentences of certain restricted grammatical forms indicates that your remark is to be taken as a polite request. Because the meanings of these words **are** given in terms of the linguistic performances they are used to make, the range of sentences in which they can meaningfully occur is highly restricted.

For example, we don't normally say any of the following: *I believe that hello; If hello, then one is friendly; I doubt whether ditto; If ditto, then there is nothing to argue about; Sam disputed Mark's claim that would you please pass the pepper; I wonder whether yes;* or *If yes, then there is an even prime number.* In some cases we can force a comprehensible interpretation onto one of these deviant sentences, as in the following dialog: A asks *Is 2 a prime number?* B responds *If yes, then there is an even prime number.* However, even here, the response would be more properly expressed *If the answer is 'yes', then there is an even prime number.*

The general point, I think, remains. Since these special words have non-descriptive, performative meanings that are given by specifying the linguistic acts they are used to perform, the range of linguistic environments in which they can meaningfully occur is severely restricted. If evaluative terms were similarly non-descriptive and performative, we should expect the range of linguistic environments in which they can meaningfully occur to be similarly restricted. Since evaluative words are **not** restricted in this way, they do **not** have the kind of meaning that the emotivist theory ascribes to them.

Revisionary Conceptions of Emotivism

If this line of argument is correct, then emotivism must be rejected, assuming that it is to be taken as a **descriptive** theory of what evaluative words really mean in ordinary language. Perhaps, however, there is another way in which it might be understood. Suppose an emotivist were to maintain that our ordinary use of evaluative language is confused and misguided. On the one hand, we use various simple sentences containing evaluative terms to give orders, make recommendations, and generally to guide action. On the other hand, we use evaluative terms in a broader class of sentences in a quite different, quasi-descriptive way—as if they were simply words standing for properties that things might have or lack. Thus, it might be maintained, our ordinary use of evaluative words presupposes both that they stand for properties of objects, and that the recognition that an object has one or another of these properties is something that is inevitably magnetic, or motivating, and action-guiding.

But, the emotivist might maintain, this is incoherent—no properties are intrinsically, and by their very nature, magnetic and action-guiding in this way. An emotivist who took this view would **reject** our ordinary evaluative notions as confused, inadequate, and ultimately inapplicable to anything.[10] In their place, he might propose that we substitute evaluative notions that really do work according to the emotivist theory. An emotivist who took this line would be a **revisionist**, whose aim was not to describe our existing evaluative language, but to replace it with something arguably preferable. Of course, one might wonder whether this is really either practical or preferable. One might also wonder what could possibly make a philosopher who took this position think that the rest of the world would follow his lead.

Historical Legacies of Emotivism

In discussing the arguments for and against emotivism, we have, implicitly, invoked two general requirements that any theory of evaluative language and evaluative judgments must satisfy.

R1. The theory must explain the role of reason, reflection, and logic in evaluative matters.

R2. The theory must explain how the use of evaluative language and the making of evaluative judgments are related to motivation, commitment, and action.

---

[10] John Mackie takes something like this view, without being a revisionist, in *Ethics* (Singapore: Pelican Books, 1977).

The tension between these two requirements is one of the central difficulties in constructing an adequate theory of evaluative language and evaluative judgments. Standard descriptivist theories, which treat evaluative language as a species of fact-stating discourse, and evaluative judgments as a species of belief and knowledge about an independent realm of fact, tend to emphasize R1, while often struggling with R2. By contrast, emotivism focused on R2, while coming to grief over R1.

There is little doubt that the theories of the original emotivists were decisively refuted by the arguments brought against them. However, that doesn't mean that non-cognitivism about value, broadly conceived, died with emotivism. As we will see in volume 2, an important brand of non-cognitivism flourished in the '50s and '60s, as part of what was called the *ordinary language school* of British philosophy. Although it too was plagued with severe problems, the idea that there is something special about evaluative language and thought that sets them apart from ordinary fact-stating discourse and knowledge of the world remains a potent force in moral philosophy to this day. In this respect, the historical legacy of emotivism continues.

A different historical effect, which was initially felt quite strongly, but which, fortunately, did not prove to be so long-lasting, was a drastic narrowing of the focus of philosophical thought on evaluative matters in the analytic tradition. One aspect of this narrowing was the restriction of attention to a very limited range of evaluative terms—*good, bad, right, wrong, ought*, and a few others—for which reductive analyses to a small base of emotions and preferences seemed (for a time) to be possible. For more than two decades after the advent of emotivism, philosophical discussions of value all too often gave the impression of having lost sight of the rich and nuanced character of the domain of evaluative language available for expressing judgments. A small sampling of evaluative terms includes, *fair, just, unjust, obligatory, permissible, valuable, praiseworthy, blameworthy, justified, excusable, forgivable, rude, polite, inconsiderate, heroic, courageous, wise, prudent, decent, slovenly, slothful, beautiful, magnificent, wonderful, charming, dainty,* and *dumpy.* When one begins to appreciate the variety of our evaluative language, one has to wonder whether the same kind of analysis will work for all evaluative expressions. Whether or not, in the long run, emotivism turns out to have contained important insights, one of its worst short-term historical effects was to encourage philosophers to ignore the many differences among evaluative terms. Fortunately, there is now a much wider appreciation among analytic philosophers that moral philosophy needs—and, happily, is now receiving—a conceptual mapping of the territory covered by different classes of evaluative terms. This mapping may or may not turn out to be compatible with an essentially non-cognitivist analysis of evaluative language. However, in order to provide it, one must do more than simply declare all evaluative judgments to be emotive.

Another temporary but historically significant effect of emotivism was the elevation of meta-ethics at the expense of normative ethics. Emotivism was not a view about which evaluative judgments one should accept, but a doctrine about what one is doing when one accepts any such judgment. Hence, the dispute over emotivism was not a dispute within ethics so much as a dispute about the nature of ethics itself. In short, emotivism was a meta-ethical thesis. Still, taking a meta-ethical position does not exempt one from the need to make ethical judgments and choose among competing ethical principles. The study of these principles and the methods for choosing among them is known as *normative ethics*. Since even emotivists are called upon to make ethical decisions and resolve moral quandaries, one might imagine that the pursuit of normative ethics by philosophers would have continued unabated, even in the emotivist era. Unfortunately, this didn't prove to be so.

Instead, a commitment to emotivism tended to discourage many philosophers from doing normative ethics. One of the best indications of this is found in the highly influential paper, "The Emotive Meaning of Ethical Terms," by C. L. Stevenson, arguably the premiere emotivist of his day. After arguing that the meaning of sentences containing 'good' is primarily emotive rather than descriptive, Stevenson ends his paper with the following paragraph.

> I may add that if 'x is good' is essentially a vehicle for suggestion, it is scarcely a statement which philosophers, any more than other men, are called upon to make. To the extent that ethics predicates the ethical terms of anything, rather than explains their meaning, **it ceases to be a reflective study**. Ethical statements are social instruments. They are used in a cooperative enterprise in which we are mutually adjusting ourselves to the interests of others. Philosophers have a part, as do all men, but not a major part.[11]

[11] P. 281 in Ayer's, *Logical Positivism*, my boldface emphasis.

Here, Stevenson seems to be suggesting

(i) that the job of the moral philosopher is to determine the meanings of ethical terms; and

(ii) that if those meanings are emotive, then the formulation and assessment of ethical principles specifying what is right, wrong, good, or bad is not a reflective enterprise, and is not a proper subject for philosophical study.

In short, Stevenson seems to be saying that if emotivism is correct, then there is no such thing as normative ethical theory, as a reflective enterprise.

But it is hard to see why this should be so. Perhaps it is true for the simplest forms of emotivism, in which assertive utterances of ethical sentences are little more than expressions of raw emotion, with little else in the way of intelligible content. However, it is not true, or at least not obviously so, for more sophisticated versions of emotivism (or non-cognitivism generally), according to which saying that something is good retains its essential magnetic or motivating force. As I have emphasized, all of us, emotivist or not, make moral choices. In making these choices we often appeal to moral principles grounded in commitments about which we feel confident and wholehearted. However, we also come up against situations in which our principles conflict with one another, or fail to give a clear result for some other reason. In these situations, we need to extrapolate from the familiar to the unfamiliar, to find a way of modifying and extending the principles we accept, which already cover many cases we feel clear about, so that they come to provide clear and consistent guidance for cases about which we are presently uncertain. Even if, in the end, our most basic ethical principles turn out to rest in part on personal interests and preferences about which there can be no rational argument, it is clear that reason, argument, and reflection play a large role in formulating, testing, modifying, and extending those principles. Since this sort of reasoning is precisely the domain of normative ethics, this normative enterprise is highly reflective, and there is plenty here for philosophers to do, whether or not they are non-cognitivists in meta-ethics.

The way to see this most clearly is to focus on the questions: *What should I do? How should I live?* and *What ethical principles should I adopt?*, as opposed to the question *What ethical principles can I demonstrate any rational agent must adopt, no matter what his or her particular interests or preferences?* Stevenson may well have thought that the truth of any form of emotivism precluded ethical principles from being demonstrably binding on every rational agent. But even if this were so, to think that it would preclude normative ethics from being a reflective enterprise that may be practiced productively by philosophers is to hold a conception of normative ethics that is far too restrictive. Unfortunately, Stevenson was far from the only emotivist, or emotivist-inspired philosopher, to hold this conception.

There were, however, others who continued to do illuminating work in normative ethics, even in the age of emotivism. One of these was the great anti-emotivist and anti-consequentialist, Sir David Ross. We turn to his work in the next chapter.

CHAPTER 15

NORMATIVE ETHICS IN THE ERA
OF EMOTIVISM:
THE ANTICONSEQUENTIALISM
OF SIR DAVID ROSS

CHAPTER OUTLINE

1. *Consequentialism*

   Basic consequentialist theses; distinction between simple and extended consequentialism

2. *Ross's challenge to consequentialism*

   Three categories of duties that conflict with maximizing good consequences; whether the goodness of a consequence is always independent of how it is produced and who receives it

3. *The scope of moral obligation*

   The normative and meta-ethical significance of a neglected range of acts: morally good but non-obligatory acts, morally bad but permissible acts, and permissible, non-obligatory, morally neutral acts

4. *Ross's positive theory of moral obligation*

   The variety of *prima facie* duties; the definition of actual duty and the problem of weighing conflicting *prima facie* duties; Ross's pessimistic conclusion and its effect

5. *Ross's moral methodology*

   The use of pre-existing moral convictions to assess moral theses; kinship with Moore's methodological conservatism in epistemology

W. D. Ross was a contemporary of A. J. Ayer and C. L. Stevenson. Like Ayer, he was a Fellow at Oxford. (He was also Provost of Oriel College.) Unlike Ayer and Stevenson, he was neither an emotivist nor a logical positivist. He believed that ethical sentences and judgments are true or false, and that those which are true state genuine facts. Thus, in trying to determine which moral principles we should accept, he took himself to be trying to determine which moral principles are true. However, because his views about the factual nature of moral judgments are largely independent of his arguments about which moral principles we should adopt, one can study his normative theses without attempting to settle the question of whether his meta-ethical position is correct. For analytical purposes, his contribution to the normative enterprise can be divided into three parts: (i) his critique of consequentialist theories of moral obligation, (ii) his own alternative theory of obligation, and (iii) his method of formulating and testing ethical theories. We will discuss all three, beginning with his critique of consequentialism.

Consequentialism

The central characteristic of consequentialist theories of moral obligation is that they take the rightness of an action to be completely determined by the goodness or badness of its consequences. Although these theories may take different forms, the simplest, most general, and purest form of consequentialism is given by (C).

> C. (i) An act x is right iff there is no alternative act y open to the agent which would produce a greater balance of good over bad consequences than that produced by x. (An act which is not right is wrong.)
>
> (ii) An act is obligatory iff it produces a greater balance of good over bad consequences than any other act open to the agent.

According to theories of this sort, if the state of affairs resulting from an act is the best state of affairs that one is able to bring about, all things considered, then that is the act one morally ought to perform. If one performs any other act which brings about a less good state of affairs, then one does something morally wrong. On this view, acts are simply means to the end of bringing about the best states of affairs possible. The nature of the act itself means nothing; its only morally relevant feature is the value of its effects.

Different versions of consequentialism result from making different decisions about what counts as good (and bad). For Ross, three simple things are good in themselves—virtue, knowledge, and pleasure. However, his arguments against strict consequentialist theories of moral obligation do not, for the most part, depend on precisely which things are taken to be good or bad. Except in special cases, we will not, therefore, be concerned with the different theories of goodness that might be adopted in conjunction with the strict consequentialist principle. However, we do need to pause for a moment over the distinction between an act and its consequences. As I have said, consequentialism views acts as means to the end of producing good consequences. Thus, it is natural, when specifying the consequences of an act, not to include the act itself, or the fact that that act has been performed, as one of its consequences. After all, the consequences of an act are things **caused**, or produced, by the act, and no act causes itself; nor does it cause the fact that it has been performed.

Although this point is often taken for granted in discussing consequentialism, occasionally it is not. As a result, it is worthwhile to contrast two different conceptions of consequence, and consequentialism. According to the first conception, which we may call *simple consequentialism*, the consequences of an act do not include the act itself. Rather, an act occurs, and then, because it has occurred, certain other things—its consequences—occur later. For example, a witness at a trial lies under oath. Among the consequences of the lie may be that the defendant is acquitted, and that the witness is later tried for perjury. However, the fact that the witness told a lie is **not** one of the consequences of the lie the witness told. The second conception of consequentialism, which we will call *extended consequentialism*, differs from the first in just this respect. On this conception, the consequences of an act include those things caused by the act, plus the act itself. So, in the case of the lie, the fact that the witness lied is one of the consequences of the lie.

The difference between these two conceptions is potentially significant because the second allows one to attach intrinsic value to an act itself, and to include this value, along with the value of the states of affairs brought about by the act, in the consequentialist calculation. This could, in principle, have a marked effect on whether the act is characterized as right or wrong. For example, a proponent of extended consequentialism might assign lies a substantial degree of intrinsic badness, independent of the states of affairs they may bring about. As a result, the "consequences" of a lie, in the extended sense of 'consequences', would always include a substantial amount of badness, which would have to be outweighed by other good results in order for the act to be judged to be right, or obligatory.

Like many writers on the subject, Ross did not always distinguish between these two conceptions of consequentialism. However, it seems clear from many passages that his main target was simple consequentialism—which is natural, since simple consequentialism seems to be what consequentialists themselves standardly have in mind, at least until they encounter Ross-like objections. Consequently, for our purposes, I will take simple consequentialism to be the default consequentialist position, and I will revert to a consideration of extended consequentialism only when the occasion demands it.

Ross's Challenge to Consequentialism

Consequentialism Is Not True by Definition

The first point Ross makes is that the consequentialist principle C does not constitute a definition (in Moore's sense) of the expressions *right act*, *obligatory act*, or *act one ought to perform*. This is the subject of chapter 1, "The Meaning of *Right*," of his famous work *The Right and the Good*. He says:

> The most deliberate claim that *right* is definable as *productive of so and so* is made by Prof. G. E. Moore, who claims in *Principia Ethica* that *right* means *productive of the greatest possible good*. Now it has often been pointed out against hedonism, and by no one more clearly than Prof. Moore, that the claim that *good* just means *pleasant* cannot seriously be maintained; that while it may or may not be true that the only things that are good are pleasant, the statement that the good is just the pleasant is a synthetic, not an analytic proposition; that the words *good* and *pleasant* stand for distinct qualities, even if the things that possess the one are precisely the things that possess the other. If this were not so, it would not be intelligible that the proposition *the good is just the pleasant* should have been maintained on the one hand, and denied on the other, with so much fervor; for we do not fight for or against analytic propositions; we take them for granted. Must not the same claim be made about the statement *being right means being an act productive of the greatest good producible in the circumstances*? Is it not plain on reflection that this is not what we mean

by *right*, even if it be a true statement about what is right? It seems clear for instance that when an ordinary man says it is right to fulfil promises he is not in the least thinking of the total consequences of such an act, about which he knows and cares little or nothing. 'Ideal utilitarianism' [i.e., consequentialism] is, it would appear, plausible only when it is understood not as an analysis or definition of the notion of *right* but as a statement that all acts that are right, and only these, possess the further characteristic of being productive of the best possible consequences, and are right because they possess this other characteristic.[1]

As we saw in chapter 4, Ross was right in holding that consequentialist principles like C do not qualify as Moorean definitions. Of course, the fact that C isn't a definition doesn't tell us anything about whether or not it is true, or acceptable. Since Ross believes it to be unacceptable, he must next produce further argument to establish this stronger point.

We begin with two kinds of *prima facie* duties involving consequences that Ross recognizes. One kind, which he calls *duties of beneficence*, "rest on the mere fact that there are other beings in the world whose condition we can make better in respect of virtue, or of intelligence, or of pleasure" (these being regarded by Ross as things that are good in themselves).[2] The other, which he calls *duties of self-improvement*, "rest on the fact that we can improve our own condition in respect of virtue or of intelligence."[3] Roughly speaking, these are the kinds of duties that consequentialist theories recognize: duties to produce the greatest good, where this includes goods both for oneself and for others.[4] Although Ross clearly recognizes that these consequentialist considerations are relevant to determining what one ought to do, he believes that there are other factors that must also be considered. These additional factors can be categorized under three main headings—duties not to harm or injure others, duties of justice, and duties of special relation.

---

[1] Ross, *The Right and the Good* (Oxford: Clarendon Press, 1930), pp. 8–9.
[2] Ibid., p. 21.
[3] Ibid., p. 21.
[4] Note, however, the different treatment of pleasure in the two cases. Ross struggled over this. See pp. 24–26.

Duties Not to Harm Others

Regarding these duties, he says:

> I think that we should distinguish from [duties of beneficence] the duties that may be summed up under the title of *not injuring others*. No doubt to injure others is incidentally to fail to do them good; but it seems to me clear that non-maleficence is apprehended as a duty distinct from that of beneficence, and as a duty of a more stringent character.[5]

Although Ross doesn't elaborate a great deal on this, it is easy enough to see his point. Pure consequentialist principles like C require one to treat individuals as means to the end of benefiting mankind; and, because of this, they run afoul of our duty not to harm some individuals in order to benefit others. As Ross puts it, "*We should not in general consider it justifiable to kill one person in order to keep another alive, or to steal from one in order to give alms to another.*"[6]

We may illustrate this point by imagining the case of a doctor with three terminally ill patients—one needing a heart transplant, one needing kidneys, and one needing a liver. We stipulate that there are no voluntary donors or recently deceased individuals available, and that the only possible sources of the needed organs are healthy people with no connection to the patients, and no wish to sacrifice their lives for them. Nevertheless the doctor realizes that her patients will surely die without transplants. What should she do? One possible course of action, fantastic though it may sound, would be to trick a healthy person, kill him, and transplant the victim's organs in the three dying patients. There might, of course, be practical difficulties with this plan—e.g., the need to properly match the donor with the patients in order to prevent organ rejection, the uncertainties of the operation itself, the possibility of being discovered, and so on. However we may suppose, for the sake of argument, that all these difficulties have been eliminated; the doctor knows a healthy person whose organs would not be rejected (one of her former patients), she knows how to kill this person without anyone finding out, she has developed an essentially foolproof technique for transplanting organs which allows her to predict with a

[5] *The Right and the Good*, p. 21.
[6] Ibid., p. 22.

high degree of certainty that the operation would be a success, and she is sure that everything could be kept secret.

In such a scenario, following the gruesome plan would result in three lives saved versus one lost, whereas not following the plan would result in three lives lost. Supposing that the lives of all four individuals are essentially comparable to one another both in their own intrinsic goodness and in the amount of good they would do for others, were they to live, one naturally supposes that following the plan, and killing the one to save the three, would produce a greater balance of good consequences over bad than any alternative open to the doctor. If so, then the consequentialist principle C tells us that the doctor is **morally obligated** to go ahead with the plan. But surely, Ross would say, this is wrong; not only is the doctor not obligated to do so, she is obligated **not** to do so.

Ross took examples like these to show that the consequentialist principle C is false. In drawing this conclusion, he was both rejecting a normative principle, and interpreting that rejection from a meta-ethical point of view that takes moral discourse to be fact-stating. In our discussion, we are separating those ideas, and considering only the first. From this perspective, one must ask whether one agrees with Ross that the doctor is **not** morally obligated to follow her murderous plan. If, as I do, one does agree with this, then one must **reject** part (ii) of C (when taken to express the position we previously called *simple consequentialism*). If one further agrees with Ross, as I do again, that it would be impermissible, and hence wrong, for the doctor to follow the plan, then one must reject part (i) of C as well. Whether or not one expresses this by calling parts (i) and (ii) of C *false* is, for present purposes, immaterial.[7]

---

[7] A die-hard consequentialist who agrees with Ross about the doctor's plan might retreat to extended consequentialism, and expand his inventory of intrinsically bad states of affairs to include any state of affairs in which someone is murdered (as opposed to simply dying, or not being saved). Provided that he assigns such states a high enough degree of badness, he might get the same results as Ross in this case. However, it is not clear that this strategy of weakening consequentialism so as to accommodate Ross-type examples would work for all cases. Suppose the example were changed so that we were faced with the choice of killing an innocent person at the behest of a terrorist in order to stop him from carrying out his threat to kill three others. If, in this case, one believes that one is not morally obligated to kill the innocent party, then one must reject part (ii) of C, even on the extended understanding of consequences. A similar test might be applied to part (i).

As Ross sees it, the problem illustrated by our example is that principle C fails to take account of the fact that our duty not to harm innocent individuals outweighs any general duty we have to benefit others. This doesn't mean that our duty not to harm is absolute, and can never be outweighed by anything else; but it does mean that there is more to determining whether an act is right, wrong, or obligatory than impersonally tallying its consequences. One does not look **only** at the end results of an act and compare them with the end results of other possible acts. Rather, one must take into consideration how those results are brought about.

Duties of Justice

The second category of duties Ross takes to raise challenges for consequentialism consists of what he calls *duties of justice*. These, he says, "rest on the fact or possibility of a distribution of pleasure or happiness (or of the means thereto) which is not in accordance with the merit of the persons concerned; in such cases there arises a duty to upset or prevent such a distribution."[8] Ross himself has his own unique take on questions of the distribution of goods, and how these questions relate to consequentialism. In examining these questions, I will first present some sample cases involving distribution, and indicate why, from a certain commonly held perspective, they raise problems for consequentialism. After that, we will examine how Ross's views about merit bear on the matter.

One form that problems concerning the distribution of goods take arises from the fact that individuals have rights, or deserve certain things, independent of their status as sentient beings who are potential beneficiaries of one's actions. If individuals do have such rights (to life, liberty, and the like), or do deserve certain things, then actions that involve unjustly depriving a few individuals of their liberty, their property, or something else that they deserve, or have a right to, may properly be judged to be not only non-obligatory, but also wrong, even if such actions produce a small increment in the total social good that is unmatched by any alternative act open to the agent. The problem with consequentialism, from this point of view, is that it leaves no room for morally robust notions of deserving, or being entitled to, something.

[8] *The Right and the Good*, p. 21.

The following three examples illustrate this point. (i) A nation institutes a draft for military service. It is argued on consequentialist grounds that the poor should be drafted, while the productive and well-off should be exempted because (a) the latter add more, in civilian life, to the total social product than the poor do, and (b) their lives are better than those of the poor anyway—in terms of pleasure enjoyed, knowledge attained, virtue practiced, etc.—hence loss of their lives in battle would diminish the quantity of goods enjoyed by the totality of sentient beings more than would the loss of the lives of the poor. Surely, this line of reasoning is wrong. Instituting a draft restricted to the poor on these grounds is **not** morally required, but is, instead, morally **prohibited**. The problem for consequentialism is that it neglects the fact that each person has an equal right to life and liberty. (ii) A man works long and hard, on his own time, using only resources that he is already entitled to, to produce something for the benefit of himself and his family (e.g., he builds a house). After he is finished, someone else—perhaps someone in authority—correctly judges that the product of the man's labors would be enjoyed more by another family—enough so that confiscating and giving the man's work to that family would increase the total amount of good enjoyed by sentient beings as a whole slightly more than allowing the man to keep what he created. Nevertheless, such action is neither morally obligatory, nor, arguably, even morally permissible. The problem for consequentialism is that it neglects the fact that, normally, goods come into the world not as manna from heaven to be distributed impartially by benevolent authorities, but as the products of human activities that give rise to rights and entitlements. (iii) Members of group B have false beliefs about members of group A, and on that basis strongly dislike and disapprove of them. Nevertheless, a family from group A plans to take jobs and live in a community overwhelmingly inhabited by B's. Because of the B's violent dislike of the A's, this would lead to a great deal of anger, unhappiness, and unproductive resistance on the part of the B's—enough, we may imagine, to more than offset the good that would accrue to the family of A's if they were to move in. According to consequentialism, it would seem that the family is morally obligated not to move in. But this seems transparently wrong; the unhappiness experienced by the B's should count for nothing in this case. The problem for consequentialism is that it measures only the total amount of good enjoyed, not who enjoys it or why.

Or does it? In presenting these criticisms of consequentialism, I have assumed that the consequentialist takes facts about which things are intrinsically good (or bad) to be independent of who experiences them, and how they are produced. Although this view about goodness is quite common, it does not accurately reflect Ross's view. In chapter 2 of *The Right and the Good*, he describes the duties of justice as duties to bring about "*a distribution of happiness between other people **in proportion to merit**.*"[9] In chapter 5, he discusses the value of pleasure, which is one of the intrinsic goods, and its relationship to merit, as follows:

> But reflection on the conception of merit does not support the view that pleasure is always good in itself and pain always bad in itself. For while this conception implies the conviction that pleasure when deserved is good, and pain when undeserved is bad, it also suggests strongly that pleasure when undeserved is bad and pain when deserved good.
>
> There is also another set of facts which casts doubt on the view that pleasure is always good and pain always bad. We have a decided conviction that there are bad pleasures and (though this is less obvious) that there are good pains. We think that the pleasure taken either by the agent or by a spectator in, for instance, a lustful or cruel action is bad; and we think it a good thing that people should be pained rather than pleased by contemplating vice or misery.[10]

So perhaps in case (iii) above, involving the A's and the B's, the pain, unhappiness, and general disutility that the B's would experience were the A's to move in would not, by Ross's lights, count as bad, because the B's **shouldn't** be feeling these things.

In chapter 5, Ross expands his account of intrinsic goodness to include exactly four things, "virtue, pleasure, the allocation of pleasure to the virtuous, and knowledge (and in a less degree right opinion)."[11] According to him, pleasure is always good, except in those cases in which certain disqualifying characteristics are present.

> A state of pleasure has the property, not necessarily of being good, but of being something that is good if the state has no other characteristic that prevents it from being good. The two characteristics that may interfere with its being good are (a) that

[9] Ibid., p. 26, my boldface emphasis.
[10] Ibid., pp. 136–37.
[11] Ibid., p. 140.

of being contrary to desert, and (b) that of being a state which is the realization of a bad disposition.[12]

Since his theory of goodness incorporates some consideration both of desert, and of how particular good states of affairs are brought about, Ross does **not** view his duties of justice as conflicting with the general consequentialist duty to maximize the good.

> The duty of justice is particularly complicated, and the word is used to cover things which are really very different—things such as the payment of debts, the reparation of injuries done by oneself to another, and the **bringing about of a distribution of happiness between other people in proportion to merit**. I use the word to denote only the last of these three. In the fifth chapter I shall try to show that besides the three (comparatively) simple goods, virtue, knowledge, and pleasure, there is a more complex good, not reducible to these, consisting in the proportionment of happiness to virtue. The bringing of this about is a duty which we owe to all men alike. . . . **This, therefore, with beneficence and self-improvement, comes under the general principle that we should produce as much good as possible, though the good here involved is different in kind from any other.**[13]

The idea that one cannot determine which states of affairs are good, once and for all, without making some judgments about the moral character of those enjoying the good, and how that good came to be enjoyed, is a powerful one that deserves more attention than we can give it here.[14] Certainly, Ross has raised a very important issue. However, he has not supplied the needed details; nor, in my opinion, has he established that our duties of justice are simply special cases of the general consequentialist duty to maximize the good. Ross's linking of the goodness of pleasure with virtue may be sufficient to allow the consequentialist to deal with some problems of just distribution—perhaps even the third of our illustrative scenarios, involving the A's and

[12] Ibid., p. 138.

[13] Ibid., p. 27, my boldface emphasis.

[14] For an interesting recent discussion of goodness, desert, and their relation to equality, see Shelly Kegan, "Equality and Desert," in *What Do We Deserve?*, O. McLeod and L. Pojman, eds. (Oxford: Oxford University Press, 1998), 277–97.

the B's. However, it is far from obvious that this link resolves the problems for consequentialism posed by the first two scenarios. The problem with drafting the poor and exempting the well-off is not that this would upset the proper balance between virtue and happiness; there is no reason to assume that the poor are more virtuous than the well-off, and the policy would be wrong even if the poor were less virtuous. The same may be true in the second scenario as well—if our hard-working producer is himself morally quite ordinary, whereas the individuals on whom the authorities wish to bestow his labors are themselves morally exemplary. In such a case confiscation and transfer of his house might even improve the general balance of happiness and virtue. However, it would neither be just, morally obligatory, nor, arguably, morally permissible. What this case illustrates is that the producer has a special claim to the fruit of his labors that is not simply a function of his overall level of moral virtue. Thus, in my judgment, the problem for consequentialism posed by just distributions remains.

Could these remaining problems be solved from a consequentialist point of view by making the account of the good even more dependent on antecedent judgments about the justice of the process by which good things are produced and distributed? Perhaps, though it is impossible to tell without a careful examination of precise and detailed proposals to this effect. At this point, it seems best to limit ourselves to two qualified conclusions. First, questions of justice and fair distributions pose *prima facie* problems for consequentialism. Although some of these problems may be solvable along roughly the lines Ross suggests, it is not clear that all such problems can be handled in this way. Second, the strategy of making one's account of the good dependent on one's account of moral virtue, justice, desert, entitlement, and the like already represents a major change in one very familiar, and attractive consequentialist picture—the one represented by G. E. Moore in *Principia Ethica*. For Moore, goodness was the fundamental notion of ethics on which other notions—including rightness, wrongness, and moral obligation—depended. Accordingly, he argued, questions of goodness could, and must, be settled before one attempts to resolve issues about rightness, wrongness, and the like. This simple conception of the priority of goodness falls by the wayside if, in response to the problems posed by justice, the consequentialist makes the account of goodness depend on antecedent decisions about fairness, desert, entitlement, and virtue. Since these decisions may themselves presuppose judgments about rightness, wrongness, and moral obligation, the right and the good become conceptually interdependent, and the simple conceptual priority envisioned by Moore is overturned.

Duties of Special Relation

Ross's final criticism of consequentialism involves what may be called *duties of special relation*. These typically involve cases in which certain actions of the agent give rise to rights in other people. The existence of these rights explains why certain further acts that maximize good consequences are, nevertheless, not morally obligatory, and may not even be morally permissible.

The first duty of special relation is to keep one's promises—where these include both implicit and explicit promises. (Ross takes lying, for example, to involve the breaking of an implicit promise one makes when one engages in a conversation.[15]) To make a promise is to make a commitment to someone. Once the commitment has been made, the person to whom we have made the promise has a special claim on us that others don't have; that person no longer has the status of being simply one member of mankind who is a possible beneficiary of our action. Thus, when the time comes for us to do what we promised, we don't think in terms of maximizing good consequences for mankind as a whole, but rather in terms of living up to a prior commitment. There may, of course, be special circumstances in which some other obligation arises which outweighs our obligation to keep our promise; e.g., the need to rush my dying friend to the hospital may preclude me from keeping my promise to meet you at the movie theater. However, special circumstances aside, we don't think that our obligation to keep promises is outweighed by small increments in value that may accrue to mankind in general. If we have promised to do something for x, we certainly don't search for someone other than x who might benefit a little more from our action than x would; we simply take ourselves to be morally required to keep our original promise. Ross suggests that in recognizing this, we are, in effect, recognizing the unacceptability of strict consequentialism.

> It might seem absurd to suggest that it could be right for any one to do an act which would produce consequences less good than

---

[15] *The Right and the Good*, p. 21.

those which would be produced by some other act in his power. Yet a little thought will convince us that this is not absurd. The type of case in which it is easiest to see that this is so is, perhaps, that in which one has made a promise. In such a case we all think that *prima facie* it is our duty to fulfil the promise irrespective of the precise goodness of the total consequences. And though we do not think it is necessarily our actual or absolute duty to do so, we are far from thinking that any, even the slightest, gain in the value of the total consequences will necessarily justify us in doing something else instead. Suppose, to simplify the case by abstraction, the fulfillment of a promise to A would produce 1,000 units of good for him, but that by doing some other act I could produce 1,001 units of good for B, to whom I have made no promise, the other consequences of the two acts being of equal value; should we really think it self-evident that it was our duty to do the second act and not the first? I think not. We should, I fancy, hold that only a much greater disparity of value between the total consequences would justify us in failing to discharge our *prima facie* duty to A. After all, a promise is a promise, and is not to be treated so lightly as the theory we are examining would imply. What, exactly, a promise is, is not so easy to determine, but we are surely agreed that it constitutes a serious moral limitation to our freedom of action. To produce the 1,001 units of good for B rather than fulfil our promise to A would be to take, not perhaps our duty as philanthropists too seriously, but certainly our duty as makers of promises too lightly.[16]

The second duty of special relation mentioned by Ross is the duty to make reparations, when one has previously injured, or otherwise wronged, someone. As in the case of promising, this duty arises from past acts of the agent which create rights in other persons. For example, if A harms an innocent person B, and later is in a position to bestow benefits, then A owes something special to B, even if the total effects of benefiting B are not quite as valuable as those of benefiting some uninvolved third party. Having harmed B, A has an obligation to set things right, before looking around for others to benefit.

The final type of duty of special relation mentioned by Ross encompasses duties of gratitude, which arise from acceptance of benefits from

---

[16] Ibid., pp. 34–35.

others—especially if the benefits are of great value, or resulted from sacrifices by the other person. These duties are ubiquitous, and are typically owed to parents, family members, and friends.

All of these duties provide graphic examples of the failures of consequentialist principles like C. According to consequentialism, everyone who could conceivably benefit from our actions has, in principle, an equal moral claim on us. But this simply is not so. People to whom we have made promises have a special moral claim on us to keep our promises; people whom we have harmed have a special claim on us to make restitution; benefactors—including family and friends—have a special claim on us to repay their good works. As Ross points out, the fact that consequentialism doesn't properly recognize this is one of its most glaring defects.

> The essential defect of the 'ideal utilitarian' theory [consequentialism] is that it ignores, or at least does not do full justice to, the highly personal character of duty. If the only duty is to produce the maximum of good, the question of who is to have the good—whether it is myself, or my benefactor, or a person to whom I have made a promise to confer that good on him, or a mere fellow man to whom I stand in no such special relation—should make no difference to my having a duty to produce that good. But we are all in fact sure that it makes a vast difference.[17]

If Ross is right about this, then consequentialism must be rejected, both as a theory of moral obligation, and as a theory of the moral rightness and wrongness of actions. As a result, a new theory is needed.

The Scope of Moral Obligation

Before turning to Ross's positive alternative to consequentialism, it is worth looking for a moment at a different defect of consequentialist principles like C—a defect which Ross does not mention, but which plagues many theories, including, I will argue, his own positive alternative. This defect involves the question of the scope of moral obliga-

---

[17] Ibid., p. 22.

tion. According to principle C (ii), every act is either obligatory or impermissible—except in those cases in which the values of the total consequences of each of two different acts open to the agent are (a) exactly the same, and (b) not exceeded by the value of the total consequences of any other act open to the agent. In these rare cases, principle C characterizes both acts as right, and neither as obligatory; in all other cases acts are characterized either as morally wrong, and hence impermissible, or as morally obligatory. But this seems highly doubtful. There are surely many acts that are neither obligatory nor wrong, but simply permissible.

If, in my free time, I decide to read a book rather than listen to music, go to the gym rather than watch television, compose a letter to the editor of the newspaper rather than surf the Internet, or start writing a new philosophy paper rather than watch the Red Sox play the Yankees, then what I do is, typically, neither obligatory nor wrong, but simply permitted. I don't have to calculate the benefits to all mankind, myself included, in order to determine what my obligations are; in these cases, the question of obligation doesn't arise. One course of action might be better for me than another, one might be more virtuous than another, one might even produce more benefits to other people in the long run than another. I might be praised, admired, or respected for doing some of these things, while being criticized or looked down upon for doing others. But that doesn't make any of these actions either morally obligatory or morally wrong.

Rather, it seems, we must recognize a distinction between acts that are morally wrong, acts that are morally permissible but not required, and acts that are morally obligatory—with the middle category of morally permissible but non-obligatory acts including a large range of acts that is capable of being subdivided into acts that are morally good, acts that are morally bad, and acts that are morally neutral. Particularly interesting is the class of permissible but non-obligatory, morally good acts.[18] These include everything from simple favors to over-subscriptions of particular duties (when one does one's duty plus a little bit more), to acts of saintliness, heroism, and self-sacrifice. For example, I might do you a favor by giving you my ticket to the sold-out

---

[18] The category of permissible but non-obligatory, morally bad acts is also interesting. These include cases of simple rudeness and lack of courtesy, cases in which one refuses to provide significant aid to someone who has no special claim on one, even when the cost to oneself of providing such assistance would be minimal, and cases in which one has a right to do x, but exercising that right would be harmful to others.

basketball game, so that you can watch your favorite team. That would be nice, something mildly good from a moral point of view. However, it is not my obligation to do it. If I don't give you the ticket, but attend the game myself, I won't have done anything morally wrong; I won't have failed to do my duty, because I have no duty in this regard.

Another kind of non-obligatory, but morally good, action involves doing one's duty, plus a little extra. For example, part of the job of a professor is to see students, to answer their questions, discuss their work, advise them in their studies, and so on. Suppose a particular professor does this and more. He converses with students during evenings and weekends by e-mail or over the phone, he lends them his books and papers, and he continues to read their work and advise them after they go on to graduate school or take up teaching jobs of their own. Up to a certain point, the actions of the professor are simply the fulfillment of his duty as a teacher. However, beyond that point they are something more—non-obligatory, but nevertheless praiseworthy and morally good. Typically it is very hard, if not impossible, to say precisely where duties end and acts of supererogation begin, but there is no question, viewing the totality of his acts, that the professor does considerably more than what is required.

Finally, there are inspiring instances of saintliness, self-sacrifice, and heroism. These include the actions of saintly figures like Albert Schweitzer and Mother Teresa, who devoted their lives to alleviating misery, as well as those of the heroic firefighters and security men, like Rick Rescorla, at the World Trade Center, who, after leading many to safety, went back inside the flaming towers, where they died attempting to rescue still others.[19] Although these rare individuals deserve the highest praise and admiration, they were not simply doing their moral duty, just as those who never rise to these heights are not; for that reason, failing to fulfill their moral obligations. One will describe them in this way only if one thinks that, except for rare instances of exact ties in the consequentialist calculus, there are just two morally significant categories of actions—those that are obligatory and those that are impermissible. But the slightest attention to the moral judgments we actually make shows that our categories of moral evaluation for actions are much richer than this. In failing to recognize this, strict consequentialist theories that incorporate C (ii) falsify and, in my opinion, distort our moral experience almost beyond recognition.

[19] James B. Stewart, "The Real Heroes are Dead," *New Yorker*, Feb. 11, 2002.

Finally, the recognition of an expanded set of categories for morally evaluating actions has ramifications not only for normative theories, but also for some meta-ethical theories—in particular, for emotivism. For example, according to the relatively crude version of emotivism put forward by Ayer, to say that stealing is wrong is just to vent one's disapproval of stealing, and to say that helping others is right is just to express a positive attitude toward helping others. However, this crude analysis doesn't have the resources to distinguish between saying that a particular case of helping others is morally obligatory and saying that it is morally good but not required. One can't analyze **both** simply as expressions of one's approval, for that would wrongly characterize the two moral statements as amounting to the same thing. How, precisely, one should analyze these claims from an emotivist point of view is a question that is not answered by the unsophisticated version of emotivism put forward by Ayer. Whether or not more sophisticated versions of the theory would be up to the task is a question we need not try to resolve.

The main point is that we must not rush to accept sweeping, but overly simple, normative or meta-ethical theses without thoroughly examining the evaluative terrain that they are meant to cover. The evaluative distinctions about the scope of moral evaluation that we have made in this section are troublesome enough for consequentialism and emotivism. But this may be only the beginning; there is little reason to think that we have done more than scratch the surface of our complex system of moral evaluations. Exploring this system further to discover the full range of morally significant distinctions to be found in ordinary moral, and legal, discourse is crucial for developing more sophisticated theories in both normative ethics and meta-ethics.[20]

Ross's Positive Theory of Moral Obligation

Having cast serious doubt on consequentialism, we are now in the market for an alternative normative theory of moral obligation. Ross's positive theory may be reconstructed as built on the following list of morally relevant features of actions.

---

[20] Two useful articles on the general topic of this section are Joel Feinberg, "Supererogation and Rules," *International Journal of Ethics* 71 (1961); and Roderick Chisholm, "Supererogation and Offense," *Ratio* 5 (1963).

MORALLY RELEVANT FEATURES

1. the value of the consequences of the act (as compared to the value of the consequences of all other acts open to the agent)

2. whether the act is an instance of lying

3. whether the act is an instance of keeping a promise or of breaking a promise

4. whether the act is an instance of making reparations, or honoring a debt of gratitude

5. whether or not the act is just[21]

6. whether or not the act harms others

Some of these morally relevant features are favorable, and some unfavorable. If an act has a favorable morally relevant feature, we say that it is an instance of a *positive morally relevant kind*. If it has an unfavorable feature, it is an instance of a *negative morally relevant kind*. These two notions are used to define *prima facie duty* and *actual duty*.

PRIMA FACIE DUTY

(i) An agent has a *prima facie* duty to do x iff x is an instance of a positive morally relevant kind.

(ii) An agent has a *prima facie* duty not to do x iff x is an instance of a negative morally relevant kind.

ACTUAL DUTY

(i) An agent has a duty to do x iff x is an instance of a positive morally relevant kind and either (a) x is not an instance of any negative morally relevant kind, or (b) the **stringency** of x's positive morally relevant kinds is greater than that of x's negative morally relevant kinds.

(ii) A has a duty not to do x iff x is an instance of a negative morally relevant kind and either (a) x is not an instance of any positive morally relevant kind, or (b) the **stringency** of x's negative morally relevant kinds is greater than that of x's positive morally relevant kinds.

---

[21] As discussed above, Ross himself probably would not list this as a separate morally relevant feature, but rather would incorporate it under MRF1, as involving the production of a special kind of good. I have included it as a separate feature because I don't think his case for incorporating it under the heading of producing good consequences is decisive.

Although this framework is attractive, and avoids certain counterexamples to consequentialism, three main causes of concern immediately present themselves. The first involves the problem of the scope of moral obligation, discussed in the previous section. It would seem that virtually every act will be of either a positive or a negative morally relevant kind, since whether or not the act has any of the morally relevant features corresponding to (2–6), it will nearly always have consequences of some (positive or negative) value, and so receive an evaluation from feature 1. Thus, even if morally relevant features 2–6 don't come into play, the first will, by itself, generally be sufficient to generate an actual duty, thereby characterizing moral obligation as ubiquitous. Consequently, Ross's theory—wrongly, in my view—characterizes nearly every situation as one in which we are under a moral obligation to perform some act or other (except in the presumably rare cases in which the relative stringencies of an act's positive and negative morally relevant kinds exactly cancel each other out). If so, then his theory fails, in more or less the same way that consequentialism fails, to take proper account of the large and interesting range of permissible but non-obligatory acts.

That Ross, himself, didn't find this range of actions problematic is indicated by the following remark.

> **It must be added, however, that if we are ever under no special obligation such as that of fidelity to a promisee or of gratitude to a benefactor, we ought to do what will produce most good**; and that even when we are under a special obligation the tendency of acts to promote general good is one of the main factors in determining whether they are right.[22]

Although I cannot agree with the emphasized portion of this passage, the remainder of the passage is surely correct. Surely, if the value of the consequences of an act, at least for others, is great enough, one's *prima facie* duty not to lie, for example, or not to break a promise, can be overridden, thereby rendering these violations of one's *prima facie* duties permissible. Thus, consideration of the consequences of one's acts does play an important role in determining rightness, wrongness, and obligation. In my opinion, it also plays an important role in determining which permissible but non-obligatory acts are morally good, and which are morally bad. The challenge, in my view, is to explain

---

[22] Ibid., p. 39, my boldface emphasis.

how the value of the consequences of one's acts can play these roles without expanding the scope of our moral obligations far beyond their proper bounds.

The second cause for concern regarding Ross's positive theory involves how we determine which features of acts are morally relevant. Ross claims that it is simply self-evident which features are morally relevant and which are not; it is self-evident not only that producing the most good possible is *prima facie* right, but also that keeping promises, making reparations, and repaying debts of gratitude are too, while and lying and harming others are *prima facie* wrong. Some philosophers believe that this appeal to self-evidence is mysterious, but it is hard to know what the alternative is supposed to be. All normative theories posit some principles that don't derive their support from anything more basic. Consequentialism, for example, takes fundamental claims about goodness, as well as the basic consequentialist principle C, to be fundamental and unexplained. If, like Ross, one is a cognitivist in meta-ethics, then presumably one will take these principles of consequentialism to be self-evident (if one believes them to be true). If one isn't a cognitivist, then, presumably, one may regard Ross's principles non-cognitively as well. In either case some normative principles are taken to be fundamental—whatever their ultimate meta-ethical status may turn out to be. The only difference is that Ross takes a few more principles to have this status. It is hard to see why this small difference in the number of allegedly self-evident principles should be viewed as particularly problematic.

There is, however, a related, and more serious, cause for concern. Since there are a number of positive and negative morally relevant features, one of which (involving the value of the consequences produced by the act) applies to virtually all acts, a great many acts will be instances of several morally relevant kinds. More importantly, in virtually all interesting cases in which one looks to normative ethical theories for guidance, the acts under consideration will be instances of at least one positive morally relevant kind and at least one negative morally relevant kind. In cases like this, Ross's theory tells us that our actual duty is determined by the relative stringencies of the positive and negative morally relevant kinds of which the acts open to the agent are instances. But what, one would like to know, are the relative stringencies of the different kinds?

Unfortunately, Ross has very little to say about this. His most definitive word on the subject seems to be the following:

It is worthwhile to try to state more definitely the nature of the acts that are right. . . . It is obvious that any of the acts that we do has countless effects, directly or indirectly, on countless people, and the probability is that any act, however right it be, will have adverse effects (though these may be very trivial) on some innocent people. Similarly, any wrong act will probably have beneficial effects on some deserving people. Every act therefore, viewed in some aspects, will be *prima facie* right, and viewed in others, *prima facie* wrong, and right acts can be distinguished from wrong acts only as being those which, of all those possible for the agent in the circumstances, have the greatest balance of *prima facie* rightness, in those respects in which they are *prima facie* right, over their *prima facie* wrongness, in those respects in which they are *prima facie* wrong. . . . **For the estimation of the comparative stringency of these *prima facie* obligations no general rules can, so far as I can see, be laid down.** We can only say that a great deal of stringency belongs to the duties of 'perfect obligation'—the duties of keeping our promises, or repairing wrongs we have done, and of returning the equivalent of services we have received. For the rest [what follows is a quote from Aristotle] 'the decision rests with perception'. This sense of our particular duty in particular circumstances, preceded and informed by the fullest reflection we can bestow on the act in all its bearings, is highly fallible, **but it is the only guide we have to our duty.**[23]

This, in the context of the rest of his theory, is a remarkably pessimistic conclusion. If Ross is right, then there is almost nothing one can do to construct a workable normative theory. If a theory of the type he has constructed does not specify the relative stringencies of the different morally relevant features of an act, then it won't be able to provide useful and informative answers about which acts are right or wrong in the overwhelming majority of cases in which we are initially uncertain—since these tend to be actions about which there is both something positive and something negative to be said.

Thus, in the end, we are left in an uncomfortable position. The arguments Ross gives against consequentialism are powerful, and his

---

[23] Ibid., pp. 41–42, my boldface emphasis. That the position Ross outlines here is essentially Aristotelian should not be surprising, since he was an eminent scholar and translator of Aristotle.

case for multiple moral principles in the evaluation of action is persuasive. But his conclusion—reached, one must say, with virtually no argument—that there is little that can be done to systematize our moral
thinking by elaborating principles that establish priorities, and resolve
conflicts between competing *prima facie* evaluations, amounts to a
counsel of despair, as far as the prospects for normative theories of
rightness, wrongness, and moral obligation are concerned. Either Ross
was mistaken about this, or the idea of constructing informative normative theories of this sort to provide moral guidance and resolve
doubts is fundamentally wrongheaded. It is, I think, fair to say that, at
the time he wrote and for many years after, opinion on the relative
merits of these two alternatives was deeply divided.

It is not hard to see something ironic in this. Ross did not, I believe,
set out to sow the seeds of further doubt about the value of normative
theory in philosophy. A man of great moral and intellectual clarity, with
a highly developed moral sensibility, he would have been the last person
to disparage a serious, intellectually disciplined approach to moral questions. However, he wrote at a time in which many important analytic
philosophers regarded normative ethics with suspicion—as something
either ultimately unintelligible or, at any rate, not really the province of
philosophy. It would be wrong to characterize Ross as sharing these
suspicions. On the contrary, he was, as we saw in chapter 14, the leading
and most insightful critic of his day of the main source—emotivism—of
philosophical skepticism about ethics. However, his own normative
theory of rightness and moral obligation ended with what seemed to
many to be a highly pessimistic conclusion about what can reasonably
be expected from philosophy in this area. For this reason, it would not,
it seems to me, be wrong to see his work as inadvertently feeding the
rather widespread suspicion about the place of normative ethics, and
other evaluative matters, in philosophy that typified the attitudes of
many important analytic philosophers in the '30s and '40s.

Ross's Moral Methodology

We close with a word about Ross's methodology in ethics, which he
describes in the following passage.

> In what has preceded, a good deal of use has been made of 'what
> we really think' about moral questions; a certain theory has been

rejected [consequentialism, or "ideal utilitarianism"] because it does not agree with what we really think. It might be said that this is in principle wrong; that we should not be content to expound what our present moral consciousness tells us but should aim at a criticism of our existing moral consciousness in the light of theory. Now I do not doubt that the moral consciousness of men has in detail undergone a good deal of modification as regards the things we think right, at the hands of moral theory. But if we are told, for instance, that we should give up our view that there is a special obligatoriness attaching to the keeping of promises because it is self-evident that the only duty is to produce as much good as possible, we have to ask ourselves whether we really, when we reflect, *are* convinced that this is self-evident, and whether we really *can* get rid of our view that promise-keeping has a bindingness independent of productiveness of maximum good. In my own experience I find that I cannot. . . . In fact it seems, on reflection, self-evident that a promise, simply as such, is something that *prima facie* ought to be kept, and it does *not*, on reflection, seem self-evident that production of maximum good is the only thing that makes an act obligatory. And to ask us to give up at the bidding of a theory our actual apprehension of what is right and what is wrong seems like asking people to repudiate their actual experience of beauty, at the bidding of a theory which says 'only that which satisfies such and such conditions can be beautiful'. If what I have called our actual apprehension is . . . truly an apprehension, i.e. an instance of knowledge, the request is nothing less than absurd.[24]

Ross continues,

I would maintain, in fact, that what we are apt to describe as 'what we think' about moral questions contains a considerable amount that we do not think but know, and that **this forms the standard by reference to which the truth of any moral theory has to be tested, instead of having itself to be tested by reference to any theory**. . . . We have no more direct way of access to the facts about rightness and goodness and about what things are right or good, than by thinking about them; **the moral convictions of thoughtful and well-educated people are the data of ethics just as sense-perceptions are the data of a natural sci-**

[24] Ibid., pp. 39–40.

ence. Just as some of the latter have to be rejected as illusory, so have some of the former; but as the latter are rejected only when they are in conflict with other more accurate sense-perceptions, the former are rejected only when they are in conflict with other convictions which stand better the test of reflection. The existing body of moral convictions of the best people is the cumulative product of the moral reflection of many generations, which has developed an extremely delicate power of appreciation of moral distinctions; and this the theorist cannot afford to treat with anything other than the greatest respect.[25]

There are two strains in this passage that may usefully be separated (without prejudice to the question of whether or not they are correct). The first is Ross's meta-ethical position of moral realism. On this view, the subject matter of ethics is moral reality, just as the subject matter of natural science is physical reality. Just as sense perception is the foundation of genuine knowledge of physical reality, so moral reflection, and pre-theoretic moral intuition, are the foundations of genuine knowledge of moral reality.

The second strain in the passage is Ross's methodological conservatism in normative ethics. He takes seriously, and treats with respect, our antecedently existing moral convictions, especially those which are both (i) not themselves based on other, more fundamental convictions, and (ii) among the convictions about which we feel the strongest. For Ross, there is no overturning all, or even most, of these convictions, or values, at once. We come to the normative enterprise already having evaluative commitments that can't be dismissed, except when they conflict with other more strongly held commitments. We can make adjustments and refinements, we can remove inconsistencies, and, in principle, we can try to modify and extend limited moral principles that we are already committed to so that they provide defensible moral classifications of a broader range of actions, including some about which we are presently uncertain. In these cases, we try to formulate new principles that correctly characterize the moral status of the overwhelming majority of actions about which we are already certain, while issuing verdicts on some actions about which we are presently unsure. If we are successful, then support for the new principles provided by the antecedently clear cases will translate into support

---

[25] Ibid., pp. 40–41, my boldface emphasis.

for the verdicts they issue on the previously unclear cases. In this way, we can hope to gradually increase the sphere of our moral confidence, and decrease our moral doubts. However, there are limits to how far any normative theory can move us from our strongest and most fundamental, antecedently held moral convictions.

The point here should be familiar, since it is analogous to two important developments in the analytic tradition we have already discussed. The first was G. E. Moore's encounter with skepticism about the external world. The lesson drawn by Moore and others was that our most basic pre-theoretic convictions about what we know constitute data against which philosophical theories of knowledge must be tested; hence no theory of knowledge—no matter how attractive it may appear when considered in the abstract—can be accepted if it contradicts too many of these convictions. The second development was the logical positivists' failed attempt to construct a new and radical theory of meaning. One of the important lessons to come from that failure was the recognition that our pre-theoretic convictions about the meanings of sentences constitute data against which theories of meaningfulness must be tested; hence no such theory—no matter how attractive it may appear in the abstract—can be correct if it contradicts too many of these pre-theoretic convictions. Ross's methodological conservatism about normative theories, and his arguments against consequentialism, are examples of the same general perspective in philosophy.

SUGGESTED FURTHER READING
FOR PART FOUR

Main Primary Sources Discussed

Ayer, A. J. *Language, Truth, and Logic.* New York: Dover, 1952 (reprinting of the 1946 2nd edition).

Carnap, Rudolf. "Testability and Meaning." *Philosophy of Science* 3 (1936) and 4 (1937).

Church, Alonzo. "Review of *Language, Truth, and Logic: Second Edition.*" *Journal of Symbolic Logic* 14 (1949): 52–53.

Hempel, Carl G. "The Empiricist Criterion of Meaning," *Revue Internationale de Philosophie* 4 (1950); reprinted in A. J. Ayer, ed., *Logical Positivism* (New York: Free Press, 1959).

Quine, W. V. "Truth by Convention." First published in O. H. Lee, ed., *Philosophical Essays for A. N. Whitehead* (New York: Longmans, 1936); reprinted in H. Feigl and W. Sellars, eds., *Readings in Philosophical Analysis* (New York: Appleton, 1949); in P. Benacerraf and H. Putnam, eds., *Readings in the Philosophy of Mathematics* (Englewood, NJ: Prentice Hall, 1964); and Quine, *The Ways of Paradox* (New York: Random House, 1966).

Stevenson, Charles L. "The Emotive Meaning of Ethical Terms." *Mind* 1937.

Additional Primary Sources

Ayer, A. J. *Logical Positivism.* New York: Free Press, 1959.

———. "Verification and Experience." *Proceedings of the Aristotelian Society* 37 (1936–37); reprinted in *Logical Positivism*; see also his introduction to the volume.

Neurath, Otto. "Protocol Sentences." *Erkenntnis* 3 (1932–33); reprinted (in English) in *Logical Positivism*.

Ross, W. David. *Foundations of Ethics.* Oxford: Clarendon Press, 1939.

———. *The Right and the Good.* Oxford: Clarendon Press, 1930.

Schlick, Moritz. "The Foundation of Knowledge." *Erkenntnis* 4 (1934); reprinted (in English) in *Logical Positivism*.

Additional Recommended Reading

Cartwright, Richard. "Propositions." In R. J. Butler, ed., *Analytical Philosophy*, 1st series (Oxford: Basil Blackwell, 1962).

Chisholm, Roderick. "Supererogation and Offense." *Ratio* 5 (1963).

Feinberg, Joel. "Supererogation and Rules." *International Journal of Ethics* 71 (1961).

Geach, Peter. "Ascriptivism." *Philosophical Review* 69 (1960).

Hare, R. M. *Freedom and Reason*. New York: Oxford University Press, 1965.

———. *The Language of Morals*. New York: Oxford University Press, 1964.

Kegan, Shelly. "Equality and Desert." In O. McLeod and L. Pojman, eds., *What Do We Deserve?* (Oxford: Oxford University Press, 1998), 277–97.

Mackie, John. *Ethics*. Singapore: Pelican Books, 1977.

Searle, John. "Meaning and Speech Acts." *Philosophical Review* 71 (1962).

PART FIVE

THE POST-POSITIVIST PERSPECTIVE
OF THE EARLY W. V. QUINE

CHAPTER 16

THE ANALYTIC AND THE SYNTHETIC, THE NECESSARY AND THE POSSIBLE, THE APRIORI AND THE APOSTERIORI

The Context

Willard Van Orman Quine taught at Harvard, first as an instructor, then as a professor, from 1936 until his retirement at age 70 in 1978, after which he continued to write and lecture on philosophy for more than twenty years. He began his academic life studying logic, and his first major philosophical publication was his well-known article, "Truth by Convention," published in 1936. By the early '40s he was an important figure on the philosophical scene, especially in America. With the publication in 1951 of his celebrated article, "Two Dogmas of Empiricism," he became the dominant philosopher in America, which he remained until January of 1970, when Saul Kripke, who had studied with Quine as an undergraduate at Harvard, gave the three lectures at Princeton that became *Naming and Necessity*. Even after the emergence of Kripke, Quine's influence on analytic philosophy remained strong for more than twenty five years.

In chapter 12, we discussed Quine's argument in "Truth by Convention," and in volume 2 we will examine the skeptical doctrines about meaning and reference developed in his major works, *Word and Object*, published in 1960, and *Ontological Relativity and Other Essays*, published in 1969.[1] In this chapter and the next we will concentrate mostly on his "Two Dogmas of Empiricism," which, among all his articles, was the most well-known and widely discussed.[2] In it Quine offers a critique of logical positivism. He isolates what he takes to be the central ideas behind positivism; he indicates which of those ideas he takes to be correct and which incorrect; and he briefly outlines the central tenets of a new philosophical view that retains much of the spirit and legacy of positivism, while, he hopes, avoiding its fundamental problems.

Although the central ideas expressed in "Two Dogmas" had been part of Quine's thinking throughout much of the '40s, the paper was not published until 1951. By that time logical positivism was finished. Nevertheless, many philosophers continued to believe that there had been something right about positivism that should be retained, whatever in the end might have to be rejected. The question was how to separate the good from the bad, and many philosophers saw Quine's article as doing just that. As one looks back now at the history of the period, one cannot help but think that an important reason "Two Dogmas" became so important and influential was that it offered a vision to an important group of philosophers precisely at the time they

---

[1] Quine, *Word and Object* (Cambridge, MA: MIT Press, 1960); *Ontological Relativity and other Essays* (New York and London: Columbia University Press, 1969).

[2] Quine, "Two Dogmas of Empiricism," *Philosophical Review* 60 (1951); reprinted in Quine, *From a Logical Point of View* (Cambridge, MA: Harvard University Press, 1953, 1961, 1980). Unless otherwise indicated, citations will be from the 1980 edition.

needed one. In examining the article we will try to build up that vision in a step-by-step way.

The best way to approach the article is to divide it into three parts. The first part includes sections 1–4, in which Quine discusses and rejects the distinction between analytic and synthetic sentences or statements. The second part consists of section 5; where he discusses the central assumptions behind the verification (or empiricist) criterion of meaning, as well as those behind a doctrine he calls *reductionism* (essentially what we have been calling *the theory of logical constructions*). Quine makes suggestions about which of these assumptions should be retained, which should be rejected, and which new assumptions should be added. The final part of the paper, section 6, contains a brief sketch of his positive theory of meaning, and his views about the nature of science.

In this chapter, we will be concerned with part 1, where Quine discusses the traditional philosophical distinction between analytic and synthetic sentences or statements. We have seen that both the logical positivists and the Wittgenstein of the *Tractatus* divided up the class of meaningful sentences, or statements, into three classes—analytic sentences (or tautologies), which were supposed to be true in virtue of meaning alone, contradictions, which were supposed to be false in virtue of meaning alone, and synthetic sentences, the truth or falsity of which was thought to depend not only on what they mean, but also on the way the world is. As we emphasized in chapter 12, it was crucial for both Wittgenstein and the positivists that the distinction between analytic and synthetic truths should coincide exactly with the necessary/contingent distinction, and the apriori/aposteriori distinction. According to them, all necessary and apriori truths are analytic, and it is only because they are analytic that they are necessary and apriori.

For Wittgenstein, the source of this view lay in his contention that for a sentence to say anything, for it to provide any information, is for its truth to exclude certain possible states that the world could be in. Since necessary truths exclude nothing, they say nothing, and since they say nothing about the way the world is, the way the world is makes no contribution to their being true. Hence their truth must be due to their meanings alone. For the positivists, all knowledge about the world is dependent on observation and sense experience. It follows that since apriori truths can be known, independent of observation and sense experience, they must not be about the world; and if they don't tell us anything about the world, their truth must be due to their meanings alone. Given the background assumption that all and only apriori truths are necessary, the positivists saw their identification of the apriori with the analytic as coinciding with Wittgenstein's identification of the necessary with the analytic.

In addition, the positivists insisted on a kind of explanatory priority; the **reason** for the necessity or aprioricity of any sentence is to be found in its analyticity. As they saw it, there simply is no explaining what necessity is, how we can know any truth to be necessary, or how we can know anything apriori without appealing to our knowledge that certain statements are true by virtue of meaning. Thus, from their point of view, necessary and apriori truths had better be analytic, since, if they aren't analytic, then one can give no intelligible account of them at all. Ironically, this theoretical weight placed on the notion of analyticity by the positivists left their doctrines about analyticity, necessity, and aprioricity vulnerable to a potentially devastating criticism. If it could be shown that analyticity cannot play the explanatory role they assigned to it, then their commitment to necessity, aprioricity, and perhaps even analyticity itself might be threatened. This was the strategy behind Quine's attack.

In chapter 12 we examined what can be seen, at least in retrospect, as the first part of that attack. There we spelled out the apparent reasoning behind the positivists' claim that knowledge that certain statements are true by virtue of meaning (or true by convention) can be used to explain all apriori knowledge. We concluded, on the basis of an argument drawn from Quine's "Truth by Convention," that this reasoning is fundamentally flawed, because any such explanation presupposes certain antecedent apriori knowledge that cannot itself be explained linguistically. If this is right, then the positivists never succeeded in showing that analyticity could do the job that made it so important to them. In itself, this doesn't prove that there is anything illegitimate about analyticity, aprioricity, or necessity. However, within the context of the positivists' guiding assumptions connecting these notions, it should have been enough to make them distinctly uneasy.

For whatever reason, they were very slow to take the lesson of "Truth by Convention" to heart. Thus, fifteen years later, in 1951, Quine presented a new, more direct, and more sweeping attack. He agreed with the positivists' fundamental premise that there is no explaining necessity and aprioricity without appealing to analyticity. However, he challenged the idea that any genuine distinction could be drawn between the analytic and the synthetic without presupposing the very distinctions they were needed to explain. Hence, he concluded that there is no way of explaining and legitimating necessity and aprioricity— or analyticity either. This meant that there is no genuine distinction to be drawn between the analytic and the synthetic, between the necessary and the contingent, or between the apriori and the aposteriori. Indeed, the idea that any such distinctions exist is one of the "two dogmas" that are targets of his article. It is the burden of sections 1–4 of the article to demonstrate that this dogma should be rejected.

The Circularity Argument against the Analytic/Synthetic Distinction

Quine begins by saying that it won't do to try to explain analyticity in terms of necessity, since the distinction between necessary and contingent truth is just as much in need of explanation as the distinction between the analytic and the synthetic (if not more). One might try to make the distinction by saying that an analytic sentence is one that is **true solely in virtue of meaning**, whereas a synthetic truth is **true in virtue of fact**. But what, Quine wonders, are we to make of this talk of meaning? Surely, he thinks, we need not suppose that there are any **things** that are the meanings of sentences and other expressions— obscure entities that somehow mediate between words, on the one hand, and the objects that words stand for, or apply to, on the other. On the contrary, Quine maintains that talk of meaning is not talk of things; when talking about meaning, we want to know which sentences and other expressions are meaningful, and which are synonymous with one another. This leads him to think that the best way to make sense of the idea of a sentence being true in virtue of meaning is to interpret it as the idea that a sentence can be turned into a logical truth by putting synonyms for synonyms. Since a logical truth is one that comes out true no matter how the non-logical words in it are understood, it follows that any sentence that satisfies this condition is logically guaranteed to be true.

This interpretation also makes sense of another traditional characterization of analyticity. Traditionally, a number of philosophers have made the distinction between the analytic and the synthetic by saying that an analytic statement is one the negation of which is contradictory. Since, on Quine's interpretation, an analytic sentence is one that can be turned into a logical truth by putting synonyms for synonyms, it is also a sentence the negation of which can be turned into a logical falsehood—i.e., a sentence logically equivalent to a simple contradiction A & $\sim A$—by putting synonyms for synonyms. Thus Quine's interpretation of analyticity offers a plausible way of understanding the doctrine that the negation of an analytic sentence is contradictory.

In this way, Quine arrives at the following proposed definition of analyticity.

PROPOSED DEFINITION OF ANALYTICITY
S is analytic iff (i) S is a logical truth, or (ii) S can be turned into a logical truth by putting synonyms for synonyms.

In order for this definition to be successful, we must be able to make sense of two crucial notions: *logical truth* and *synonymy*. Quine takes the notion of a logical truth to be unproblematic, provided that we are given an inventory of the logical constants in advance—e.g., *and, either . . . or, not, all, at least one*, the material conditional and biconditional. Given such an inventory, we can define *logical truth* as follows.

LOGICAL TRUTH
S is a logical truth iff it is a substitution instance of a schema all of the substitution instances of which are true.

A schema, like *Either S or not S*, is a formula constructed using schematic letters plus two logical constants. A substitution instance of a schema is a sentence that results from replacing schematic letters with expressions of the language—e.g., replacing sentential schematic letters with sentences of the language, replacing predicative schematic letters with predicates of the language, and replacing nominative schematic letters with names of the language. Examples of logical truths, in this sense, are (1) and (2).[3]

1. Either it is raining or it is not raining.   Either S or not S

2. No man who is not married   No F who is not
   is married.   G is G

The other notion needed to make sense of the proposed definition of analyticity is synonymy. If synonymy is a clear and intelligible

---

[3] Sometimes, as in (1), a little adjustment of the grammar is needed in getting instances from the schema.

notion, then we can use the synonymy of *bachelor* with the phrase *man who is not married* to turn sentence (3) into a logical truth of the form (2).[4]

3. No bachelor is married.

However, this will work only if synonymy is a legitimate notion; and Quine will grant its legitimacy only if we can give it a clear, non-circular definition.

This leads him to examine the following proposal.

PROPOSED DEFINITION OF SYNONYMY

An expression A is synonymous with an expression B iff A can be substituted for B in all linguistic environments (except within quotes) without changing truth value.

Is this an adequate definition of synonymy? Quine's answer is that it depends on what kind of language the definition is applied to—an extensional language or an intensional language. An *extensional* language is one in which expressions that refer, or apply, to the same objects can always be substituted for one another without changing the truth values of any sentence in which they occur. Examples of such languages are Russell's language of formal logic, the languages of mathematics, and, by some accounts, much of the language in which physical science is done. By contrast, an *intensional* language is one in which substitution of expressions that refer, or apply, to the same objects sometimes changes the truth values of sentences in which they occur. Natural languages, like English, are intensional. First we will consider how the proposed definition of synonymy fares when it is applied to an extensional language, and then we will consider how it fares when applied to intensional languages.

In applying the definition to an extensional language, it is useful to consider the following expression pairs.

---

[4] Here, and in what follows, I take it for granted that *bachelor* is synonymous with *man who is not married*, and *unmarried man*, if any expressions are synonymous. I do this only because the example is frequently used in the literature (by Quine and others), not because I think that there aren't better examples of synonymy. I think there are much better examples—e.g., *a blue ball* is synonymous with *a ball that is blue*. If the *bachelor* example seems worrisome to you, substitute your favorite example.

the planet seen in the morning sky	*the planet seen in the evening sky*
Ben Franklin	*the first postmaster general of the United States*
is a creature with kidneys	*is a creature with a heart*

Astronomical discovery has shown that one and the same planet is seen in the morning sky (at a certain place and time) and in the evening sky (at a certain place and time). Thus, the singular definite descriptions *the planet seen in the morning sky* and *the planet seen in the evening sky* are coreferential. In an extensional language, one can always be substituted for the other without changing the truth value of any sentence. The same is true of the name *Ben Franklin* and the singular definite description *the first postmaster general of the United States*. The predicates *is a creature with kidneys* and *is a creature with a heart* illustrate another version of the same point. It seems to be a contingent fact of biology that every creature with a heart is a creature with kidneys, and vice versa. (At any rate, Quine takes this to be so.) Hence the two predicates apply to exactly the same objects. In an extensional language, this means that one predicate can always be substituted for the other in any sentence without affecting truth value.

It follows that if the proposed definition of synonymy is applied to an extensional language, then all three pairs will be classified as pairs of synonyms, and the sentences in (4) and (5) will be declared to be analytic.

4a. For any object whatsoever, it is the planet seen in the morning sky iff it is the planet seen in the evening sky.

 b. Any descendant of Ben Franklin is a descendant of the first postmaster general of the United States.

5. Every creature with a heart is a creature with kidneys.

But these results are wrong. Defenders of analyticity would argue that since the truths in (4) and (5) are contingent, rather than necessary, and since they cannot be known to be true simply on the basis of knowing the meanings of the words they contain, they are not analytic. Hence, defenders of analyticity and synonymy would reject the proposed definition of synonymy, when it is applied to an extensional language.

Suppose, however, that the definition of synonymy is applied to an intensional language (like English), and in particular to a language that contains the linguistic construction (6).

6. It is a necessary truth that . . .

Note that substitution of terms that refer to the same object sometimes changes truth value in this kind of construction.

7a. It is a necessary truth that if a single planet is seen in the morning sky, then the planet seen in the morning sky is seen in the morning. (true)

b. It is a necessary truth that if a single planet is seen in the morning sky, then the planet seen in the evening sky is seen in the morning. (false)

This means that the terms *the planet seen in the morning sky* and *the planet seen in the evening sky* are correctly characterized as non-synonymous by the proposed definition, when it is applied to a language that contains the construction (6). Similarly for the other pairs of expressions we have looked at.

8a. It is a necessary truth that Ben Franklin was Ben Franklin. (true)

b. It is a necessary truth that Ben Franklin was the first postmaster general of the United States. (false)

9a. It is a necessary truth that a creature with a heart is a creature with a heart. (true)

b. It is a necessary truth that a creature with a heart is a creature with kidneys. (false)

In general, the proposed definition of synonymy will have the consequence that sameness of reference (extension) is not sufficient for synonymy when a language contains constructions like (6).[5] By contrast, genuine synonyms like *bachelor* and *unmarried man* are substitutable in (6) without change of truth value.

10a. It is a necessary truth that if someone is a bachelor then that person is an unmarried man. (true)

b. It is a necessary truth that if someone is an unmarried man then that person is an unmarried man. (true)

So, the definition correctly characterizes these as synonymous.

[5] The extension of a singular term is the thing it denotes, the extension of a predicate is the class of things it applies to.

Quine concludes from this that the proposed definition is an adequate account of synonymy, which in turn will allow us to define analyticity, provided that the language we are talking about includes the notion of necessity. But what about necessity? What does it mean? According to Quine,

11. It is a necessary truth that S.

just means

12. The statement that S is analytic.

But now we have gone in a circle. To explain analyticity, we must first make sense of synonymy. To make proper sense of synonymy, we must appeal to an antecedently understood notion of necessity. But to explain necessity, Quine thinks that we have to presuppose analyticity, which means we have gotten nowhere. Given any one term in the family—*analyticity, synonymy, necessity*—we could define the others. But since we can't explain any of the terms except by using the others, and since Quine thinks that all are equally in need of explanation, he concludes that all of these notions must be rejected.

Evaluating the Circularity Argument

We begin with the observation that Quine's argument is effective, at best, only against positions that accept two of the positivists' fundamental theses.

T1. All necessary (and all apriori) truths are analytic. (For all sentences S, if S expresses a necessary (apriori) truth, then S is analytic.)

T2. Analyticity is needed to explain and legitimate necessity (and aprioricity).

The argument is designed to show that no such position can be correct, since the only way to make sense of analyticity involves presupposing the very notions of necessity and aprioricity that it was intended to explain. In assessing this argument, and understanding the impact it had, nothing is more important than keeping this historical background in mind. Very few philosophers today would accept either T1 or T2, both of which now seem decidedly antique. Nowadays, the prevailing view—derived substantially from Saul Kripke's *Naming and Necessity* (which will be discussed in volume 2)—is that necessity and aprioricity are, respectively, metaphysical and epistemological notions that can stand on their own; moreover, although some truths are both necessary and apriori, there are many examples of each that are not examples of the other. As for analyticity, opinions vary; many now assume that when sentences containing indexical expressions (e.g., *I, now, here, actually*) are excluded, the analytic truths are a subset of the truths that are both necessary and apriori. (Things become more complicated when indexicals are introduced.[6]) For these reasons, the positivists' attempt to explain necessity and aprioricity in terms of analyticity now appears badly mistaken. Quine's circularity argument hardly comes off better. Since it presupposes the positivists' mistaken assumption that necessity (aprioricity) and analyticity make sense only if T1 and T2 are correct, it shares their error, and is largely irrelevant to contemporary understandings of these notions. From our present perspective, Quine doesn't attempt, let alone succeed, in giving a general argument against analyticity. At most he succeeds in undermining a particular conception of analyticity, and a particular set of theses that the positivists, and others, held regarding it.

Lest that seem to be a small achievement, one must remember that T1 and T2 were very popular at the time Quine wrote. For one thing, the influence of positivists, and former positivists, remained strong, especially in America. For another, T1 and T2 were accepted by many important non-positivists as well. Not only can their roots be traced to the *Tractatus*, but Wittgenstein retained them in his later philosophy, including the *Philosophical Investigations*. In addition, the identification of necessity and aprioricity, and the belief in the linguistic source of both, persisted in the philosophy of the ordinary language school, centered at Oxford from the late '40s through the early '60s, which was so much influenced by the later Wittgenstein. All of this work was well within the target of Quine's circularity argument. Thus, the fact that the argument was, and was seen to be, such a powerful objection to the then dominant conception of analyticity was no small historical achievement.

There were, of course, contemporary responses to Quine that raised important critical objections. Since we will be examining those later in

---

[6] For an illuminating discussion of indexicals, see David Kaplan, "Demonstratives," in J. Almog, J. Perry, and H. Wettstein, eds., *Themes From Kaplan* (New York and Oxford: Oxford University Press, 1989).

this chapter, we need not, at this stage, prejudge the question of just how successful his circle argument was against those originally targeted. Before we take up that question, I will examine further the idea of trying to define analyticity without assuming either T1 or T2. How, one might wonder, would the force of Quinean considerations bear on such attempts?

An Alternative Definition of Synonymy
(and Thereby Analyticity)

In looking for an alternative definition of analyticity, we may start with the notion of synonymy (within a single language). As we have seen, in presenting the circularity argument Quine says that if we are given the notion of necessity, we can define synonymy in terms of substitutivity, preserving truth value in the linguistic construction (6)—*it is a necessary truth that.* . . . In particular, Quine thinks that if we could make sense of examples like (13), and if some such statements were true, then the predicates A and B would count as synonymous, as would the singular terms, n and m.

13a. It is a necessary truth that all and only A's are B's.

   b. It is a necessary truth that n = m.

However, this is not our normal notion of synonymy, as is indicated by (14a–b).

14a. It is a necessary truth that all and only *equilateral triangles* are *equiangular triangles.*

   b. It is a necessary truth that $2^{10} = 1024.$

Although each of these sentences is true, the italicized expressions are **not** normally taken to mean the very same thing—i.e., to be synonymous.

An important reason why we don't take these expressions to be synonymous is that we take the statements in (14) to be significant discoveries. A person could know that a triangle was equilateral without knowing that it was equiangular. Similarly, a person could know that a book had 1024 pages without knowing that the number of pages that the book had was 2^{10}. What these examples show is that there are certain expressions that can always be substituted for one another without changing truth value in the construction (6), but which cannot always be substituted without changing truth value in the constructions in (15).

15. x knows/believes/thinks/says that. . . .

Many philosophers hold that our ordinary notion of synonymy is one that requires synonyms to be interchangeable not only in modal constructions like (6), but also in epistemic constructions like (15). Thus, they would maintain that the proposed definition of synonymy in terms of substitutivity will give correct results only if substitution in the constructions in (15) are included. When these are included, 2^{10} and *1024* are correctly characterized as not being synonymous. These philosophers would add that *bachelor* and *unmarried man* do pass the substitutivity test, and so are correctly characterized as synonyms. The idea is that anyone who believes that Jones is an unmarried man thereby believes that he is a bachelor, and vice versa. Believing that someone is a bachelor doesn't require any inference; it is nothing more than believing that he is an unmarried man.

On this view, the notion of synonymy that Quine defines in terms of necessity is a different and weaker notion than our ordinary notion of synonymy, which may be defined in terms of substitutivity in the constructions in (15). When the definition of synonymy is understood in this way, it does a reasonably good job of capturing our notion of sameness of meaning, without presupposing anything about necessity. Thus, if an analytic sentence continues to be defined as one that can be turned into a logical truth by putting synonyms for synonyms, then we have a definition of analyticity that does not presuppose necessity, and so escapes Quine's circularity argument.

Of course, the conception of analyticity that results from the new definition is much narrower than the one endorsed by the positivists. In my view, the best way to understand it is to see it as giving up the theses T1 and T2 that were common ground for both Quine and the philosophers he was criticizing. For example, under the new definition, very few of the necessary, apriori truths of arithmetic end up being classified as analytic. The same is true of philosophical theses, even when they are true. This is important for a certain conception of philosophy. Many logical positivists, as well as other analytic philosophers of Quine's day, thought that since philosophical theses are not empirical, they must be analytic, if true. The job of the philosopher was thought to consist in ferreting out hidden but significant analytic truths, using the method of linguistic or conceptual analysis. If analyticity turns out to be a much narrower notion than originally thought, then this conception of philosophy is indefensible. Thus, if anything like the modified position on analyticity just outlined is the position to which defenders of analyticity are forced to retreat in the face of Quine's argument, then one must judge his argument to have been substantially successful—even though he may have been wrong in thinking that there is no distinction at all to be drawn between the analytic and the synthetic.

However, Quine himself would not have been content with this limited victory. In "Two Dogmas of Empiricism" he does not discuss the strategy of defining synonymy in terms of substitutivity in constructions other than *it is a necessary truth that*. However, he did discuss this possibility nineteen years later in his book *Philosophy of Logic*, published in 1970, where he discusses examples (16) and (17).[7]

16. Necessarily, cordates are cordates.

17. Tom thinks that cordates are cordates.

In discussing these examples, Quine uses *cordate* as short for *creature with a heart* and *renate* as short for *creature with kidneys*. It is supposed to be a truth of biology that all and only creatures with hearts are creatures with kidneys, so the two expressions, *cordate* and *renate*, are supposed to apply to the same things, without, of course, being synonymous. It is amusing that Quine indicates that *cordate* is short for *creature with a heart*. What he means, of course,—though he doesn't say it—is that as he uses these terms, they are **synonymous**. But if that is what he means, then there must be such a thing as synonymy after all. So his very example seems to presuppose the position which he uses the example to argue against.[8]

---

[7] Willard Van Orman Quine, *The Philosophy of Logic* (Englewood Cliffs, NJ: Prentice Hall, 1970), pp. 8–10.

[8] Quine inadvertently allowed the same presupposition to creep into section 2 of "Two Dogmas." The section is concerned with the notion of definition, and Quine's main point is that since the most familiar definitions—e.g., dictionary definitions and philosopher's *explications*—either report, or depend on, belief in pre-existing instances of synonymy, an attempt to define an analytic truth to be one which, by virtue of the definitions of its words, is equivalent to a logical truth would not avoid relying on the problematic notion of synonymy. However, at one stage in this discussion Quine notes an exception to the idea that definitions rely on a belief in pre-existing instances of synonymy. On pp. 25–26, he says:

> There does, however, remain still an extreme sort of definition which does not hark back to prior synonymies at all: namely the explicitly conventional introduction of novel notations for purposes of sheer abbreviation. Hence the definiendum becomes

Be that as it may, after pointing out how substitution of the term *renates* for one of the occurrences of the term *cordates* in (16) would change truth value, Quine says the following:

> True, other examples could be cited. The example [17] serves as well as [16], since Tom might well **not** think that all cordates are renates, while still recognizing that all cordates have hearts.[9]

What Quine is saying here is that in the case of (17), as in the case of (16), substitution of *renates* for one of the occurrences of *cordates* may change truth value—which means that we could define synonymy in terms of substitutivity in (17), as opposed to (16), and still get the desired result that *cordate* and *renate* are not synonymous. But then Quine goes on to say the following:

> And [17] has the advantage of being couched in more innocent language than [16], with its cooked-up sense of necessity. However, innocence is one thing, clarity another. The *thinks* idiom in [17], for all its ordinariness, is heir to all the obscurities of the notion of synonymy . . . and more.[10]

On the face of it, this passage seems to be a *reductio ad absurdum* of Quine's position. He says that *think*, and presumably other verbs like *believe* and *know*, have all the obscurity of synonymy and necessity **and more**. But he rejects the notions of synonymy and necessity

---

synonymous with the definiens because it has been created expressly for the purpose of being synonymous with the definiens. Here we have a really transparent case of synonymy created by definition; would that all species of synonymy were as intelligible.

Although the main point here is surely unobjectionable to anyone who believes in synonymy, Quine here seems to have forgotten that the issue that is central to his overall argument is not how synonymies get created, but whether the notion of synonymy—i.e., sameness of meaning—makes sense. His position is that it doesn't. But if it doesn't, then to grant that explicitly stipulated synonyms are genuinely synonymous is to say something inconsistent with his overall conclusion. It is telling, I think, that even Quine's dedication to his larger, negative, argumentative purpose was not enough to prevent a glimpse of the denied truth from breaking through.

[9] *The Philosophy of Logic*, p. 9. Note the implicit substitution here. In the final sentence of the passage Tom is described as (i) as not believing all cordates are renates while (ii) believing that all cordates have hearts—i.e., that all cordates are creatures with hearts. Quine takes this to show how substitution in (17), *Tom believes that cordates are cordates*, can change truth value. This all makes sense only if Quine assumes that believing that all cordates are creatures with hearts just is believing that all cordates are cordates, which in turn rests on his assumption that *creature with a heart* is synonymous with *cordate*. Again, Quine's discussion presupposes synonymy while disparaging it.

[10] *The Philosophy of Logic*, p. 9.

because they are obscure. If the notions of thinking, believing, and knowing are even more obscure, then, by parity of reasoning, they should be rejected as well. But from this it would seem to follow that, according to Quine, whenever we say that someone thinks, believes, or knows that so and so, we are saying something incorrect, unintelligible, and certainly untrue. If that is his position, then surely, it is absurd.

There are reasons to think that it was Quine's position. In the period between the publication of "Two Dogmas" and the publication of *The Philosophy of Logic*, Quine produced his most striking and influential book, *Word and Object*, published in 1960.[11] In that work he developed an independent argument, based on a doctrine called the *Indeterminacy of Translation*, that leads to the conclusion that there is no such thing as meaning, reference, or belief, in the sense that we ordinarily understand those notions. The implication of Quine's conclusion is that insofar as we are interested in accurately describing reality, our ordinary notions of meaning, reference, and belief must be replaced with drastically weakened and sanitized behavioristic substitutes. In volume 2, I will discuss those conclusions in detail, and explain why they are ill-motivated and ultimately self-defeating. For now, I simply note that in discussing the possibility of defining analyticity and synonymy in terms of substitution in belief contexts, Quine seemed, in 1970, to be thoroughly under the sway of those radical conclusions, and, for that reason, to be willing to go to what otherwise would seem to be great lengths to reject any approach to defining synonymy and, thereby, analyticity, in terms of belief.

It is a pity that Quine was willing to go overboard, because there is a point that could be made on his behalf that does not require going so far. Consider (18) and (19).

18. Jones is an unmarried man.

19. Jones is a bachelor.

Surely, it is conceivable that one could show these two sentences to someone, ask him if he believes what they say, and have him tell you that he believes (18) but not (19). But then, one might wonder, how can substitution in the construction *x believes that* . . . be an adequate test for synonymy? Many philosophers would answer this question by distinguishing between *sincerely assenting to a sentence*, on the one hand, and *believing that which the sentence expresses*, on the other. For

---

[11] Quine, *Word and Object*.

example, if I were to ask Manuel, a monolingual speaker of Spanish, whether he believes what is said by the sentence *The earth is round*, he would not know whether to answer *yes* or *no*, since he wouldn't know what that English sentence means. Still it would probably be correct to describe Manuel as believing that the earth is round, especially if he accepted the corresponding sentence of Spanish. Consequently, the fact that one fails to assent to a sentence S does not always show that one doesn't believe that which the sentence expresses. One may believe what S expresses, while failing to assent to S because one does not know what S means.

Many defenders of synonymy would apply similar reasoning to (18) and (19). They would say that anyone who sincerely assents to (18) but not (19) thereby shows either that he does not understand the expression *unmarried man* or that he does not understand *bachelor*, or both. But if he doesn't understand the meaning of these expressions, then his assent or dissent will not be a reliable indicator of what he really believes. In particular, if he assents to (18), understanding what it means, then he really does believe that Jones is an unmarried man. And if he believes that, he thereby believes that Jones is a bachelor, whether he understands the word *bachelor*, and assents to (19), or not.

That is how many defenders of synonymy would argue. Two things need to be noted about this position. First, this defense of using sub-stitutivity in belief constructions to define synonymy depends on assuming that there is a genuine distinction to be made between **not accepting a sentence because one does not understand what it means** and **not accepting a sentence because one does not believe what it says**. Though I think it is reasonable to assume that there is such a distinction, Quine would, I believe, reject it if pressed. (So much the worse for Quine.) Second, this defense of using substitution in belief constructions to define synonymy will work, and will give us results that we want—like the result that *bachelor* and *unmarried man* are synonymous—only if we are sure that anyone who believes that Jones is an unmarried man believes that Jones is a bachelor (even a person who accepts sentence (18) while rejecting sentence (19)). But if we ask ourselves why we are so sure that this is so, it is hard to resist the following answer: since (18) and (19) mean the same thing, anyone who believes what one of them expresses must believe what the other expresses—in which case anyone who believes that Jones is an unmarried man must believe that Jones is a bachelor, whatever he may say. But if this really is our reason for thinking that *bachelor* is always substitutable for *unmarried man* without change in truth value in belief constructions, then our definition of synonymy in terms of substitutivity in such contexts will presuppose an antecedent grasp and application of the very notion we are supposed to be defining—sameness of meaning. So it would seem that there is a kind of circle here after all, even if it is not the one that Quine focused on.

What should one conclude from this? The conclusion I would draw is that our notions of *belief, knowledge, assertion, what someone says, meaning, what a sentence means or says,* and *what an expression means* are interdependent. Truths about each of these notions are tied up with truths about the others. Questions, unclarities, or indeterminacies involving any of these notions translate into corresponding questions, unclarities, and indeterminacies about the others. All the notions are genuine and intelligible, but neither the propositional attitude family—*belief, knowledge, assertion, what someone says*—nor the semantic family—*meaning, what a sentences means or says, what an expression means*—is conceptually prior to the other. For each notion, there is a genuine distinction between cases that definitely fall under it and cases that definitely do not. In addition, for each notion there are cases in which it is doubtful, or perhaps even indeterminate, whether the notion applies. Thus, if we define analyticity in terms of synonymy, and if we relate synonymy to notions like belief, then there will be some sentences that definitely count as analytic, some that definitely are not analytic, and some in which it is doubtful or even indeterminate whether they are analytic. Of course, in saying this I have gone far beyond both Quine's explicit argument, and what he would accept. Nevertheless, this is where Quine's famous circularity argument in the first four sections of "Two Dogmas" naturally leads, once it is divorced from the background assumptions, T1 and T2, that Quine shared with the positivists.

The Response to Quine by Paul Grice
and Peter Strawson

The critical response to Quine that I have just outlined was not made in the period just after the publication of "Two Dogmas," largely, I suspect, because it would have required giving up theses T1 and T2, which at the time were assumed by both Quine and his opponents. Moreover, adopting this criticism would have meant accepting a greatly diminished conception of analyticity, as well as giving up the conception of philosophy as purely linguistic analysis, aimed at the discovery of significant and illuminating analytic truths. Most of Quine's opponents at the time were too wedded to this conception of philosophy to give it up. For that reason, they missed some of the most effective criticisms that can be made of his argument.

Nevertheless, some interesting, and telling, contemporary critical responses were made. Two in particular stand out as raising issues from which there is something important to be learned. Both were made in an article by Paul Grice and Peter Strawson, called "In Defense of a Dogma," published in 1956.[12] The first of the criticisms begins with an attempt to clarify what Quine's position really is. In the first paragraph of "Two Dogmas" Quine announces that the *"belief in some fundamental cleavage between truths which are analytic, or grounded in meanings independently of matters of fact, and truths which are synthetic, or grounded in fact,"* is an ill-founded dogma that should be abandoned.[13] At the end of section 4, he concludes his argument against the distinction by saying: *"But for all its apriori reasonableness, a boundary between analytic and synthetic statements simply has not been drawn. That there is such a distinction to be drawn at all is an unempirical dogma of empiricists, a metaphysical article of faith."*[14] What is it to say that the idea that there is a distinction at all between analytic and synthetic statements is ill-founded, and that the distinction should be abandoned? What precisely is Quine's conclusion? Grice and Strawson point out that it can be given either a strong or a weak interpretation.

Criticism 1: The Strong and Weak Interpretations

On the strong interpretation, what Quine asserts is that there is **no** distinction between analytic and synthetic statements—i.e., no difference at all between the class of statements to which philosophers have attached the label *analytic* and the class of statements to which they

[12] H. P. Grice and P. F. Strawson, "In Defense of a Dogma," *Philosophical Review* 65 (1956), reprinted in James F. Harris, Jr. and Richard H. Severens, eds., *Analyticity* (Chicago: Quadrangle Books, 1970). Another important criticism which played a role in prompting Quine to develop the views presented in *Word and Object* is found in Rudolph Carnap, "Meaning and Synonymy in Natural Languages," Appendix D, second edition of Meaning and Necessity (Chicago: University of Chicago Press, 1956). This is taken up in volume 2.
[13] "Two Dogmas of Empiricism," p. 20.
[14] Ibid., p. 37.

have attached the label *synthetic* (perhaps because there really are no analytic or synthetic statements). By the same token, there is no distinction between synonymous and non-synonymous expressions—i.e., there is no difference at all between pairs of expressions that are said to have the same meaning and pairs of expressions that are said to have different meanings. Similarly, there is no distinction between necessary and contingent truths. On the weak interpretation, Quine is not denying that these distinctions exist. Rather, his point is that although there are genuine differences marked by these distinctions, the nature of these differences, and hence the reasons for making the distinctions, have been misunderstood by philosophers who have talked about them. On this interpretation, there **is** some sort of difference between statements that have been characterized as *analytic* and those that have been characterized as *synthetic*, but philosophers have misdescribed the distinction.

Having distinguished these two interpretations, Grice and Strawson go on to argue that the view expressed by the strong interpretation is false. Of course, they say, there is a difference between analytic sentences or statements and synthetic sentences or statements, as well as a difference between synonymous expressions and non-synonymous expressions. The existence of these differences is shown by the fact that, in each case, there is an established practice characterized by widespread agreement regarding which examples belong in one category and which belong in the other. Take the analytic/synthetic distinction, for example. There is widespread agreement that *Bachelors are unmarried, Triangles are three-sided, Either it is raining or it isn't,* and *If Sam gave a watch to Mary, then Sam gave Mary a watch,* belong in one class, whereas *The book is on the table, It rains in Seattle, There are people in the room,* and *I have a hand* belong in another. Moreover, and this is crucial, the sentences assigned to the two classes do not form a closed list. Rather, different people who are familiar with the distinction classify new sentences in roughly the same way—even though they may never have encountered those particular examples before, and certainly were not told whether or not they were analytic when they learned the distinction. This shows that in learning the analytic/synthetic distinction, people do not simply memorize a small list of sentences to which philosophers have attached arbitrary labels. Rather, they acquire a genuine ability—roughly the same for each person— that allows them to differentiate two different kinds of sentences given an open list of new examples.

According to Grice and Strawson, this fact—that different people make markedly similar discriminations—calls for explanation. Surely, they argue, the natural explanation is that some features of the sentences themselves must call forth similar judgments on the part of different agents. Some features common to sentences the agents classify as synthetic must be responsible for the fact that different agents classify them in the same way, and other features, common to sentences the agents classify as analytic, must be responsible for the fact that different agents agree in grouping them together. Thus, it is wrong to claim that there is **no** distinction between these two classes of sentences or statements—i.e., no distinction between statements philosophers call *analytic* and those they call *synthetic*. There may well be serious questions about what exactly the distinction comes to, and how it should be described. However, that there is a distinction to be made at all is, Grice and Strawson maintain, beyond doubt. Thus, the view expressed by the strong interpretation of Quine's conclusion is false.

Let us pause for a moment to evaluate this argument before going on to see what Grice and Strawson have to say about the weak interpretation of Quine's conclusion. The argument rests on the supposed fact that the sentences classified by philosophers as analytic are a more or less homogeneous collection that would be recognized by virtually anyone who had been given a rudimentary introduction to the distinction. Being philosophers, Grice and Strawson didn't carry out any empirical research to validate this claim. Rather, they simply assumed their observation was beyond serious doubt. Although there may well be a kernel of truth in their assumption, there is reason to think that matters are more complicated than they realized.

As for the kernel of truth, if we started two lists—one consisting of **simple, obvious, necessary truths that are also knowable apriori**, and the other consisting of **simple, obvious, contingent truths that are knowable only aposteriori**—and then presented subjects with new example sentences randomly drawn from both categories, it is, I suspect, very likely to be true that we would find a considerable degree of agreement in the classification of the new examples. It is also true that this result would support the claim that there is some distinction to be drawn between the statements grouped together in one class by speakers and the statements grouped together in the other class. If, as a philosopher, you simply took it for granted that the necessary, the apriori, and the analytic are one and the same, and to be contrasted with the contingent, the aposteriori, and the synthetic, which are also one and the same, then you might naturally take these observations to support your contention that there must be some distinction to be drawn between the analytic and the synthetic.

However, there are two serious reservations that severely limit the force of this argument. First, as I have repeatedly pointed out, these identifications—of the necessary, the apriori, and the analytic, on the one hand, and of the contingent, the aposteriori, and the synthetic, on the other—are neither inevitable, nor, in the end, even natural. Rather, they were parochial artifacts of a particular period in analytic philosophy. From our perspective today, we can see that not all necessary truths are apriori, not all apriori truths are necessary, and not all members of either class are transparently so. In many cases it takes careful analysis and argument to come to the correct classification. For these reasons, it is simply **not** to be expected that ordinary speakers, given only rudimentary introductions to the necessary/contingent distinction and the apriori/aposteriori distinction, and provided with new examples randomly selected from the four resulting categories, would classify them with high degrees of accuracy or uniformity.

Second, there are limits to what can be concluded from even the most carefully drawn experimental test of uniformities in speakers' judgments of the type that Grice and Strawson imagine. Suppose that W is some word or phrase in common use, and that a Grice and Strawson–style test for uniformity in speaker judgments revealed that speakers reliably apply W to randomly selected new cases in largely uniform ways. This would show (i) that there is a genuine distinction between objects to which speakers would apply W and objects to which they would not, and hence (ii) that there are properties possessed by objects in the first class that distinguish them from objects in the second class. However, the uniformity of speaker judgments would not always show (iii) that these properties constitute the meaning of W, (iv) that W truly applies to the objects that speakers call W, or (v) that the sentence *There are W's* is true. To see this, imagine that W is the predicate *is a witch*, that speakers in a certain community reliably apply this predicate to certain types of women and not to others, and that it is part of the definition of *witch* that to be one is to be a woman whose alliance with the Devil gives her supernatural powers. Although on this understanding there are, in fact, no witches, there is a genuine distinction between individuals to whom speakers would apply the word (because, perhaps, of some suspicious-seeming speech and behavior) and individuals to whom they would not. By parity of reasoning, the Quinean might claim that the mere fact that there is uniformity in the ways speakers apply terms like *analytic* and *necessary* to new cases (supposing this could be established) doesn't show that there are any analytic or necessary truths, or that there is any genuine distinction between the analytic and the synthetic, or the necessary and the contingent—even if there is a distinction between sentences speakers would call *analytic* and those they would call *synthetic*, or those they would call *necessary* vs. those they would call *contingent*.[15]

This Quinean response is correct, as far as it goes; however, it is not the last word. A crucial factor in the *witch* example is the stipulation that to be a witch a woman must satisfy a condition that no one in fact satisfies. It is only because speakers have false beliefs, which are assumed to be definitional, that the genuine distinction between women who are called *witches* by speakers and women who are not does not translate into a genuine distinction between witches and non-witches. To apply the same reasoning to *analytic*, the Quinean would have to show that speakers have similarly false beliefs, which are properly regarded as definitional of *analytic*; and the circularity argument does not do that—unless it is built into the case that the speakers assume the philosophical theses T1 and T2, which is pretty unlikely unless they are professional philosophers.[16] The upshot of all this is that neither Quine nor his critics, Grice and Strawson, fully succeeded. The circularity argument doesn't establish that there is no analytic/synthetic distinction, nor does it locate any false beliefs about analyticity (aside from T1 and T2). Grice and Strawson's argument about uniformity of speaker application at most establishes the presumption that there is some distinction to be made, but it doesn't rule out the possibility that there may be no analytic truths. With T1 and T2 off the table, there was simply nothing further to be gotten from this argument on its own.

This leaves us with a mixed assessment of Grice and Strawson's argument against the view expressed by the strong interpretation of Quine's conclusion. On the one hand, their argument from uniform classification of an open list of examples is flawed both by failure to note complications that were invisible to them because they shared Quine's problematic presuppositions, and by failure to fully appreciate

---

[15] This is, essentially, Gil Harman's response to the Grice and Strawson argument. Thanks to Jeff Speaks for a very useful discussion of this.

[16] Moreover, the Quinean would have to explain how, according to his extreme position, anything can be definitional of anything else.

complications in the move from uniform classification involving a pair of terms to the existence of a genuine distinction marked by those terms. On the other hand, it may very well be possible to construct restricted versions of their argument that lend a degree of support to the claim that there is some distinction to be made between the necessary apriori and the contingent aposteriori, and a different distinction between synonymous and non-synonymous expressions.[17] Whether we can get from there to support for the idea that there is a genuine distinction between the analytic and the synthetic all depends on how analyticity is defined, and what it is used to explain. Grice and Strawson don't help us with that.

With this verdict on their argument against the strong interpretation of Quine's conclusion under our belts, we can move on to what they say about the weak interpretation of his conclusion. On this interpretation, there **is** a distinction between the analytic and the synthetic, the necessary and the contingent, and the synonymous and the non-synonymous, but these distinctions have been widely misunderstood and misdescribed. According to the weak interpretation, this was Quine's point. However, if that was his point, then Grice and Strawson ask, *What exactly was wrong with the ways that other philosophers have understood and described these distinctions?* Is it wrong, on the weak interpretation, to hold that analytic truths reduce to logical truths by putting synonyms for synonyms? To hold that they do is, of course, to appeal to the notion of synonymy. But, on the weak interpretation, that's all right, for, on this interpretation, there is a genuine distinction between expressions that are synonymous and those that are not. Granted, we would like to have a more complete and accurate understanding of synonymy, necessity, and analyticity, but that is another matter.

Grice and Strawson conclude that, on the weak interpretation of Quine, the most he has shown by the circularity argument is that these notions form a family of interdefinable notions. If he is right about this, then it is not wrong to say that analytic truths reduce to logical truths by putting synonyms for synonyms; it is not wrong to say that synonymy is definable in terms of necessity; and so on. Rather, all these claims are true. Thus, if we admit that all the distinctions exist, and that it is just a matter of correcting the false statements that

[17] Even in the case of the synonymous and the non-synonymous, there is reason to think that the distinction is not one that is entirely transparent to ordinary speakers. See chapter 3 of my *Beyond Rigidity* (New York: Oxford University Press, 2002).

philosophers have made about the distinctions, then we must also conclude that Quine's interdefinability argument in sections 1–4 does not identify such statements. That is the lesson that Grice and Strawson draw from the weak interpretation.

Again, although they have a point, it needs to be qualified. Certainly to show that a set of notions is interdefinable is not, in general, to show that the notions are questionable. Nor is it to show that they have been wrongly described, or wrongly understood, unless one of these notions has been taken to be conceptually prior to the others, and assumed to constitute the basis for understanding them. However, this is how analyticity had been treated, not only by the positivists, but by philosophers of the ordinary language school, to which Grice and Strawson were attached. Since this was Quine's target, his interdefinability argument was to the point.

To reiterate, the most that can be claimed for the interdefinability argument is that it shows that the conjunction of T1 and T2 is false— it is not the case both that all necessary (and all apriori) truths are analytic and that analyticity can be used to explain and legitimate necessity (and apriority). Of course, if one does not accept T1 and T2 to begin with—as many philosophers now do not—one will not conclude that Quine's argument establishes that there is no analytic/synthetic distinction, nor that it establishes that the other distinctions he discusses do not exist. One may grant, however, that it does show that a certain conception of the relationship between analyticity, necessity, and apriority is incoherent. Although this achievement is much less ambitious than the one Quine set for himself, it is no small thing. The reason Grice and Strawson missed it is that they (wrongly) shared his problematic assumptions, T1 and T2, while remaining (rightly) convinced that there must really be some necessary truths, some apriori truths, and some synonymous expressions.

Criticism 2: Skepticism about Meaning

The second criticism Grice and Strawson make of the circle argument focuses on meaning and synonymy, rather than analyticity and necessity. Their point is that Quine's skepticism about synonymy leads directly to an absurd skepticism about meaning in general. This time their criticism is, it seems to me, not only dead on, but historically prophetic. They argue that it is absurd to reject the notion of synonymy as unintelligible because that would require rejecting the notion of meaning altogether—a position that is obviously untenable. The argument establishing this connection is simple. If expressions can have meanings at all, then surely there must, in principle, be true answers to the question *What does this, or that, expression mean?* But if there are true answers to such questions, then we can identify synonymous expressions as those for which answers to these questions are the same.

Here is what Grice and Strawson say in a somewhat broader context.

> To say that two expressions x and y are cognitively synonymous seems to correspond, at any rate roughly, to what we should ordinarily express by saying that x and y have the same meaning or that x means the same as y. If Quine is to be consistent in his adherence to the extreme thesis [the strong interpretation] then it appears that he must maintain not only that the distinction we suppose ourselves to be marking by the use of the terms "analytic" and "synthetic" does not exist, but also that the distinction we suppose ourselves to be marking by the use of the expressions "means the same as," "does not mean the same as" does not exist either. At least, he must maintain this insofar as the notion of *meaning the same as*, in its application to predicate-expressions, is supposed to differ from and go beyond the notion of *being true of just the same objects.* . . . Yet the denial that the distinction (taken as different from the distinction between the coextensional and the non-coextensional) really exists, is extremely paradoxical. . . . But the paradox is more violent than this. For we frequently talk of the presence or absence of relations of synonymy between kinds of expressions—for example, conjunctions, particles of many kinds, whole sentences—where there does not appear to be any obvious substitute for the ordinary notion of synonymy, in the way in which coextensionality is said to be a substitute for synonymy of predicates. **Is all such talk meaningless? Is all talk of correct or incorrect *translation* of sentences of one language into sentences of another meaningless?** It is hard to believe that it is. But if we do successfully make the effort to believe it, we have still harder renunciations before us. **If talk of sentence-synonymy is meaningless, then it seems that talk of sentences having a meaning at all must be meaningless too. For if it made sense to talk of a sentence having a meaning, or meaning something, then presumably it would make sense**

to ask "What does it mean?" and if it made sense to ask "What does it mean?" of a sentence, then sentence-synonymy could be roughly defined as follows: Two sentences are synonymous if and only if any true answer to the question "What does it mean?" asked of one of them, is a true answer to the same question, asked of the other.[18]

The argument here is powerful: one can give up synonymy only if one is willing to give up meaning and translation entirely. Moreover, Quine seems to have felt its power, since four years after this criticism appeared, he published *Word and Object*, in which he does advocate—in a somewhat backhanded way—giving up meaning and translation entirely. We must wait until volume 2 to explain that disastrous choice.

[18] Grice and Strawson, "In Defense of a Dogma," pp. 60–62 in *Analyticity*, my boldface emphasis.

CHAPTER 17

MEANING AND HOLISTIC VERIFICATIONISM

CHAPTER OUTLINE

Quine's Positive Doctrines
in Sections 5 and 6 of "Two Dogmas"

In the last chapter, we examined the famous circle argument given in
the first four sections of "Two Dogmas of Empiricism." As I presented
the argument, its main lesson is that there is no way of explaining, or
defining, what it is to be an analytic sentence that is consistent with
two fundamental theses that were widely presupposed by defenders of
analyticity at the time.

T1. All necessary (and all apriori) truths are analytic. (For all sentences S, if S expresses a necessary (apriori) truth, then S is
analytic.)

T2. Analyticity is needed to explain and legitimate necessity (and
aprioricity).

Since Quine himself accepted these theses, he concluded that the ana-
lytic/synthetic distinction, along with the necessary/contingent and
the apriori/aposteriori distinctions, must be rejected.

So much for one dogma of empiricism. In section 5, Quine turns his
attention to the second so-called dogma, which he dubs *radical re-*

ductionism. This is the view that every meaningful sentence is translatable into sentences about sense experience. (Radical reductionism is, roughly, what we have been calling *the doctrine of logical constructions out of sense data*.) Quine's first major point is that the two dogmas—(i) that there is a genuine analytic/synthetic distinction, and (ii) radical reductionism—are linked in empiricist thinking by verificationism as a theory of meaning. Roughly speaking, according to verificationism two sentences have the same meaning iff they would be verified or falsified—confirmed or disconfirmed—by the same experiences. Given this notion of synonymy, one could define analyticity by saying that a sentence is analytic iff it is synonymous with a logical truth. Thus, if verificationism were correct, then the analytic/synthetic distinction would be safe. Similarly, if verificationism, or at any rate a particularly simple version of verificationism, were correct, then any empirical sentence would be translatable, without loss of meaning, into a set of sentences about sense data that would confirm the original sentence. But that, in essence, is just the doctrine of radical reductionism. For these reasons, Quine concludes, if verificationism were correct, then the two dogmas of empiricism would be expected corollaries.

Of course verificationism, as a theory of meaning, had already failed, and was quite dead, by the time Quine wrote "Two Dogmas." The same was true of radical reductionism. Nevertheless, he noted that some philosophers still maintained certain modified versions of them.

> But the dogma of reductionism has, in a subtler and more tenuous form, continued to influence the thought of empiricists. The notion lingers that to each statement, or each synthetic statement, there is associated a unique range of possible sensory events such that the occurrence of any of them would add to the likelihood of truth of the statement, and that there is associated also another unique range of possible sensory events whose occurrence would detract from that likelihood. This notion is of course implicit in the verification theory of meaning.
>
> The dogma of reductionism survives in the supposition that each statement, taken in isolation from its fellows, can admit of confirmation or infirmation at all. My countersuggestion, issuing essentially from Carnap's doctrine of the physical world in the *Aufbau*, is that our statements about the external world face the tribunal of sense experience not individually but only as a corporate body.[1]

---

[1] Quine, "Two Dogmas of Empiricism," pp. 40–41.

It follows from these remarks that someone who knows the meaning of a sentence might **not** know precisely which experiences or observations would count in its favor, and which would count against it; and surely, for some statements at least, Quine is right about this. The best example of what he has in mind is a highly theoretical scientific hypothesis. One might understand the hypothesis, and thereby know how it functions in the relevant scientific theory, without knowing exactly which possible observations would count for or against it; the hypothesis itself might be too abstract and theoretical to logically entail observational predictions on its own. To generate observational predictions it must be combined both with further, subsidiary statements (some of which may themselves be observational) and with other hypotheses of the theory. With this in mind, let us suppose that the combination of hypothesis H with further statements T_1 through T_n entails observational predictions that run contrary to what we actually observe. If the predictions are false, then we know that at least one of the statements used in making them must be rejected. But which? According to Quine, there is no hard and fast rule here. Which statement we reject will depend on a variety of desiderata—including the simplicity of the resulting system, the ease with which it can be applied to new cases, and the ways it might be modified in the future. On this picture, individual statements are not confirmed or disconfirmed by directly comparing them with experience. Rather, a statement's connection with experience typically is mediated by a larger body of accepted fact and theory.

This conclusion may be expressed roughly as follows:

A. The unit of confirmation is not the individual sentence or statement, but the theory as a whole.

Quine does not stop here; from (A) he concludes (B).

B. The unit of meaning is not the individual sentence, but the whole theory.

Thus, he closes section 5 of "Two Dogmas" with the following remarks:

We lately reflected that in general the truth of statements does obviously depend both on language and upon extralinguistic fact; and we noted that this obvious circumstance carries in its train, not logically but all too naturally, a feeling that the truth of a statement is somehow analyzable into a linguistic component and a factual component. The factual component must, if we are empiricists, boil down to a range of confirmatory experiences. . . . My present suggestion is that it is nonsense, and the root of much nonsense, to speak of a linguistic component and a factual component in the truth of any individual statement. Taken collectively, science has its double dependence upon language and experience; but this duality is not significantly traceable into the statements of science taken one by one.

The idea of defining a symbol in use was, as remarked, an advance over the impossible term-by-term empiricism of Locke and Hume. The statement, rather than the term, came with Frege to be recognized as the unit accountable to an empiricist critique. But what I am now urging is that even taking the statement as unit we have drawn our grid too finely. The unit of empirical significance is the whole of science.[2]

Let us take this passage slowly, paraphrasing as we go. Quine begins by endorsing a general doctrine,

in general the truth of statements does obviously depend both on language and upon extralinguistic fact,

which may be paraphrased as (1).

1. The truth of a set of sentences depends on (a) what the sentences mean, and hence what they say about the world, and (b) the world's being the way the sentences say that it is.

Next Quine draws attention to a certain conclusion one might naturally be tempted to draw on the basis of this correct general doctrine. The conclusion is that

the truth of a statement is somehow analyzable into a linguistic component and a factual component,

which may be paraphrased as (2).

2. For each individual true sentence S, the truth of S depends on (a) what S means, and hence what S says about the world, and (b) the world's being the way S says it to be.

---

[2] Ibid., pp. 41–42.

Next Quine tells us how empiricists must construe the notion of the world's being the way it is said to be by a sentence or set of sentences.

> The factual component must, if we are empiricists, boil down to a range of confirmatory experiences.

This may be paraphrased as (3).

> 3. The condition that the world be the way it is said to be by a sentence or set of sentences is the condition that the sensory or observable events that would confirm the sentence or set of sentences actually occur.

Quine closes the paragraph by rejecting (2), while endorsing versions of (1) and (3) in which the sets of sentences in question are scientific theories of the world.

> My present suggestion is that it is nonsense, and the root of much nonsense, to speak of a linguistic component and a factual component in the truth of any individual statement. Taken collectively, science has its double dependence upon language and experience; but this duality is not significantly traceable into the statements of science taken one by one.

The final paragraph in the quoted passage simply reiterates this conclusion, and places it in historical perspective. When, in the passage, Quine speaks of *the impossible term-by-term empiricism of Locke and Hume,* he is referring to the view that each significant word stands for a collection of possible sensory experiences, and nothing more. Quine contends that it was a significant advance—and in particular an advance for empiricism—when it was realized that one could "define a symbol in use," without associating the word with any nonlinguistic entity which is its meaning, or any set of entities to which it applies. To define a symbol *in use*, one gives a rule that specifies the contribution the word makes to the meaning of every sentence in which it occurs. A paradigm example of such a definition is Russell's analysis of the definite article 'the'. We also saw this idea employed in the doctrine that material objects sentences can be analyzed in terms of sense data sentences. The key to the analysis was the attempt to specify how material object sentences could be translated, as wholes, into corresponding sense data statements, without having to associate each material object word with a synonymous phrase about sense data.

This is the kind of advance that Quine is talking about when he says:

The idea of defining a symbol in use was, as remarked, an advance over the impossible term-by-term empiricism of Locke and Hume. The statement, rather than the term, came with Frege to be recognized as the unit accountable to an empiricist critique.

The reference here to Gottlob Frege is to one of the first philosophically significant instances of defining symbols in use—even though, unlike Russell, Frege himself did not link this to any sort of empiricism. When Quine talks about the statement, rather than the term, coming to be *recognized as the unit accountable to an empiricist critique,* he is referring to the pair of doctrines given in (4).

4a. The primary units of meaning are individual sentences; words have meaning only by virtue of the contributions they make to the meanings of sentences.

b. The meaning of a sentence is to be understood in terms of the sensory or observational events that would confirm it.

These are doctrines that the logical positivists were seen as having accepted, in one form or another. Quine finishes up the passage by repudiating the doctrines (4a) and (4b), and replacing them with (5a) and (5b).

5a. The primary units of meaning are entire scientific theories; sentences have meaning only by virtue of the contributions they make to the meanings of theories.

b. The meaning of a theory is the set of sensory or observational events that would confirm it.

This is essentially what he means when he says,

But what I am now urging is that even taking the statement as unit we have drawn our grid too finely. The unit of empirical significance is the whole of science.

We are now in a position to step back and put the entire picture together. Consider again Quine's general conclusion B—that the unit of meaning is not the individual sentence, but the theory. (This is also, of course, expressed by (5a).) What does this doctrine mean, and why does Quine accept it? At first glance it seems like a strange claim. It seems to imply that one can't understand a single sentence S until one has understood a whole range of other sentences with which S has been combined to form a theory. Although this may seem odd, Quine would, I think, accept it. His point, I believe, is that to understand S one really does have to know what would be evidence for or against S. However, the connection of a sentence with evidence typically is not direct, but rather is mediated through other sentences. Thus, knowing what would be evidence for or against S reduces to knowing how S functions in one's total theory or system of beliefs, which as a whole generates observational predictions. Since knowing the meaning of S is knowing what would confirm or disconfirm S, and since knowing what would confirm or disconfirm S amounts to knowing how S contributes to the observational predications made by one's total theory of the world, Quine concludes that the meaning of S is its contribution to the observational predictions made by the total system of science that one accepts.

Another way to make essentially the same point is to ask what premise is needed to draw Quine's general conclusion (B) from his premise (A). What Quine needs, and what he accepts, is (C).

C. The unit, or primary object, of confirmation is the unit, or primary bearer, of meaning; its meaning is the set of sensory or observable events that would confirm it.

This identification of meaning with evidence is essentially the identification that was shown to be mistaken by the failure of the verifiability criterion of meaning, as applied to individual sentences. Quine maintains that what was wrong with the verifiability criterion was not the identification of meaning with evidence, which he accepts without argument as axiomatic; rather what was wrong was the location of the unit of meaning with the individual sentence. According to Quine, the proper view is that the basic unit of meaning is the entire theory.

The resulting version of verificationism is expressed by QT1.

QT1. HOLISTIC VERIFICATIONISM

a. The meaning of a theory = the class of possible observations it fits.

b. Two theories have the same meaning iff they fit the same class of possible observations.

In understanding these theses, we will take the class of possible observations that a theory fits to be given by the class of observational conditionals entailed by the theory—where such a conditional is one the antecedent of which specifies some observable event or events and the consequent specifies a further observable event. The set of all such conditionals entailed by a theory is the set of empirical predictions made by the theory. In order for the theory to be true, it is necessary that all these conditionals be true. In order for two theories to mean the same thing, it is necessary and sufficient that they entail the same observational conditionals.

So understood, these theses are essentially the simple, old verificationist doctrines updated to apply to theories rather than individual sentences. Once this adjustment is made, various corollaries follow relatively naturally. Quine discusses these in section 6, the final section of "Two Dogmas."

QT2. The totality of our beliefs is a "man-made fabric which impinges on experience only along the edges."[3]

QT3. Any statement can be held true come what may (by making adjustments elsewhere in the theory).

QT4. Any statement can be rejected, or held to be false (by making adjustments elsewhere in the theory). Thus, no statement is immune from revision.

QT5 UNDERDETERMINATION
For any consistent theory T_1, and class of possible observations O that fit it, there is a theory T_2, logically incompatible with T_1, which also fits O.

QT2, with which Quine begins section 6, is just a metaphorical way of asserting QT1a. The totality of our beliefs constitute a theory or system. This system is confirmed only by predictions it makes about experience. Indeed, the meaning or content of the system is simply the class of potential experiences it fits. The reasoning behind QT3 and QT4 is also clear. First consider QT3. Imagine a theory T containing a statement S, which is not an observation statement. Suppose that T makes a false prediction, and that S is one of the statements involved in generating that prediction. Since S doesn't make the prediction all by itself, but does so only in conjunction with other statements P, Q, and R of the theory, Quine reasons that one can always, if one wishes, retain S and reject one or more of the subsidiary hypotheses P, Q, and R. Of course, rejecting these may require other

[3] Ibid., p. 42.

adjustments, but Quine thinks that such adjustments can always be made. Hence any (non-observational) statement can be held true "come what may."

The same sort of reasoning applies to QT4. Suppose that T_1 is a theory that makes the right predictions. Suppose also that T_1 contains some non-observational sentence S. Quine thinks that given any such theory, one can always, in principle, construct another theory T_2 that makes the same observational predictions as T_1 in a different way. In fact, T_2 can always be constructed so as to make observational predictions that match T_1, while at the same time denying S. If this is right, then, since by QT1b the two theories mean the same thing, there is no issue of truth or falsity separating them—no question of one making a true claim about the world that the other does not. Thus, any non-observational sentence S can always be denied without resulting in falsehood. This may sound paradoxical, but according to Quine, the reason it does is that we are accustomed to thinking of sentences as having meanings on their own, independent of larger theories in which they are embedded. If we give up this view, and accept holistic verificationism, then it is much more natural to suppose that no sentence is immune from revision in Quine's sense. Finally, this discussion of QT4 also illustrates the underdetermination thesis, QT5, which we tacitly relied upon in illustrating QT4.

With Quine's positive views in place, we can also amplify his criticism of the analytic/synthetic distinction. Recall that the original criticism in sections 1–4 of the paper presupposed two theses commonly accepted at the time Quine wrote.

T1. All necessary (and all apriori) truths are analytic.
(For all sentences S, if S expresses a necessary (apriori) truth, then S is analytic.)

T2. Analyticity is needed to explain and legitimate necessity (and aprioricity).

In essence, Quine's argument was that analyticity cannot explain and legitimate necessity, because it can be explained and legitimated only by presupposing necessity. Since neither notion can be legitimated without presupposing the other, no legitimation is possible, and both must be rejected as confused or incoherent. Given holistic verificationism, Quine can now add another layer to his criticism of the analytic/synthetic distinction; he can pinpoint precisely where traditional descriptions of the distinction have, supposedly, gone wrong.

As Quine sees it, traditional defenders of the analytic/synthetic distinction (like Ayer) hold (6a–c).

6a. Experience is relevant to the confirmation of individual synthetic, but not analytic, sentences.

b. Analytic sentences can, without error, and without change of meaning, be held true in the face of any experience. Synthetic sentences cannot be.

c. Analytic sentences cannot be rejected without error, unless we change what we mean by those sentences. Synthetic sentences can be so rejected.

By contrast, Quine's doctrines of holistic verificationism and underdetermination lead him to deny the claims in (6), and replace them with those in (7).

7a. Experience is never relevant to the confirmation of non-observation sentences, taken individually. However, it is relevant to the confirmation of all such sentences, taken in their role as contributing to our total theory of the world.

b. Any non-observation sentence, can, without error, be held true in the face of any experience (by making compensatory changes elsewhere).

c. Insofar as it makes sense to talk of the meanings of individual sentences at all, changes in one's total theory (which will involve changes in which sentences one accepts and which one rejects) should be seen as implicitly changing the meanings of all one's sentences.

One way to sum up this aspect of Quine's critique of the analytic/synthetic distinction is to say that he rejects a sharp and definitive— one might say, **an absolute**—distinction between sentences the confirmation of which depends on experience, and sentences for which confirmatory experience is irrelevant. However, this does not mean that he takes experience to be relevant to every sentence in the same way, or to the same degree. As Quine puts it, our system of beliefs can be thought of as a sort of web that touches experience only at the edges. Different sentences occupy different places in the web. Some are, as he puts it, near the periphery. These are statements we are most ready to revise in the face of new experience, such as observation sentences and low-level generalizations. Other statements play a more central role in our conceptual scheme—e.g., highly theoretical scientific hypotheses, and even the laws of logic. These are among the statements we are most unwilling to give up. However, the difference between statements at the periphery and statements near the center of the web is one of degree, rather than kind. The laws of logic are an extreme example. Some philosophers have proposed that certain logical laws should be modified in order to account for quantum mechanics. Quine himself doesn't think that quantum mechanics requires this, and hence he keeps logic as is. However, he does claim that it is appropriate to evaluate the correctness or incorrectness of logical laws by reference to the role they play in empirical scientific theories.

Thus, Quine's final criticism of the analytic/synthetic distinction may be put as follows. There are differences regarding the degrees to which experience is relevant to the confirmation of different sentences, but it is incorrect to describe these differences as amounting to a distinction between sentences that are immune from revision (i.e., analytic sentences) and sentences that are not (synthetic sentences). No sentences are immune from revision; rather, there is a continuum. Sentences that have typically been regarded as analytic lie toward one end of the continuum, whereas sentences that have typically been regarded as synthetic lie toward the other end. Moreover, the distinction is drawn within the context of a theory of meaning in which the unit of meaning is the entire theory, and meaning is identified with evidence.

Taken as a whole, Quine's two-pronged critique of analyticity was historically very influential. The reason for this was that the assumptions it rested upon were widely shared. Holistic verificationism, upon which the second part of the critique rested, was popular with logical positivists and their followers, who saw in it a means of salvaging what they took to be the most important insights of their formerly flawed system. To be sure, by 1951 a good many other philosophers had lost faith in positivism, and had given up verificationism entirely. However, most of these anti-verificationist philosophers continued to subscribe to the view that philosophy was nothing more than linguistic analysis, that all necessity was linguistic necessity, and that all aprioricity was linguistically based. Since these philosophers continued to accept theses T1 and T2 relating necessity and aprioricity to analyticity, the first part of Quine's critique (the circularity argument) posed a serious challenge to them.

Looking back today from a perspective of 50 years later, the debate is apt to seem outdated, and the furor caused by Quine's attack on the analytic/synthetic distinction may seem difficult to understand. Today, there are very few proponents of either holistic verificationism, or the linguistic analysis of necessity and aprioricity expressed by theses T1 and T2. Since Quine's critique rested on these claims, which he took entirely for granted, the critique no longer has the significance it once did. However, it did have a real effect on the philosophy of his day.

Critique of Quine's Positive Views

We now turn to certain problems that arise for the positive view expressed by Quine in sections 5 and 6 of "Two Dogmas." The first problem comes in the form of a paradox that results from combining his thesis of holistic verificationism with his underdetermination thesis.[4]

A Paradox

QT1. HOLISTIC VERIFICATIONISM

a. The meaning of a theory = the class of possible observations it fits.

b. Two theories have the same meaning iff they fit the same class of possible observations.

QT5. UNDERDETERMINATION

For any consistent theory T_1, and class of possible observations O that fit it, there is a theory T_2, logically incompatible with T_1, which also fits O.

From these two principles it follows that for any consistent theory T_1 there is another theory T_2 that means the same as T_1 while being logically inconsistent with T_1. That's odd. One would have thought that if two theories meant the same thing, then they would be consistent with the same things, and hence that one would be inconsistent with

---

[4] The paradox, which is usefully discussed in Gil Harman, "Meaning and Theory" (*Southwestern Journal of Philosophy* 9:2 [1979]: 9–20), can be traced to an observation by Barbara Humphries in her "Indeterminacy of Translation and Theory" (*Journal of Philosophy* 67 [1970]: 167–78), pp. 169–70.

the other only if it were inconsistent with itself—which can't be the case, since, by hypothesis, T_1 is consistent.

But there is more than oddity here. With the help of three apparently trivial supplementary premises, we can derive a contradiction from QT1 and QT5. Remember, we have used these two doctrines to show that a certain consistent theory T_1 means the same as T_2 while being logically incompatible with T_2. But clearly, two theories that mean the same thing must make the same claim about the world, and so must agree in truth value, while two theories that are logically incompatible with one another cannot both be true. These are our first two supplementary premises.

SP1. If two theories mean the same thing, then they make the same claim about the world, in which case they cannot differ in truth value. Hence one is true if and only if the other is true; similarly, one is false iff the other is false.

SP2. If two theories are logically incompatible, then they cannot both be true.

It follows from this that T_1 and T_2 are both false. But that is strange. Surely there are some true theories of something. This is our third supplementary premise.

SP3. Some theories of some subject matters are true.

Given this, we may simply select some true theory T_1, and some theory T_2 that is observationally equivalent but logically inconsistent with it, and run the argument as before. We then get the result that T_1 and T_2 must both be true, because they have the same meaning, while also getting the result that they cannot both be true, because they are logically incompatible. Since this is a contradiction, at least one of the principles that led to it must be incorrect.

Another way of expressing the paradox is this. Consider Quine himself. Surely, there are some scientific theories that he accepts, and is willing to assert. In fact, he tells us as much. Let T_1 be one of the theories that he does accept. But then, by his own underdetermination thesis, it follows that there must be some other theory T_2, logically incompatible with T_1, that makes the same empirical predictions as T_1. But now, given that Quine-the-scientist accepts T_1 as true, he must reject T_2 as false. But this conflicts with his philosophical thesis of holistic verificationism, or at any rate it does if we accept the seemingly obvious premise SP1. Thus, it would seem that Quine-the-scientist contradicts Quine-the-philosopher. The question we must address is whether this contradiction can be avoided, and the paradox resolved, while adhering to the spirit, if not the letter, of Quine's views.

A possible Quinean resolution to this problem can be reconstructed along the lines of a suggestion made by Gilbert Harman in his insightful article, "Meaning and Theory."[5] The resolution relies on the following three Quinean principles.

P1. Theories are sets, or conjunctions, of sentences.

P2. What a sentence means, and accordingly whether it is true or not, are matters that are relativized to the language in which the sentence is used.

P3. The meaning of one's words, and hence the language one speaks, is affected by one's total system of beliefs and the sentences one accepts. In particular, the meaning of a theoretical term like *electron* depends on what laws one accepts that include the term. If one changes the laws, one changes the meaning of the term, as well as the meanings of sentences, and theories, containing it.

We may illustrate the use of these principles in responding to our paradox by considering a simple example discussed by Quine in his paper, "On Empirically Equivalent Systems of the World."

> Take some theory formulation and select two of its terms, say 'electron' and 'molecule.' I am supposing that these do not figure essentially in any observation sentences; they are purely theoretical. Now let us transform our theory formulation merely by switching these terms throughout. The new theory formulation will be logically incompatible with the old: it will affirm things about so-called electrons that the other denies. . . . Clearly . . . the two theory formulations are *empirically equivalent*—that is, they imply the same observation conditionals.[6]

Let us examine how we would describe this case. In this examination, we will use the term *theory* in the same way that Quine uses the

---

[5] In what follows, I reconstruct Harman's suggestion, using slightly different terminology than his, and ignoring certain auxiliary issues with which he was concerned.

[6] Quine, "On Empirically Equivalent Systems of the World" *Erkenntnis* 9 (1975): 319.

expression *theory formulation* in the passage—that is, as applying to sets or conjunctions of sentences used to do theoretical work, including the making of observational predictions. We will let T_1 be our standard system of science and T_2 be a slightly modified theory in which the terms *electron* and *molecule* have been systematically permuted in the laws of the theory. The two are logically incompatible, since T_1 logically entails the (non-observational) sentence *Electrons are constituents of atoms, which in turn are constituents of molecules,* whereas T_2 entails the negation of that sentence. Given that T_1 is the standard scientific theory that we all are familiar with and believe to be true, we will reject T_2, which is inconsistent with it. Suppose, however, we were to meet some people living in an isolated part of the world who had never studied standard physics as we know it, but had developed a physical theory entirely on their own. Quite miraculously, the theory they have come up with is precisely the set of sentences T_2. When they tell us this, we are astounded. Clearly their theory—considered as a set of sentences—is not identical with ours, since the words *electron* and *molecule* are permuted in the two theories. However, the difference between the theories seems to be entirely verbal. What our new friends mean by the word *electron* is what we mean by the word *molecule,* and what they mean by the word *molecule* is what we mean by the word *electron*. Aside from this purely verbal difference, there is no disagreement between us about the world. Clearly, what is important is not what words they use to express their view, but what their view is, which is reflected by what their words mean. In a case like this, we would say that although our new friends speak a slightly different language than we do, the theory they express in their language means the same as the theory we express in our language, and hence makes the same claim about the world as ours does.

So what should we say about these two theories, T_1 and T_2? If they mean the same thing, then surely they can't be logically incompatible, can they? But how can they not be logically incompatible, since the sentence *Electrons are constituents of atoms, which in turn are constituents of molecules* is a theorem of T_1, whereas the negation of that sentence, *It is not the case that electrons are constituents of atoms, which in turn are constituents of molecules,* is a theorem of T_2? In answering these questions, it is crucial to keep one important fact clearly in mind. The two theories, T_1 and T_2, considered simply as sets of grammatical sentences, occur in both the language L_{us} that we speak, and the language L_{them} that they speak. Since the sentences that make up the two theories mean different things in the two languages, we must relativize our questions to the particular languages we are talking about, when we ask whether these theories mean the same thing, and whether they are logically incompatible.

We may ask any of the following questions.

Q1. Is the meaning of T_1 in L_{us} the same as the meaning of T_2 in L_{us}? Are the two theories, taken as sets of sentences in L_{us}, logically incompatible?

Q2. Is the meaning of T_1 in L_{them} the same as the meaning of T_2 in L_{them}? Are the two theories, taken as sets of sentences in L_{them}, logically incompatible?

Q3. Is the meaning of T_1 in L_{us} the same as the meaning of T_2 in L_{them}? Is T_1, taken as a set of sentences of L_{us}, logically incompatible with T_2, taken as a set of sentences of L_{them}?

The answers to these questions are the following:

A1. Since we accept T_1 as true in L_{us}, whereas we reject T_2 as false in L_{us}, the two theories do not mean the same thing in L_{us} (even though they entail precisely the same observational conditionals, and so make identical observational predictions). Moreover, since T_2 contains a theorem that is the negation of a theorem of T_1, the two theories are logically incompatible, taken as sets of sentences of L_{us}.

A2. Since they accept T_2 as true in L_{them}, whereas they reject T_1 as false in L_{them}, the two theories do not mean the same thing in L_{them} (even though they entail precisely the same observational conditionals). Moreover, since T_2 contains a theorem that is the negation of a theorem of T_1, the two theories are logically incompatible, taken as sets of sentences of L_{them}.

A3. Since T_1, understood as a set of sentences of L_{us}, differs only verbally from T_2, understood as a set of sentences of L_{them}, the meaning of T_1 in L_{us} is the same as the meaning of T_2 in L_{them}. However, when understood in this way, T_1 and T_2 are not logically incompatible; sentences, or sets of sentences, can be logically incompatible only when they are taken as belonging to the same language.

These are the answers that a Quinean, following Harman's suggestion and utilizing principles P1–P3, would naturally give to questions Q1–Q3. Moreover, as a description of this particular case—involving the permutation of the words *molecule* and *electron* and nothing more—the answers seem to be correct. Since in this case our use of the sentences in T_1 matches our new friends' use of the corresponding sentences in T_2 in every respect, the meaning of T_1 in L_{us} is obviously the same as the meaning of T_2 in L_{them}. The surprising thing about the Quinean, however, is that he treats this sort of example as paradigmatic. He holds that no matter how different two theories, T_a and T_b might be, and hence no matter how different the uses of their individual sentences by proponents of the two theories might be, so long as the theories entail the same observational conditionals (and so make the same observational predictions), the meaning of T_a in the language of someone who accepts it is the same as the meaning of T_b in the language of someone who accepts it. The difference between them is purely verbal. According to the Quinean, the choice between them is never a choice about substance; it is a choice about which language one finds simplest, most convenient, and most efficient to use. Theoretical choices between theories that make the same observational predictions become pragmatic choices between languages. This is what Quine's pragmatism, based on holistic verificationism, amounts to.

With this in mind, we can state the Quinean resolution of the original paradox. The contradiction was derived from the original Quinean principles QT1 and QT5 plus the supplementary premises SP1–SP3.

QT1. HOLISTIC VERIFICATIONISM

a. The meaning of a theory = the class of possible observations it fits (given by the class of observational conditionals entailed by the theory).

b. Two theories have the same meaning iff they fit the same class of possible observations (i.e., iff they entail the same class of observational conditionals).

QT5. UNDERDETERMINATION

For any consistent theory T_1, and class of possible observations O that fit it, there is a theory T_2 logically incompatible with T_1 which also fits O.

SP1. If two theories mean the same thing, then they make the same claim about the world, in which case they cannot differ in truth value. Hence one is true if and only if the other is true; similarly, one is false iff the other is false.

SP2. If two theories are logically incompatible, then they cannot both be true.

SP3. Some theories of some subject matters are true.

The Quinean resolution of the paradox that we have just explored gives up the original formulation, QT1, of holistic verificationism, and replaces it with the following weakened version, QT1′, of that thesis.

QT1′. WEAK HOLISTIC VERIFICATIONISM

a. The meaning of a theory in the language of someone who accepts it = the class of possible observations that it fits (given by the class of observational conditionals entailed by the theory).

b. The meaning of a theory T_1 in the language of someone who accepts T_1 = the meaning of a theory T_2 in the language of someone who accepts T_2 iff T_1 and T_2 fit the same class of possible observations (i.e., iff they entail the same class of observational conditionals).

The underdetermination thesis, QT5, does not need substantial change, but may simply be clarified to avoid ambiguity as follows.

QT5′. UNDERDETERMINATION

For any consistent theory T_1, in the language L_1 of someone who accepts it, and for any class of possible observations O that fit it, there is a theory T_2, also in L_1, logically incompatible with T_1, which fits O as well.

The contradiction is blocked because the weakened version of holistic verification does not entail that the theory T_2, which has precisely the same observational consequences as T_1, has the same meaning in L_1 as T_1 has in L_1—where L_1 is the language spoken by those who accept T_1. If, as we assumed in the original statement of the paradox, T_1 is true in L_1, then T_2 is false in L_1, and so, by SP1, the meaning of T_2 in L_1 differs from the meaning of T_1 in L_1.[7] What does T_2 mean in L_1? The weakened version of holistic verificationism does not say. But

---

[7] In light of our reformulation of the other principles, SP1 might now be stated as follows: *If T means the same thing in L that T′ means in L′, then the claim about the world made by T*

whatever it means, it is not what T_1 means in L_1. Precisely analogous points can be made about L_2. Since T_2 means the same in L_2 as T_1 means in L_1, SP1 together with the truth of T_1 in L_1 ensures that T_2 is true in L_2. Thus, T_1 is false in L_2, and its meaning in L_2 differs from the meaning of T_2 in L_2. As before, the weakened version of holistic verificationism is silent about the meaning of the false theory, T_1, in L_2. It is even silent about whether the meaning in L_1 of the false T_2 is the same as the meaning in L_2 of the false T_1. Perhaps the Quinean should remind us that whereof one cannot speak, one must be silent.

That is, I think, about the best we can do in constructing a response on Quine's behalf to the paradox generated by his original principles. The position we have ended up with is both coherent and Quinean. It also receives some support from the *electron-molecule* example. But is it correct? Here, we may content ourselves with three critical observations.

First, very little positive justification has been given for even the weakened version of holistic verificationism. True, the *electron-molecule* example is one in which the two theories do, in fact, both mean the same thing and entail the same observational conditionals. But do they mean the same thing **because** they entail the same observational conditionals? Neither Quine himself, nor other Quineans, have made any serious attempt to show this. Moreover, alternative explanations exist. If, as many philosophers hold, meaning is determined by use, then the fact that the two theories obviously mean the same thing may be due to the fact that the sentences that make them up can be put in a 1-to-1 correspondence, where the paired sentences are used in exactly the same ways by the proponents of the two theories in their different communities. If this is the right explanation of this example, then in a case in which two very different theories cannot be put into this kind of a correspondence, they may well differ in meaning (as used in their respective communities) even though they entail the same observational conditionals. In order to establish the weak version of holistic verificationism, one would have to rule out this possibility. To date, this has not been done.

Second, the weakened version of holistic verification needed to avoid the original paradox is not fully general. As we have seen, it is silent about the meanings of theories in languages in which those theories are

---

in L is the same as the claim about the world made by T' in L', in which case the truth value of T in L cannot differ from the truth value of T' in L'. SP2 will now read: *If two theories in the same language are logically incompatible, then they cannot both be true in that language.*

not accepted. Since the sentences of such theories are fully meaningful sentences of those languages, the theories themselves must have meanings in the languages. Moreover, according to the weakened version of holistic verificationism, those meanings cannot be identified with the observational predictions they entail. The unanswered challenge for the proponent of this version of verificationism is to specify what the meanings of these theories are, and why the meanings of some theories are identified with the totality of their observational predictions, whereas the meanings of other theories must be something quite different.

Finally, the original paradox may not have been fully put to rest. The proposed solution makes the meaning of a theory in a language depend on whether or not speakers of the language accept it as true. But speakers are neither empirically nor logically omniscient, and sometimes sets of sentences, or theories, have logical properties speakers do not notice or recognize. With this in mind, consider the following possible case. T_1 is a true theory of some domain. T_2 is a different theory that entails the same set of observational conditionals as T_1, while being logically incompatible with T_1 (though not obviously so). In this case, a certain speaker x believes that the two theories are observationally equivalent, and x believes that all their predictions are true. However, x has failed to notice their incompatibility, and wrongly takes them to be consistent with one another. Because of this, x accepts both T_1 and T_2 as true. Thus, the language L spoken by x is both the language of someone who accepts T_1 and the language of someone who accepts T_2. This is all that is needed to re-create the paradox using the weakened version of holistic verificationism, instead of Quine's original version. According to the weakened version, the two theories have the same meaning in L (and hence, by SP1, the same truth value in L) even though they are logically incompatible in L. This, of course, is impossible. It is plausible to think that if the original paradox showed that Quine's initial version of holistic verificationism was incorrect, then this re-creation of the paradox shows that the weakened version of holistic verificationism is also incorrect. Of course, one might try to avoid this result: one might dispute the claim that two theories really could be related in the way here imagined; alternatively, one might claim that in any such case the agent x, without realizing it, really speaks, and oscillates back and forth between, two different languages, one corresponding to each theory; or, one might search for some still weaker version of holistic verificationism that would avoid refutation by such a scenario. All these responses are theoretically possible. Still, with holistic verificationism becoming so baroque, it is hard to avoid the thought the one should give it up altogether as simply being on the wrong track.

Quine's Problematic Empiricist Heritage

At this point I will leave aside further questions about the issues raised by the paradox, and take up a set of issues involving the broader philosophical significance of Quine's holistic verificationism. I have suggested that we view his position as an extension of the project initiated by early verificationists. Since Quine endorses the verificationists' identification of meaning with sensory evidence, one might wonder whether the verificationists' radical attack on metaphysics carries over to Quine.

To see that it does, we begin with a simple example. Consider a theory T consisting of physics as we know it, purged of any inconsistencies it might contain. Let D be the set of observational conditionals entailed by T. Now imagine another theory T+, which differs from T only in the addition of purely metaphysical claims about God, divine purposes, and the relation of human beings to the divine. Let us suppose that adding these metaphysical claims does not change the observational conditionals logically entailed by the theory. Thus, T and T+ entail the same set D of observational conditionals, and so make the same observational predictions. Given all this, Quine's holistic verificationism will tell us that T and T+ mean the same thing, and so make the same claims about reality (in the languages of those who accept them). Thus, in adding the metaphysical statements that result in T+, we have not added any further claims about reality. The additional sentences in T+ are just useless, and empty of new content. Because of this there would, I suppose, be pragmatic grounds to reject them—since they do no work. But even if one doesn't realize this, or finds them pleasing and, for that reason, doesn't reject them, they raise no issue of substance, and are utterly trivial. Surely this Quinean conclusion is one that Ayer could happily have accepted. As Ayer might put it, *one who endorses physics while adding statements about God says nothing more than one who simply endorses physics; it is as if what one was doing was asserting the propositions of physics in a soothing tone of voice.*[8] To the extent to which all metaphysical claims can be treated in this way, one might reconstruct the early verificationists' attack on meta-

[8] Compare with Ayer's gloss of *You acted wrongly in stealing that money* on p. 107 of *Language, Truth, and Logic.*

physics in general within the framework of Quine's holistic verificationism. If such a project could be carried through, then much of the
spirit of the verificationists' rejection of traditional metaphysics could
be seen as vindicated by Quine's positive theses.

Quine himself seems to press this line of attack to rather extreme
conclusions in connection with traditional philosophical questions
about the existence and nature of physical objects. In section 6 of "Two
Dogmas," he tells us that physical objects are "myths," comparable to
Homer's gods. We are told that the only salient difference between the
two is that the *myth* of physical objects is more useful than the myth of
anthropomorphic gods. Moreover, it is useful in quite a specific respect.
He says:

> As an empiricist I continue to think of the conceptual scheme of
> science as a tool, ultimately, for predicting future experience in
> the light of past experience. Physical objects are conceptually im-
> ported into the situation as convenient intermediaries—not by
> definition in terms of experience, but simply as irreducible posits
> comparable, epistemologically, to the gods of Homer. For my part I
> do, qua lay physicist, believe in physical objects and not in Homer's
> gods; and I consider it a scientific error to believe otherwise. But in
> point of epistemological footing the physical objects and the gods
> differ only in degree and not in kind. Both sorts of entities enter
> our conception only as cultural posits. The myth of physical ob-
> jects is epistemologically superior to most in that it has proved
> more efficacious than other myths as a device for working a man-
> ageable structure into the flux of experience.[9]

In saying that the "myth of physical objects" is useful, Quine is saying
that stating scientific laws in terms of physical objects is a useful way of
making predictions about sensory experience. We may put Quine's
point in the following way. Our ordinary physical theory T can be
thought of as an elaborate mechanism for making predictions about
our own sense experiences. However, we shouldn't think that T is the
only way of making these predictions. Quine seems to believe that it is
possible, in principle, to construct an alternative theory T− which
doesn't talk about physical objects at all, but rather states all laws directly in terms of sense experience. Suppose we could imagine such a
theory. The idea is that T and T− could make the same predictions

[9] P. 44.

about sense experience, while using very different theoretical tools to make those predictions. Since these theories fit the same class of possible sensory evidence, holistic verificationism tells us, they make the same claims about reality. Thus the theory that freely employs physical-object talk really doesn't say anything more (in the language of someone who accepts it) than the theory that employs only sense data language says (in the language of someone who accepts it).

On the Quinean picture, T and T− do not differ regarding any objective fact. Thus, the only basis for choosing between them is pragmatic. The question is not which theory is true, or correct, or accurate—both are. Rather, the question is which theoretical apparatus is the simplest and most efficient tool for deriving the predictions about sense experience that both are capable of making. Quine's answer is that the theory that employs physical-object talk is the one that best exemplifies these virtues. However, he is at pains to point out that this is the only respect in which the physical-object theory is superior.

Here is a passage from a different essay, "On What There Is," published in 1948.

> The physical conceptual scheme simplifies our account of experience because of the way myriad scattered sense events come to be associated with single so-called objects. . . . Physical objects are postulated entities which round out and simplify our account of the flux of experience, just as the introduction of irrational numbers simplifies laws of arithmetic. From the point of view of the conceptual scheme of the elementary arithmetic of rational numbers alone, the broader arithmetic of rational and irrational numbers would have the status of a convenient myth, simpler than the literal truth (namely, the arithmetic of rationals) and yet containing that literal truth as a scattered part. Similarly, from a phenomenalistic point of view, the conceptual scheme of physical objects is a convenient myth, simpler than the literal truth and yet containing that literal truth as a scattered part.[10]

Here, Quine develops a parallel. The phenomenalistic—i.e., sense data—theory of nature is to the physicalistic theory of nature as the arithmetical theory of the rational numbers (i.e., those expressible as

---

[10] Quine, "On What There Is," *Review of Metaphysics* 2 (1948): 21–38; reprinted in Quine, *From a Logical Point of View*, rev. 2nd ed. (Cambridge, MA: Harvard University Press, 1980), 1–19, at pp. 17–18.

fractions) is to the broader theory that includes both rational numbers and irrational numbers (like the square root of 2). Quine comes close to saying that the literal truth is expressed by the theory of rational numbers and the phenomenalistic theory of nature. The broader arithmetical theory is just a more simplified way of stating that same literal truth; by the same token, the broader physicalistic theory of nature is just a more simplified way of expressing the literal truth about nature that is expressed by the phenomenalistic theory.[11]

It is interesting to note that Quine presented the same analogy in greater detail in the original version of "Two Dogmas of Empiricism," published in the *Philosophical Review*. He deleted the discussion of that analogy in the version of the essay reprinted in *From a Logical Point of View*, because, he says, it overlapped with the section just cited from "On What There Is," which is also cited there.[12] This deletion is unfortunate, since the discussion of the analogy in the original version of "Two Dogmas" was more extensive and illuminating than the one in "On What There Is." Here is the relevant passage:

Imagine, for the sake of analogy, that we are given the rational numbers. We develop an algebraic theory for reasoning about them, but we find it inconveniently complex, because certain functions such as square root lack values for some arguments. Then it is discovered that the rules of our algebra can be much simplified by conceptually augmenting our ontology with some mythical entities, to be called irrational numbers. **All we continue to be really interested in, first and last, are rational numbers**; but

---

[11] Quine later had qualms about this. Referring to this passage in the forward to the 1980 edition of *From a Logical Point of View* (p. viii), he writes, "But I shall improve the opportunity in this preface for a few caveats. One is that 'On what there is' is nominalistic neither in doctrine nor in motivation. I was concerned rather with ascribing ontologies than with evaluating them. Moreover, in likening the physicalists' posits to the gods of Homer, in that essay and in 'Two dogmas', I was talking epistemology and not metaphysics. Posited objects can be real. As I wrote elsewhere, to call a posit a posit is not to patronize it." To me, these words thirty-two years after the fact sound more like second thoughts than mere elucidation. To be sure, the "reality" of physical objects and the truth of statements involving physical-object language could have been readily admitted in 1948. But given Quine's commitment to holistic verificationism, plus his phenomenalistic characterization of the experience against which theories are tested, the content of these admissions would not have amounted to much. Quine tried (in my opinion not very successfully) to deal with these issues much earlier, in "Posits and Reality," written (he says) in 1955, first published in 1960, and reprinted in Quine, *The Ways of Paradox and Other Essays* (New York: Random House, 1966).

[12] See p. 169 in the section "Origins of These Essays," in *From a Logical Point of View*.

we find that we can commonly get from one law about rational numbers to another much more quickly and simply by **pretending** that the irrational numbers are there too.

I think this a fair account of the introduction of irrational numbers and other extensions of the number system. The fact that the mythical status of irrational numbers eventually gave way to the Dedekind-Russell version of them as certain infinite classes of ratios is irrelevant to my analogy. That version is impossible anyway as long as reality is limited to the rational numbers and not extended to classes of them.

Now I suggest that experience is analogous to the rational numbers and that the physical objects, in analogy to the irrational numbers, are posits which serve merely to simplify our treatment of experience. The physical objects are no more reducible to experience than the irrational numbers to rational numbers, but their incorporation into the theory enables us to get more easily from one statement about experience to another.

The salient differences between the positing of physical objects and the positing of irrational numbers are, I think, **just two**. First, the factor of simplification is more overwhelming in the case of physical objects than in the numerical case. Second, the positing of physical objects is far more archaic, being indeed coeval, I expect, with language itself. For language is social and so depends for its development upon intersubjective reference.[13]

If we take this analogy seriously in the sense that Quine seems to have intended it, we arrive at the view

(i) that the phenomenalistic theory of nature tells us the whole truth and nothing but the truth;

(ii) that the elements talked about by the phenomenalistic theory—i.e., sense experiences or sense data—are "all that we are really interested in, first and last";

and

(iii) that talk about physical objects is justified only in its being such a vastly simpler way of making predictions about what we are really interested in—sense data, or sense experience. In positing

---

[13] Quine, "Two Dogmas of Empiricism," pp. 41–42, my boldface emphasis.

physical objects, we "pretend" that there are such things so as to make our tool for predicting sense experience simpler.

In my judgment, these views locate the position Quine took in 1951 as standing at the end of a long and distinguished empiricist tradition of philosophical error. We have already seen how Quine accepted a key component of the empiricist view of meaning championed by the logic-al positivists, in order to extend and reshape it into holistic verificationism. This doctrine in turn led him to accept a key element of the positivists' reductionist program about material objects, which he extends and reshapes. The reductionist, empiricist tradition of which Quine is a part can be characterized by three stages of its development. With Berkeley, the primary unit of meaning or analysis was the term, the basic elements of reality that terms were used to talk about were sense data, and material objects were characterized as sets of sense data. With Russell and Ayer, the primary unit of meaning was the sentence, the basic elements of reality (at least in their phenomenalistic phases) continued to be sense data, and material objects were said to be logical constructions out of sense data—which meant that statements purporting to be about material objects were regarded as translatable into sense data statements. When we reach the Quine of "On What There Is" and "Two Dogmas," we are told that the primary unit of meaning is the entire theory, that sense data or sensory experiences are the things in reality "we are really interested in," and that material objects are myths, or theoretical posits, "on a par with the gods of Homer"—which meant that physical-object theories had the same content as phenomenalistic theories that made identical predictions about sense experiences. A thoroughly familiar idea, put in new form.

Thus, it is not surprising that old difficulties should reappear. Consider, for example, other people. Presumably, everything Quine says about material objects could be said about them. Surely, we know about other people through knowing of their bodies. Thus, it would seem that any reason for holding that physical objects are convenient myths would also be a reason for holding that other people are too. In other words, if T is a theory that makes observational predictions about my own sense experience, without recognizing the existence of other people at all, and if T* makes the same predictions while allowing for other people, then by Quine's lights the two theories should have the same meaning, and hence agree on all objective facts. To paraphrase Quine on physical objects—all of you, dear readers, are simply convenient myths on the same epistemological footing as the gods of Homer.[14]

That is a view I don't expect any of you to accept. And if you don't accept it, then you must reject at least one of the Quinean theses that led to it. They are holistic verificationism, in either its strong or weak form, the underdetermination of our theory of nature by data, and the characterization of the data statements, used to specify the contents of theories, as statements that report private sense experience, rather than statements about public objects. Confronted with this choice, most people would naturally respond by giving up at least the last of these claims. Quine himself did so; at any rate, after the early 1950s he pretty much stopped talking about private sense experiences or phenomenalistic ontologies. To maintain holistic verificationism, one has the option of dropping sense data statements and characterizing observation statements as a subclass of physical object statements. If one does this, then some of the worst problems for Quine's holistic verificationism go away—along with the exciting talk about myths and the gods of Homer.

But where should one stop? If, according to holistic verificationism, statements reporting ordinary, unaided observations of physical objects can play the role of data statements that give empirical content to theories, how far should we go? Do observations using magnifying glasses count? How about binoculars, telescopes, microscopes, electron microscopes, radio telescopes, Geiger counters, and x-ray machines? The more we include in the observational base of theories, the less radical, but also the less interesting, holistic verificationism about the non-observational parts of theories becomes. One wonders whether there could be any principled basis for drawing the line between the observational and non-observational that would render even weakened holistic verificationism at all plausible.

With this in mind, consider a final objection to Quine's positive views. He offers a general theory of meaning that is supposed to apply across the board. But what happens when we turn his philosophical views about meaning on themselves? As before, let T be our total scientific theory of the world. Let TQ be the result of adding Quine's philosophical views to that theory. Let T~Q be the result of adding the

[14] Quine recognizes this issue in "Posits and Reality," and tries to disarm it. I don't think he is entirely successful, because it is not clear precisely which of the central doctrines leading to this result he wishes to reject. There are indeed passages that seem to indicate a lessened reliance on sense data, but even the import of these is not fully clear.

negation of Quine's philosophical views to T. Do these theories make different observational predictions? If so, Quine should point them out and we can then decide whether his philosophy should be accepted. Although Quine did, from time to time, make some gestures in this direction,[15] he never attempted to do this in a careful or systematic way—probably because neither his philosophy nor its negation plays any very straightforward or significant role in making observational predictions about the world. If that is so, then the three theories—one without any philosophy, one with Quine's philosophy, and one with the negation of Quine's philosophy—all make more or less the same observational predictions. According to holistic verificationism, this means that they all mean more or less the same thing, and hence make more or less the same claims about the world, in the languages of their respective proponents. If this is right, then Quine's philosophy should be regarded as virtually empty in more or less the sense in which sentences about God or the Absolute were claimed to be. Surely, there is something wrong here. It is hard to resist the conclusion that it is Quine's holistic verificationism itself.

[15] See "Epistemology Naturalized," in Quine, *Ontological Relativity and Other Essays* (New York and London: Columbia University Press, 1969).

SUGGESTED FURTHER READING
FOR PART FIVE

Main Primary Sources Discussed

Grice, H. P., and P. F. Strawson. "In Defense of a Dogma." *Philosophical Review* 65 (1956); reprinted in James F. Harris, Jr., and Richard H. Severens, eds., *Analyticity* (Chicago: Quadrangle Books, 1970).

Quine, W. V. "On What There Is." *Review of Metaphysics* 2 (1948): 21–38; reprinted in Quine, *From a Logical Point of View*, rev. 2nd edition (Cambridge, MA: Harvard University Press, 1980).

———. "Two Dogmas of Empiricism." *Philosophical Review* 60 (1951); revised and reprinted in Quine, *From a Logical Point of View* (Cambridge, MA: Harvard University Press, 1953, 1961, 1980).

Additional Primary Sources

Quine, W. V. "Epistemology Naturalized." In *Ontological Relativity and Other Essays* (New York and London: Columbia University Press, 1969).

———. "On Empirically Equivalent Systems of the World." *Erkenntnis* 9 (1975): 313–28.

———. *The Philosophy of Logic*. Englewood Cliffs, NJ: Prentice Hall, 1970.

———. "Posits and Reality." Reprinted in *The Ways of Paradox and Other Essays* (New York: Random House, 1966).

———. "Truth by Convention." First published in O. H. Lee, ed., *Philosophical Essays for A. N. Whitehead* (New York: Longmans, 1936); reprinted in H. Feigl and W. Sellars, eds., *Readings in Philosophical Analysis* (New York: Appleton, 1949); in P. Benacerraf and H. Putnam, eds., *Readings in the Philosophy of Mathematics*

(Englewood, NJ: Prentice Hall, 1964); and Quine, *The Ways of Paradox* (New York: Random House, 1966).

Additional Recommended Reading

Harman, Gilbert. "Meaning and Theory." *Southwestern Journal of Philosophy* 9:2 (1979): 9–20.

INDEX